THE LAND I CAME THROUGH LAST

POETRY BOOKS BY ROBERT GRAY

CREEKWATER JOURNAL

GRASS SCRIPT

THE SKYLIGHT

SELECTED POEMS

PIANO

CERTAIN THINGS

NEW AND SELECTED POEMS

LINEATIONS

NEW SELECTED POEMS

GRASS SCRIPT: SELECTED EARLIER POEMS (UK)

AFTERIMAGES

NAMELESS EARTH (UK)

ROBERT GRAY

The Land
I Came Through
Last

GIRAMONDO

FIRST PUBLISHED 2008
FOR THE WRITING & SOCIETY RESEARCH GROUP
AT THE UNIVERSITY OF WESTERN SYDNEY
BY THE GIRAMONDO PUBLISHING COMPANY
PO BOX 752
ARTARMON NSW 1570 AUSTRALIA
WWW.GIRAMONDOPUBLISHING.COM

© ROBERT GRAY 2008

DESIGNED BY HARRY WILLIAMSON
TYPESET BY ANDREW DAVIES
IN 10/17 PT BASKERVILLE

PRINTED AND BOUND BY LIGARE BOOK PRINTERS
DISTRIBUTED IN AUSTRALIA BY TOWER BOOKS

NATIONAL LIBRARY OF AUSTRALIA
CATALOGUING-IN-PUBLICATION DATA:

GRAY, ROBERT, 1945–
THE LAND I CAME THROUGH LAST

ISBN 978 1 920882 35 8.

GRAY, ROBERT, 1945– – CHILDHOOD AND YOUTH.
POETS, AUSTRALIAN – BIOGRAPHY.

A821.4

To my brothers and sister, chosen people

I am the family face;
Flesh perishes, I live on
…leaping from place to place
Over oblivion…
Thomas Hardy

It seems I was called for this:
To glorify things just because they are.
Czeslaw Milosz

ACKNOWLEDGEMENTS

To Lily Cameron and Amanda Simons for their
editorial assistance and advice, to Len Bartulin
and John Carrick for invaluable comments on the
manuscript, to the Literature Board of the Australia
Council for a grant and the University of Technology
Sydney for a scholarship, to Euan Macleod, for
allowing the use on the cover of a detail from his
painting, to Ivor Indyk, exceptional publisher, for his
sustaining enthusiasm and forbearance, and to Dee
Jones, who exceeded even him in the latter quality
– my lasting gratitude.

The quotation from C. P. Cavafy's 'Ithaka' is
translated by Edmund Keeley and Philip Sherrard in
the *Collected Poems* (Princeton University Press, 1992);
those from David Marr in chapter 18 are from his
Patrick White: A Life (Vintage, 1992).

CONTENTS

Preface **1**

1. Rumours of War **3**

2. The Waters in the Earth **25**

3. A Religious Wound **52**

4. Memories of Tropical Fruit **76**

5. The Spilt Horizon **94**

6. An Ineffectual Love **128**

7. Sisters of Limited Mercy **154**

8. A Jungle Boy **165**

9. In a Cold Haven **186**

10. 'The Church of the Midnight Cry' **203**

11. *Off the Bitumen* **221**

12. *The Reeking Sun* **246**

13. *With Cords of Water* **259**

14. *By Craft Alone* **272**

15. *Walking after Dark* **292**

16. *A Vacant Possession* **313**

17. *The Sufficient Place* **328**

18. *White Continent* **352**

19. *Extreme People* **384**

20. *How It Is Night* **395**

21. *A Tomb in the Winds* **414**

PHOTOGRAPHS

My father's first plantation, photographed by him. **8**

My father as a young man, at home in Sydney. **17**

My great-grandparents with family, my grandfather to the left. **28**

'Tweed Villa', my great-grandparents' house. **31**

My grandfather's friends: a 'gun culture.' **34**

Margaret, her younger sisters and my father. **37**

'Toby' with Dorothy and Olga; my father standing. **49**

This picture shows how I think my father felt to himself. **55**

My mother and father at the time of their marriage. **61**

My father in the air force. **63**

A family group. **72**

Max and me, with borrowed props: a studio portrait. **84**

The dairy farm, with me on the front fence. **96**

My mother and me in Sydney. **114**

My maternal grandparents. **147**

The three boys; Billy to the fore. **178**

Our backyard in town; Billy inspecting the crop. **183**

Max and his wife 'Bonny'. **215**

My sister Alicia in her last year at school. **244**

My brother Billy with his son Nathan. **278**

Ted working on a large triptych, 'Glenreagh Bush'. **282**

'Paperbark Creek' by Joe Conroy. **287**

'The Breakwater' by Ted Hillyer. **288**

In 'hippie' days. **290, 314, 318**

Dee in a motel room. **332**

Harriet and me. **333**

Harriet doing her homework in Europe. **335**

Hilary Armstrong in Scotland. **348**

The explorer. **367**

Dee, somewhere in time. **371**

Patrick White (1980) by William Yang. **381**

Percy with two of his conquests. **389**

My father at the nursing home. **405**

My mother with Billy's son, Nathan. **417**

My mother in the nursing home, in her nineties. **427**

Me, more recently. **433**

Preface

This book was meant to be mainly about my parents, although I and others have obtruded within it, and was intended neither to vindicate nor to vilify them, but to retain a sense of them as they were. It originated in the desire to write for writing's sake: I believed with Bertolt Brecht that 'someone who wants to write will be glad to have a subject', and found I had inherited one.

At first, I thought I could treat my appearances in the book curtly, in the second person; autobiography seemed distasteful and too difficult. But that resistance was pushed aside in the midst of writing, as memories opened, 'lighting one candle with another's flame'.

In gathering people's lives from about the keyboard, I felt a need for objectivity, but was assured by friends who knew the intellectual fashion that it was impossible to be accurate about another's past or even one's own.

It seems to me that memory must be as we find it, pragmatically: something that can usually be relied upon. To deny this, in principle, is to deny there is a distinction between fantasy and empirical fact. We could not function unless it were so. Memory is a particular ability, which differs among individuals. For some, images will step forth in detachment and speak as themselves.

Yet while we may be able to recall things a person did, and draw inferences from them, we cannot experience what it means for another to be him or her self. There is no possibility that someone's sense of the weight and the texture of life could be communicated, in its dailiness. We are each a pin on which a universe is balanced. It happens somewhere unreachable in everyone.

A writer can only hope to create a sense of his subjects by accumulating their gestures; he has to trust that within his encircling imagery, if it is insistent enough, the dead will appear for a moment, like a glimmer on the waves.

1. Rumours of War

My father was a remittance man in his own country. In earlier times than his, during colonial days, wealthy British families sent their unruly sons to Australia and maintained them on instalments, so long as they stayed away. My father's family extended this tradition, in the late 1920s, within a continent that was still an outpost, by forcing him to move four hundred miles north of Sydney, to an isolated place on the coast of New South Wales. They bought him a plantation there, beyond a small town, up among the eucalyptus hillsides, and above an empty sea, on condition that he not return to the city; and when he risked losing this property, to further gambling and carousing, they set him up again, rather than have the embarrassment of him in the harbour-side avenues of Vaucluse.

It was apparently a torment for my father to be tethered outside Sydney, despite the perfect sub-tropical climate into which he had been sent. He knew the beauty of that place, Korora, but would have felt, in the folded heat of one of its close valleys of an afternoon, as if life had passed to another shore. Everything seemed embalmed in a bright stagnant fluid, where the occasional bubble broke loose, and that was all.

My mother, in telling me of the early days of her friendship with my father, whom she met on the coast, remembered how whenever he began to slip beyond her into drunkenness he would mutter about the Metropole Hotel, which once stood at the centre of the city, and would name the mates he imagined lining the bar. All of them, she said, had easily lost contact with him.

When he did break the family's edict and return to Sydney, on two or three occasions while his father lived, it was never done unobtrusively enough. So my grandfather, a much tougher man than his son, although at times equally a drunkard, could at once have his will re-enforced on my father, through hired men, without even needing to appear. Within a day or two of arriving in town, my father was debarred and brusquely treated in all the better drinking places. And then he was found: if not among the potted palms and marble of the Metropole or of Adams Hotel, at a bar somewhere, perhaps down by the produce markets, with some immediate cronies. He would have looked like a puppet that for the moment was able to hold itself upright in its strings, as I have so often seen him, his face foolish with the effort of keeping its features in balance. Or he was found collapsed at a tram stop or in a park. Wherever it was, unknown hands hauled him to his feet, straightened him up, put a ticket into his pocket, and with his kitbag forgotten about, loaded him onto the early evening train from Central; all without his understanding the extent of the conspiracy that was ranged against him. He woke in the morning to the guard's impatience, and was urged to step down onto a small platform; and he sat there on a bench until he came to himself, out among the wide-open paddocks, in the immense light.

This used to happen long before his life with our family: it was after his first wife and children had gone, and had cut off all contact with him. He was then receiving a monthly allowance from his father, as a reminder of their agreement, which continued for years, even after the plantation was well able to pay.

My father never attempted to escape the constriction he felt in this arrangement by offering to leave Australia entirely. He must have known that he was too hampered in his 'weakness for drink' to be a traveller and survive in foreign places. He had read and re-read Robert Louis Stevenson, his favourite author, and could have visualised himself becoming stranded and confused, as desperately lost as those men who had to live on the beach at Papeete, in the story 'The Ebb-Tide'.

From the time of his arrival at the plantation, when in his late twenties, my father's only contact with his previous life was through letters from two of his sisters, who remained spinsters and who always lived together. One or other sister would correspond with him every fortnight, and as regularly he replied. He was still writing to them in the week of his death, when in his seventies.

It was a strict condition of my aunts for these letters that nothing they might think 'unpleasant' and nothing complaining should be mentioned; otherwise, there would be a drawn-out silence. I became aware that such a punishment had occurred, more than once, when I was a boy, and I remember the anxiety my father then showed, in asking about or watching for the mail.

He himself entirely believed in his sisters' ideal of reticence, since it accorded with his imaginings of himself as a 'gentleman', but it was part of his nature that he must betray this – that he must cheat on any agreement. He felt, I suppose, that the odds were always too much against him. So his sisters, despite their implicit sympathy, had to be subtly reminded of how the all but perfect trajectory of his decline was a farce they too, in their time, had helped to stage. I think my father wished that everyone he could possibly incriminate in his failure, however unreasonably, should know of and carry an apportioned blame.

Always in those letters of his he would manage to insinuate, with a seeming unconsciousness, details implying his frustration, and fleeting innuendos about the past, and some casuistry, in self-exoneration, before the long passages that served for smoothing-over, and his affectionate wishes.

'Your father writes such clever letters,' Margaret, my favourite aunt, said to me, with an edge, during one of my boyhood visits to Sydney. I saw she had an example of these in hand, and was skimming it warily – sipping it, as though with lips that tested something hot. Then she appreciated aloud a passage of his elaborate prose, and sighed quickly over a nicely turned anecdote, before folding it all firmly away. (His sisters' letters to him, none of which my mother kept, would have been full of family chauvinism, and of the sentimentalities of positive thinking.)

I was in my forties, and Margaret, the last of that family, had just died, when I discovered the manner in which my father had written to his sisters. I sat on the stripped-off mattress in her room, at a nursing home, sorting through her papers, and I recognised of a sudden a shockingly gnarled, ornate handwriting, that was like blackened matchsticks. The bundled letters were all from the late fifties and early sixties, and had apparently been kept because they mentioned some small triumphs of his, when we were living in government housing on the edge of a country town – with his flowers, in the local agricultural show, or his garden, photographed for the council's calendar, or the butcher's – and sometimes of mine, at school, or of my brothers, their more practical achievements. (These were much contrasted with mine, to my disadvantage, I was still pained to see.) And as I read those pages they seemed to belly like sails in my hands, with their gusts of self-pity and frustration.

My father belonged among the generations of Australians whose ideal of behaviour was their image of an English gentleman. The gentleman was proverbial in this country until the 1950s, invoked in homes, in schools, in the streets. (As a boy, I heard a prostitute in Sydney shout after someone, 'You ain't no gentleman!') Those who experienced this ideal through their imaginative reading, as my father did, were surely the most susceptible to it. (My father was never influenced by the precepts of his family; he might have been slightly more so by those of his private school.) Obviously, he wanted to conform to the gentlemanly image, or at least to some part of it, for the sake of his self-respect, but what was unusual about him was the insistence of the fantasy he created around this idea of himself. It was something he single-mindedly reaffirmed, in all of his rituals, every day. The gentleman as someone considerate of others was not his concern, however; it was only the gentleman as possessing a certain coded manner, a style, which preoccupied him.

On his first plantation, which was already established when my grandfather bought it, mainly with banana palms, but also with mango and papaya trees, my father could afford to leave all of the real work to labourers, and to live an imaginary Somerset Maugham life. He spent most of the day on the verandah of his 'bungalow', as he would have liked to think of that tin-roofed weatherboard shack, giving occasional instructions to a foreman. The place had a galvanised-iron watertank, on a wooden stand, and a vegetable garden close by. Built on posts at the front, it stood almost in the shining, restless plantation, which rose abruptly on the hillside behind it – a horde of upright, broad leaves, quickly tattered, quickly replaced, each one like the flourish of a man-sized New Guinea shield. Downhill, there was a view across an orange dirt road, along a widening, forested valley, with cannon-bursts of dark eucalyptus foliage floating onto the sky, and out to sea.

On the verandahs, which fitted around two sides of the shack, moving from the sun, my father spent his days reading, having

7

had sent from libraries, or on account from second-hand dealers, many literary novels, and some histories, biographies, and Latin classics. His legs out in a planter's chair, a glass on its arm beside him, a bottle on the floor, he paced himself, so as not to become fully drunk until late afternoon, or else not until he was in the town, at the bar.

These habits of my father were known to the man who would become my maternal grandfather, and to his grown sons, at the next plantation, further into the hills. (All of the hillsides around there, in the coastal range, had their northern ridges and gullies, to about two-thirds of their height, taken over by banana plantations, in orderly rows, below the blue-black, corroded skyline of eucalyptus forest.) That next family, as well as being growers, were the district's produce carriers, who shifted truck-loads of fruit to the railway. Its men called regularly on my father, to load up, or for payment. They were derisive at their dinner table about what they saw as the profligacy and pretension of my father's way of life. This was how my mother, twenty-one at the time, coming home on her days off from working as a housekeeper in another town, first heard of her future husband.

My father, often wanting to drink in the town at night, would afterwards have to drive back along the highway, and then on a steep dirt road that was almost a lane. He usually gave up along the way, pulling over by the roadside trees, and would sleep there until well into the morning; until the sun rose high enough out of the sea to reach him, tilted beneath the undergrowth.

I cannot say how many accidents my father had, although he owned a series of cars – Buicks and Studebakers – but surprisingly none could have been too serious. All of that was later thought by my mother too shameful, and a temptation of fate, to speak about lightly. She did say that he was a fool ever to have started out from the town on those evenings, or even to have left home, and admitted that he had all kinds of mishaps on the way. Among these, I gradually gathered, were his running into livestock, for which he was fined, pulling into places where he became bogged down, and leaving the rear of the car too far out, when he had stopped, with a violent result.

There is one notorious story about his driving that was still raised in the town when I was a boy. I would hear people reminiscing and laughing over what they called his 'last ride'. When I think of this story, I also think of the bushman's poem, *The Man from Snowy River*, which tells of a stockman careening on horseback down a stony hillside in pursuit of wild horses, or of a valuable runaway among them, while the rest of the party reined back and held their breaths.

He sent the flint-stones flying, but the pony kept his feet,
    He cleared the fallen timber in his stride,
And the man from Snowy River never shifted in his seat –
    It was grand to see that mountain horseman ride.
Through the stringy barks and saplings, on the rough and broken ground,
Down the hillside at a racing pace he went;

And he never drew the bridle till he landed safe and sound
At the bottom of that terrible descent.

I think of this because my father's ride was the opposite of such a heroic one. It was bungling and inadvertent, risible, and quite useless – and yet it exemplified something about him that was more than just these things. It was a debacle, but one that he must try to redeem, with a gesture.

On his way home that night, going too fast, my father drove his car off the side of the steep road and plunged down a forty-five degree slope through someone's banana plantation. Swaying and sliding on the easily knocked-down palms, which were fibrous and slippery, accumulating beneath him, he tobogganed all the way to within a few yards of a lighted back door, at the bottom of the long hill. In the sudden quietness, after the regular swishing fall of the swathe of trees, and the clang and scrape of the rear of his car on stony ground, a young woman had gradually appeared in the light, with a child in her arms. My father is supposed to have struggled out of the car, which was prised widely apart from the earth, like a mouth filled with a gag, and steadying himself on its open door, to have raised his hat and said, with a slight bow (a slur was usually affected here, in the telling), 'Dear madam, I – abjectly before you – to apologise, un – forgivable but – can assure – unintentional – intrusion.' Or words of that sort.

From then on, my father had to rely on his workmen, or on someone else, to drive him home. He did buy another car, but often on the day following a binge he would be at the roadside, hitching a lift – sometimes from one of my mother's family – going to collect it.

When I was a child, my father had another plantation, in a different part of the district, about three miles inland from the town, and his solution to his transport problem in those days was to own an ex-racehorse (a fine animal, it was said), which would bring him home, slumped in the saddle. God knows how he climbed on board, let alone stayed there. Getting him seated must have been done with much staggering about and hilarity, among his helpers, in the backyard of the pub. The horse trotted back, joggling its dozing rider, along the side of the road, through occasional headlights. It came in the left-open gate of the property, and strode upwards on a track through the paddocks, to our lighted front door, and snorted, and my mother would go out and drag my father from his place, his head dangling beside the mane. (He had often lost his hat; it was sometimes returned to him. 'This your old man's, missus?') She was always as disgusted with him, I remember, as she was solicitous for 'the poor creature', the horse.

My father was not by a long way the only drunkard on the roads in that place and time. I can see, from a later period, his sudden complete soberness, one morning, after a neighbour told us the news about three of his drinking mates, with whom he had been the night before. These men, riding in one car after closing time, in heavy fog, had missed the approach to a bridge, burst through guide-posts, and gone straight down into deep water. All were drowned; all had had families. My father came home that night incoherent from eulogising them.

As for his other interest, which always came off second best, his reading, it would still be fair to say that he was formidably well-read. This seems the right word for such a jealously possessed distinction. He used to hint at the many mysterious corridors he had been down, in a great, rambling house of books, which was his by right of long and solitary habitation. At times, for me, who was interested, he would open a room there (as I visualised it), take a particular book from a shelf, reminisce briefly over it, too briefly, then return it, and put off the light.

When I wanted to read these books, almost all of them had gone – they were 'lost' he said, which meant sold off, mostly, or eaten by white ants, or found to be mildewed and abandoned in moving house.

Over the years, I gathered a lot about my father's reading. It was done mainly in the time of his exile, or earlier, when he had had a youthful avidity, he said, to know about people and history. He was able to refer, for instance, to the whole rugged landscape of Sir Walter Scott's novels – he could recount the plots of *Quentin Durward*, *Ivanhoe*, *The Heart of Midlothian*, *Rob Roy*, *Waverley*, and probably others, because his family had owned a complete set of Scott's work, out of nationalistic pride. Through questioning him, as I grew up, I also found he was able to make knowledge-able remarks on almost anything that I thought I might want to read, or had read: on Fielding, Jane Austen, Dickens (whose most quoted book was *The Pickwick Papers*), Wilkie Collins, Trollope, Kipling, Hardy...He revered, above all, Stevenson, for his style, and particularly *The Master of Ballantrae*, but he praised everything by that author, including the stories and essays, and what I later found very minor books, *Catriona*, *St Ives*, and *The Black Arrow*. Conrad, too, was spoken of reverently – in a tone only books could elicit – and Bennett; but also (just as much, it seemed) Galsworthy, Wells, Buchan, Rider Haggard (mostly for a book called *Nada the Lily*), and Maugham. He admired at least the first few novels by D. H. Lawrence; but had a particular dislike for James Joyce and Virginia Woolf – he detested, I should think, modernist self-consciousness. In his last years I remember him reading Graham Greene, Evelyn Waugh, Anthony Powell, and Pasternak's Nobel prize novel *Doctor Zhivago* (although normally he had no time for 'foreign tome-stones', meaning Russian novels, in particular).

The book he most often called his favourite was *Vanity Fair*. Anything he really liked, he read repeatedly, always in a way that suggested he was merely glancing down the page in search of some reference, but which, if you asked him about it, showed his close absorption. He appeared not to enjoy lighter fiction. He had read fewer American authors, I found: Fenimore Cooper, Mark Twain (including the less usual novels), some early Henry James, Jack London, *The Red Badge of Courage*, and, not long after they appeared, books by Fitzgerald and Hemingway. He quoted often, of course, from Poe, the most theatrical of them.

Remembering this last-mentioned enthusiasm, I took him, when he was ultimately in a nursing home, in the early seventies, a collection of Poe's short stories, among other books – apparently my idea, at the time, of invalid's food.

'Ah, yes,' he said, accepting it, '"The Cask of Amontillado" – I know something about that sort of experience.'

The allusion, to being buried alive with only drink for comfort, was the one mention he made to me about the 'banishment' of his younger days. He would have known I had heard of it, though; and his remark seemed, on the occasion, too typically self-dramatising, too self-indulgent, to let pass. Before I could consider, I retorted with an adaptation of the first line of that story, in our old quoting, competitive way – 'The thousand injuries of Fortunato they had borne as they best could' I reminded him. He looked startled, and hurt, an old shame flushing him without colour, and after a few moments he said coldly, 'I think "The Narrative of Arthur Gordon Pym" is the one I would like to read again. Thank you for your consideration.'

Poetry was not his usual reading, although he had a good memory for many passages of it. These he admitted came mainly from anthologies, like Palgrave's or Wavell's. He seems to have read, in their own books, only a couple of the more boisterous, 'manly' poets, Browning and Kipling (whose very names seem participles), and also A. E. Housman. I have heard him declaim, for seemingly no reason, while walking about in the house:

What's become of Waring
Since he gave us all the slip,
Chose land-travel or seafaring...
Rather than pace up and down
Any longer London town?

Or in an exaggerated, sententious tone:

As it will be in the future, it was at the birth of Man –
There are only four things certain since Social Progress began:
That the Dog returns to his Vomit and the Sow returns to her Mire,
And the burnt Fool's bandaged finger goes wobbling back to the Fire...

My father often referred to the short stories of Henry Lawson, and claimed their author was by far the best Australian writer, as long as he stayed in that medium. When my father was a boy, my grandfather had pointed out Lawson to him on a city street, who they saw was cadging money for drinks from passers-by, and told my father this was a great man, and had fervently pressed paper money into the writer's hand. My father remembered Lawson's buffoonish, bleary salute.

In my teenage years, my mother confided to me, prompted by some association – as she dabbed gentian violet on bleeding oyster cuts in my hands and knees, after I'd come home from the beach – that my father had had one other diversion in his early days on the coast. She said that he was known to have joined in nude swimming parties.

I sustained for a little while the shocked pause that she expected. Then I heard, in answer to my insistent and more and more irritating questions, that these revels were held at isolated coves along the coast, and from the banks of creeks, in the summer evenings. The participants amounted to three or four men and the daughters of some local dairy farmers. The entire purpose of her telling me this was to say that such behaviour was disgusting, when people had 'all that hair' on their bodies. (This conversation would be the extent of my sexual education from her.) She also told me that my father had been known for 'showing off' on such occasions, but because of her relative lack of embarrassment with this part of the story – indeed, her slight relief – I think she believed she was referring to demonstrations of his famous swimming prowess.

My father loved the surf, and would swim fearlessly in heavy breakers, at the town beach, when everyone else had obeyed the order to come out. My mother, who never learned to swim, could remember lifesavers blowing whistles and gesturing furiously at him, a dark spot out among the smoky, crashing sea, and my father ignoring them, until they began to get the belt-man ready, to go after him. Then, when he came walking nonchalantly up the beach and was berated by a lifesaver, he had told the man, inappropriately, to 'Bloody well mind your own business.' People were standing around in towels, glaring at him, or grinning, my mother said.

I remember him coming out from swimming, and drying his legs with a towel, making the hair on them stand out against the sunlight. His legs seemed as heavily furred as those of the god Pan in illustrations. He saw me staring at him and said, in a warning tone, 'That's what comes of shaving your legs when you're young.' I have no idea from out of what experience this remark arose.

When I was a child, my father lifted me onto his shoulders, waded into the surf, and swam outwards with me, my legs astride his neck and my hands holding his skull − like a steering wheel, as I seem to remember he suggested. We went out into the rank, windy sea, well beyond the breakers. Although I whimpered, he told me to keep still, and said it would be all right. I kept twisting my head toward the shore, where I could see the small figure of my mother, anxiously waving a towel that looked like a wisp of smoke. Once out there, he rolled onto his back, in the weirdly inflating and sinking ocean, which kept wiping away my glimpses of safety, and held me at the end of his arm, by as little as one finger. I was dangled there, complaining and crying, with all the unimaginable dark cavern of the ocean underneath me. He let me cling to his freckled back while he trod water and repeated to me how wonderful it was in the water, and how safe I was. My mother, when we got back to shore, shouted wildly at him.

Such a small town scandal as that about his nude swimming must have helped cause my mother's long resistance to her suitor. But she told me at another time that for all his faults my father had never been 'a ladies' man'. I can imagine he was not – he could hardly have been considered fun by the sort of young woman who would join his friends and him naked on the beach: not by the normal, hedonistic, and therefore moody, essentially conservative country girl, of the time. Not with his disconcertingly educated demeanour, his elaborate but faintly mocking 'good manners', his looks that were too peculiar to be called ugly; and not when he preferred to be drunk by the end of the evening.

My father's ideal woman was the person who was always closest to him, from his point of view: his elder sister, Margaret. She was a spinster because of a broken engagement, and because of having had to look after her invalid mother for years. But she was attractive, slim, witty, impeccable; 'someone who never went out without gloves', as she was described to me. She was always referred to by my father as 'a lady'. He used very cruelly and pointedly to say, at home, 'My sister Margaret, who is a lady, of course...'

My father once informed me that he could never be called a drunkard while ever his shoes were clean. He was fastidious to the end of his life about cleanliness and dress. In his country role, he wore creased khaki cotton trousers and a shirt that was immaculately white and pressed (my mother's work), a tweed jacket, often a tie, highly polished short riding boots or brogues, and a grey felt hat. He smoked constantly, mostly a pipe. One hand was always kept elegantly in the pocket of his jacket: wherever he was walking, even in the house, and even between courses at dinner, or while drinking tea, he would be idly turning over and over a lighter or some coins there.

His appearance was unusual not only for the care that he took with it. He had a long, bony face (which in age developed a warp, like an image in a flawed mirror), a great French aquiline nose, that had been broken, long ears, and an extraordinarily high-domed forehead. He looked like the classic illustrations of Sherlock Holmes, slightly caricatured; and he wore his hair, that receded at the temples, brushed back tightly in the Holmesian style. But this first general impressiveness was then spoiled, because beneath the striking brow his eyes were small, dark and wary, and his mouth was thin and hard. While he had a long, narrow head, his body was barely of average height, for the time, about five foot eight inches, and was stocky and strong, at least when he was younger. He was always sun-browned, but close up had fine dark freckled spots all over him, like foxing.

Despite his looks, my father was vain. He said on numerous occasions that a doctor in the army had remarked to him about never having previously seen a cranium so large and finely shaped as his, and had taken its measurements. He was vain about his auburn hair, which shone like French-polished timber, and which he treated every day with bay rum and brushing, and about his well-kept hands – he always carried a nail-file in his pocket. He was even vain about his feet, and once when drunk and in a good mood took off a shoe to draw his family's attention to his foot's elegant silhouette.

My father's expression, at first sight, mixed intelligence with arrogance, but that look was undermined, for me, as I grew aware of how underneath it there was a secretive discomfort. There was always about him, I felt, for all the authority of his talk, a subtle embarrassment, a consciousness of what would have been thought his moral weakness. Most people, however, who had only the heroes of the cinema for reference, seem to remember him as a person of notable suavity.

With his great facility for the cutting remark, with his instinct for one's vulnerability, with the constant edge of cynicism beneath his politeness, he was not a prospect the ordinary country girl would have been quick to claim, nor an older woman, looking for comfort. My mother was only in her background an ordinary person.

Most striking of all my father's attributes, I came to think, apart from his profligacy, was his sense of humour – although it was often so private as to be narcissistic. His humour usually passed everyone by, in the company he kept, but this never deterred him. (I discovered it was a good thing that most of his quick, allusive comments were missed, because of their sarcastic implications.)

I was curious about my father, and struck by the things he said, and used to puzzle over them. As an adult, prompted by chance associations, I remembered his remarks, and only then saw the point of many of them. His humour was almost invariably based in language, in puns and literary references. It was a solitary pleasure, like a crossword puzzle, employed for his self-regard. I think he enjoyed it that others were often unable to follow him.

It is not at all for their merit that I recall my father's puns; I know they vary in quality, although I am unsure of what is merit in the device, it has so little content. I suppose a good pun is startling. The best I can think of, at the moment, is in *Ulysses*, where Buck Mulligan says to the old housekeeper, 'Did you make the tea yourself, my dear?' and she replies, 'Yes, and the water, too.' I have recorded my father's puns for what they reveal about him; which is, I think, a desire to insist that things are not merely as they seem.

'Dad,' I said, 'what's an opossum – why is it different to a possum?' I must have been twelve, and remember turning the pages of a magazine on the bare dining room table. My father was examining by touch the knot in his tie, checking his finger-nails, and the length of his shirt-cuffs, about to go out. He did not hesitate for a moment, but without becoming any less cold, mannered and fastidious, pronounced, as established fact, 'An opossum, you will find, properly spelt with an inverted comma, is the offspring of an itinerant Irish labourer and of some of the more appealing local fauna.'

'Geoffrey,' said my mother, 'I will not stand for that sort of talk…'

My father re-emphasised the dent in the prow of his grey felt hat. He gave me a dry, considering glance, and perhaps the hint of a smile.

Once, my mother was haranguing my father, who was drunk,

at the dinner table, and he did what he would normally never have done at such a time, took up some cutlery, to begin to eat. As he did so, he explained to me, in a stage whisper, 'I can only look on this Gorgon in the bowl of my spoon.'

He and I were at the beach together, which again was something unusual; I was about nine, and we were sitting on a grassy bank under a pine tree, waiting for my mother to bring the other children from the changing shed. A young woman came onto a short flight of wooden steps, carrying a towel, ready for the beach, slipped and sat down on her amply cushioned behind. Some boys, playing nearby, burst into laughter, pointing. The young woman said something to them, and included us in her glare; then she went on, with much dignity, her buttocks grinding softly in her swimming costume. My father at once instructed me, in a voice I saw as like the capital lettering in the Bible, his forefinger lifted: 'Oftentimes, a fall goeth before pride.'

Again in the fifties, when we lived in the town, my mother one night commented that she had seen a newly arrived Jewish couple in the main street. She had noticed them previously, and was interested because of having worked for a Jewish family, and because Jews were then almost unknown in the countryside. These new people had come to run a small motel, she had heard. They had a child, and were, my mother said, a close couple – she was surprised and touched by the parents holding hands, though middle-aged, while out walking. My mother returned to this subject, in round-about ways, over several nights. She imagined the newcomers must be refugees, they seemed so foreign. (The terrible revelations concerning the Jews that came with the end of the War were not yet ten years behind us.) No doubt my father thought she was being sentimental, over the couple's 'display', as he would have called it.

A few days after my mother's remarks, I met my father by chance in the main street, after school. We never went out as a family, and it was unusual for me even to come across him, like this, while on an errand. He stepped out of the newsagent's with a paper, already slightly stupefied by drink. 'What are you up to, boy?' he said, making a good-humoured public display. He took hold of the back of my neck with a cleft hand, as he often did, and walked me along the street a little. I could smell the beer, and tried for a moment to wriggle free. 'I want you to go home,' he announced redundantly, 'and give your mother a hand. Help with preparing the dinner. Get the wood chopped for your baths...' Just then, the Jewish family appeared, among the shoppers, looking as they had been described at home – their stockiness, heavy clothing, and round glasses. They were coming along beneath the awnings, toward us. The small, walking child was a girl. My father touched his hat as they passed, and introduced himself politely: he invited the newcomer and his wife to the lounge bar for a drink, if they should be near the hotel. The strangers were startled, and impatient. The man shook his head, maybe muttered, looked away. All three continued moving, sidling past us. Perhaps their disquiet was caused, despite his well-meaning tone, by my father's introductory remark. Only recently have I understood what he said: it had seemed mere foolishness at the time. What he must really have commented was: 'Ah, the duet – and the Jewette!' That was why, even though he had been ignored, my father looked pleased with himself.

Later, on a visit I made to Sydney with him, we took a tram from Central in the early morning and went out along Old South Head Road, going to my aunts through the Jewish neighbourhood. It must have been a Saturday. 'Who are those people?' I asked my father, my finger on the glass, indicating a group of Hasidic Jews walking in the street, sombre, ringleted and bearded, in their black hats and coats. My father, as an answer, made one of his jokes (either spontaneously or recalled from earlier use, since this was an area close to where he had grown up). I knew what he said was in verse, by the rhythm and his elevated tone, but only many years later did I discover that it had been a distortion of some lines of A. E. Housman's (about 'heartless, witless Nature'). Glancing out at the people I had noticed, my father told me gravely, 'It is the Jews of mourning,/ That weep, but not for thee.'

(He was noticeably pro-Semitic, attracted to Jewish people, I gathered from all of his comments about them, because he thought, presumptuously, that both they and he were sometimes looked down upon, narrow-mindedly, while of more sensibility than their detractors.)

My father was constantly alert for the chance of a pun or an allusion, as if he thought these were evidence of a superior inward life. Yet when, as a teenager, I cheekily responded to one of his word plays by enquiring whether or not he agreed that the pun was the lowest form of humour, as the cliché had it, he said seriously, 'I do, indeed.' He continued: 'It's a pity that authors and critics don't remember this. We would have been spared a great deal of nonsense about that side-show spruiker James Joyce, if they did.' (At the time, he had *Ulysses*, which was banned in Australia, on his shelves – I believe it was borrowed – and for a while he regularly expressed at the dinner table his dislike of that book, to which we had no response.)

Strangely, it was this small, passing comment about puns which first made me conscious of my father's deep pessimism toward himself – I seemed to catch a sudden glimpse of his self-distaste, beneath what I had taken to be invulnerable conceit.

In his earlier days, after he had been living for more than ten years on the coast, my father thought he saw a way to escape his exile, when war was declared. He imagined he could exonerate himself by joining the army, and even win a sympathy that might be played upon – or such was my mother's perception, at the time, which she always maintained.

She was then still solidly resisting the ten years siege he had laid against her, to have her marry him. For almost that whole time she was away in the city, working, followed there by his letters and telephone calls; but on hearing the relentless news of the War, she had decided to return home to her parents – only to find that her suitor was rushing off, out of the countryside, and into uniform.

Almost immediately he regretted what he had done. 'His feet became very chilly,' my mother said, fifty years later, with a moonlight smile. 'He thought the War would be over quickly. Misjudging his bets, as usual.' Once under canvas, my father realised the fighting could go on for years, and because in 1939 he was thirty-seven, he need not have felt the pressure to be drafted, at all.

Soon there was talk around the Sydney Agricultural Show-ground, where he and many other troops were camped, that an overseas posting was imminent for his division. This news did win sympathy from my mother. The War seems to have played greatly on her religious, apocalyptic imagination. She agreed to come back to the city to visit him. And there, when they came out of a cinema one rainy evening, to the newsboys shouting about some fresh disaster, my parents were suddenly overcome with emotion for each other, and declared themselves engaged.

Still, the wedding did not occur in a hurry: it was not performed until 1941, when my father was at last definitely about to embark, for New Guinea. My mother, in the meantime, withdrew again to her parents' farm. She might have been prepared to lend an ear, in my father's troubles, but certainly no other organ.

Earlier, when my father had first joined up, and announced to his sisters where he was, a further extent of his miscalculation was revealed to him. His sisters let it be known that their father had recently collapsed and was now seriously ill in his bed, from which he refused to be moved to hospital. So my father at once requested leave, and went around in uniform to his boyhood home. But those same women, always so excusing, so blind-eyed in his direction (as long as nothing was actually spoken about), now had to be unmoved as servants, in conveying the old man's refusal of anything to do with 'some prodigal son's return'. My father was turned away by them, on the doorstep – as he was again immediately after the War, when his mother was dying. (It had become a family tradition by then, he explained to me, decades later. This was once at twilight, the confidential hour, on the verandah of the nursing home, during what I think of as the New Frankness, which came upon him and Margaret in their final years. He spoke flippantly, with a half-smile, but above that he gave me a sharp, embarrassed glare.)

When my father left the North Coast, answering with such eagerness the call to arms, he put his property up for sale, without waiting for an outcome. It had only recently been transferred into his name – a premonitory, tax-avoiding gesture by his family. The first offer, clearly an opening move, was niggardly, for the large tract of land he owned, yet he accepted it. I suppose he was surrounded then by many drinking mates – people of his own 'kind', at last – in those transient days, before the plain of war, and needed money in his pockets to make an impression. My mother said that the troops camped in Sydney behaved 'disgracefully', whenever they went on leave.

Word of my father's latest dereliction, the 'throwing away' of his land, reached my grandfather, who was a property speculator and real estate agent, through his connections, and it would have been this that caused him to harden his feelings against his enlisted and only son. It was also, my aunts believed, the cause of what almost immediately followed, the final hardening of his arteries.

2. The Waters in the Earth

All those on my mother's side of the family used to protest, in exasperation and bitterness, that my father had been given 'every chance in life'. But this was only superficially true. The claim did not allow for genetic hazard, which can appear as ruinously as salt water from beneath the earth.

By the time he was born, in 1902, my father's family owned a two-storey brick house that overlooked Sydney Harbour. They were surrounded by a garden, with poplars and jacarandas, in a terrace of similar properties.

Across the water, a mile off, was a bush reserve, as there is today, reaching right along the foreshores, the smoky-blue eucalyptus making a single, diminishing brushstroke. The hazy shore rose steeply from water that was as white as ice-slush, on the many brilliant days. In the lower left-hand corner of their view stood the downtown city, low-rise, of sepia-coloured sandstone, Georgian and Victorian in style, and without the famous bridge, as yet. The sky in that part was often brick-dust brown with smoke, but old photographs show this easily contained by the light.

The family was well-off, in a middle-class way, mostly because of inheritance. Their main distinction, which was always spoken of, was the mother's extraordinary snobbishness. This must have been due, to some extent, to her having met her future husband while working as 'help' in his parents' house. (She would explain that her family, from the north of Ireland, had acquired a 'country property' in New South Wales, but she had left home early, after her parents died, because of her brothers' drinking.)

My mother remembered my father's mother, whom she met during the War, as even at that age a caricature of vanity. She could never have imagined, my mother said, anyone outside a play with so many affectations. My grandmother was known as 'The Duchess of Vaucluse', among shopkeepers in the Eastern Suburbs, because of what my mother called her 'preposterously dignified carryings-on'.

My grandfather's decorum was entirely superficial. Everyone speaks of him as relentlessly jovial, hedonistic, and rash. He would reassert his commitment to the middle-class ideal on occasion, under domestic pressure, and censure his employees and children, but would blaspheme in his own behaviour at the first chance. He certainly did so by the next weekend, all of which he spent, though he had a young family, partying at his beach shack, a suburb away, on the northern headland of Bondi Beach.

That area is now covered with blocks of flats, and from a distance looks as crowded as an Italian hill town, but then it was a place reserved for 'bucks' camps'. The allotments had to be approached on foot, over the close-grassed, treeless, long promontory. Those whitewashed timber shacks were each mainly an open verandah; many had a low picket fence, some a flagpole, with the flag flying for an owner in residence. Of an evening lanterns were strung out; shouts and singing could be heard at the shops on the beach-front; barbecue smoke drifted as if a farmer were burning off. The surf was phosphorescent on the beach, and turned to momentary blossom against the cliffs.

A photograph shows my father in the camp, at seven years of age, sitting side-saddle on a verandah rail. His bare legs are crossed girlishly at the ankles, and he squints from under a sash of white hair. Behind him stands a row of men, all cavernous-eyed, with felt hats and plush moustaches; all except one, who leans beside the boy, himself smooth-faced and tousled-headed. This is Jack London, the American novelist, on his visit to Sydney in 1909, in his yacht, the *Sea Wolf*. He and my grandfather became 'boon companions', and my grandfather introduced him into the 'camp' at Bondi, where married men went to escape women and families; where they were shouldered about and could laugh and yarn, compete and belong, in the athleticism of alcohol.

A family story is that my grandfather went on a binge with London, and out-drank the great writer, the tough man of the Klondike, causing him to be hospitalised. He had to be shipped home by liner to the United States, breaking off his world voyage. It was not mentioned that London had TB at the time.

My grandfather used not to leave his wassail until the last minute, or later, of a Sunday evening. My father told my mother of having been driven by him wildly, in a sulky, after a day at the headland – rushing towards Ethel, wife and mother, who would be waiting at the dinner table, in they knew what mood. (My grandmother, as street photographs show, had developed by middle age an expression like a triggered, frustrated rat-trap. Why were such grim pictures kept? Were they left shuffled among his collection by my grandfather, as a sly exoneration of himself?)

My father, it seems, always remembered his father standing up and shouting in the gig, flogging his horse at full-tilt along Old South Head Road, with the shopkeepers coming out to look, and people staring and shouting back. The boy crouched low in the rocking vehicle, taking care of his father's hat. Nothing he held could save him. The last amber glow of a summer day came under the fronds of the cabbage tree palms, along the road; and the horse, my father said, turned back its eye and skewed its neck furiously at them, while his father let the whip run out along its rump, and peeled it away again. They went whooping and clattering beyond the shops, into the deep shadow of Vaucluse hill; taking the long, slow-curving ascent, with the horse slowing, but still whipped on, and hearing now all the dogs left behind them, in the Sunday dinner-time stillness.

It was his father's money that established my grandfather in the wealthy Eastern Suburbs. John Gray had come to Australia when thirty-three, at the start of the 1850s gold rush. He was born and grew up at Berwick-upon-Tweed, on the Scottish-English border. It was perhaps this barest of footholds on his country that made him so nationalistic about it. He had been a printer, in Glasgow, and I was pleased to find even such a crude access of ink into my lineage, as printers in those days were often well-read; he seems to have been though, from his later journalism, only average in

his literary gifts. In Australia, he went straight to Beechworth, in up-country Victoria, to the 'diggings', but decided at once that downwards with pick and shovel in the mine shaft was not the direction he wanted to take. He chose what might have been a more abruptly downwards course, working as an armed guard on carriages that took the gold to Melbourne. If there were excitement from bushrangers on those trips, his later family had heard nothing of it; but at least he was prepared that there might be.

The pay for such work must have been good, and he most likely brought money from home, because he soon opened a general store in Beechworth, for the miners. This proved a true and reliable mine. The business specialised, before long, as a draper's, and advertised in the local newspaper a stock of Paris fashions and of fabrics. The printer's thumb measured silks and brocades.

In Beechworth, in 1857, John Gray married Elizabeth Lyons, the governess to a clergyman's family. She was from Liverpool, her father an Anglican minister, and her mother previously a widow, Mrs Aspinall. Elizabeth claimed in later life that the Reverend Lyons was not her real father, mainly on the grounds that she had been entirely brought up and educated by nuns at a convent in France, which an Anglican clergyman would not have wanted for his daughter, nor have been able to afford. Hers was a thorough and finished education. She promised that one day she would reveal her suspicions about her true paternity, but seems to have forgotten about this with age. She always claimed that she was French. Perhaps some of the grandiosity enters the family with her.

Elizabeth came to Australia accompanied by two half-brothers, who were lawyers. On arrival in Melbourne, the men immediately deserted her for the goldfields, leaving her short of money. This is how she came to be working for the Reverend Symons, at

Beechworth, who performed her wedding in his home, when she was twenty-four.

A year after their marriage, the Grays moved to Albury, on the border of Victoria and New South Wales, where along with a junior partner John Gray bought and himself became the editor of a newspaper, the *Border Post*. This had eight pages an issue and appeared several times a week. After the new owners took it on, it became as boldly laid out as an old-style theatre poster. The paper published a large proportion of advertisements, and also poems, short stories, and serialised novels, with titles such as *She Was Wrong*, *A Moonlight Tryst*, and *The Tea Cup Controversy*. The news stories often recounted raids by Aboriginals against isolated farms. Among the other reports, one I noticed was 'Father's Quick Thinking Saves Boy', an account of how a 'working lad' had picked up a stone in a paddock and found under it a venomous brown snake, which had bitten his finger. By the time he ran home, his hand was swollen and discoloured, and the family was far from a doctor. So the father took a knife, while the boy was held down by his brother, and the mother and daughters fled the house, and chopped off the poisoned finger on the kitchen table. Also in the files are stories of bushfires, storms, drought, robberies, and murder, but little of the outside world.

An editorial in a rival newspaper, in 1858, comments on my great-grandfather's paper, as the 'disgraceful publication' which had printed a 'scurrilous' story about a local doctor. For this, it says, the 'unconscionable' editor was waylaid by the doctor in the street, and beaten with an umbrella. Because the editor 'developed the matter', the police were called.

When John Gray retired, his paper was bought out, secretively, by a competitor, and incorporated with the other's journal. This was remembered by the family as a great disappointment to him.

Elizabeth Gray became a friend in Albury of the town's magistrate, Thomas Alexander Browne, who as 'Rolf Boldrewood' wrote one of the two best-regarded nineteenth-century Australian novels, *Robbery Under Arms*. (The other is *For the Term of His Natural Life* by Marcus Clarke.) Elizabeth proofread this book, for its first edition, and again in its revised form. Family story has it that she made a number of suggestions which were taken to be improvements by the author.

Elizabeth established a salon, in that wealthy pastoralists' town: she was an excellent pianist and French conversationalist, and a great reader, who loved to discuss books. Above all, she was an enthusiast for amateur theatricals, and was constantly involved in rehearsals at her house. Her husband admired her tastes, and shared them, as much as his shyness allowed, but during his retirement was mainly concerned with breeding horses, on a property near Albury. This ended up being his most lucrative enterprise.

The house they had built, Tweed Villa, looks from photographs to have been beautiful; with deep verandahs all around, fringed with iron lace, and its deep gardens, it was like a hill-station in India.

John Gray always spoke with a marked Scottish accent, but his

31

four children kept none of his expressions, under their mother's reproofs. His coming to Australia was a speculation that matured well: he would have been thought of in the colonies as an exemplary if middle-ranking success.

The eldest of the Grays' five children, William, used his share of their inheritance to establish a well-known legal practice in Sydney, in the city. The youngest son, Percy, became a society florist, also in Sydney, although this was something of a front with him, I have been told. He was really a programmatic seducer of widows – an exponent of the Lambeth Walk, at Farmer's Tearooms, a pianist, and a baritone. He managed to marry only once, when in his seventies, despite his copious liaisons, and he ended up by far the richest of the family, from his many legacies. My grandfather, Albert, the second youngest, moved to Sydney, also, and began his career dubiously. He worked in the bank there, but was such a heavy gambler on the racecourse that it was brought to his employer's notice. His integrity was considered at risk, and he was dismissed. So he began making his property deals. He bought all that he could in what was the working-class suburb of Paddington. Today, on those hillsides, the high terraced houses, in cement-rendered stone, with their decorative ironwork, have been mostly restored, and are hugely expensive; but in the suburb's middle period, it was a slum, and my grandfather a flourishing landlord there.

Almost every photograph I have of my grandfather is a hunting scene. For one of them, in a studio, he is formally posed, a virile shotgun on his arm; a stocky man in a slightly hip-tilted, classical pose, wearing tweeds, gaiters, tweed cap and drooping moustache, against a painted backdrop of misty highlands. A broken Doric column is arranged behind him, as though it were part of the landscape. With his raised and distant gaze, undaunted in the wilderness, the picture is a version of 'The Monarch of the Glen'. Most of his photographs, though, are snapshots, taken along one bush track or another, usually with an open T-model Ford nearby, parked on wheel tracks in the sandy earth. The foliage of the stunted and twisted banksia trees is like almost scraped-away paint, in the early light.

For these pictures, my grandfather often holds a brace of rabbits, or the animals are laid like a bouquet on a car's bonnet, against which he leans. Sometimes the car and a similar one drawn up behind it are filled with smiling, full-fleshed young women, glancing sideways, in broad hats and boas, as though they were parked at the races. Four or five men are standing around, with lairish grins and deferential weapons, and with an essential uncouthness about them, in their jauntiness, which the knickerbocker suits and cloth caps emphasise. In one of the photographs, a man in a suit and tie, bare-headed, leans against a hard-topped car that is parked on the edge of a highway, with a shotgun hanging matter-of-factly in his hand, like a member of the Bonny and Clyde gang. In most of the pictures there are dead animals everywhere – rabbits are held awkwardly downwards, in bunches, are hung at the corners of the cars, or are piled along the running boards, sometimes with the long shadow of the photographer across them. An eagle is stretched, wing-tip to wing-tip, in two men's hands, as if they are displaying a banner. There is a wallaby, the tail held up at the end of someone's arm, the bent-back head laid in the dirt. Speckled birds that look like guinea fowl are suddenly shocking when you distinguish how many of them there are, in neat sheaves, on what had seemed to be light-dappled ground. A slim fox has its lanky killer standing over it facetiously, arms folded, his foot planted on the small, sharp head. There is nothing written on the backs of these pictures: I have no idea who the people are, except for my grandfather, who appears in a number of them, perfectly at ease, although older or somehow more substantial than the others. In several, a thin, hard-faced man, in white shirt, bow tie and black waistcoat, leans back among the ladies, who incline around him, or stands with one foot on the running board, smoking a cigar. It looks as though they have brought the head waiter or the croupier with them, after a night on the town. There are no bottles to be seen, but raucous good times, the aura that my grandfather seems to have trailed, reverberate out of these nicotine-brown, creased, small prints.

My aunt Margaret, in old age, once plucked from the tangle of her tapestry box, as we were talking, and passed over to me, a medal. She said that I should keep it. It was gold, in the shape of the Iron Cross, and was inscribed to my grandfather, A. E. Gray, with the date November 5th, 1903. On that day, it said, my grandfather had 'dived into a heavy sea' from a ship, off Timaru Breakwater, in New Zealand, and had rescued from drowning the 'only boy' of a couple named Biscard. The medal had a loop attached, so that it could be worn on a chain, but Margaret said my grandfather had never mentioned it to anyone, nor the event it named, which had occurred during his marriage. It was found in his safe after he died.

In his boyhood, my father was brought up among domestic 'help' – a woman who was cook and housemaid, another who came part-time, an occasional gardener, and in some periods a nanny – and it was mainly in relation to these people that he first showed the character he would retain. He continually provoked and discomforted the household, just as later on, with my mother and her children, he would do so again.

Once, coming in from prep school, he found a woman on her hands and knees, waxing the floor, and dropping his schoolbag he immediately gave her a fully indulged-in smack across the behind with his cricket bat. Then he ran, with her screaming after him, through the house and into the garden, and escaped over the back fence. Such malicious 'jokes' of his were so common at the time that his parents decided to let the staff chase and beat him, if he were cruel to them, but only immediately on his performing some outrage. Otherwise, he was to be reported to his father: there could be no vendettas. The father, though, was usually not around, and when he was, for a late dinner, was most often in a state too like embers to be interested in exercise or strife. Nor was a cold justice, at this stage of his life, part of my grandfather's nature.

So my father could play his game of truces and sudden attacks, mostly on the domestic staff, but on his mother and his elder and two younger sisters, also. His sisters were more often amused, or awe-struck, than they were upset, over what he had done. From some young age, my father slept with the door to his room locked, and would never give up the key, not even if taken by the ear, claiming that this time it really had been lost. Once, when his parents had the lock of his room changed, one of his sisters straight away stole the new key, on her own account, and gave it to him.

It might be thought those were merely boyish pranks he got up to, but there was always a colouring of cruelty to them. He would knock over a bucket of dirty mop-water onto someone, from a balcony; or sneak into the kitchen and put more heat under a meal; or fire sloppy missiles or the hose at people, when they came into the garden for the newspaper; or turn the black rubber hose on hard, to wash the path, as he had been told to do, and then pretend it was out of control, and struggle with it, as if it were a sea serpent, and manage to drench his mother; or he would fill the female underwear on the line with mud; or carve faces into the broad leaves in the garden, and spear the trees, and continually swap the plants around there, confusing his mother and causing them to fail. Having committed himself in these ways, he then used to escape, and frisk with the family's dogs on the beaches of the nearby coves. Often he came home soaked or filthy, or in the forced company of some irate neighbour. My aunts said that he was widely known as 'a right bugger of a kid'.

His mother would have liked to take her responsibilities for discipline seriously, and once when she came upon him by chance, with some offence still in mind, and with a sulky whip to hand, she began to use it freely on him – until, screeching, flailing, he broke free, dragging the whip away from her. He ran with it to her back-yard flower garden and thrashed that to shreds; then he went to the woodpile and chopped the whip into small pieces and in tears came and threw them at the conservatory glass, behind which the women of the house were watching. Holding the axe, he strode up to the back steps and split the wooden knobs on the banister posts. Then with derisory cat-calls he exited by his usual route, over the back fence.

There must have been amiable times for him, too, among all of those women, because in a studio photograph, taken when he was about ten, of him and his three sisters, he is not at all resentful or abashed. Rather, dressed in his knickerbocker suit, he is full of self-confidence, and seems almost preening. One knows, without needing to have been told, that this was a family

in which a son, whatever his faults, had a special standing.

The knickerbocker suit is part of another story about him. Dressed in this, and with his blond hair slicked tightly sideways, he and his sisters were being taken out by their mother when he decided to throw himself across the tramlines and refuse to get up. He kicked and squirmed there, despite the fast-approaching tram with its clanging bell, and despite his sisters' cries. Dragged to his feet, he ran off, further along the line, and did the same thing again. It was all in the cause of being left at home. His father, when told of this, decided, in his detachment, that the incident showed character in the boy.

It was probably his mother who experienced the worst of his nature and was his particular enemy. His eldest sister told me that their mother had hauled him out of a cab, once, and into a public park, where despite the little girl's pleas she had begun to flog him about the legs with a snatched-up stick. Holding onto him by the clothing, encumbered herself in a long jacket and fur, her hat and net veil falling askew, she struggled to beat him, until a passer-by threatened to report her to the police. My aunt Margaret's comment on this memory, when in her ninetieth year, was 'Poor mother.' She and I were riding in a taxi through the city at the time, and she nudged me and pointed. 'That was the place.'

By his early teenage years, my father had become a particularly strong swimmer. At Sydney Grammar School he was a champion of the sport, and is said to have swum seven miles up the Lane Cove River, which leads into Sydney Harbour, in waters where sharks had been known. This was for a bet, and was adjudicated, unofficially, by the school's rowing team, at training. Sporting ability brings popularity, of course, and so my father was by no means alienated, when young.

Life-long, one of my father's vanities was his school, and his prowess there. 'At my school, Grammar, you know...' he would begin a reminiscence, in later life, for the discomfort and edification of his disrespectful children, who went to the small-town, meagrely funded government provision. It was true, as he said, that his school had been the best and most expensive in Sydney, and true also, his family confirmed, that he had been an excellent scholar, outstanding in English and classics, but also in maths. Judging from his repetitive anecdotes, his swimming feats at school were later of no more importance to him than was his ability in Latin.

He kept what I thought a strange obsession with that language, reading over a relatively few texts all his life; but I think now that however much he may have admired Caesar's strategies in Gaul, the obsession was really with a past achievement of his own.

In my father's high school days, when he was thirteen or fourteen, after a particular argument with his parents, he raged from the house, late one afternoon, crossed the road, and went down to the beach, wrenching off his clothing on the way. He began to swim outwards, into the harbour. The old man, he knew, would be watching him, who had been looking all afternoon through his binoculars at the yachts from his front garden. The harbour is often choppy there, a couple of miles in from the ponderous Heads, which open widely onto the sea, and it was even in those days crowded at the weekends with international ships, ferries, yachts, and fishing boats, but my father kept swimming straight on, amongst it all, toward the navy-coloured opposite shore. Finally he rose from the water, in his father's glasses, against sandstone boulders, and sat on a small beach; but not for long. He began to swim back, disappearing behind a passing wooden ferry, and among the enormous yachts, with sails puffed out like pantaloons, and vanishing within the shoals of late sunlight. My grandfather, watching with his girls gathered about him, sent them down to the beach to wait with a towel and warmer clothing. When my father came into the house, in the dark – the lights had been left off, and his mother taken away to bed – no word was said to him by his father, who soon afterwards went out for dinner at his club. He came home, Margaret said, with the basted, roasting face that would become permanent in his later years, and in a surprisingly jovial mood.

In my father's late teens, Olga, his youngest sister, announced at a Sunday lunch that a group of her friends was coming to the house for tennis, and that she would prefer her brother were out, rather than he made himself familiar, in his usual way, which embarrassed her. After a few moments consideration, everyone grown still, my father rose quickly from the table, without speaking, grabbed the central dish of goulash, and with abbreviated ceremony poured it all over her head and tennis clothes. He strode briskly from the room, affecting a whistle, as she threw herself onto the table, screaming. That night my father came home so drunk he was oblivious to any reprimand, and he continued to do this until he became the object of concern, and Olga's insensitivity was the scandal.

This is the earliest story of my father and the uses of drunkenness. There was much social drinking among his circle, in his youth. He seems to have been a normal young hedonist of the Jazz Age, in its loose-limbed antipodean version. At weekends he would borrow a car from his family, in which he picked up his friends, or he rode with them, and they collected some girls, and went to the Rugby or the races, and on to parties. Most weekends they partied in one or other of the neighbours' long, slanting gardens, under lanterns, amid the smell of frangipani and sea-ooze. No doubt, as with everyone, but the young most of all, my father and his friends were the porcupines of Schopenhauer's parable, who are compelled to draw closer for a living warmth, but who at the same time are inadvertently repelled by each other's spines. Smarting, dissatisfied, at times elated, they played their tennis and drank and were raucous together. They came to Bondi, to go surfing, the men leaping from the running boards of the trams; and the young males met outside the dance halls, carrying their black jackets and ties. Somewhere my father found his first kiss – perhaps on one of those spring evenings in Sydney that are worn as lightly as a silk shirt. The bats go over at that time in silent flocks, twitching above the orange and lemon windows of houses and blocks of flats – over the palms that are like party hooters, and the vast pachydermatous fig trees with their impossibly broad canopies and their roots bulging along the ground. A weekend ferry might have gone by, floating string music, on the melted bullion of its lights. Or the rite may have occurred in a shadowy hallway, before his leaving by the front door, of a rainy afternoon. Even when it rains in Sydney, the sky is immensely high. There seems everywhere the space for possibilities, if one is adequate to them. Of course, a day or a month later she would have refused to speak to him, or the other way around. It was a common enough youth, although with 'every advantage'.

My father came from a family that shared definite preferences. My grandfather set the style, and my grandmother was given exemption, allowed to be 'dignified'. Margaret was the true disciple, who kept all of their tastes. Things they liked were prawns, beer, sherry, the races, card games, a dance band, offal (particularly for breakfast – kidneys, tripe, brains, tongue, or 'lamb's fry', with toast), detective stories (read in copious numbers and circulated through the family), and a jocular, bantering manner. On religion, they thought there was definitely Someone – otherwise life would not make any sense – but going to church, thinking on such things, was not considered 'normal'. Normality was a condition they greatly prized and considered themselves to embody. The family was only insistent, in the matter of religion, that they were Anglicans. My father's default from their standards was his 'heavy' reading (which his father always said was of 'Dostoyevsky', having been told once that was who was being read), and perhaps his joining the Drama Society, when he was at the university: these things were considered, later, to have been indicative of unsoundness. Part of the credo was not to take anything too seriously, except 'getting ahead', of course, which out of superstition one never talked about. Olga's heresy was to be humourless and teetotal.

The life my father later sought to escape, working his plantation, was a fate he solicited, because for years in his young manhood he claimed, against his parents' scepticism, that agriculture was his metier.

He started to protest this in his university days, when he studied law, and was articled to his uncle William's firm. All at once, in the last year of his course, he disappeared into the backblocks of New South Wales, to become a jackaroo on a sheep station. It was a position that had been casually found for him by a university friend. He mentioned the experience to me once, obliquely, in his remark that any God who could create sheep was a complete incompetent. He was persuaded all too easily to return home. Taken on in his father's property dealings, this was not farming, either, and he did no work at all. He hardly ever turned up at the office, and then only after a 'business lunch', to bother the secretaries. Still, he seems to have been paid. For a year he claimed that he was trying to decide what to do with himself, while mostly reading and swimming in the day and going out of an evening. Suddenly, he announced to his parents that a 'lady friend' was pregnant by him, and that he was going to be married. He was in his early twenties; she was ten years older, had already been married, and worked in a dress shop in the city. When the family met her, they found she had all her self-assurance. This was a cool head, they decided, a business woman. So, despite the uproar it caused, they ruled that my father was to have no settlement, but only the opportunity of a job that had good prospects, with another firm.

Perhaps it was partly because of this disappointing start that the marriage, which soon produced a second child, was constantly off and on, and lasted only four or five years. The couple lived in a flat at Kings Cross, the bohemian part of town. Whatever else they quarrelled over, my father, I know, objected that his children were to be raised as 'bigoted Catholics': this was the only kind, he seems to have believed, from his invariable use of the adjective. His own religion, he used later to say, was 'just to do the right thing' (to which he would add that he was 'lapsed').

I first met my half-sister when in my late thirties. My father, who had died, had never mentioned his earlier family to me. Nor did my mother, until one day as a boy I heard the story from her at the cost of revealing that I had been searching through the private possessions in my father's bureau. I was looking, I suppose, for some traces of him, and was struck, as always, by the orderliness of all his things: the precise arrangement of his papers, the exact placement of his souvenirs, the obsessive neatness of his folded clothes, which he would fold again after my mother had ironed them. In one of his drawers, I came on a society pages clipping of a bride, someone who was named as his daughter. My mother told me, while she berated my lack of morals and checked I had left no trace of prying, that my father had only discovered this picture by chance. Then, long after, my half-sister introduced herself to me at a poetry reading I gave, with the broad bones in her face of the newspaper picture, so unlike my father's and my own. One of the first things she said was that her mother, when in financially comfortable old age (having married a wealthy man, and outlived him) told her: 'Your father had the best sense of humour, and was the most fun, of any man I've known. Geoffrey was a simply marvellous man.' I had to say, 'He wasn't like that for us,' and after the intermission I read a poem on the disaster of my father's later life. I saw my half-sister's discomfort, in the front row, where she had been smiling, but we became friends.

During his first marriage, my father managed to hold on to work in real estate by regularly changing his employer and by the business connections he could claim. He became renowned, among his family, because of a deal that he made for himself. He bought a block of land on Pittwater, a large bay north of Sydney Harbour, but when he went back to look at his beach-front bargain, he found the tide was high and the place had been diminished by half. 'They took him to lunch before the inspection,' my grandfather explained, uproariously. It seemed like something I had seen in a cartoon, when I first heard of this, but my aunt's face, in the telling, stayed all too straight.

In the decline of his marriage, my father ran up large gambling debts. I was not able to discover the amount of these: Margaret fluttered and twittered and assured herself that she had forgotten. He had to reveal the problem to his parents, and explained that he had been trying to win the money they had not allowed him, to support his wife as she had a right to expect, since she had known of his background when their attachment was formed. My father was taking the break-up badly, which meant that he was having to be half carried home by strangers to his parents' house each night.

It was decided that my grandfather would settle my father's debts, and my father would be given his chance at farming, on condition it was done somewhere far out of the way, and he not return. His sisters would help with his children, of whom he was going to lose custody, and if his ex-wife agreed, would bring them to visit him. This part of the plan seems to have happened not more than once, and then only with his daughter. His ex-wife's attitude to my father was somewhat different then, no doubt, from what she would later tell my half-sister.

My aunts decided that my father had been tricked and shabbily treated by his first wife. 'Belle was her name, and that tells you her nature,' Margaret said. '*La belle dame sans merci*, your father used

THE WATERS IN THE EARTH

to call her,' Olga told me. 'It's Tennyson – but you'd know that, wouldn't you.'

I have found only one picture of my father's first wife: it was among his sisters' collection of loose photographs. The main subject of the snapshot is a small boy, in his low chair, out on the grass; but a woman with curly bobbed hair is crouching beside him, cut off at the edge of the frame. She looks pretty, unaffected, and 'normal', as she glances sideways into the camera. The surprise about this picture is the tone of the writing on the back. It must have been sent off, once, to someone, because it reads, 'Geoff's wife squatting on our lawn. The boy looks a hundred years old. Toby.' (Toby was my grandfather's nickname, in later life, when he became as portly as a jug.) The choice of verb, the detachment, the cold humour add some detail to my grandfather's nature.

My mother believed she understood the failure of my father's relationship with my grandfather. My father was not able to understand it, she thought, because it was too simple and too unflattering of him. For him, it was a mystery that his father, so relentlessly drawn to a good time, was prepared to accept anyone else's riotous living, and to be anyone's friend, but his own. I am not sure whether my mother ever tried to tell my father what she knew, or if she only had her insight in old age. She told me: 'Your father had really just one fault, in the old man's eyes – he couldn't hold his liquor. That's a thing those people won't forgive. Someone who's an embarrassment to them. It's not what you do, it's always how you do it, with their kind.'

My mother used to call her father-in-law 'the old rogue', though she knew him almost entirely from my father's reports. This was said without connotations of warmth, or amusement, or even a begrudged respect. My grandfather and she met only twice,

both times in the country, before her marriage. Once he came
there to oversee improvements to the plantation he had recently
bought, and once he turned up briefly when my father was getting
into financial strife again, to berate him, straighten out his affairs,
reassert the arrangement. After that last occasion the two men
never met again.

On his second visit north, my grandfather considered buying
further land there: a tract which ran untouched right along the sea-
front, over several headlands, out in front of the tall hillsides and
their plantations. Unfortunately for his descendants, he decided
against it. My mother heard that he had grown more than usually
impatient with his son, on that occasion, and had cut his visit short.
By the time I was a boy, tourists had begun to come to the area in
numbers that compounded every year, and motels were appearing there as though by cell division. These have now been added
to with large-scale holiday resorts, spread along the foreshores.
In his old age, my father remarked on how his family could have
owned 'all of that', waving his hand from his nursing home bed,
northwards across the town, toward the sun. That they did not was
a tragedy he lay and contemplated. He would not have been old
and dying and poor and sober, but for 'something or other' that
had happened once.

Back in those days, my mother said, when the father and son
had finished their inspection of the plantation for the day, they
would go into town together and compete at regaling the locals in
the bar. The trouble between them would have once again been
apparent there.

My father hardly knew my mother at that time, but during the
first of my grandfather's visits he went to the dress shop where she
was working and asked her to join them in the pub's lounge, when
she was free. He invited her again, more formally, on his father's
second trip. My mother was not impressed on meeting my grand-

father. 'The old rogue,' she explained, 'he thought he had charm.'

Despite my mother's low opinion of him, my grandfather does seem to have been 'good value', for men at least. To both him and his son, what was important was how they stood in other men's eyes – how much bonhomie they asserted, how generous they were, how 'manly' in their drinking, how forceful as raconteurs. Such primitive command is most convincing if backed up by physical accomplishment, and my father had his swimming, my grandfather his shooting, and evidently swimming, too. Male camaraderie of such an overt kind used often to be thought a particularly Australian trait, but surely the Greeks gathered on the beach at Ilium not just in the hope of loot, but in response to such an atavism.

My grandfather, as he got older, regularly used to announce, in a sentimental mood that came upon him, somewhere down the blue shift towards drunkenness, that all he wanted from life was to be able to put his hand into his pocket, whenever anyone asked for help, and to find a twenty pound note there. As it turned out, this was literally what he had formed the habit of doing, through his later years, except usually with larger currency. He became known as an easy mark. People promised to pay him back the next day, or the next week, but he would not remember who they were, or what they owed. When he died, during the War, his daughters opened the safe in his office and found it crammed with IOUs, almost all of them drunkenly illegible, written on his card, on pub stationery, on beer coasters, often unwitnessed, and many for amounts for which he would have had to write cheques. My aunts already knew his business had gone 'a bit close to the edge' during the Depression, but that morning, shaking out shoeboxes full of scraps of paper, one imagines their stomachs lurched, with the realisation that their fortunes had left the road and were airborne. Olga, who had worked for him, crouched on the carpet in the Sunday morning light that came through the blinds, and piled up the evidence, calculating with urgent glances the company's lack of resource.

Margaret and Olga never liked to talk about their father to me, obviously because of his failure in responsibility toward them; but once, when I was in my twenties, and the topic came up, and after Margaret had left the room, to dab her eyes, Olga turned to me with a frankness that came of long bitterness. 'It was all your father's fault, what happened to Dad: it was because he didn't really have a son. As you have no doubt noticed, Geoffrey has managed to wreck the lives of everybody who...'

Fortunately, just then, with a bright, wet smile, Margaret returned.

The family's shame, its business failure, presented to my aunts as almost their entire inheritance, was made less glaring by the tragedies of the War around them. They could hide their distress in the general lowering of heads, against the hot, animal breath coming out of Europe and Asia.

The 'girls' and their mother, it was found, would have to sell the family house and rent a flat. There would be some income from shares, but jobs would need to be taken. Still, they were not going to be moved from Vaucluse, from among their sort of people.

Almost immediately after Toby's death, the second daughter, Dorothy, or Bill as she was always called, decided to marry. She chose from among her various suitors the blandest of them, but the wealthiest. He owned pharmacies in country towns and had rural investments, and they withdrew to a pastoral district and joined the polo set. Her main problem in life was thought to have been solved; wrongly, as it turned out.

The two remaining sisters were so absurdly dissimilar they should never have kept a close relationship, but were forced to by

circumstance. Their mother was dying of a slow, inoperable cancer, and begged not to be put among strangers. Margaret, not just for lack of other talent, but because of her solicitude, stayed at home with her, while Olga went to work for them all.

Margaret was tall and thin, described as a 'beanpole' until late in life, and her features were piquant and small. In earlier photographs she has heavy brown hair. She was frivolous and witty, and her wafted, tottering walk, on thin ankles, made people solicitous for her. She was vague, thought not to have much brains, but she contradicted that with her humour, and with the way she managed as her mother's nurse, learning to give injections of morphine and attending to everything alone. Her only relief was in the last days of the ordeal, when a nurse was brought in to allow her some sleep. After their mother died, Margaret fled from housekeeping for Olga, and went to northern Queensland, a rough frontier then, unqualified and into the unknown. She had finished school at thirteen, education thought to be wasted on her, and was by then in her late thirties. She had never been out in the world. Finally, Olga traced her to a hotel in the dry, remote town of Charters Towers, where she was the housekeeper. It took more than a year of appeals to win her back.

Olga was the one to be the breadwinner: although barely five feet tall, she had masculine force and a hard efficiency. Previously only employed by her father, she improved her skills at business college, then found a job with a large insurance firm. She became head of the typing pool there, and in a hairdo like Captain Bligh's wig, as my father pointed out, strode the quarterdeck for many years.

Olga was the most difficult person I have known. One felt a constant disquiet when around her, waiting for the next complaint. She seemed swollen with discontent, within her compact shape, and was always flushed, so that she reminded me of a tourniqueted finger. When about the house, if not actively complaining, she would often sigh ('Nothing...it's nothing...it doesn't matter...'). If she was angry, she tilted her finely painted brows together, like an actor in a Noh play, and held herself rigid, as though she wanted to deliver a slap. During my boyhood visits, Margaret and I sometimes looked at one another, of a day, and merely smiled – realising, unspokenly, how we enjoyed the office hours.

In the Depression, when the family still lived in 'the old house', Olga had been willing to go around the tough streets of Paddington alone, to collect her father's rents. More surprisingly, he had allowed her to do so. She perched on a cushion in the car and went, it seems, without any reflection on being chosen for the job. I can see her astride the front doorsteps, as she looks in photographs of the time – her bonnet like a helmet; her fur as big as a horse collar; her shoulders seemingly over-padded, but all her own; her remarkably wedge-shaped physique, bust-heavy, tapering to flat, narrow hips, and then to calf muscles like Indian clubs. She had a tight, angry-looking little Roman nose, rolled like a snail shell at the nostrils; pretty, softly waved hair, worn in a close style; a large beauty spot, lacquered black; and cheeks that were permanently hectic. Margaret said to me late in her life, embarrassed, looking at a photograph from that period, 'God help anyone who got behind with their rent – she let them know where they stood.'

'Wasn't she ever robbed?' I asked.

My father said that she was never robbed because it was obvious she carried a knuckleduster. (I looked a question at my mother; she shook her head.) His nickname for her in their youth, I learned, had been 'Knuckle'. It seemed to me accurate; her profile was abrupt as a bulldog's and her jaw was square. He said that you knew at once she was trouble by her walk, which was staccato even in slippers. I am sure he was afraid of her. He also called her 'a pocket Hercules'. This description was used much later: it was borrowed from the publicity for a strongman, hardly taller than Olga, called Don Athaldo, who was famous in my boyhood. He advertised his course of home exercises in magazines, with photographs of himself, fists on hips, looking as though he were built of cobblestones. I remember my father saying to my mother, 'Just look at that neck,' pointing to an advertisement, which was headed 'The Mighty Atom, Australia's Strongest Man'. It was on a page of *Pix* magazine, taken from around the butcher's meat. My father had picked up the paper, folded it back, held it out to my mother. 'My God, who does that neck, and those shoulders, remind you of?'

My mother said, 'Don't exaggerate, in front of the child.' But she gave an assenting, bleak shake of the head, which I thought conveyed how 'fed up' she was with us all.

3. A Religious Wound

My mother and father first met soon after he appeared on the coast, at a party he gave in the packing shed of his plantation. She went along invited by a girlfriend, on a Saturday afternoon, and was greeted with a *lai* of frangipani flowers: he was placing one around the neck of each young woman who arrived. My mother was surprised at the thought of a man gathering all the blossoms needed for this and carefully stringing them together. Everyone, she believed, thought him strange; they certainly considered him an extraordinary 'toff'. My mother said she and her girlfriend withdrew into a corner of the shed, by one of the large, propped-out wooden shutters that would close the empty window frame, and while the others were dancing to the wind-up record player, they sat and giggled and pulled their *lais* to pieces.

Despite this, and although they had hardly spoken together, my father asked to see her again, as she was leaving. They became friends, but only cautiously on my mother's part; she had the defensive scepticism of country people in those times. From my father's elaborate story, which she thought was told with self-pity, she separated the facts: that he had been married due to immorality, had two children, whom he was now unable to visit, and was not welcome in his parents' house, nor even in the same city as them. She also discovered that he 'liked to booze', although it took time for her to understand he was more than simply unhappy, but an alcoholic. From her brothers she heard how they, and most people, thought him conceited. What impressed her about him was his 'gentlemanly' manner, even when he was drunk.

To him, she must have seemed someone his mother and sisters would have been aghast at, for her naivety. Certainly, she was far removed from his former wife's stylishness and social ease. But he would have noticed she was gentle, unspoiled, and comely; and, quite soon, that she was sympathetic, even against her will.

My mother was not entirely an ordinary person, although from appearances she seemed to be. Twenty-one at this time, she was five foot two inches tall and had a maternal build, on which the flesh was still light. Her face was more round than narrow, her eyes good-sized and hazel, her nose straight, definite, slightly fleshy at the end, and her dark brown hair was worn in bangs, like that of most girls then. (Later she wore her hair in two long plaits, wrapped over her head from opposite directions and pinned in place – a style that remained outside fashion and that she kept for most of her life.) Her best feature was always her smile, which was sincere and soft, and came and went like music blown about out-doors. All her tastes were normal (except in one regard) and she had none of the distortions that are caused by talent. She had been to school for only four years.

What was unusual about my mother was that from childhood she had a spiritual craving; and not as a whim, but with constancy. It seems she knew early, and as though directly on her senses, the unsatisfactoriness of the world, and wanted in some way to trans-cend this. The desire for spiritual security, kept private all through her youth, occupied her more as she learned more of the cruelties of 'our man-made system'. The world's injustices were constantly barging up against her, but a political response to them, although relieving, she would have found superficial.

Her religious preoccupation had much to do with an equally constant, disquieted sense – that of being in flight toward life's target, death. This single overwhelming fact, I believe, caused every situation she experienced, up until marriage and childbirth, to seem unreal.

My mother was about as unworldly as one could be, while carried along by the everyday course of things. She told me that during her young days she was much troubled by the conflict between 'purity' and a desire for children, and had decided, with the world as it was, that her maternal urge should be 'put aside'.

Her longing for sanctity made my mother dissatisfied with any commonplace, lightly held religion. Brought up an old-style Presbyterian, she retained their belief that the Roman Catholic Church, in which many of her temperament have taken refuge, was 'the whore of Babylon', a corrupted thing, and too grossly sensuous. Christianity, for her, could only be authentic if experienced at a small meeting of 'the meek of the Earth'; in the linoleum-floored sitting room of a working-class family, or on a folding chair at a rented, hollow municipal hall.

After she met my father, my mother would sometimes hear his 'plummy' voice, while passing one of the pubs in town, raised above those of the other men. When she finally accepted his invitation and went for a drink in a lounge bar, she alone seemed to notice, from the edge of things, that during the loud conversations, he had a peculiar mannerism. It was one she disliked. He would stand with his free hand inside his jacket, holding onto the side of his chest, and would secretly caress himself there, moving his hand slightly, appreciatively, while he unwound his eloquence. He stood with his head in the air, overwhelmed all competition, and acted 'the real I am', she told me. As he grew drunker, with a half-embarrassed look, he seemed to try to talk his unsteadiness down.

My mother soon went away to Sydney, to work as a 'domestic', and only came home briefly for holidays, when between jobs, or every few years. My father wrote to her, with lapses, for all of the ten years she was gone, but she kept none of his letters. I said to her this was a long time for him to have continued writing, and she said he had probably needed someone to whom he could complain. (But the remark was made after she had been old and alone for decades and had grown acerbic.) He would also telephone sometimes, from the post office, to her work. She could not remember how often  she answered his letters, but agreed it was probably to almost every one, 'as a person does'. During this time he gave her an emerald ring, the stone in a setting of wrought silver that he had designed, which he liked because it was 'unusual', and which she said he 'might have thought' was an engagement ring. My mother said her life was good then, and she had been in no hurry to settle down.

The life she led in the city would not have been thought of as a good time by most young women. Living-in with the families she worked for, she had little to do with friends, which seems to have been as she preferred. On her day off, a treat might be to see her cousins, Jean, Ivy and Heather, the Anderson girls, who had also moved to Sydney, to work as hotel maids, and one of them in a bar. They used to go to the pictures together and then to a tea shop.

When their days off did not coincide, my mother would go into town on the tram to speak to one or other of them at work, 'just to say hullo'. That was considered an outing. What she remembered liking most, though, was to sit alone by the harbour of an early morning, to watch the boats. I have done this, also, at the place she went to. One can see, from there, the few yachts bowing before the great door of Sydney Harbour, entering and reemerging from the outer world of light.

My mother said she liked working in the Eastern Suburbs because you could live in a big house and look out on the water. She worked longest for a Jewish family, for whom she cleaned, helped in the kitchen, cared for the children, and opened the house early, before they rose, and to whom she was known, she overheard (or was to the patriarch), as 'the Christian girl'. She admired their warmth among themselves, and recalled them as having been good to her.

At this time my mother joined a religious sect called British Israel, which believes that the Anglo-Saxon people are the lost twelfth tribe of the Jews; that they are the 'chosen race', and the British monarch sits on the throne of David. (Was she, in this belief, secretly asserting herself, usurping the people whom she served?) Going alone to meetings of this religion, in a stunted church in the back streets of Darlinghurst, occupied her leisure, also. I know about this involvement because my father used later regularly to scoff, at my mother's interest in what he called 'the more crazy' religions. She tried numerous other sects, including the Mormons and the Plymouth Brethren, but after she discovered 'the Truth', in middle age, she grew shy of mentioning her earlier false starts.

My mother claimed that she never had any male friend but my father. There used to be a photograph of her as a young woman, taken in a Sydney studio, which my father had asked her to have made. Closest to the viewer was a large fur stole, almost certainly a prop, with her gazing sideways from behind it, and from behind a bare shoulder. The fur looked all the more soft because it was slightly out of focus. She wore the close-fitting round bonnet of the thirties, and had very dark eyes and a soft expression, slightly bashful, slightly amused. It was a warm and innocent face. She had been flattered, relaxed, and made to shine. The picture was never sent. I once said to my mother, as an adult, holding the photograph (which was kept for years in a drawer in her room, and was later said to have been lost), that she was beautiful. She said, no, she was never beautiful. I said I thought I could be objective. She smiled tightly and put an end to the matter: 'Oh yes, you're something of a judge of women's attractions – I'm forgetting that.' I had been divorced.

All her life my mother disliked being short and complained about it. She claimed she would have grown taller except for an accident she had had when twelve years old. The family was living in Queensland then, on a cattle property her father managed, and once at dusk she took one of his best horses and ambled away quietly on it, to a racetrack that lay nearby, in the bush. There she began to ride wildly. Some cattle had got onto the course and were invisible, browsing in the dark. Her horse suddenly tried to leap over a cow lying by the rail, as it had startled up. She was thrown heavily. Later her father found her, after the horse had gone home, wandering dazed in the fringe of the bush. He carried her home, stumbling, unable to mount his horse with her in his arms. She lay back, and the vast, brightly starred, insect-riddled Queensland night seemed to be slopping over her. The feeling was one of strange detachment. Her father was anxious at the slurred silliness she talked, and came home speaking to her soothingly and calling across the paddocks, alternately. Laying her down, he knelt and stroked her face, giving brusque orders to the others. He never, later on, scolded her for what she had done. It was an experience she often spoke about.

My mother was born in 1909, with the help of a bush nurse, at the cattle station's homestead, inland on the Tropic of Capricorn. It was a scrubby, flat, sandy landscape, in which the tin roofs of the few clustered buildings blazed like drops of solder, in the vastness and in her memory. When she was twelve, the family moved down to the more lush country on the northern coast of New South Wales, to start a banana plantation. They arrived by passenger steamer, and came ashore, several at a time, in a canvas sling, hung beneath a 'flying fox' wire. It carried them 'a long way' just above the surf and onto the beach. My mother was terrified.

Then she was frightened by the dingoes that wailed to each other at night, from hill to hill, in that forested, steep country.

My mother left school around this time, to help in the house, as she was the eldest. All her life she kept her maroon, hard-covered school reader, along with her Bible, and these were probably the only books, as distinct from Bible-study aids, that she ever read. The poem in her reader about Mary calling 'the cattle home, across the sands of Dee' was always fascinating to her, and she also talked of the one by Longfellow, about 'a banner with the strange device, Excelsior'.

After a few years in their new locality, her father saw the prospects for a carrying business, handling produce. While continuing to grow his own fruit, he would eventually run six trucks, using hired men. He took on his two sons to work as soon as they were teenagers. A big workshop was put up, in corrugated iron, along from the house, on a shelf of land beneath the plant-ation; a gravel driveway barely skirted my grandmother's picketed front garden, and became oil-stained and in need of regular renewal, under heavy wheels. Within the compound stood petrol pumps, workmen and trucks; the ground was scored and turned to mud; motors were made to roar, dogs barked, and blue smoke drifted, all through my mother's earlier days.

When her younger sister was old enough to help full-time in the house, my mother, in her late teens, took her first paid job. She went to a larger town, further north, to work in the home of people who owned the general emporium. Sometimes she came back for a day or two, by train. She particularly missed her sister, and her father, who was always busy, but thought of her mother as remote and severe.

Then she went away to the city, and the years passed, and when she came home again, to stay for more than a week or so, it was because she was disturbed by what she had seen of the War in newsreel cinemas.

And then she was to be married, to someone known for a decade yet hardly known or understood. She went off alone to Sydney on the train, for the wedding, without any enthusiasm from her family, among a crowd of rowdy boys going to enlist. She was a woman of thirty-two, who had been on her own for many years.

The ceremony was held in the central Wesleyan chapel, my mother being at the time in transition between more extreme beliefs. The War perhaps promised enough fire and brimstone to give her a sense of authenticity, just then. There were no guests: my father, in uniform, persuaded two idlers off the street to be witnesses, and gave them money for the pub. My parents stayed the night in a hotel, then my father went back to camp, to pack his gear for New Guinea, and my mother began looking for work. She was unusually old to be marrying, for those days, and my father was thirty-nine.

My father always scoffed at my mother's religious faith, but it was surely her being drawn to Christian values that helped make her attractive to him, and caused him to persist so long in wanting to marry her. Such doctrines led her to think she could redeem him, which was her intention with the marriage, so they ought to have been encouraged by him. My mother was that very person to whom, in an earlier incarnation, the Christian ideas were first preached – one of the 'meek', the 'poor in spirit', the spiritually 'heavy-laden'. It is understandable that in a later world, still insecure in much the same ways, such a person would again be attracted by a plain form of what seem to me entirely compensatory beliefs.

My father saw the children of his first marriage, after ten years, on a few brief and final occasions, when he was stationed in Sydney. There is a photograph of him in uniform, while out with them, taken by a street photographer. No one thinks to smile. The girl is round-faced and mild, with sweetly looped-up plaits, and she holds his hand while gazing off intently, as though searching in the crowd. The son is a teenager, already much taller than his father: white-faced and Jesuitical-looking, he bends sideways, graciously martyred, into the frame. He has large, stony knees, between his school socks and overly tight shorts, which are strangely intrusive – they suggest something furious and inarticulate about him. Cold-thighed, intensely inward, he floats upwards, diminishing, remote, as though an El Greco figure. My father's uniform fits perfectly, and he appears to have just swaggered into his pose. He stands tilted a little on one hip, his hand around the bowl of a pipe, jutting beside his jaw.

The son is said to have been such an ardent Catholic that once while staying at his aunts' flat he slashed the pages of a book his father had sent him there, in disagreement with its theology, or what he thought its implications. I saw this book when I was young and staying in my turn with my aunts. I took out of a cupboard a heavy volume, *The Jungle Book Omnibus*, of Rudyard Kipling,

illustrated in black-and-white and with colour plates, and turning through it I came on places where pages had been deeply carved away, or where the pictures had had their faces slit. I showed Margaret what I had found, enquiringly, and she grew flustered, took it from me, and brought me biscuits and milk. She tucked the book back again deeply into the linen press – as evidence, one felt.

My father was at first drafted into the army, and made the driver of a staff car, but he wanted something more prestigious, and set out to ingratiate himself with the officers he ferried. He was able to impress someone of influence, to the extent where he could ask a favour. His request was supposedly unheard of, a transfer into the air force, but it was soon arranged. Old school connections may have helped. In the new service, he became a sergeant major and eventually a flight lieutenant. It turned out that the War was for my father, as for many, the best time of his life. His drinking was controlled for him and he had signs of respect from other men.

I asked my mother why he had wanted to change to the air force, and she answered, surprised at my innocence, 'Vanity.'

'The smarter uniform,' she said. 'He thought he would look better in it. Also, of course, there was less chance of fighting.'

But he was sent to New Guinea, just the same, while the Japanese invasion was going on there. He went by ship to Port Moresby, and then, in charge of a few others from his company, was flown with American troops across the island to Rabaul, to build an airstrip, with native labour. There was a good chance when flying of being attacked by enemy fighters, but what they ran into was an exploding tropical storm. The transport plane rolled and plunged like a tanker in a heavy sea. Lightning struck the plane and flickered back and forth along its wings and fuselage, unable to escape. Those looking out the windows saw the whole machine glow supernaturally, like an illuminated Cross. 'That was a sign and a wonder,' my father remarked, 'for those boys from the south. They fell on their knees in their vomit and prayed aloud.' He spoke with a dismissive grimace, which implied that he had remained aloof. I believe he did. His disdain for religion increased, the worse things became for him.

There remained a thrill of fear, you could sense, in the stories he told about New Guinea. At Rabaul, my father met the soldiers

coming in from the jungle, where unknown numbers of Japanese were, although most had been driven back along the Kokoda Trail. Some Australian soldiers told my father that when on patrol they had found the newly severed hand of one of their men, wedged in the fork of a tree, above the track. The body was nearby, in tall grass. It was covered with flies – as excited as bees, is the impression I have. The leader of the patrol, my father said, took the cigarette from his lips and placed it between the fingers of that rigid hand. As the smoke drifted away into the glare, each soldier passing beneath contributed a remark or a salute. One took the hand down and shook it, then replaced it and the cigarette. The bravado of the soldiers, in this story, contrasted with my father's subdued manner in telling it.

My father tried to sustain his comrades' morale, while at war. He had a photograph of himself taken, later kept deep in his bureau, which at first seems merely of him in profile, on a rock shelf, before an almost sideways view of a stringy, many-branching waterfall. The water spreads like a giant creeper among boulders, and in places is bounding from them. Dressed in full uniform, in pith helmet, jacket, shorts, and long socks, with one foot stepping forward, my father gazes off as nobly as a Victorian explorer, above a camp site taking up half the background. But he has positioned himself exactly, so that a prominent stream, breaking out of the falls, seems to emerge from his crotch, and his folded hand is hung casually in the right position. The headquarters tent, with its flag raised, and the soldiers and natives milling about, can be read, with a little indulgence, as being pissed on, prodigiously.

This picture is surprising, because my father was the least vulgar of men. He had deeply cultivated inhibitions. He never swore, no matter how drunk he might be, or how provoked; he never raised his voice, in his family life (his sarcasm made that unnecessary); no mention, no evidence, of private bodily functions was tolerated in our house (fortunately the lavatory was outside); he looked repelled if a workman spat on the ground; his children were contemptuously rebuked for the slightest sniffle.

That such a puerile photograph was taken suggests he felt a need to ingratiate himself; that the picture was kept implies the joke was popular and this had gratified him. Perhaps another story my father told us, of his life in the services, is revealing here. He said a sergeant major, in Australia, was so abusive to his men, physically and psychologically, that a group of them, wearing bala-clavas, dragged him up into an empty football grandstand, while they were on leave, and threw him from the top, breaking his spine. This was also recounted with an uncomfortable look. Such anecdotes, and the photograph, are the only clues to my father's inner life while in the forces.

I have some pictures of my father with another white man among tribesmen in New Guinea. Each native wears a small wooden lid over his genitals, or else a truss of cloth. They are short, bandy and powerful, and each has a crescent-shaped disc strung from his neck and lying on the striated muscles of his chest. Finer crescents, the horns turned downward, are stuck through their nasal septums. The natives are fuzzy-haired, have tuberous noses, and are beautifully muscular, the separation between muscle-groups like fine, darker lines drawn on their bodies. They wear bunches of long, upright feathers in their headbands, overtopped by spears with wooden splinter-tips.

My father said to me casually, when he was sorting through his papers and had these photographs in hand, 'I ruined one of those head-dresses for a fellow, one time.' After my question, he went on, 'We were building an airstrip. I was the only white man there, at the finishing stage, in charge of a labour gang. I was in my tent at night and this chap got drunk and came after me. He'd been giving a lot of trouble, stirring up the others. The people there were pretty fierce – they'd been cannibals, headhunters. This fellow came blundering around my tent in the dark, shouting. I sat up, and he swung at the canvas with an axe. Fortunately, he staggered in the same moment, and fell forward. Brought the tent down on top of me. I punched and kicked and wriggled out the side – I was expecting my head to be split open, any moment. I got to my feet as he was lurching up, and he chased me, bellowing and swinging. The other boys all drew away. I was completely alone. I ran to the work site, falling about in the dark, snatched up the first thing I could lay hands on, a shovel, turned around – it was as dark as he was – the old "whites of the eyes" – let him have it, right in the crown. The shovel must have been edge-on. I felt it jar, in my heels.'

'Did you kill him?'

My father looked embarrassed, then his expression turned cold, seeing me so full of awe. 'Allow me a closet in my skeleton,' he said.

'There wasn't any fuss made,' he added curtly, after a while.

My mother told me her question had been, 'How did the native get drink in the camp? That's what there could have been some fuss about.'

She said my father was transferred straight back to Australia, and glad of it. He was stationed in various country towns, drilling recruits, for the rest of the War.

When he complained about a meal at home, which he ritually did, as if looking for self-justification, my father would sometimes announce, 'This is not the worst meal I have had, however, bad though it is. The worst was…'

We children would chant, 'New Guinea, Christmas Day, 1943.'

He always looked surprised. 'That's right. And it might have done you lot some good, if you had been there.'

He would press on. 'I had for lunch on that occasion a tin of Captain's Crab, before hiding in the bush near the airstrip we had begun building. I lay stretched-out flat, with just my shoulders against a tree, because of Jap planes buzzing all around the sky like wasps. Though I kept yelling at my native boys to keep still, suddenly some more of them would make a break for the jungle. Then the bombers arrived and came in across the airfield and began to pound it. I was bounced right off the ground, like a kid tossed in a blanket. I can tell you, my lunch and I were separated, quite soon.'

'Oh, really Dad! Do you mind!' We kids would play it up, though we had heard it all before. But our mother put a reserve of bitterness into her voice. 'And you're supposed to be a man of some background. So we're told.'

Our father smirked, in this brief abandon to uncouthness.

My mother found work in Sydney, while the War was going on, in a munitions factory. This bothered her, then and afterwards. Every day she felt nauseated by the pieces of dense, smooth metal that she had to handle; but she had been directed to work there by the government employment agency. She also remembered, from her time in this job, that 'Some women are very rude.'

Now that she was married, my mother was completely given up to marriage. As much as she had been resistant and elusive with my father, she became devoted to him. After his return from New Guinea, she several times made the thousand-mile trip from Sydney into Queensland, by blacked-out train, to visit him at Maryborough, where he was finally based; and she met him mid-way, in Brisbane, when he went there on leave.

My mother had realised that the purpose of her existence was to have children – doing so would redeem my father's life, and her own. It seems she believed that the good qualities in my father's character, as she perceived them, could be chosen and made reliable in her offspring: they could be separated from his weak, self-indulgent traits through her influence and care.

My father did not immediately see, apparently, what her sub-mission to him was about – he did not realise that after a short time he might be put aside. I think he could have imagined, briefly, that his self-centredness had found its appropriate earth.

My mother was prepared, in those early days, to go to hotels out by the Brisbane racetrack, with my father, and to spend much of the day waiting for him there. He would mingle with the jockeys and trainers, buying them drinks, for the sake of what might be whispered or overheard. His father, long before, had done the same thing, near the Sydney racecourse, although had never taken his wife along.

In later life, my mother was scornful of her 'romantic' days, and of the backsliding from her beliefs that allowed her to compromise with my father's habits. She particularly regretted and was embarrassed by the time wasted at hotels, sipping lemonade and making desultory talk with other women. 'A person was such a fool,' she would say, quietly. And on several occasions she added, with an indignant stir, 'Cheeky little men, jockeys.'

My mother went to visit my father's sisters, when he was in the air force, invited after they heard of the marriage, and on several occasions while she was pregnant. Her travel concessions for visiting my father had all been used, by those later times; she was living alone in a room, working at the munitions factory, and saving. Going to her new relatives' flat, she found it was the cause of much sighing and grumbling, amid descriptions of how the family formerly lived. My mother thought the place large and comfortable, but overburdened with possessions.

She ingenuously answered her sisters-in-law's questions, revealing that she had no experience of life, no social circle, and no property, apart from clothing and small things like pictures and vases. It did not bother her that she lived on the surface of life, reading a magazine or listening to the radio in the evening, occasionally going alone to a film, because she was preoccupied with understanding the Bible and what God expected of her. She said that she had previously been employed, for years, by a well-known Jewish family, further up the road in which the Grays had lived. Of course, she never thought, during all the time they were neighbours, of calling on the family of her 'fiancé'. He would not have encouraged her to do so, and she would not have taken the relationship seriously enough. She admitted to often passing the Grays' house, when walking down to the harbour on her days off, but one can believe she was not seriously reproved for that.

My mother's name, Nina, was pronounced by her family and herself 'Nine-ah'. When she introduced herself in this way to my father's sisters, Olga was aghast. There was no such name. My mother had to explain that her father had named her Nina May because she had been born on the ninth of May; she now guessed that he must never have heard the name spoken, only have read it. Olga ruled that to them she would be 'Nee-nah'. One did not play around loosely with names. My mother, however, always pronounced her name the way her family did.

A distant relative has told me that as a girl she felt drawn to my mother, on meeting her in the anxious household of my father's family. This woman, sixteen then, was staying for a time with my aunts while her father was at the War. She noticed that my mother, when visiting them, had no need to be entertained, but would sit quietly knitting, unabashed by the formality around her. On an early occasion, my mother had glanced up and seen she was being watched by the girl and had said, 'Come and sit with me and I'll show you how it's done.' Her manner and voice were warm; but even more, the woman said, one felt she was reliably like that. The girl had overheard the witticisms and noticed the discomfort about my mother, among the family, but said the person herself seemed remote from pettiness. I can see my mother sitting, on those occasions, each time noticeably more swollen, amid the pretensions and fuss of a widow and virgins, her eyes cast down, her smile always ready. She must have had, for her hosts, the discomforting fragility and the complacency of an egg.

Although the 'Gray girls' implied their superiority to my mother

– Margaret by not becoming too friendly, Olga by disallowing altogether the possibility of friendship – they made it clear how grateful they were that she would take care of their brother. They spoke as though he had acquired a nurse. I think they were baffled that anyone would choose such a task: selflessness always made them uncomfortable, as if it were a vice.

My mother was unintimidated by the Grays, because privately she did not respect their morality. She knew about the 'unnatural' way they had treated their son and brother, who could have been redeemed when young by a Christian example. It was the 'vanity' of the household in which he had grown up, the 'profligacy' he had seen, which had made him as he was. The matriarch, when she could make an entrance, on my mother's visits, 'tried very hard to be nice,' but even in illness was 'simply ridiculous' in her manner – 'like one of those birds at the Easter Show with too many long feathers, which keep getting in its way.'

The last time my mother and father met, before she went to her married sister's, in readiness for the birth, was disturbing for her; all her brief confidence began to buckle, as though beneath the weight of Queensland heat.

Soon after arriving at Maryborough, she was told she had influenza, and spent a week in her room; then the doctor decided, sombrely, that her illness was German measles. My mother knew that in someone pregnant this condition often caused birth defects and threw herself upon prayer. She was calmed by the thought that she was doing something redeeming, and so surely Providence would not let her down. Later she realised how subtle Satan was: how he can lead mortals into the sin of bargaining with God.

My mother was staying close to the air force base, on a tree-lined street, her boarding house one of the typical big airy wooden buildings of the town, painted white, raised above man-height on stilts, lattice enclosing it to verandah-rail height, all around. She convalesced in a cane chair on the breeze-way, her lunch brought by the landlady, who was stolidly comforting and unworried by infection; the place was all but empty. The traffic going past was as desultory, one imagines, as the awkward child whom my mother chatted with every day – a girl whose parents had called and asked that she be allowed to become infected, and who would therefore hit a tennis ball against the fence for hours, in the building's shade, chatting, and then come upstairs and limply embrace my mother. She proved to be resistant.

My mother said that from the verandah, while knitting or reading, waiting for my father to visit, she would hear his voice, bellowing at the recruits as he put them through their drill. The sound carried over the paling fences of the backyards, in the stillness and heat. Although unable to make out much of what was shouted, she could distinguish many sarcastic inflections. The voice made her uncomfortable. She could not help wondering what it would be like, after he had had such an experience, to live with a sergeant major.

A telegram that had a secret meaning was sent to my father to announce my birth, since he had agreed to avoid celebrations and to arrive at the hospital sober. He travelled down on the train, for a day and a night, to where my mother was, with her sister and brother-in-law, at a small fishing port in New South Wales (a place now overrun by a thousand motels), and appeared at the house, upright and steady. After dropping off his gear and cleaning up, my father was loaned a car – his brother-in-law worked as a motor mechanic from his garage at home – and set out for the hospital.

He later explained that he took an indirect route because he wanted to drive by the river, under the rows of dark old pine

trees for which the town was known. Coming around a corner, on a brilliant, blustery day, glittering with the aftermath of a storm, he found one of the century-old pines fallen on the road. It must have just come down. Beneath it, a car was crushed; and going up to look, my father found the occupants barely visible, but blood-coated and certainly dead. He was joined by another motorist, who went straight away for the police; and my father decided that he would leave too, since he had an appointment, and needed first to steady his nerves.

When he did finally arrive at the hospital, he was, to my mother's shame, by far the most incapable person in the ward. He came in stupidly, clutching at unstable things, causing shrieks, and went crashing to the floor. My introduction to him, I was told, was a blast of his beery cigarette-cough, for which all the women turned on him.

My mother never believed his story about the crushed car. (Her seemingly wildest intuitions about my father – this was hugely frustrating for him, I later saw – would usually turn out to be right.) Her feeling, on this occasion, was that he had heard talk of the accident while in the pub, and had decided to stay there longer, on the strength of the alibi it could provide.

This was early in 1945; our family life did not really begin until more than a year later, when my father was finally demobbed. In the meanwhile, my mother stayed on with her sister, who had always been the closest person to her. The sister, Alice, had a small boy of her own, a couple of years older than I was, and a 'decent husband'. A year after my mother and I left their house, her sister, who was not much more than thirty, fell down on the kitchen floor, as if to a sniper, dead of a cerebral haemorrhage.

My earliest memory is of that woman. We are at the beach; I have been told she was visiting the house my parents had found in Sydney. She and my mother are somewhere in the sunlight, in frocks, and my cousin must be with us, too. Then I roll down a sandhill, a short way, and I have cut my forehead on a tin can. I can see the thing – its serrated lid is brandished like a crab's fighting claw. I yell and my aunt is the first to come to me. I must be a bit over two years old, so my mother will have been pregnant again. I see Alice as a dark, human-shaped cut-out, kneeling over me – her wavy, bobbed hair – embracing me, and I feel a different warmth to that of the day. I feel the thick substance of benevolence. I have no other image of the person, and nor did my mother keep her photograph: I have just this feeling I associate with her (my mother long afterwards confirmed it was Alice who picked me up). She is the vaguest shadow, the most mysterious touch, and yet is there, tenaciously. I think of the final line of a Philip Larkin poem, which he says is 'almost true': 'What will survive of us is love.' In her case, it is so.

When liberation came to the larger world, my father felt himself doubly liberated – he believed he could now continue with his life from where his parents had interrupted it, long before the War.

He would set up as a real estate agent in Sydney. (It was seemingly much easier to do so then.)

For his operations, he chose the city's developing southern edge. He rented, as the family house, what was considered a weekend cottage, behind the sandhills at Bundeena, among a scattering of similar fibro shacks. It was an isolated place, at the southmost end of Port Hacking Bay (which runs parallel to the ocean), where a national park comes down to the water. There was, and still is, a sombre, packed eucalyptus forest there, then broad heathland, with tin roofs among it (many more now), sand dunes, a cantaloupe-coloured beach, and the saturated blueness of what might be a lake, in its 'clear, heavenly reaches'. Nowadays, of course, my father's predictions for the district have all come true: among the trees on the steep side of the bay there are everywhere great stilted, glass-walled, timber-decked houses, which look as though they could put to sea.

The most direct way into Bundeena was by a small wooden ferry, which ran the half-hour length of the bay, from the railway station and shops at Cronulla. Life for the newly married might have been idyllic there.

In another memory from around then, I must be three years old. My brother is not long born, and my mother has brought us to stay with one of her brothers, who lives in Sydney, too, in a small suburban brick house. There is a hot and noisy highway outside. She has left my father, as I understand now (the only time that she did), because he is unreliable at bringing groceries home, in his resurgent drunkenness, and because she is afraid the cottage is too isolated for her, with a new child. I remember myself as play-ing in the backyard of that house, with my cousin, when my father suddenly appears, staggering, a brown paper bag of bottles in his arms. Then my uncle is shouting at him, forcing him off the back step and pushing him in the back and down the driveway. I follow them, through the shadow of the house, afraid that my father, who is reeling about, will fall. His bottles have been snatched from him. He catches sight of me, beyond my uncle, while he is half turned, trying to argue his case, and he pauses to grin foolishly at me. I intensely dislike my uncle, who is bellowing at my father, and bumping him along with one great hand, then grabbing a sleeve, to hold him upright. My cousin, who is a little older than I am, gives me a look of both shame and challenge.

My father, it seems, brought little acquired knowledge or inherited ability to the real estate business. Few vendors or buyers appear to have been persuaded by him, for all his easy talk. He saw his capital quickly dwindling, and had the idea that my mother could help, by baking cakes and pies at home, in the wood-burning stove, for him to sell. These products of her sweated labour he drove, in a hired van, on the rough bush track out of Bundeena, to offer at shops, and failing that, from door to door. But it was like bailing out a foundering rowboat with one's hands. The only solution, given his age, was clear – he would have to apply to the Soldiers Resettlement Scheme for a grant, and return to what he could claim to know something about, a banana plantation on the coast. Less than two years after his discharge from the air force, my father found himself back, by his own choice, in the life he thought he had escaped at the start of the War.

4. Memories of Tropical Fruit

It took barely three years for my father to establish his new plantation, and then to lose it, in a game of cards. By that time my mother had given birth to her third son.

My father used to go to illegal gambling, held on certain nights in a shed at the railway yards. I knew that place, growing up: it was the size of a small aircraft hangar, and had a railway siding down one length, under an over-hanging tin roof. Within there, many cases of bananas and other produce were briefly stacked. The building was so matte with coal dust that even at midday it seemed a silhouette. Behind it was a yard, where paspalum grew higher than the strung wire fence, and then a field with rickety tall Rugby goalposts, but no seating, reaching to the paling fences at the back of low houses. A road nearby, leading to the harbour, the fishing boats and jetty, had a few shops gathered on it, these an outrigger of the town.

I was told the gamblers went down a lane beside the football field at night; it was barely lit with a couple of weak street lamps. They left their cars in the streets around and arrived quietly on foot. I imagined them in the ocean wind and the sound of the breakers. The shed would have been a smear of darkness on the dark. The nightwatchman was said to be mainly alert for the police, who sometimes felt they should assert themselves.

After a losing stretch, accumulating debt, my father took a last chance with a single game. He was then compelled to sign over his property, to the owner of the local hardware store, one of the prominent men in the town. There was no possibility he could have avoided paying and still bought supplies, or have drunk at the pub, or probably have gone about safely. The property he lost, three miles inland from town, was the one to which he went on horseback, while in a stupor.

When my mother was told they would be moving out, she took her new infant in arms to the hardware store and tried to plead with the owner, and yet (she said) not make a scene. She was kept standing on the floorboards of the loading dock, among passing workmen, and when eventually called in, was brusquely treated. My father, hearing what she had done, was uncharacteristically furious – much more upset, my mother told me, than he had seemed to be at the loss of the plantation. What outraged him was her sentimentality – the baby in arms – which he claimed to find 'worse than anything in Dickens'. Perhaps he had been the butt of remarks in the pub.

I have illuminated memories of that plantation. Coming home from town, we got off the long-nosed bus, always without my father, and went up a double wheel-track, between red clay banks; above us were the white marble pillars of great eucalyptus trees, out of virulent green lantana bushes, and a cobalt sky.

Lantana, imported from India, with its impenetrable, swirling canes and closely packed, fretted small leaves, overwhelms the native plants and the fences, rising taller than a man. It is considered a weed, but has a great many flowers scattered over it, each the size of a large coin, each made up of red, orange and yellow florets, like hundreds and thousands, and it has in the heat a secretive perfume.

My mother used to pick those flowers, which fall apart easily into trumpet shapes, and crush them in her hand, to let me smell them. She tried it, too. I would hold one of her hands and inhale from the palm of the other that sweetly rounded, restrained scent, while she carried a second child in the crook of her arm, and probably a third in her belly. Then she walked on, refreshed, or claimed to be.

Our place was a fibro shack, the size of a garage, set crosswise in a long, narrow paddock that was draped on the ridge. The paddock went on with slight undulations toward the top of the hill, to the tall, dark blue water-stains of the forest there. An extension had been built onto the shack at one end, in corrugated iron, to house a stove and chimney flue; at the other was a corrugated iron water tank, raised on a wooden platform. It was all, including the tin roof, painted a dull maroon. Bright short grass came right to the door, without a fence or a path, and beside the posts under the lower side of the shack stood bushes and plants in tins. Among these was my own garden, which my mother had made, in hollowed-out pumpkin shells and grapefruit rinds. I also had a tortoise, under the tank stand, among the ferns and damp stones, secured by a long string through a hole my father had bored in its shell, but I was too aghast to play with this.

The ridge where we lived fell away steeply to one side, beneath the fronds of a neighbour's banana plantation, and rose again nearby, as the next slope, still under close planting. On the other side, it declined roundly and gradually, beneath a tall forest, with many cavities and much of the scaffolding of the trees showing.

Turning about, on arriving home, in the direction we faced of a morning, you could see along a façade of tall eucalyptus poles, strung with its floating parcels of leaves, over the crest of the track, and straight into a broad valley. There was a scatter of tin roofs embedded there, often smeared with smoke; and beyond that the blue arc of the hills, rising onto a third of the sky. Those hills were so darkly forested they seemed to me, in some lights, to be great cavern mouths, hollowed into the bright surface of the day. Along the base of the hills, the smoke of a train would occasionally be drawn, disappearing into tunnels or cuttings, and reappearing. I remember all that as indescribably poignant, suggesting as it did a whole world I could not understand.

I have only rare glimpses of my father from this time: almost everything seems to have been done with my mother alone. It was she who took me out onto the hill slope, one night, while my brother slept below, where our light burned, so that I could see the preternatural clarity of the stars. They were looped across the sky like daisy chains, and behind that were strewn like clover. As we distinguished stars beyond stars, it suddenly felt to me that we were sinking, plunging further and further downwards, and I clutched at my mother's leg and cried out. She soothed me, by pointing to the reclining smoke, level with our shack, to a fried moon, low in the sky, and to all the tenderness of the dew.

From when I was three years old, or almost as early as I can remember, my mother set about teaching me to read. Every morning and evening I read to her, while she continued her work. I followed her about for hours of the day, my finger under different sounds in a book, and she corrected and answered me, with what I felt even then was the life-supporting gift of her patience. When we went into town, she always bought me a Little Golden Book, one of a cheap, flat, hardcover series, luridly illustrated, that had become available with improved printing after the War. But also, it seems now, she would extend her generosity to any book I wanted, after poking around in her purse. I remember being given a larger-format book, about two gnomes, a married couple, who had built their house under some wonderfully baroque tree roots, and who used mushrooms for umbrellas. And one on a boy artist, dressed in a beret, a smock, and a big loose bow tie, with a paintbrush that dripped colour as deliciously as if it were ice cream. I envied him his commanding stance, his self-importance, his happy occupation. I remember the lacquered smell of the colours in those books. In a book of rhymes I was bought was a poem with the thrillingly sad refrain 'Over the hills and far away'. An elf, green as a string bean, was shown reclining along the bottom of the page, holding a musical pipe; loose-limbed and confident, he smiled a mocking sideways smile, as sharp-tasting and strange as the juice of a weed. At the end of the poem, he was drawn in silhouette on a grassy, blown hill, dancing supremely, with children cavorting behind him.

The book that affected me most, at this time, as must surely be the case for all children who have seen it, was a collection of fairytales illustrated by Arthur Rackham. I opened it irresistibly, and was always caught between elation and fear, as I came to its coloured plates. Of these, I remember mainly a distracted knight, stern but gentle, speaking from his horse with a girl, one of many in the book who looked alike, beautiful and pure-faced, and yet as listless and pale as cobwebs. The rider and the maiden had met while wandering on a river bank, among the flags of bulrushes; then they were each alone in a cramped forest, under the sinister, emotion-ridden trees. And there were drawings of witches, with noses like blood-stained icicles, hair like brambles, long chicken's feet for hands; and of lumpy-looking goblins, their legs in silk pantaloons as thin as frogs' legs. I recall also great winds that darkly starred the sky with leaves, lifted out the maidens' hair in lapidary shapes, and billowed their vaguely diaphanous gowns far before them, toward distant valleys.

Each of these scenes was painted in colours as drained as those of pressed flowers. 'Much have I travelled in the realms of gold' since then, I have seen many masterpieces of art, but none has affected me more, physically, than the illustrations in that book. They had an overwhelming strangeness.

My mother, when she taught me to read, told me not to say the words as she did, because she was often tired, but with each sound made more clearly, as my father said them. We used to ask him the right pronunciation of certain words, in the mornings. (From a later time, I remember him reproving my mother for not saying the word 'actually' with four syllables, and about her pronunciation of 'nude' – which she refused to be corrected on, saying he made it sound embarrassing – and over 'auction' and 'massacre' and 'reconnoitre', and many others.)

A connection between the emotional reliability of a parent in one's early childhood and being at home in the world is spoken of by Wordsworth, in *The Prelude*:

Blest the infant Babe
...who with his soul
Drinks in the feelings of his Mother's eye!
For him, in one dear Presence, there exists
A virtue which irradiates and exalts
Objects...
No outcast he, bewildered and depressed:
Along his infant veins are interfused
The gravitation and the filial bond
Of nature that connect him with the world.

Yet I knew there was something wrong with my mother. It was as plain as when a person has the flu, although no fuss is being made.

I knew my father was to blame, but began to realise her anxiety had something to do with me, also. I remembered having been taken by her to doctors when we visited her brother in Sydney: to a group of them, gathered at a hospital, and then to just the most imposing one, and each time being half-stripped, and poked, and sounded, and X-rayed, and then patted on the head; and I remembered a feeling I had on those occasions, that despite my mother's effort at restraint she was grasping after help. I remained, during such visits, passive and remote. I liked the extreme clean-liness of the men's hands. But things were kept from me, and as I had no power of finding them out; I accepted my ignorance. I was conscious of being a centre of interest, as if I were something rare. I had that feeling oftentimes at home, too, when my mother and grandmother conducted what might have seemed 'whispering campaigns', but with tenderness in their glances toward me.

Then, I remember something like panic in my mother, and like despair, when she discovered that the doctor she had put her trust in was dead. Even my father took an interest in this. They learned it from the newspapers I think, or perhaps from a letter my aunts sent: the doctor had been found hanged in the scaffold-ing of a house he was having built. This news seemed to wilt my mother, inwardly, for a long while, although the effect could only be glimpsed when she was unguarded; her manner toward me remained always solicitous and artificially calm.

It was more apparent that my father caused her worry. 'Let's have the radio,' she would say, in the long evenings. It had a bakelite casing, and looked like a chocolate out of a box. But she would soon switch it off, and go along with things quietly, and would seem then to be really listening.

My father hated the radio, especially in the mornings. My mother would only put it on, to a women's programme, after he had gone as soon as he could to the plantation, disappearing down a track among the trees (where he would sit, no doubt, for a long while, in the packing shed).

The radio often played, in those days, a lilting song called 'Mockingbird Hill', and I remember hearing this while eating my porridge on the sunlit doorstep, looking over grass as silver as an ocean, and how it expressed my feelings. My father's horse and a few of someone else's cows cropped before me. A single electricity wire, lit like a thread of spider's web, ran to the house, bringing us our music, I thought. As soon as possible, I would leave off eating, which I disliked, and clean my teeth, and have my face wiped again with a damp cloth, and my hair brushed, again, and would run out onto the hill, above a valley that was the purple of a morning glory flower. I would wheel or saunter about in play at the edge of the bush: dry vines were strung from the trees like broken nets, there were tendons in the smooth trunks, and a sleekness to the silvery, fissured logs. The warmth in the stones was almost breath. I used to stand and feel as though I were being absorbed by the warmth and the light.

There was also fear in that place, but not of any predator. The bush in itself was innocent, toward humans. My parents, like all those who lived in the region, were untroubled about such elusive creatures as snakes, or by the rarest of dangers, a spider. Fear was in the mysterious ways of adults, their tangible sadness. Or it lay hidden in the commonplace. As I was going doubled-over one morning, under low branches, through wet grass, all at once, right beneath my face, and smelling as though it were a taste, I came on death. In a nest of oily, hollowed-out feathers, entangled there, and raking at itself, were the rolling white digits of some incredible greed. Just as dew of a morning was intrinsically good, this was bad, as even animals knew. I staggered, weeping and spitting, away from it.

My mother was heavily pregnant with my brother William when she stepped outside at night, taking a broom, to chase a feral cat, and fell jarringly on her back, and her labour began. Fortunately, my father was at home; and although he had been drinking, he could reel through the dark to a neighbour's house, a quarter of a mile away, to a telephone. When the ambulance came, rolling in the paddock, its headlights bleaching the long, cleared ground before the house, my mother fearfully insisted that my younger brother, three years old, and I should come with her in the ambulance, and not be looked after by our father. She probably thought he had more alcohol somewhere. So we rushed through the dark with her, the siren on, while she lay and moaned and looked apologetically at us, where we sat hunched on the floor in pyjamas and pullovers. I held her bare foot.

At the hospital, we children ate biscuits and slept in the waiting room chairs, until our grandfather came. He was retired by then, living with my grandmother on the edge of town. He carried us for two miles to his place, one drowsing on either shoulder, along the dark, blue-metal streets, never thinking to take a cab. He remained strong, in his seventies, and only paused a few times that night, as I remember it, to shift his load. I wanted to get down and walk, but he pointed out that my feet were bare.

The next day, to our embarrassment, we had to play in his yard in our pyjamas. I remember the neighbouring kids coming to look at us over the fence of the half-acre block, and them shouting raucous, derisory questions, and laughing. My brother and I hid, without acknowledging to each other what we were doing, between the chickens' shelter and a tool shed, and played a quiet game. We had to wait for our father to bring us clothing, which he was to leave at the hospital; he was not welcome at our grandparents' house. It took him, I am told, almost a week to do this. I remember we were wrapped in bedsheets, while our grandmother washed what we had to wear.

My father owned, around that time, an Australian cattle dog, or kelpie, kept not for work but as a pet, which my mother said was an unfair thing for him to do. My father loved dogs, but having this breed play around the doorstep was like owning a Ferrari sports car in the back streets of Yokohama. The dog coursed throughout his body with an excess of intelligence. He was alert like some spiny seed that is impossible to hold. Although he acted as if he were just visiting for a while, he was devoted to my father. I knew that he was far smarter than I was: I could feel him patronise me. I thought that he did not speak only because he had no need to. This brilliant creature was fed linseed oil with his meat, and his black coat, like his swaggering, insolent tongue, ran with light. Whatever life could have offered him, I felt, it would have been too little. He constantly brought home rabbits, hung from his jaws, and stood back from his work, grinning and unrepentant. No one else ever saw those creatures there. He danced in every limb and every movement, or lay and watched us, where he was allowed to come, on a rug by the door, easily encompassing each exchange, looking from one person to another, blackly radiant and dignified.

The dog took up the diversion of chasing cars and trucks, down on the road, and nipping their tyres, which he did with great joy. Once he went with my mother and brother and me, cheekily disdaining her orders to stay behind (my parents could not bear to see so much life put on a chain), when we were going for the bread that the bus driver left in our letterbox. The kelpie, named by my father Lucky, for his exploits, instead of Nigger, as he had been when he came to us, disappeared ahead. When we reached the road, a neighbour was walking around a bend towards us, and she waved, as if coming for a chat, bringing her small daughter by the hand. But as she came up close, we saw she was agitated, and she said, 'That dog of yours – just now – he's as flat as a pancake. Just a minute ago. Flat as a pancake. Around there on the bridge.'

I remember it clearly. 'This had to happen,' my mother said, shakily, squeezing my shoulder.

'He was caught by a truck,' we were told. 'It was coming in the opposite direction, while he was on the bridge, after a car. There was nowhere to jump.' The bridge had wooden sides to it. We had just seen a loaded timber-jinker going past, moments before, dangling shreds of dusty bark, like hide, with the logs on it as big as pylons.

My mother went along the road to see for herself that he was properly dead, but she only needed to go to the corner, for that, and she came back. (She later told my father that Lucky was lying 'unpacked' on the road; my father went and cleaned him away with a shovel.) I was so oppressed I could not cry or speak. My brother, too, was silenced. My mother said it seemed 'too ridiculous' that Lucky should have been caught in such a simple way, and I saw what she meant. All of that extraordinary smartness had been made nothing, in an instant, by a situation that was completely lumbering and pointless. This was just the empty way of things, I realised. I glimpsed that what mattered in life was not what you were, but the place you happened to be, at a particular moment. We kept stepping from trapdoor to trapdoor, while these were dropping open at random, all around us. I felt myself swimming with the horror of it, and yet I was standing upright and steady – like a top spinning so rapidly it seems almost unmoved on its stem. I knew I must never hint to my mother about such feelings. She was talking to us, at that moment, of a heaven for dogs, but I could not imagine it; it did not fit with what had just happened. The two concepts grated in my head. What about rabbits, in that dogs' heaven? It seems to me now that I never believed in my mother's consolations, and that one is determined to believe or not to believe by temperament alone.

This incident was my baptism in reality. I would have been six years old. I stood on a place where there was a hard, bare floor. But when I looked out from there, I thought the dew on the grass more brilliant than ever.

My mother and brother and I used to visit my father at the plant-ation around noon, on the days he was working, taking him lunch. We started off down the paddock, then turned aside into what felt like a secret track, holding apart leafy branches to enter; and we went downwards, steeply, among the close shafts of trees, the giant ferns, the tall splashed-up grasses. Long, burrowing lights were sunk through the dimness. The bare earth track was like a boot-lace being undone, drawn back and forth. Birds leapt and shouted among the leaves, lizards crackled out of our way, and we came to the packing shed at the bottom of the slope, bringing my father's thermos and sandwiches, and our own. We approached the shed horizontally, for the last bit of our walk, through the straight, close timber, calling out now, making the dog bark. Suddenly, the dim bush was replaced, up ahead, from the valley's floor to its summit, with an amphitheatre of bright green banana palms. The fountains of the banana leaves overlapped in seemingly endless progression, going on from plantation to plantation, across the hills. My father worked alone, or with an occasional day labourer, wearing a singlet and smelling as salty as corned beef.

Even when my father was no longer a banana grower, that way of life was a welcome, neutral topic of conversation between my parents. My mother had grown up amid 'the industry' and its problems were subjects on which she could have an opinion – how the present season was looking, new techniques being adopted, the challenge from other districts, and growers' returns. I took an interest in all of that myself, as a teenager, because the days of my father's plantation-owning were our last respectability, the last mentionable means of family support. When I was in high school, I used to say that my father was a 'grower', if asked his occupation, and would name with apparent boredom some outlying area as the location of his property.

The banana plant was brought to Australia from Fiji, and grows best, in sub-tropical New South Wales, on steep slopes, where it can have a sustained northern light. The ground should be stony, to hold the soil, because the slopes used are often of forty-five degrees. The roughness of the ground and its angle are part of what makes the work so heavy – 'only fit for a blackfella', in the idiom of the time, although hardly any Aboriginals wanted to work for the poor wages. Banana trees are shallow-rooted, succulent palms, and have upstanding fronds, six feet or more in length. A healthy tree stands about fifteen or eighteen feet, overall. The leaves appear out of the centre of the trunk, rolled tightly as a newspaper, open into green, pristine forms, become yellowed, take on a brown age-blight, and finally are dangling trash, weathered to a canvas-grey, all stages of the process visible at once.

They are irrigated through thin metal pipes laid on the slopes: the water in a dam, on the catchment ground, is driven back up the hills by a rapidly firing pump, which keeps on rattling all morning. The pipes spray into the sunlight, at intervals, a peacock's tail of mist, and each of those settles over a small precinct of trees.

A banana palm bears only once, burdened with a great pine-cone-shaped bunch, which can fell the tree, so that it often has to be propped with stakes. The fruit is tiered around the stalk in tight, upcurving rows. A thin fibrous tail hangs beneath the bunch, a big, purple bud at its end, called a 'bell'. This, the size of a turnip, gradually scrolls back layer after plastic-hard layer of sepals, dropping them, to drip from its centre a yellow filament of seeds. The offspring appear beneath the tree. These 'suckers' are culled by the farmer for the strongest one, and the parent tree is chopped down with a blow or two of a machete.

The heavy bunch, lopped off while the tree is standing, its stalk reached from the ground with an overhand swing of the machete, is handled carefully, to avoid bruising. It is loaded onto an open dray, behind a steeply tilted tractor, or else lugged on one's back along the hillside to a flying fox wire, the more common way in my father's time. Hooked onto a pulley, the bunch runs away under its own weight, causing a zinging sound on the cable, through numerous deep, slowing-down lapses, between posts, far down the hill, and right into the packing shed. Someone there grabs each bunch by the neck as it arrives and lays it down. A bunch can be almost as tall as a man. (There used to be sun-bleached photographs in the windows of the co-operative produce shops, in the towns at the top end of the state, of men standing beside famous banana bunches, looking like game fishermen with their catch.)

At the sheds, packing cases are made up from lengths of deal, with heavier wood for the ends (now it is done by simply unfolding cardboard boxes). Hundreds upon hundreds of cases need to be knocked together at a plantation, with a single blow for each nail used. The green fruit is cut off the bunch in 'hands' and arranged 'palm down' in a case lined with newspaper. The bulging cases, nailed shut, are drenched in a vat of chemicals, with the help of a pulley and a clamp. Each case is stencilled with the grower's code, and they are piled ready for the carrier to take to the railway yard, on its way to the Sydney markets. There, everything depends for the grower on the bidding of the day. His agent sends a cheque, and many an envelope is opened on a hot night at the end of the month and a piece of paper thrown contemptuously onto the kitchen table, for the wife to begin her diatribe about. Her complaints are directed at the weather, the agent's greed, the choice that brought them such a life, but mostly at the drinking man, who is already turning toward the door, on his way to the pub.

Just as we were having to leave my father's property, small, brash aircraft began to arrive in the district, to take over the job of spraying herbicides, at the larger plantations. In the fifties, people were more careless about chemicals than now, mostly because of marvellous promises made them on the radio, in confident, manly voices, or with a chirruping female enthusiasm, about the new inventions – plastics and nylons and pills and smoother cigarettes. For a while no one seemed to have the confidence, or the evidence, to ask questions concerning the poisons drifting on the wind, in agricultural districts. A plane would sweep up and down the steep valleys just outside the town where we were then living, in the peaceful mid-morning sun, trailing its silvery cape, dwindling to a sound like that of the new motor-mowers in the gardens, up into the glare, and then drop back, as if down a chute, with a growing steel-bladed noise. The sky, behind the plane, took on the lacquered sheen of stockings. In the local newspaper there was argument about statistics, as I overheard for years: no one could agree, it seemed, whether a larger number of deformed babies was being born in the district or not. My grandfather, when we kids were at his house, and the planes were out, swore that he could smell DDT on the air, even though the wind was meant to be blowing it away, and he would urge us inside. Then, of course, Rachel Carson's book *Silent Spring* was published, excerpts appeared in the city papers, and the crop-dusting planes disappeared.

My father climbed on the hillside at his plantation and sprayed his weeds from a metal 'knapsack', a hose in one hand and a pumping lever in the other. He chipped with a hoe at whatever weeds escaped the chemicals, striking sparks on the stones. Plantations had to be kept rigorously clear of weeds, which robbed the trees of nutrition and threatened a disease that could ruin everyone. Inspectors regularly played the taskmaster with growers and were resented by many.

I sometimes used to trail behind my father, through the crackling banana trash, while he chipped, or propped up trees, or lopped off bunches, taken with him of a morning despite my mother's protests. I would be driven on a gradual track up the hill, behind a petrol-reeking tractor, in a trailer, with a canvas canopy tied over its framework. I wore my carefully ironed cloth hat. Put down, I clambered on the volcanic, rubble-strewn ground, poking with a stick, flinging stones about, and talking constantly, for a small return of answers, until lunch-time when my mother arrived. My father remarked that she always turned up early when I was with him. I remember mainly the wonderful aroma of the plantation, of the old toasted leaves: something between the smell of chickens' mash and of dry straw.

High on that slope, I saw the sun being cranked up out of a ceramic-bright passage of the sea. It rose beside my father's bowed figure, as he moved slowly along, chipping, in his sodden shirt, or as he straightened and held his back, calling for the canteen it was my job to bring him, not confusing it with my own. Then I went back into the shade as told: I would usually climb into the trailer, and gesture and talk to myself there. If he came by, or if he had to move the tractor further along, he would make what I knew were humorous comments, and which even then I regretted missing. Standing out on the hillside, my father seemed as if he were speaking to me from behind a bright pane of glass. Not for many years would I feel so close to him again.

Almost everything to do with a banana plantation had to be won from nature with chemical help (the mosquitoes alone would have driven anyone from the packing shed if the dam were not regularly sprayed), but the mice and rats my father could control by keeping a sleepy carpet snake, swagged yard upon yard among the rafters of his shed.

Carpet snakes are constrictors, and are usually no more than the thickness of a man's arm, so they are not interested in humans, even children. If they bite, through being provoked, they leave a sore, that regularly recurs, I was told. They have a beautiful Persian carpet patterning, in green and gold, and when grown are on average six feet long. Their distinctly musty smell, if they live in a close shed, terrifies mice, and cats, and even discomforts dogs. Children are in awe of them, too.

I remember my father taking me out at night, along with my mother, to see a thick carpet snake that had lowered itself deeply from a branch, at the edge of the bush. Its red eyes hung in the misty torchlight, at the end of a long art nouveau curve. I see the eyes as wolfish, in their wariness; they were close-set, within a narrowing head, which seemed all the more nasty for being relatively small.

At his shed, my father once encouraged a slimmer one of those snakes to entwine his arm, while my mother and her children stood back against the wall, and then unwound it, with some effort, holding it behind the head, and directed it away again, into its sedate freedom. I can see the snake retaining its kinked shapes in the air, against a blank square of daylight, as it was peeled off by my father. I thought it was like one that Moses held up in our Illustrated Bible. I had seen a drawing of such a hieratic gesture in that book (they were coldly-incised steel engravings, which I disliked), and my mother had read me the passages about it. God had sent a plague of snakes among the Israelites, as punishment, but then rescinded his judgement. 'And the Lord said unto Moses, Make thee a fiery serpent, and set it upon a pole; and it shall come to pass, that every one that is bitten, when he looketh upon it, shall live.' (Numbers 21:8.) Something obscure was stirred in me by this, but I could not yet understand or face what it was.

5. The Spilt Horizon

We moved a mile closer to the town, to a dairy farm that my father was given the job of running for an elderly 'gentleman', as my mother fervently called him. This man had rescued us.

Mr Sharp wore a thin, white moustache, a polka-dot bow tie, and a variety of hats, among which my father identified for me a kepi, a boater, and a stetson, tied beneath the chin. He drove a trap with the whip standing beside him like an aerial, which he regularly snatched up, to write his initials sharply in the air.

But he was anything other than a taskmaster. He never came to check on my father's work, just took the income of the farm, and called in unfailingly to pay my father what was owed him. He was a thin, silvery old man with seemingly nicotine-stained hair, chopped off squarely at neck level, who knocked on the door lightly and called out but would not come inside. His striped shirts were unironed, and his pale suits were loose-fitting and always stained. He left an envelope, or he and my father spoke in the yard, leaning their backs against the fence rails. His voice was English and juicy, as if the words were berries softly squashed on his palate. (When I remarked once that Mr Sharp looked dirty, my father instructed me that a gentleman, no matter what he wore, was always dressed in his voice.) Mr Sharp allowed us to live in the farmhouse rent-free. My mother made a thankful remark about his nature whenever she glanced up, from the front garden or the kitchen, at the quick, chipped sounds of him passing along the road.

Mr Sharp had a house opposite the farm, on the top side of the road, where the red-painted iron roof was all that was shown to the world: it was packed around tightly with frangipani, hibiscus and oleander bushes, and stood in a grove of ruled-up long palm trees. He had retired there to look after his invalid wife. Sometimes they went driving together in his trap, she hidden under a big hat and a blanket. His farm, where we lived, was called 'The Pines', for the tall black row of the Norfolk Island variety of those trees that grew along its frontage, some of them higher than the topmast of a windjammer, judging from a book on the sea that I had, and wider than a mainsail.

My father milked Mr Sharp's remaining herd of twelve cows by hand, every morning and afternoon. In the mornings, he separated the cream in a churn, with the strength of his arm, and dragged the heavy milk cans on a sled, behind an old draught horse, up the runnelled lane to the road. There he again waltzed with them, ponderously, this time onto a wooden platform that had a pitched, shady roof to it, like a wayside shrine. They were picked up by a milk truck that was as big as a circus van. My father later collected the empty, clanging cans and rode on the sled with them back to the dairy.

The afternoon milk all went to the pigs that the farm kept, and to the calves. My father poured buckets of pure milk over a fence into a filthy tin trough, and the pigs trampled and slithered upon each other and shrieked, with unbelievable greed. The milk was brandished in the air, from bucket after bucket, and seemed to hang there a moment, as curved, fluted and tapering as a cleaned,

fresh bone. He splattered its purity in seeming contempt onto the pigs' heads and backs and forefeet, but he once told me not to look with such dislike at those animals – there were situations that could make people behave in that way, also. I denied it, inwardly, for myself.

The house where we now lived, from when I was six years old until I was nine, was an old, disjointed-looking weatherboard place of grey planks, the paint, if there had been any, long since gone. Along one side of it was a verandah, built in to waist height, facing the mornings and the distant edge of town. The view was through a gap in the camphor laurel trees, which lined the drive so densely they made a tunnel. The lane went past the side of the house and around into the open light that stood above the paddocks, to the dairy, the yards and the sheds, set well behind us.

Our house was on its own allotment, through a suburban wire gate and along a path, in which each brick was outlined with fluorescent moss. It had hooded awnings over the two front windows, in bare grey tin, with scalloped edges. The corrugated iron roof was so steep it seemed to have been trickled up to its point, and it was rusted the orange tone of the stains in an old bathtub.

On the other side of the house, over a mossy paling fence, was a huge Moreton Bay fig tree, shading the whole of its stony yard and half of where we lived. This coarse, dark-grey tree, with lustre-less canopy, was held in the earth by exaggerated tendons. Where the flat-sided roots emerged from the trunk, they were taller than a child, and they ran out unbelievably far, before tapering under-ground. They went on protruding from the earth as far as the branches continued overhead. Each leaf was about three times larger than a garden trowel. That tree could easily have held the tree house of the Swiss Family Robinson.

The sun was able to come unobstructed into our long backyard, where the shrubs grew unbounded and where there were flung-out spines and canes and tendrils. There was a vegetable garden there, like a page from a ruled exercise book written on in my mother's neat, rounded hand; and there was a lavatory, which was being hauled off sideways by a rampaging wisteria vine, towards the sun-smoke of the pastures.

At the front of the house, we looked slightly upwards to the road and the dark pine trees, across a paddock in which at some seasons the grass was olive and at others ivory.

My father worked the dairy farm and grew and harvested a regular paddock of corn, for three years, before he had to give up the job because of his health and a new man was brought in. We were able to continue living at the farmhouse for almost a year after that. The workman who took over was not interested in children, never spoke to us, and came and went unannounced. My father looked after the cows at weekends.

At this time he was about fifty. He had been forty-three when I was born and forty-six when he moved back to the country after the War. Before taking on his second plantation he had never done hard work, or what amounted to work at all. His fastidious nature made him unsuited to 'a real job', my mother thought. The labour of running the plantation by himself had begun to break him physically, and there was his connivance in such an outcome by other means.

Finding he could not keep on with the dairy farm, my father was luckily able to get a relatively light job, as a foreman, helping to build a large airstrip near the town. For this he cited his wartime experience. He had by now been diagnosed with TB, perhaps because of drinking the unpasteurised milk at the dairy, for his ulcers, but more likely, since my brother and I sometimes managed to get hold of unboiled milk without ill-effect, through sleeping rough when drunk at night.

After his afternoon milking, my father used to walk into the town (I have no idea what happened to his horse), having bathed and dressed up, with a handkerchief in his breast pocket. He would stamp his feet on the bitumen every little while, as he went along, to keep the dust off his shoes. When the returned servicemen's club closed at ten, friends brought him in a car to an intersection fairly near the farm, where they turned off for a new housing subdivision. My father would have insisted that was close enough, since they were running late themselves, and there were other such deliveries to be made. But he mostly failed to manage the remaining half a mile on foot.

From when I was about seven, I used regularly to go out at night with my mother, after closing time, to search for him by the road. We poked with sticks in the dark under the lantana bushes, down from the verge, where he would often have rolled; or we found him lying in the long, damp grass on the side of the bank. Once, he was neatly laid out, as if moonbathing, on the frosty front lawn of one of the last houses of town.

If he was at a card game, however, my father might start for home at any hour, and my mother used to wake up late, from sleeping at the kitchen table, or on the top of their bed, and hurry out to look for him, in our vicinity. I would try to stay awake so as to go with her, listening from my bedroom for her to make a move, but would usually wake deep in the night, startled, with the realisation that I had been asleep, and drag myself from bed to check on her. If she was not in the house, I set off up the dark lane in pyjamas and along the road, aflame with imagining that she had been murdered or kidnapped or run over. Before starting out in the lane, I took a stick with me, which was always kept hidden at the same place. When I was hurrying by the road, if a car's headlights approached, I would crouch down on the weed-grown bank. Usually I found her, in the dark near the five-barred gate, watching the road. On occasion there was no sign of her, and I had to go back in a panic, hobbling barefooted in the stony drive – always neglectful of shoes in my haste to find her – and would discover her dozing somewhere unusual about the house. She would be in the sparsely furnished, almost unused living room, on a cane lounge under a lifted window, or on hot nights in a canvas chair on the dark verandah, with a strained-looking neck, a coil of mosquito repellent smoking nearby. Before I went back to collapse into bed, I carefully trickled water into the bottom of the bathtub, to wash my feet, so as not to spoil the sheets.

But the sheets were spoiled, anyway. I developed the habit of bed-wetting. There is nothing more disappointing to a child than realising that the paddy field of warmth he vaguely feels spread around him in the night is becoming, yet again, soggy and chill. I even wet the bed twice in a night, to my mother's long-suffering despair. There were stained bedsheets constantly on the line, the great white rolling flags of my humiliation. My father, with a headache, glaring and hostile, proposed rubbing my nose in the sodden sheets as a cure.

A doctor sent my father away to the Soldiers Repatriation Hospital in Sydney for treatment of his TB. He was gone for many months, which was a relief to us at home, like a modest win in the lottery. But my mother would have had only some unemployment benefit and child endowment to manage on, and things must have been hard. He was treated, I remember, with a new drug, streptomycin, a word that fascinated me – it was like a chemical taste on the tongue. I have read recently that a few years before that, as late as 1950, the writer George Orwell died of TB, at the age of forty-six, and that he was given the same experimental treatment.

When my father came home, he still had, and would always keep, his seemingly constant cough, caused by smoking. He told people it was the aftermath of pleurisy. His coughing was like the theme tune of a character in a film: we heard it when he was about to appear, and while he spoke during family meals, and through-out the night: a dry, hard, assertive tattoo. Or else a racketing cough, ratcheted upwards as it went on and on. After his return from Sydney, my father had to go for regular X-rays, and for further treatment at the local hospital, but he made no effort to stop smoking: following the War, he constantly smoked cigarettes. Nor did he modify his drinking, of course.

It was at this time that he took on the job at the aerodrome, for a couple of years, which mainly involved talking to the engineers and then to the men, and going to the pub with both parties after work. This job supported us for a time, after we left the farm.

I was considered a prime risk for TB, and was supposed not to get too close to my father. My mother often berated him for coughing near me. But although my thin chest was pressed regularly to the cold X-ray plate, and although one of the local doctors managed to get away with my tonsils, adenoids, and appendix, and to put me into hospital for sinus drainage, he was never able to find the disease that had brought me into his power. (From later hearing others reminisce about his abilities, that doctor seems to have been something of a valet to the mortician.)

When my father worked at the aerodrome he earned better money than usual, but his family did not benefit. My mother said he would rather buy himself a new tie or shoes than put more food on the table, and certainly would rather drink. She had to demand her housekeeping from him, and never knew what he really earned. This provoked her into taking out a prohibition order against him in the court, to prevent him entering a hotel or club, and anyone serving him alcohol. The first time she appeared at a hearing, supported by my grandfather, her request failed, because she had not known she needed a specific record of occasions on which my father had been drunk – 'Every night,' she told the magistrate, surprised – and of the times at which he had arrived home, and whether he was expected for a meal, and of his behaviour in the house, what he had said, who might have seen him, and so on. My father came home on the night of the failed case defiantly; which is to say, as drunk as a jelly. I remember him being supercilious, condescending, self-righteous, and yet hurt and frightened. He had been 'snaky', I heard my mother tell my grandfather. That was one of the few occasions on which I recall my father being really angry, though it was in a cold way. My mother learned from her first court appearance: thereafter, she kept a detailed list of his drinking, written in pencil where he would not find it, on the back of a dark cupboard door, near the sink, which she herself could only read by sunlight. The next time she went before the court she succeeded, producing even his medical record in her testimony; but the order handed down was for only six months. I vaguely remember my father's hauteur, on that night, also, but he was not too disturbed: he had realised that although his friendships might suffer, he would still be able to get drink. It would be easy to have someone buy it for him, since there was almost a club of men who were willing to help each other in such a situation.

Once, during the third order that my mother managed to have served on him, we happened to see my father being provided with booze in the backyard of a pub. We lived in the town then and were walking home after dark, my mother, and four children, one in arms, coming from my grandparents. We passed a short lane that led into a gravelled, tyre-scored parking lot, a white streetlight shining in its puddles, on a cold night, white as lard, and we saw my father leaned against a fence, and a man hurrying over to him with a big, full glass and a short bottle in a paper bag. He was obviously a delegated 'runner', begrudging the time. As we stood looking, the back door of the hotel opened again – on a scene that I remember was yellow, steamy and congested, like a Chinese omelette – and some men came out on stiff legs, and stepped as if they were sore toward my father, and began affably talking to him and laughing. The man who had brought the drink hurried off-stage, taking an empty glass. My mother sighed, as if forcibly compressed, and we walked on. She did not continue her part in the war of attrition on my father, she later said to me, because she had decided it was too cruel for him not to have men to talk with.

While we were still living on the dairy farm, in his prohibition days, my father would go to bed sober and wake up drunk. He was now sleeping alone on the verandah, isolated in the white fog of a mosquito net, which also kept off moths and beetles. Once I went to say goodnight to him there, while he was reading in bed, and I saw him take a swig from a squat bottle, his finger in the pages of a similar-shaped book that I knew to be his Livy, in Latin. He winked at me, guiltily, and I did not report anything. I am sure one of his diversions, on the night, got more of him than the other.

From that time, as far as we children knew, our parents slept apart, although there must have been a physical encounter between them at least once more, to produce my sister. It was my mother's punitive decision that they should have separate beds, but my father turned the situation to his advantage: we began finding empty rum and whisky bottles, tossed over the verandah rail, behind the hydrangea bushes. Once I came on a full bottle of brandy with my bare foot, hidden in the wide cleft of a tree that I was climbing, which he would have had to stand in a wheelbarrow to reach. Numerous times, we kids turned up bottles of spirits, full or empty, in the deep piles of dry camphor laurel leaves beside the lane, or in the disused sheds, behind machine parts or under stacks of rotting bags. Sometimes we told my mother, with a conspiratorial excitement and self-righteousness; but if I alone found his secret, I used not to speak about it, even though I was the eldest.

When my father took to sleeping on the verandah, his bed was put where the sun shone onto him early, through a gap in the leaves, but I still often needed to shake him, to bring him into sodden wakefulness. It was better that I woke him, at around six-thirty on summer mornings, than my mother did, since she had once returned to his bedside with a big saucepan and its lid and had crashed them together close beside his head. I usually would not realise how drunk or hung-over he was until I saw him in the hall, coming out of the bathroom's dry-ice smoke: then I would know by the affectation of his greeting and by his stilted gait.

'Oh, you imbecile of a man,' I remember my mother greeting him in the kitchen after a glance in his direction. She often used such expressions. Immediately, she was despairing, utterly blackened, in the bright sunlight of the room. She stood barefooted on the linoleum, stopped in the act of making breakfast.

'Put some slippers on, for God's sake, woman,' my father begged her, in pain. He claimed to have a horror of my mother's bare feet, which were flat, broad, and dryly cracked at the heels, since she loved going barefoot, as she had done as a child. She would go into the garden like that, and 'potter'. He often pointed out that she had the feet of a peasant; that her ancestry in Scotland and Germany had gone barefooted, even in those climates, and this was why she was intractable in the habit.

'I can't afford any slippers, you fool. I can hardly afford to feed and clothe these children of yours. If they weren't here, I'd give you a crack across the head you'd never forget. Now get out of my sight. There's no food for you here. Get out!'

My father dabbed at a rash of shaving cuts around his neck, using a clean square of handkerchief, his long-jawed face naked-looking and sleek after his shave. 'What a fine religious way to speak. See, you've made all the wounds of your lord to bleed...All right, all right. I'm going.'

One hung-over morning, to pre-empt the situation, my father went straight to the kitchen window and looked out at a thin white-wash of frost on the emerald grass. He said with a heavy sigh, 'Ah, there it is again – much adew about nothing.' The joke found no response.

On what must have been a holiday from school, I was outside before breakfast when I saw my father come out of the house, with an unsteady dignity, and heard my mother's angry voice following him. I was in the first of a row of persimmon trees, just beyond the high chicken wire that fenced our back garden. From there, I could look over the dairy, which was like a ramshackle covered wharf, the paddocks, in their icing-sugar dusting of frost, the dark expedition of trees, escorting the creek, and across the smeared blue forest, to clear navy blue mountains. My father came by and pulled down a ripe persimmon, parted it softly between his thumbs, and turned the half-fruit on its skin inside out, to release into his mouth the firm, apricot-coloured jelly. He remarked, without looking up,

'Your Aunt Margaret's favourite fruit,' and found himself another one, and ate it. Then he went around the corner of a shed, and came back carrying a shovel. He went past, to the outdoor lavatory in the bottom corner of the yard, propped its door open with the shovel, shimmied out the can, screechingly, on the cement floor, and after a tense, staggering, groaning moment had it planted on his shoulder, like a water-carrier. He carefully took up the shovel again, with his free hand, and set out toward the dairy, then turned aside through a barred gate, lying open, and went across a short paddock, to a ploughed field, treading warily. As he passed under the persimmon tree, without looking up, he began to speak in his reciting voice. It was a performance for my benefit; and yet he had no way of knowing that I would listen, and years afterwards recognise in a book what he had said, and laugh aloud.

It was a poem, which he declaimed, going out of earshot; one that perhaps he had learned at school: 'The Burial of Sir John Moore at Corunna'.

Not a drum was heard, not a funeral note,
As his corpse to the rampart we hurried;
Not a soldier discharged his farewell shot
O'er the grave where our hero we buried...

My father was, unsurprisingly, accident-prone. It was not from drinking during the working day, but because he was left so unsteady by the previous evening. While he was running the farm, we would often hear sudden commotions that involved him. My brother and I played on the bare earth and the grass beneath the persimmon trees, with a view of all the property, and we witnessed many outbursts: most memorably, his backing the tractor into a ditch and getting its rear wheels stuck, deeper and deeper, as he furiously made them spin, and the tractor rear steeply, and mud fly like water from a fireman's hose, my mother coming out to shout furiously at him; or his knocking down a high stack of empty kerosene tins in the barn, which made a huge shimmering sound, like auditory lightning, in a place as dim as a mine shaft. Often it was something that brought howls of agony from him. We would look up, startled, in the midst of a game, and our mother would come rushing onto the back steps. 'What?' she would shout. After a while, he appeared from the barn, or one of the sheds, or the dairy, holding his knee, perhaps, in which case he would drop onto the ground, whooping and massaging it; or he would come out gingerly into the light, pulling up his trouser leg to look at his shin; or would hold up a hand, or even a finger, to show some blood. Once he limped from having a cow step on his foot in a crush and refuse to move. Invariably, what had happened was disproportionate to the sound effect. I found the same sort of noises transcribed, later, in the old-fashioned stories about English schoolboys that I developed a taste for and managed to get hold of, second-hand. '"Yaaarooo! Whooop! Aaargh!" The halls of Greyfriars school resounded to the cries of Billy Bunter, the fat Owl of the Remove...'

My mother would shout, 'Be a bit more careful, then,' in a mollified tone, seeing the minor nature of his damage, and go back inside. My father would sit for a while on some old planks, smoking a cigarette, shaking his hand and examining it, and would wash it under a tap by the dairy, and perhaps decide to go to the house to get it bandaged, or he would limp back to his job. 'So, you're all right there, boys?' he would call, over his shoulder. 'Yes, thank you,' we answered, barely glancing up.

My mother used to say that my father was a coward; alternatively, she often said that he seemed to feel pain more than other people. She thought he was a coward, ungratefully enough, because when she was angry and threatened him, he would not fight back, but 'made himself scarce'. He probably saw that he had little grounds for argument. When he was too maddeningly drunk and she struck him, he never looked as if he even considered retaliation, although his nose or mouth bled. He staggered, and then merely said something ridiculous, like 'That's not very decent,' in a propitiating tone. Or else he would protest, 'Don't be ridiculous. There are children here. What's the matter with you?' This was when it had really hurt him. Of course, his children intervened, with screams, shouts, and tears.

The boards and linoleum of the house were always being mopped, by my mother, the rugs shaken, the back steps washed down, the meagre things of the household dusted and straightened up, the windows sluiced with a wet, vinegar-smelling cloth, and the cobwebs scooped from under the eaves (she stood on a chair when at the back of the house), using a small brush tied on a bamboo pole. My father was not given any chance to complain to his sisters about her housekeeping.

I never knew my father to go to the 'pictures', as we called the cinema, except once, and that was on the occasion of my first film, when I was seven. What attracted him was Robert Louis Stevenson's *Treasure Island*: the Walt Disney version, live-acted, with Robert Newton. On our way there, just the two of us, the only time we ever had such an outing, my father held me around the back of the neck, so that I kept up his pace, and then he took my hand when we were on the pavement in front of houses and I was slackening. He told me that the author of this story was the man after whom I had been named. (Years later, I found that Stevenson's family and friends always called him Louis, pronounced Lewis.)

In those days, before television, there was a flourishing cinema in the town: its building was larger than the department store. Films were the only public entertainment, apart from the pubs, the beach, the Rugby game (on our town's rostered winter Saturday afternoon), the monthly horserace meeting, and a brass band. I stood up beside my father, in the matinee, for what must still have been, by a year or two, 'God Save the King'. Then, right at the start of the film, the black-cloaked and cowled figure of blind Pew appeared, with his bandaged eyes, groping hand and tapping stick. He snatched hold of Jim Hawkins and twisted the boy's arm, enquiring about Billy Bones, the drunken sailor who was staying at the family's inn. I got under the seat, immediately. My father was not having any nonsense: hardly taking his eyes from the screen, he grabbed me by the hair, encouraged me back into place, and hissed at me to stay there. So I watched everything, flinching and agog.

I can still clearly see Jim climbing the rigging of the almost-deserted ship, and turning with a pistol to face the pirate who was following him, and then, wounded in the shoulder by a flung knife, firing his gun, and the pirate bouncing off a cannon below and into the sea; and Jim being treated for his wound, under a flag of truce, outside the stockade, by Dr Livesey; and Jim captive, tied by a rope behind Long John Silver, who swings on his crutch across the sands of the island, in a greatcoat; and Silver's vast, bristly, haunch-of-bacon face, and winning, treacherous charm; and Jim breaking out of the group of his victorious friends and running to push Long John's dinghy off the beach, to let him escape; and Long John getting the sail of the boat raised, and standing to lift his arm in farewell. I remember it in detail, indissolubly. I think I must have felt from the start who Long John Silver was.

The experience of the film was so moving that as soon as I could I became an obsessive film-goer. All through my boyhood and teenage years I went to the cinema every week, no matter what was on, as long as it was rated General, and often twice a week. I had my mother's support, at a shilling and then later two shillings a time. As a young adult in the city, I would sometimes see two or three films in a day, at weekends, most of it nondescript Hollywood stuff.

The soul must feed on something for its dreams
In those brick suburbs, and there wasn't much:
It can make do with little, so it seems.
JAMES McAULEY

My mother had heard about Robert Louis Stevenson, too, and when she made me stay in bed with every minor symptom, she told me that he had been a sick boy, like me, unable to go out and play, and that he had amused himself by making up marvellous stories. I was happy to take on that role, and allowed my mother to abet my imagination with books she brought back when she went shopping, and with the blue and green bedsheets I requested, so that one of those could be the sea and one the land, in my daylong, confined games.

I seemed to catch every common childhood disease that was available, measles, chicken pox, mumps, bronchitis, whooping cough, because I was thin and 'run down'; but never the serious ones, not TB, and not polio, which was around in panic-causing proportions. When I had measles, blankets were hung over the windows of the bedroom, to protect my sight, and later my mother said I had to wear dark glasses while outside, such as on my way to school or in the playground. No one else seemed to be taken care of to this extent. The warnings I was given about not going without my glasses were like those against looking at a solar eclipse.

'Circumstances conspired to make me shy and solitary,' Siegfried Sassoon wrote, as the opening to *Memoirs of a Fox-Hunting Man*, and at the other end of the world and the social scale, that was my experience, also. Having to wear long trousers and shoes to school, and dark glasses, even if they remained unbroken for

only a short while, precluded me from games in the barefoot playground. Recess and lunchtime became too long, as classes were:
they meant keeping out of the way of rough boys, beneath the trees
in a far corner of the paddock-sized ground. There I was among
the children who were really sick: a boy with wheezing asthma who
had the startled, staring look of a chicken, another with a withered
leg, and a listless girl. I was regularly accosted by visitors to that
area, by certain sandy-coloured, sly, already bitter-looking boys,
with an irritated, uncertain derision in their voices. 'You blind, are
yuh? Eh? You blind? Y' goin' blind? C'mon, y' can tell us.' Or else,
'Why y' wearin' them duds? What's the matter w' yuh? You want
a punch? You need a good punch in the guts?' I pretended I was
eating my neat little triangular sandwiches, with the crusts taken
off, and barely looked up, hoping not to be thrown down and
dragged in the dirt.

My lunches, in particular, invited derision. Where other kids
unwrapped two slabs of bread glued together with jam or peanut
butter, my meals came in varied courses, each perfectly wrapped:
there would be dried fruit or carrot or celery sticks for recess, to go
with the flavoured milk the school provided; then, at midday, two
sandwiches, cut in quarters, of tinned fish or Vegemite or banana
and peanut butter or lettuce and cold meat; then a hard-boiled
egg, with salt twisted in a piece of greaseproof paper, or a cheese
wedge, or boiled sausage; and finally a chocolate rice crackle or
a lamington, and an apple, or an orange peeled in one continuous take and wound again in its peel. I could never eat as much
lunch as was given, ate hardly any, and so, drenched with shame,
I emptied the food in a bin, rather than take it home untouched.
Once I forgot to do that and got off the bus with lunch still in my
bag. I remembered it when about to climb through our gate, and
so I waded off into long grass nearby and threw it there. Unnoticed
by me, my mother was coming along the road from a general store,

half a mile back: she saw me in the weeds and then, after I had gone, some greaseproof paper blowing, and went to look. I have not forgotten how baffled and saddened she was, when she came into the house.

My mother fussed over my appearance, and that of my brothers, too, in a similar way. Women used to stop us in the street, when we went shopping together. 'Oh, those children, they look as if they've just come out of a band box.' Because I was very blond, the women exclaimed, 'That's the cleanest little boy I've ever seen!' They would examine my hands and turn me around. They tutted over our immaculate clothes and our smiles. All the money to dress and care for us came from our grandfather, of course.

Going to or coming from school, the bus was more riotous than an aviary at feeding time. I was exempted from bullying on these trips because one or other of the big girls from the high school would take me literally under her arm, or on her lap, pressing me against her bosom, sinking me between her thighs, while she screamed back-chat above my head. She snuffled in my white hair, nuzzled at my cheek, and held me in a grip that was only slightly less immobilising than my embarrassment.

Once, when I had been away from school with some minor sickness, I was sent back in my herringbone-patterned, fawn-coloured long trousers, only to discover on the bus that it was district sports carnival day, and everyone was in white shorts. I became opaque, dulled my feelings, locked my eyes inwards, stood ready to strike back, since I must play the freak. An officious teacher at the sports ground, under a loudspeaker that reverberated like scaffolding being nailed up, was unsympathetic. She was not from our school. Was I sick? No? Then I must be marshalled into a house group, and then into a smaller group, and then lined up for one of the waves of foot races. A shriek of mirth went up, when I was seen in my trousers and polished shoes, at the starting line, where everyone assumed the position to run. The bunting clattered in the wind. There was a pistol shot and I was convulsed into life and was running as if being dragged out of myself, as if free-falling down a hillside, the grass reeling beneath me; running as I did through the paddocks at home in the long dusks; running in a fury, going into the highest possible gear. I easily won.

'Who let this boy run? Who let him run?' My class teacher came rushing over to me, where I was standing with my arms braced against my thighs, feeling almost entirely a pair of lungs. 'Are you all right, dear? Are you sure? Come and sit down. Lie down. Just relax. Tell me if you feel strange, won't you? Let me know at once. All right?' My mother had been talking to the school. When I went home that afternoon I told her I had won a race in my long trousers, but had not been allowed to run in the final. I could have won that, too, if I had been barefoot. She looked at me dubiously for a moment, then with pity, that I needed to say such things, but mainly with fear, because I had forgotten all of her warnings against 'exertion'.

I had not been sent to school until I was seven, at which time my mother decided I should know my medical story. I needed to be told since I must now be responsible for myself, for 'being careful'. My mother's way of telling me was to explain the situation to the headmistress in my presence: that she had had German measles when pregnant, and as a result I had been born with a hole in the inner wall of the heart, 'the size of a two shilling piece', which was inoperable. Because of this, ordinary illnesses had to be carefully watched in me, and I might often be absent from school. (I doubt this was the doctors' opinion: they seem never to have committed themselves to any definite advice. I think it was my mother's and grandmother's theory.)

Soon after that, a new young doctor arrived in the town, and

I was taken to him for a check-up about something. When I had put my shirt on again, it was suggested I go and sit in the waiting room, for a little while. I went out the door, but before I had clicked it shut decided to ask if could wait in the park opposite. I began to open the door again and glimpsed the doctor and my mother standing before his desk, he with his hand on her back; he was saying flatly that someone with my diagnosis could not be expected to live to more than twenty-one. My mother's head was lowered; she said 'I know.' I pulled the door to, without a sound.

I was later able both to believe and disbelieve this, at once. Mainly, I ignored the whole thing.

The interviews about me with specialists in Sydney, which I would continue to have, always ended with them smiling bluffly in my reserved and self-conscious direction and patting me on the head, as if to say they were proud of me. They made me feel I had won some dull prize that I did not want. I did not want all the attention. I did not want, as it were, to have to get up in front of the whole school, while it stood in neat rows, and have it announced that I had been made the protégé of a renowned, mysterious and interfering figure called Death. I did not like being singled out for special respect. I wanted to be just one more anonymous seed within the plain furrows of normal children.

I had always had an amorphous suspicion that something like the local doctor's remark must be the case, because of my maternal grandmother's attitude toward me. She was at times a visitor to our house when I was sick in bed, and although it would only be the flu I had, I would notice her considering me with a steady, sombre, Scottish gaze, which I knew saw disaster within the horizon.

Those trips to Sydney to see specialists began when I was about six. I went into hospital there and while under anaesthetic tubes were inserted into the inside of both my elbows and floated through

the arteries to the heart. These sites were opened again on later occasions for the same purpose, the last time when I was twelve. Most of my visits, though, did not involve going to hospital; the operation was not a treatment, but an investigation. Most times, I just went to have my heart listened to and X-rayed and to be questioned. All the treatment I received was an iron tonic, which I took off the spoon twice a day for many years. It tasted exactly the way that iron filings smell. My mother also gave me, on her own account, regular doses of liquid calcium in a glass of milk, and this tasted like washed, dried, sun-bleached seashells.

I was tall for my age but very slight, and so when we went into town I was always weighed on a penny scale at the chemist's. The result was nodded over by my mother and grandmother and taken as somehow indicative of my heart condition. Then I would be plied with more porridge, to which creamy milk and raisins and nutmeg were added, and urged to eat, not to puddle, turning it around as I did, in a slow grey vortex, for what seemed hours.

I was taken by my father to Sydney for a few of my medical check-ups, because we stayed with his sisters, but these trips proved such debacles that by the time I was nine I was going on the twelve-hour train journey alone.

The first time we went to the city together, my father got off the train at the next station from ours, to buy beer from the refreshment room, and failed to get back on. A young couple, the only other people in the compartment, who had been merely holding hands before, seemed greatly pleased by this, and began passionately kissing and grappling with each other. They looked at me for a moment and the man said not to worry, my father would catch the following train; then they applied their attention to each other again. I tried not to think about what would happen to me, but stretched out on the hard leather seat, in the sour smell of coal dust, and listened to the moans and sighs from opposite me in the dark, to the whining of wind along the telephone wires, and to the dark vistas in the train's sound.

In Sydney, in the morning, the guard took me and our suitcase to a bench within the great, reverberating half-cylinder of Central Station. The place was crowded with idle and hurrying people. He told me to sit and wait and he would send someone from the Station Master's office, but no official came. Occasionally different people walked back and forth past me a few times and then came up and tried to get me to talk, but I refused to be drawn. I kept one arm over the suitcase on the seat beside me. I did speak to a youngish woman with some children, conceding that I was waiting for my father, and she bought me a pie. She said that undoubtedly my father would have rung his relatives in Sydney and someone must be along soon. But finally, late in the day, it was my father who was there: approaching like an exclamation mark at the end of a paragraph, among all the grey typeface.

He bought me a milkshake, making light of everything in his embarrassment. Then we took a double-decker bus, to go to his sisters'. We rode on the top deck, but before long I was feeling ill, and desperately though I tried to fight it I vomited out of the window, down the side of the bus. At my aunts', I was so wan, and our late arrival so suspicious, that the story soon had to be told, and Olga pushed my father out of the room, for a talk.

On another trip we made together, I remember my father

leaving me to wait for him in a park, seated on the grass, with a cupcake in a paper bag, while he went apologetically 'to see someone he had to meet, just across the road.' The park was near Central Station, and in it a few men were stretched out on the ground asleep, empty bottles beside them, or sitting hunched-over, holding their heads, and every now and then looking up to call out at the trees or a passer-by. I stood and waited in the furthest angle of the grass, near the road. These days, hardly anyone would be so trusting as my father was then.

In Sydney, my father and I filled in time in the uptown park called the Domain, walking across the bright grass and under a row of black, prehistoric Moreton Bay fig trees, their limbs drawn-out and viscous-looking. We stopped at a statue on a high pedestal, of a man in breeches and stockings, who held a quill and leaned against a plough, and my father raised his hat. 'Bobby Burns,' he told me, taking the back of my neck. He began to recite, in brogue: 'A man's a man for a' that and a' that...' (the import of which occurs to me now). I glanced about to see if anyone was watching us, and looked at the fine shells of the rose petals, scattered on the tips of the lawn.

The most peculiar experience of those times was a ferry ride that we took in rough weather. I learned much later that this was something my father used to do as a young man: when the weather was bad, he would try to be in the last ferry allowed to make the run from Manly, passing near the Heads and the open sea.

He and I went down the length of the harbour to Manly in the rain and darkness of an early afternoon, in a swell, supposedly to go to a funfair. It was raining too much for that, and so we went to a newsreel and ate ice cream and walked under an umbrella on the shiny concrete esplanade, among the pine trees. We watched from the outer side of the peninsula on which Manly was built the overflowing ocean come spilling inwards. He told me that he had always liked this suburb. It was obvious he enjoyed looking at the bruise-coloured, rough-housing surf. He stood inhaling the salt air, lifting his head into it. Then we sat alone on the front, in a picnic shelter, above the flooded beach. I was exhilarated by the weather, too. The water surged far up onto the sand, a weird lime colour among its foam; there were fast slashes of rain across everything; and there was the sea's vast smoky breath. We lingered on and on, and my father drank occasionally from a bottle in a paper bag, taken from his raincoat pocket.

When we went to catch the ferry back to the city, the day was almost dark; the rain had drawn heavy drapes for an early night. There was hardly anyone on the boat. My father was half asleep, as we waited to leave. He said that I would find the trip home much better than a ride at the funfair.

As we passed opposite the Heads, I started to feel the whole bellied shape of the boat beneath me. It wallowed downwards and downwards through something too yielding, not finding its proper resistance. Then we were lifted, and paused as though gasping, and shuddered, and started falling heavily again. The grey sea broke on us and covered the boat with an avalanche, blocking out the windows, as if we had gone under. We seemed, terrifyingly, much too heavy, too awkward, to be supported. My father slumped in the weak light, uninvolved, drowsy, and despondent. He did not encourage me, but told me to keep a tight grip on the slats of the see-sawing bench, in the way I noticed he did. I became completely passive myself; enduring moment to moment, hardly adding an inhalation to our burden. The ferry rose one-sidedly, like an arm flung upwards, and fell, and rolled deeply below the escarpment of the waves, and then reared up on its other side, as if with a groan; swimming overarm, exhausted. The sliding door, onto the outer walk, was yanked open, by no one, and water and foam swirled in, as when a water main bursts, and rushed across the width of the boat, soaking us both below the knees (my legs hung free of the floor). A man in a raincoat and sou-wester came at once and struggled with the door, and he shouted that we should go upstairs, but just then things grew a little easier, with the Heads behind us. The rain and spray continued to clatter at the grey windows and the glass looked as though it were rapidly melting. The rough passage would have lasted ten or fifteen minutes. At the Quay, my father said, 'Are you all right, boy? You look a bit white.' I would never say other than that I was fine, about anything; but I was shivering with cold, and felt I was walking strangely – my legs seemed to have water-softened bones.

When we got home to Vaucluse we were both wet, anyway, from the driving rain, and my father, who was noticeably unsteady, said only that while we were on the harbour we had found the weather rougher than anyone expected. I had been a good sailor, he said; a real Jim Hawkins. Margaret's main worry, as I remember, was to get me into a hot bath. Then she went out, leaving the door ajar. There were distant, subdued voices. She no doubt wanted to know why we were on a ferry at all, in such weather. Coming back into the bathroom, Margaret looked moist and flushed, as though she were the one in a steaming tub.

Although my father took me on a few of my early visits to Sydney, he never mentioned, nor alluded to, what 'all the traipsing about' to the Children's Hospital was for. At no time in his life did he raise the subject with me, and neither did I with him. After his death, my mother told me that he had not liked to speak about my illness even to her. She said a girl with a similar heart disease to mine had been reported by the newspapers as being sent to the United States for an advanced operation, on money raised by an appeal, and my mother had wanted the same for me, but my father had been embarrassed and had tried to dissuade her from 'making any fuss'. He felt vindicated when the doctors told my mother that the hole in the girl's heart was differently located to mine, and that my case was inoperable in America, too.

I felt that I had more the looming of a serious illness than the actual thing. The lethal flaw was secretive and stalking: there was little evidence of it, as yet. I had no shortness of breath, no 'blue-ness', even at birth, no lethargy, no slowness of reactions. I did have a debilitating number of the usual childhood complaints though, and each of them was treated as some ominous sign.

Once at my grandparents', when I was about nine, my cousin and I were chasing each other around and around in the big yard, in the dusk of a hot day. (One of my uncles and his family were visiting the town.) We ran on and on, despite my grandmother calling on us to stop and making my mother and my uncle try to grab me as I came by. Then all at once my nose began to gush blood, and I leaned forward and spat it away from my mouth. There was a wail from my grandmother: 'Oh my God, his heart has burst!' My heart went on pounding, perfectly all right in my chest. I stood up, grinning, wiping blood on my hands and forearms, raising my arms like a boxer. People rushed up to me, and I sprang away from them again, and ran on, shaking blood from the ends of my fingers, evading my heavy cousin, who was sent to tackle me; triumphant, taunting.

My brother told a boy at school that I was going to die young, who announced this to seemingly everybody, and I had to deny it, when a crowd of them gathered around me. Boys shoved each other out of the way in front of me, hoping to glimpse a sign. After that I wanted to avoid them. For a time I spent my lunch breaks at the library; but I had found I could catch a tennis ball, and was drawn to the playground games. At home, I loved the quickness of my reactions when the ball sprang at unexpected angles off the rough shed wall, and I practised for hours. Someone who can catch a ball and can run will not have such a bad time at school. I practised at home how to bowl, too, so I fitted into the makeshift games of cricket, played at every spare moment. Children quickly forget: for them, you are simply what you do.

To be set apart, I later learned from the Bible, means to be 'sanctified'. I felt like that: isolated, but significant. I felt not so much defective as in some ways more than usually effective; good at registering things. I seemed like a wound that can feel even someone breathing on it.

When I was in hospital in my home town, to have my appendix or tonsils removed, I was introduced by the boy in the next bed to comic books. A whole new richness appeared in the world. I was avid, for years afterwards, to read and collect my favourites among these, and gradually achieved neat piles of them in a corner of my room. What I mainly liked was to pore over the drawings: the stories were seldom as satisfying as those. If a story was really engrossing, I realised, it was because I had only read it in part, and had stopped while it was unresolved. Just to read here and there and to look was best. (This influenced my manner of reading novels, later: I would read isolated portions of them only, not minding that I did not fully understand what was going on; I preferred mysteriousness. Only a few novels made me want to give up my own imaginings for them.)

The drawings in comic books seemed to make me more conscious of common things in life. I liked particularly the details in some Walt Disney comics, and in his animated films: the way the artists had drawn fallen sticks, rotting logs, weathered fence posts, broken cement, fronds, tree roots, dead trees, and boulders (that were cracked and smooth as old cakes of soap). There were things like these where I lived, and they felt to me enhanced through being represented. I saw, at the same time, the transcendence of the real-life things: how much they exceeded any renderings of them, and so appeared more deeply themselves.

The farm where we lived was suited perfectly to such an involvement. Everything lay easily displayed and was falling apart. All surfaces had been used until they had the significance of old leather. I drifted among the barn, sheds, sprawling yards with crooked fences, and paddocks, found a rusty harrow deep in juicy-green weeds, stacks of abandoned grey fencing timber, over which small lizards skittered, tall grass around fence posts, claw-marks of light between the planks of the dairy, a cowyard heavily pocked with hoof-prints that held the vegetable water of cows, or rain, dead logs lying higher than I stood that were broken-spurred and hollowed-out by termites, bark hanging in loops about the boles of great trees, rusted bits of trucks, a car radiator like an empty honey-comb, bleached hipbones, thighbones, skulls, scattered vertebrae of cattle, termite nests in the shape of medieval beehives, balconies of meaty dull-red fungi at the base of trees and on posts, tussocks of coarse reeds stippling the paddocks, a creek with light on its shadowy surface like a swarm of bees, stands of sinuous eucalyptus that had a loose foliage like grey-green smoke, tall fire-blackened stumps, blue pumpkins on their vines as heavy as wood, a passion-fruit creeper over a wrecked chicken hutch, the lane piled deep with toasted leaves, and many dead trees, diminishing to fili-gree in the light. 'The greatest poverty is not to live in a physical world,' Wallace Stevens has said. In my childhood I had no such privation.

If I told my mother I was not feeling well in the mornings, she would dutifully allow me to stay home from school; and if, after the

bus had gone, I found myself feeling much better, in the immemorial way of children, I would be allowed to wander outdoors.

I had an advantage in this game, since my mother had to
allow that the mornings might be bad for me. I was urged by
both my mother and grandmother never to sleep on my left side
(which I still cannot do). So I was all too easily able to indulge
an inheritance from my mother, my self-sufficient nature. When
I went out of the house at mid-morning, not able to wait any
longer, I crossed a rise in the paddocks, to one side of the house,
and was soon out of sight. Then I did what was forbidden, unable
to restrain myself – I began running wildly, exulting in the space
and the light. My father had remarked to me that the hills beyond
our place were without any human life, and even without trace
of an earlier people. The Aboriginals had left no monuments,
no artefacts, almost no artworks. He said that if you walked in
a straight line beyond where we lived, you could possibly cross
the whole continent, the inland pastures and the great deserts of
the Centre, and not meet anyone, going on and on to the empty
beaches of the Indian Ocean. This idea greatly interested me.
I looked up at the blue forest on the hills and thought of the stillness and freshness there, among the calm trees, where bark idly
stripped itself from the trunks, grassy headlands blazed in the
afternoon sun, leaves dripped like the tickings of a different time,
and streams and creeks were quietly let down between boulders
and banks of fern and under fallen logs.

After standing for a time, imagining, I felt life assert itself again,
and I saw my brown legs and bare feet begin rotating effortlessly
across the grass and my shadow leading me on.

My mother dressed not much differently from her mother, except
that my grandmother wore corsets to go into town. They both
owned floral, spotted and single-coloured cotton frocks, broad-

heeled shoes, and a cardigan or two. My mother often had her brown arms bared, and very seldom wore stockings, although women usually did then when going shopping. Around the house she wore a wool skirt and a blouse. Neither owned a topcoat, nor felt they needed it, for the few cold days we had. People put on singlets in winter; if I was cold as a boy I wore a pullover. Each of them owned a jacket that was sometimes worn when going out. My mother kept one good suit from her days in the city but it was never used.

I see my mother always with a solicitous downwards tilt of her head, except when she is defying my father, and then her head is raised like a creature that makes a stand for its life. I did not like her striking my father, which was rare, but I am glad that she was not abject.

There was almost no fighting between my brothers and me. I was too engaged in inward talk to take them for rivals, or even to play with them much, and naturally we hated discord. I always felt I was special for my mother, when I was young; and when at times she turned against me, as I was growing up, it was because of things about me that reminded her too much of my father, and I felt she was right.

This was the sort of thing that irritated my mother. I once made a joke, referring to a habit of my father's: I said that if he were travelling through the jungle and heard a voice calling for help, from a man who had fallen into an elephant trap, he would go to the edge of the pit and say to the man in a pained voice, 'I wonder if you would mind modulating your voice a bit, old chap.' My father was always telling us to modulate our voices. The remark must have impressed my second brother, because one night, years afterwards, when we were living in the town and a friend of my father's came to dinner, a rare thing, my brother, who was known for being charming, made the remark to our guest at the dinner table, as his own. The guest, a handsome man, a former pilot in the Dam Busters squadron, a heavy drinker, laughed greatly. I was stung by this. 'That's my story,' I shouted into the merriment, in which I saw my father had joined, proudly. My mother wanted Billy to have his moment. 'Robert thinks he's the only one who has any ability around here. He can get a bit carried away with himself,' she said.

Of my two brothers, my father was saying, 'One of them has charm and one has looks. Max is the good-looking one, as you see.' In his cups he was patting my brother's black hair.

'Yes, he's like my side,' my mother laughed. She was dressed up, with powder and lipstick, and the Englishman was being flattering to her. He kept saying how much he had enjoyed the meal. How rarely she did, that much.

I knew, although it stung at the time, that my mother had been right about my egotism. My father saw into my vanity, too. He was always ready to discomfort me with it, though even I understood it was compensatory.

When I was nine, my mother took me, on one of my self-appointed days off school, to the draw of a lottery. Without asking my father, she had entered us for tenancy of one of the new, government-funded Housing Commission houses being built on the edge of town. We had earlier walked together to see their scaffolding, in a raw new street, backing onto the golf course and heath land, near the aerodrome. The draw was held at the Presbyterian church hall, where I paid little attention to the speeches and the clapping; but all at once I felt pass through my mother's hand, as it held my shoulder, an electrical charge. I came out of my daydream to hear her saying that our number had been chosen from the barrel. She kept looking from a ticket she held to the numbers being written on a blackboard. I was asked to check that her number really was among them. Then we left rapidly, as if some official might change his mind, hurrying away to tell her parents. In the street, her steps seemed freshly oiled. 'Fancy that! Fancy that!' she kept on saying, and smiling. 'It's the only time I've ever won anything in my life.' I encouraged her mood. I raised an imaginary hat and bowed, skipping along a few paces ahead of her, threw the hat up and caught it, settled it on my head, and then doffed it again. 'The winner! Ladies and gentlemen, the winner!' She told me there were actually twelve winners, this time; and there would be chances for other people, later.

My father did not want to move into town: he hated the idea of having neighbours. My mother said that she was taking the kids and going to a clean, new house and he could do as he wished.

On our last night at the farm, in the midst of packing things into tea-chests, my father took me out into the dark, and collected a shovel and a bucket made from a kerosene tin. We walked up the paddock, toward the road, and he started examining sapling pine trees by moonlight, searching along the edge of the darkness under the great castle wall of trees, for the perfect offspring. He dug one up carefully and put it, as tall as I was, into the kerosene tin with earth, as though it were Christmas. He said we had to take some of the old place with us. This tree, he told me, could be mine.

When we got to the Housing Commission house, on its quarter acre block of scalped earth, he planted the young pine in a front corner of the yard. The house was one of the larger ones of its type, with four bedrooms; two of them on an enclosed verandah. It was in weatherboard, painted green, with a concrete path to a concrete front porch, a wire-and-post fence around the front half of the yard, palings around the back. There was a wide verge outside, big enough for another housing block, with a gravel driveway across its dusty grass. My father would plant a pair of coral trees at the gate, which have very red, beak-shaped blossoms; he was the only person in the street of nine houses, all of them along one side, to plant trees.

The street was unsealed and dust lifted off it in the wind or if a car went by: it hung and settled and rose again in feathery shapes in the sunlight. There were a couple of houses opposite us and beyond them the silvery roofs of the town could be glimpsed, going down a slope toward the close-set roofs of the shops. Diagonally opposite our street corner was a public park with trees and a football field. Behind us stood a dark round hill, great trees over it, each like a Rorschach blot.

The pine tree my father planted grew quickly, above the lawn and the numerous garden beds and rockeries. By the time I was a teenager it could be scaled like the rigging of a ship, to the height of our roof, and I sometimes did this after school and looked across the park, to see if my mother was coming from her cleaning job. When she was, I would go to meet her. My mother used to say, at this time, that if we children quarrelled, which we did a little as we grew older, she was going to leave us, just disappear; so when I came home from school and she was not there, I used to count the dresses in her wardrobe and then climb my lookout to watch for her. The tree eventually grew to be the biggest in the town. My mother, in whom the pioneering spirit was strong, often wanted to have it cut down, over the years, but I argued against that by saying it was mine. It is still standing.

We never had holidays (except for my constrained visits to Sydney), or visitors, birthdays, Christmas, music, eating out, family outings, TV (that came to the district after I left home), nor the telephone. We had, more than other children we knew, the bush, church meetings, the Bible, library books, films, grandparental and maternal love.

In winter we had hot-water bottles; we wore shoes; chunks of stone-heavy wood were put onto an open fire in the living room, of an evening. Some mornings, the yards would be lightly coated with frost, each of its innumerable drops yellow-lit, like the oily casing of tiny insects.

In summer there was the mosquito net, smelling slightly of dust; sleep on top of the sheets; pushing up the shirtsleeve to eat a mango, outdoors, with one's elbow dripping, or a half-moon of watermelon, its flesh almost as sweet and ephemeral in the mouth as fairy floss; stone bruises on the heel; sticky grass seeds in the fine, bleached hair of the legs, looking like ticks, while looking for ticks; calamine lotion for insect bites; going to bed, bathed, tight-skinned from the sun, the skin of one's arm warm and aromatic as fresh bread, and feeling as though one were quietly glowing in the dark, and that the sleeping younger children were adding to the heat of the house, too, each a small radiator left on.

If I go back to the town on a visit now, I always walk on one of my evenings there along what used to be our street. I come to a stop in the dark on the bitumen road and look at the pumpkin-coloured lights of the houses, and at the pine tree, beneath the ground glass of the stars. I hear the tones of young voices and of adult ones. In the different, open houses, people become restless about a figure lingering outside, and I have to move on. I had been listening, but not to them.

6. An Ineffectual Love

My mother's father never visited our house, although we now all lived in the town. He was too intimidated by my father's sarcasm – by whether this or that might be sarcastic – by the insidious way his mispronunciations and lack of education were shown up, and by my father's talk in general, to risk calling on us.

Nor would his sons go near their sister's place, when revisiting that district in middle age, for the same reason; yet they were prepared to fight a bushfire with only hessian bags, or to fish off a rock shelf in the face of a pounding sea. They were all derisive of my father's drinking, but their anger always shifted, before long, to his snobbery. As working-class people, they needed to retain a sense of worth. My father knew well how to use such vulnerability for his protection.

My grandfather would come to my mother's aid, but felt he must be careful not to interfere. He would try to give her 'a little money', when things were at their worst, but she would refuse, saying her situation was caused by not having listened to him. Sometimes, though, she would have to go back and accept money.

My grandfather had built up and run his carrying business

over many years, but he never managed to make much profit from it. When he came to retire, he bought a large wooden house in the town and rented it out, and a small fibro cottage next door, for my grandmother and himself. On a third, extensive block of land, behind these, he 'put out to grass' the rusting chassis of his favourite trucks, and he strewed there his large collection of empty petrol drums. These were half-submerged in an otherwise unusable yard, a reed-bed, along with a few dispirited paperbark trees, peeling like bleached wallpaper in a wrecked house. He did some 'tinkering' for a garage in town, so as to get out of the house, or 'to keep his hands in grease,' his wife said. To help my mother, he had to carve from thin savings.

My mother's father was born in the 1880s, one of numerous children of a veterinary surgeon, who cared for the horses of the Sydney Tram Company. They lived not far from the stables, on the edge of Paddington. My great-grandfather used to be famous for treating his horses with herbal medicines. He was an Englishman, and his wife was German, from a German-speaking South Australian community. She died relatively young, in childbirth, and he never remarried. The eldest children, daughters, helped to bring up the younger ones. My mother remembered her grandfather as a white-bearded man who spoke to everyone as though soothing a horse, and who in his old age used to walk hand in hand in the street with another old Englishman, more feeble than himself, his life-long friend.

My grandfather's name was Victor Allan – English-sounding, but in him the Teutonic side showed strongly, both in appearance and in manner. I remember him mainly from his seventies and eighties, with a large, weighed-forward head, a fleshiness at the nose, and a benign expression, like Albert Schweitzer's. His hair, still entirely black when he died, was so straight that it broke at once out of the oiled shapes he combed into it and hung in fibres on his forehead, and it stuck out like the bristles of an old shaving brush at the sides of his head. His face and neck, like his hands and forearms, were brown and weathered, and his wrinkles, I thought as a child, without any aesthetic complaint, were as deeply folded-in and as shadowed as the stitching between the panels of a football. All his other skin, when he drew up his trouser cuffs or stripped off his flannel singlet, was hairless, smooth and luminously white, like lobster flesh. His eyes were grey, very clear and firm, and had amber flecks adrift within them.

When I was at primary school and first saw in a book a reproduction of that painting by Ghirlandaio of the old man with the bulbous, diseased nose, gazing tenderly at his grandson, who responds with an affectionate look and touch, I thought immediately of my grandfather and myself, although he was not deformed, with a wasps' nest on his nose, and I was not demonstrative. But it was then that I consciously realised my relationship with him.

It was a relationship that was unaffected, on either side, by his slight yet steady discomfort with me. I once, at about twelve years old, walked back unexpectedly into a room where he and his sons and their families were sitting, as he was saying, 'Bob is a very strange boy...' I smiled kindly on their embarrassment, and asked for the newspaper. Both he and I thought the strangeness was the outcome of my illness, and accepted it.

My grandfather was particularly reliable in saving the newspapers for me, until I was able to come to his house, so that I could keep up with the daily comic strip page. He knew of my obsession with 'Dick Tracy', its sad and sordid poetry, 'Little Orphan Annie', in which I loved the strange shadows that almost enveloped everything, and 'Joe Palooka', about a gentle heavyweight champion of the world. On Sundays he would buy two different papers, so that I could have both comic strip colour supplements. I particularly admired the dynamic drawings of Burne Hogarth for 'Tarzan of the Apes', in which the hero's swirling, surging athleticism, in his leopard skin briefs, was strangely contradicted by the soulful, decadent eye shadow he appeared to wear. My grandmother relentlessly threw out even recent newspapers, wherever they might be hidden, and my grandfather had to be continually alert to keep every issue until I had seen it. Our economies at home did not allow us a newspaper, when we had the radio.

My grandfather is the reason I have always felt defensive, even in casual conversation, about Germans, if people speak loosely of them as a race. It had somehow been decided by his family that he was 'a German', although he did not remember his mother and had no knowledge of such a background. It was his European-looking head, perhaps, and the way his voice seemed to us guttural. My grandmother used to refer to him regularly, behind his back, as a 'pig-headed German'.

I remember my grandfather's personality as gentle, questioning, methodical: it seemed as though he were intent on finding out, in every situation, what was right, for its own sake. Most people, I think, found his empiricism a bit slow. I understood something of his character when as a boy I watched his patiently self-taught interest in woodwork, and saw how his attitude to that was continuous with everything he did. This perhaps racial preoccupation with wood, developed in his retirement, was practised in a shed he had built down by the chicken run, at the end of his long backyard. I was allowed to sit in there with him and watch him at his craft, in the hope I suppose that I might be lured into practicality, away from so much time 'off with the fairies'. But I preferred to leaf through his piles of old magazines, *Pix* and *Australasian Post*, even though these were thought to be sleazy, and I knew I made him uncomfortable by doing so.

It was impossible for me not to read. My grandfather once remarked to someone, half proudly, that he had seen me reading years-old advertisement pages, because there was no other print. He could not forbid me to browse through his magazines, as that would have drawn too much attention to them, and though he 'tidied them away', I always found them. I used politely to decline his offer of pieces of timber, a spare vice and a wood-plane. We would sit indoors together quietly on sunny afternoons, a page turned by me, an outburst of mallet-hammering from him, the main sound the creaking of hens outside, like a gate in the wind.

Those were only mildly 'girly' magazines my grandfather collected, but he had to explain to me that they had been bought for their 'Australiana', for their stories on crocodile hunting, rabbit plagues, sporting heroes and racehorses. I skimmed over the pictures of girls in bikinis, anyway, looking for the cartoons, most of them about fly-blown bushmen carrying rabbit traps, and for any interesting articles. I do remember, though, that Sabrina, a blonde English phenomenon of the time, had an eighteen-inch waist, according to a caption (only mildly curious to me), and a bust that I am unable to recall the size of, but that even I knew lunged forward extraordinarily far. It looked like two racehorses straining nose and nose for the line. While I browsed among these obscurely unsettling pictures my grandfather would some-times look over my shoulder and say something like 'God help you if you get interested in that sort of thing.' Otherwise, he was busy learning from his mistakes, as I knew by the muttering that sometimes went on. He would be working on more of his 'artistic', primitive-looking gifts, intended for wife and neighbours, but mainly for our family.

My grandfather sawed by hand, laboriously fitted together, lumpishly glued, decorated with asymmetrical carving, and garishly painted, every possible household item, of relatively small scale, which could be made from wood. From his workshop came tea-pot stands, pot racks, breakfast trays, bookends, inlaid chopping boards, shoe lockers, and hinged boxes with many intended uses, from keeping sewing equipment tidy to displaying the samples of minerals he included with one of them, as a present for my brother. We had more carved breakfast trays than we could use, since no one ever ate breakfast in bed (except me, when I was ill, and I could have had one for every day of the week and still not have tried them all). We brought them out of a Sunday evening and ate toasted sandwiches from them for dinner, listening to the radio, while our father was at the pub. The trays were coated thickly in a globular blond paint, which seemed their creator's favourite colour, with a badly fitting geometrical inlay as their centrepiece, wavering blue or red or green stripes painted along their edging, and carved handles. They were decorated with transfers of flowers, scattered about in bunches, or of animals, and lacquered. My father said they showed my mother's father had a secret inclination after 'tarts', because of their colour – 'big, coarse German blondes' – much to my mother's disgust. She hissed at him and glared anxiously at me. My father insisted that all such 'remedial handiwork' be kept out of his sight. Once, when he had a headache in the morning, he flung a breadboard, made of rectangular pieces with the petrified glue oozed between them, and a wobbly teapot stand, in long parabolas out of the back door.

Although my grandfather had lived by manual skill all his life he seemed strangely unaware of the bumbling quality of his aesthetic work. It was not as if there were some matching decline in his other faculties; it must have been that his standards for this type of object were utterly naïve. What mattered to him, above all, I think, was to express his goodwill toward his daughter and her children, with gifts. He meant to signal his reliable presence to our household. We had to store most of his offerings at the top of the linen press, or in the laundry, where my father never looked.

When I became boyishly fanatical about soccer in the fifties, from reading English schoolboys' magazines, *The Champion*, *Wizard*, and *Hotspur*, it was a game of apparently no interest to anyone else in the town. It was a 'refo's' game, only played by migrants, and only where there were enough of them, in the cities. Still, my grandfather was prepared to convert an old pair of Rugby boots for me (the boots of a 'real' game, my father said) into soccer boots – he replaced a V-formation of tapering aluminium studs with three squared-off rows of leather ones. This was to enable me to get my toe cleanly under the soccer ball that I had brought home from the city. He built each stud like a doner kebab, carving out the separate thin layers of leather and then nailing them all together onto the boot. But quite soon the studs began falling off, while I was practising alone in the paddocks or against a backyard fence, and then the boots lay abandoned in the laundry, looking gap-toothed and imbecilic. I was unable to report this to my grandfather, but went on training every afternoon for my future professional career, barefooted, or wearing sandshoes – dribbling the ball among a tight arrangement of stakes, or aiming a shot at the end of an over-turned drum, while hearing monsoonal applause.

My mother and we kids often walked two miles across town, by-passing the shops, to visit her parents, taking it on ourselves to do so; wandering off separately, most often, or two of us together. We went along the edge of tarred streets, through the sun-flattened, thinly spread-out suburb of nowhere (the population of the whole district then, in the fifties, was about sixteen hundred), passing tin-roofed wooden bungalows or flat-roofed newer brick places, on their quarter-acre blocks, under high, blatant electricity wires. We waited to cross the highway, melted tar at its edges, then went down more streets, on the public grass, under jacarandas and ragged eucalyptus trees, or beneath the bare sky. In the gardens of the houses there were, most commonly, geraniums and frangipani.

Walking in those days, if you passed someone else on foot you made eye contact with them and muttered a greeting, even to a child.

My grandparents lived on a low-lying edge of town, in what looked like a fibro beach shack, of two rooms, in the middle of half an acre of spongy grass. Theirs was the last house: behind them were open paddocks, gradually rising, on which a few cows were always scattered, and a smoky-blue line of hills, like the foreheads and rolling bodies of dolphins. I was told that the glistening atmosphere, westward, through the long afternoons, was caused by simmering eucalyptus oil in the forests beyond the slope. My grandmother insisted on using a wood-burning stove, so when you came down the last street, in view of my grandparents' place, there would usually be lying above it a spar of blue smoke. My mother did not like her parents living in that hollow, which she said was unhealthy.

Instead of a cement path, their place had a boardwalk, and was surrounded by boardwalk, as though built on a raft. Two voracious white goats kept down the moisture-darkened yard, helped occasionally by my grandfather with a scythe. At dusk, the frogs and crickets would begin, and the whole yard became like food bubbling in a pan.

Each house in the white dirt street had a footbridge, across a large rainwater ditch, and planks for a car or truck. Coming there at dusk, I occasionally found a few bigger boys revelling waist-deep in the drains, where water always flowed, the bulrushes trampled down. There was mud smeared on their hard, thin torsos and up their bare legs and arms. Jubilant, hilarious, they were catching eels by hand. The wet, black catch, bloated-looking and evil, was rolling angrily upon itself, as if just awakened, in kerosene-tin buckets by the road.

The dusk at that misty edge of town was engrossing and mysterious, and was my favourite time to visit there. The house next to my grandparents' had a steep-pitched roof, vaguely silver, and a deep-set, dark verandah, and often a couple leaned on its rail smoking, he powerful and bare-chested and she bare-armed and also of classical solidity. They watched me pass and never spoke, with a glow-worm drifting up to either face and brushed away. At the bottom of their yard I could see a thick palisade of paperbark trees, clay-white in the smoky twilight. I told myself this was really a temple or a sacred grove that hid the entrance to another world, and I half expected to be called into it by those two watchful and sombre guardians. My back used to creep as I walked past them, barefoot in the dust, feeling their eyes on me and wondering if they would speak the secret word.

All through my boyhood I lived obsessively on fantasies, engrossed by them to the extent where I as good as convinced myself that my imaginings were realities. All possibilities existed somewhere, I vaguely philosophised, and the imagination was actually glimpses into some of these. I could not believe my invented beings were flimsy nothings, because they seemed more intensely present than my daily surroundings. I systematised these waking dreams into a complex other-world, of which I drew maps and illustrations. I made up characters of my own, or I borrowed them from comic books and novels, and introduced them into each others' schemes, in a complex cross-referencing that I found especially enjoyable. To have time on my own, so as to enter this imaginary place, was my greatest pleasure. I used to struggle against falling asleep at night.

Imagination obviously brought benefits to the hunters, shamen and storytellers who were gifted with this mutation, but it easily overreaches itself. Its presumptions become destructive. For years, as a boy, I was hardly ever where I really was. The actual people I knew were not allowed to be themselves: I made them more 'interesting' by putting them into my stories, and

I often sustained the effort of talking to them on a double level, becoming ridiculously cryptic. I have seen real dubiousness appear in people's faces as they listened to me. I would modify my words back into 'single sense' and the puzzlement would clear, but they would almost shake their heads, and a discomfort remained. I hardly had genuine contact with another person. All children play imaginative games, but when I look back on myself and recall the absorption and isolation of that boy, I am frightened for him.

At my grandparents', if it was only me who turned up, I would often be persuaded to stay for a meal. This would be something like sausages with boiled pumpkin and peas, and bread and butter, or tinned meat and a hard-boiled egg with a lettuce leaf, a split radish, and some tomato, or rissoles with tomato sauce, boiled potatoes and green beans, or fish cakes with fried onion and mashed potato, these always followed by a dessert, of jelly and ice cream, or custard with banana and nutmeg, or tinned peaches and runny cream. I was not particularly attracted by the food – with the addition of chops and of a greater variety of boiled vegetables, and of minced meat stews, it was much the same as we children ate at home. (Our father had a different menu because of his ulcers.) Chicken, called 'chook', was only for special occasions, at either house, as was bacon or roast leg of lamb with roasted potatoes. What I liked about eating at my grandparents' was sitting next to my grandfather in silence (at a table covered by a plastic 'cloth', never removed but just wiped off). My grandparents hardly spoke to each other, and they included me, at mealtimes, in this arrangement. My grandmother rose continually, to serve herself further tiny portions of food, or to make tea or more bread and butter. What I liked was that 'nobody picked on me' there, as I explained to my grandfather, when he asked why I had come visiting again.

The products of my grandfather's workshop introduced me to aesthetic incredulity and into danger as well. The hazard he presented to his two eldest grandchildren was a series of bicycles, made of pieces he was allowed to scavenge from behind the town's cycle shop. My brother and I never compared stories on the narrow escapes we had in using these, but I was aware that another bike had collapsed beneath him, also. We were too embarrassed to mention the experience to each other, or to anyone else. My grandfather only used to remark, on learning we had no transport again, that such old, free bicycles must have a short life. He never thought to enquire into the circumstances in which they had fallen apart. Instead, he became immediately preoccupied by the problem of fitting together another and better machine, with all the detachment of an armaments scientist.

When I was twelve, I applied for, and insisted to my mother I could take on, the town's newspaper delivery run. She accepted that she could not prevent me joining in life, and twenty-five shillings a week would help with my expenses. I had left behind my run of childhood illnesses. The job took me, five afternoons a week, along mostly unsealed roads, a satchel full of rolled newspapers on the handlebars, so I needed a strong bike. But the bikes I was provided with by my proud grandfather – hand-painted in pink and blue, or mauve and green, or such colours, but never in silver and black, as I asked – regularly broke down beneath me. The pedals would start to run loosely, every few turns, or would freeze up with a cranking sound, or I would shed the chain, stubbing my foot into the road – toes dragged backwards, once, without shoes. Putting on the brake in that situation, with a front-heavy load, laid the bike down sideways on the street and sent me staggering free of it, if I was lucky. On one memorable occasion, a right-hand piece of the handlebar broke completely off in my grip. It was rusted through, but that had been hidden by thick paint. I had nearly a full load on the handlebars and was freewheeling fast, with an occasional flurry on the pedals, down a long, thirty-degree slope of bitumen highway, with plenty of traffic behind. Suddenly I was holding a piece of handlebar loosely in the air, the brake handle out of reach on it, and I began to wobble, unbalanced. I was catching up fast on traffic ahead. I jerked the bike with my left hand towards the steep bank beside the road, struck it almost front on, was thrown over the wheel, and landed upside down on a bare clay slope, down which I then slid backwards. I got up fast, to see carloads of people, slowed down, pointing and agog, who had begun to laugh. I stood amazed and laughing myself. The paper run was finished on my brother's bike, long after dark, and I only explained that I had had a bit of an accident; no scratches.

Nor did I report it when the back-pedal brake failed on another bike, while I was riding at full-tilt through the town. Just ahead, a semi-trailer had swerved in front of me, to pull into a service station, and I found that pressing the brake was like flicking the switch on a blown light bulb. Cars were parked closely beside me. Standing on the pedals, I tried to swing aside, shadowing the truck, but I was going too fast, its tray hit me in the chest, and threw me backwards, as the bike continued underneath the wheels. I landed on the road and rolled sideways in the same moment, drawing up my bare legs (head lifted to watch), as the bike was crushed beside me. The truck driver swept on smoothly, up to the petrol pumps, unaware of what had happened. I stood up quickly, in embarrassment, not even conscious of the gravel embedded in my elbows, of the torn flesh on my arm and hip, picked up the bike, which was as curled and stiff as a potato crisp, and dumped it in the gutter. My grandfather was told that the bike had been stolen, but my mother had to hear something of the story while she was treating my wounds.

When I was twelve, my grandfather made a full-scale canoe for me, because I was reading the 'Swallows and Amazons' books and had become desperate to take to the water, even if not under sail. This canoe was his masterpiece: it had a completely strutted frame, the plywood was screwed on in counter-sunk style, the tar seals were almost invisible, it was built-in at either end like a racing skiff, and was elegant. But in practice it proved too shallow and was difficult to balance. I can see now it looked like something off a Bavarian carousel, all pink and blue, with 'Swallow' written on its bow in proliferating curlicues. It no doubt warranted the boisterous remarks it received from adults and older boys, which I loyally and scornfully, and sometimes excessively, answered, risking 'a good hiding', as I was warned by one of them. I was defensive because of my suppressed disappointment. I would take it down to the creek in the early morning (thereby acknowledging its rococo appearance), carrying it turtle-style, and launch it in the reeds near a sawmill, among sawdust heaps and trickling smoke. Then I poled it along a tributary, through grey mangroves – this was the Congo, in my imagination – out into what we called a creek, a waterway as broad as an English river. The creek was shaped like a billow of smoke, with a tight eucalyptus forest, dangling tattered bark and grey-green foliage, right to its banks.

Imagination alight, I became 'Deerfoot on the River'; or passing beneath the back of the cemetery, I glimpsed among the trees a sinister lost African city. I would dig my way, double-bladed, for a winding couple of miles, down to the estuary and the edge of the surf. After resting there, under the sandhills, I cranked back upstream, wobbling along the windblown surface. For a rest, mainly from the concentration of balancing the boat, I explored quietly the tunnel underneath the overhanging trees, going off into light-speckled tributaries. Or went among the stilt roots of the mangroves, at high tide, half expecting to meet a sea serpent or a mad escapee, in that flickering maze. I saw, once, a long black snake, swimming away from underneath my boat, watching me like a periscope. My 'supplies', a few sandwiches, were carried between my feet, wrapped in plastic, along with spears for fishing (never effective), and a kitchen knife. Paddling with my hands through the flooded, low-ceilinged labyrinth, ducking my head, drawing myself along by roots and low branches, I moved among shadows and across sparse ripples of light, in a place where probably no one had ever been.

But I had to come out of there and manage my boat on choppy water, with the tide running heavily of an afternoon. The current would draw me into midstream, on a corner a hundred metres wide, and I would have to let it, and hardly dare shift my aching behind, so closely was the water lapping at the gunwale. I swam about as well as lead on a fishing line. Not to be able to swim, for someone at school in that place, was a stubborn achievement. I had failed to tell my grandfather about this aversion, and he had forgotten to enquire about my safety, just as he never considered the hydrodynamics of his craft.

It seemed to me, at times, that I would never get to shore again. Small waves were ignited by the wind and rushed along the water toward me, and I dared not make directly for the bank, as I was tempted to do, in near panic. I realised I must kneel up, toward the back of the canoe, tilting its nose just a little, and fend off the waves with the paddle, progressing at a tangent gradually across the current.

I had come even closer to drowning in that creek. Idling alone on the bank one day, I walked down the causeway of a fallen tree trunk that reached far out into the water, slipped, fell in, and struck the side of my head on a branch below the surface. This caused me to panic and I pedalled and pawed wildly but could not rise. I held a membrane of air in my throat, frantically thrashing at the green murk, not to be made to eat water. Somehow I climbed a short ladder, through strata of coldness, dog-paddled through the serrated current, and grabbed onto tree roots in the bank. Years later, middle-aged, I stood on that same log, and urinated into the creek, which was much silted-up by then and looked paltry.

I was nearly drowned about five times, while growing up; at the creek, once or twice, but mostly out from the town's surfing beach, where my brother and I went to play among the breakers and would inevitably go in up to our necks. He could swim better than I could; I had a horror of burying my face in the water, but no one was taught to swim other than overarm, in 'the Australian crawl', when there was instruction at school. We would no more have used breaststroke than ride on a girl's style of bike. All of a sudden, Max and I were caught in a rip; we would feel ourselves being carried off, the way iron filings are dragged by a magnet. Lifted out of our depth and standing upright, we were moved backwards, scrabbling for toe-holds, within a chill corridor. We knew not to struggle. I would dog-paddle frantically, to keep my head above water. The current buoyed me. We shouted to each other. 'Keep your head up. Keep your head up. Put your hand up. Wave it more. Wave it. Have they seen you?' We were becoming tired. Then two lifesavers each put on a vest with a line attached to it, and came swimming outwards, like lizards running akimbo across the water.

A neighbour of ours told my mother she was at the beach when she heard the alarm bell clang, from the tallest sandhill, and saw a couple of lifesavers run down to the shore. 'How many?' they shouted to those in the shelter above. 'There's two of them. It's the Gray kids again.'

Yet we kept going to the beach. My brother became a good swimmer, while I continued to avoid the outings at school for those needing to learn. I would take the day off, rather than attend. I have no idea about the origin of this phobia, except that I could not bear even a sheet over my face: perhaps there is a clue in that. Or in the fact that when I was in my early thirties, after my father had died, while sunbathing one day at Bondi Beach, I all of a sudden went in and swam, quite normally – I had been instructed enough by Max – going easily out behind the breakers, as if it were something I had always done.

I put myself into many foolish situations as a boy because I thought it was beholden on me to be adventurous, like the beaming, 'plucky', strong-jawed heroes in my English magazines. The prospect of growing up to even a few years of an unadventurous life, in which I was not the hero of my own story, but merely someone ordinary, made life seem not worthwhile.

At the end of a curved breakwater, which created the best harbour along the coast, for the fishing fleet, there was an island, the size of a small stadium. Children were warned off this place by the rumour that death adders lived on it: we all heard the story of the man who was bitten by an adder while out there and who was dead before he could reach the causeway. I see now the story was used to protect the eggs of the mutton birds that nested there seasonally (and no longer do). I decided to circumnavigate the steep, treeless island by climbing over the large boulders of its shoreline. On the far side, I came to a seemingly impassable chasm, wedge-shaped, like a vast axe-blow, into which the sea was driven and where it exploded, with deep rumbling. I saw above, just over the chasm, along the moist, black stone of an almost perpendicular cliff, what was like a goat path. I demanded of myself that I cross that way. I can still barely face writing about this: my flesh wants to dissolve on my bones and vanish from the thought. What seemed a ledge on which I could fit from bare heel to toe, while shuffling sideways, became when I was halfway across, suddenly half that width – and this right above where the vertiginous, swelling sea came smashing its way in, above where it burst and roared up at me, a reverse avalanche, and dropped away, dizzyingly, like suction, soaking the track and me with spray. I could not move. I tried to plaster myself onto the wall. A few gulls hung idly in the air, just opposite where I was stalled, and I saw their evil incurious eyes. The waves roared again, tunnelling beneath me, filling the air with their head-scouring smoke. I managed to take hold of my viscera and squeeze until it grew steady, and then to make a half-inch move to go on, balancing on my heels, as on tottery stilts, along the slipperiness...I will probably dream of that place tonight, its gullet lined with dripping fangs, its gorge rising between my feet.

I chose a place where I thought I could keep the canoe hidden, in the reed-beds near the sawmill, but of course I left a track going in and out and one day I found the bottom stamped out of the boat and its sides splintered. Whoever did this had not thought it worth stealing. I realised that I felt relief. I knew that I was probably going to go down with the boat, sooner or later. Now I need not keep up at least one of my self-imposed 'adventures'. I let my grandfather believe the canoe was safe at home, under the house.

About ten years later, when I was working in the city, I returned home on one of my infrequent visits. My grandfather had died years before, while I was still at school. On this occasion, walking by the creek in the late afternoon, I passed the place where the sawmill had stood, and saw it was the site of a housing project. The work was deserted at that hour and I wandered in. Bulldozing the mangroves and the paperbarks had begun, the frontline fallen, ramparts of earth driven over them. I thought how black the water looked, before the driven-back trees. Then I saw nearby, in the devastated reed-beds, among a jumble of planks, tyres, a rusted chassis, wild scrawls of galvanised wire, floating bottles and tin cans, all piled there as landfill, a surprising thing. It was a fragment of splintery-edged wood, lying askew on the backs of the reeds, along with bits of styrofoam and plastic bags. Someone appeared to have evenly shaped this scrap of wreckage before they had tossed it into the reeds again. I drew it to me with a long batten. It was oval, like a tapestry or a sampler from some old living room, bleached but still decipherable, with embroidered on it in tendrils a one-word homily, 'Swallow'. The message seemed to be, 'Know your place. Don't get above yourself.'

The bulldozed earth on which I stood, with night almost completely lowered, smelled rankly. Some light was being wrung out of the evening star. Aeons of listlessness hung as mist in the paperbark trees. Across the low tree-tops, a few unfamiliar neon signs had begun to run – a roasted chicken with wriggles of steam, a group of snooker balls scattered. Headlights volleyed back and forth on the road behind me. I was filled with disgust, about something I could not limit or name – at the sordidness of everything. It included my own ingratitude. My grandfather was lying in the graveyard on the hillside nearby, and I stood holding the work of his hands, and of more than his hands.

My mother's mother was an Anderson, who must have reported favourably on the part of the North Coast where she settled with her husband, because a number of her immediate clan soon followed her there. They were dairy farmers, established south of Sydney, in the Kangaroo Valley, where my grandparents had met, before going to Queensland. My grandmother had not been happy with that move, away from her family.

The Andersons were crude people, according to my mother, who disliked them from childhood. They had bitter, cold and arrogant manners, and when I was a boy my mother could feel even a single dark presence from among them, across a sunlit, crowded Saturday shopping street. She would subtly indicate someone to me with a nudge, a slight nod of the head, as she tugged me aside, into a shop or down a lane. The Anderson 'boys', my great uncles, were greasy and dark, with something uncouth and adolescent about them, even in their sixties. They were scarred by the weather, black-haired as crows, had absent and yet watchful eyes. They used to spit into the open fire, my mother told me, as they stood around in her parents' house, just to show their general estimate of things. The old man of the clan, she remembered, from having been taken to visit him, would slap his leg and cackle, with a toothless mouth, at the way the police walked all over the top of his whisky still, but could never find it. Though only a child, she thought it shocking that his animus, greed, self-serving should never have been mellowed by age.

I remember one of the Anderson men, grown old and skewed, weathered like a Red Indian, but with fully black, plebeian hair, following me as a child into the backyard of his house, where my mother and I were for some reason reluctantly visiting, and asking me quietly to show him my 'pencil', blocking my return. 'You know, your pencil,' touching his fly. 'Has it got any lead in it?' Then suddenly urgent: 'Come on, then, get it out.' I ducked away, under some big oleander bushes, and came up against the paling fence, crawled rapidly to one side, under the lowest branches, went out over the front fence, and ran up a brown grass slope, to stand by the road, scratched and abraded. I drew in the dust with a broken-off weed stalk, watching him watch me, where he had settled on the front porch. My mother came and called me to come in, but I only shook my head. She thought that I was bored. I knew what he had meant although I had never heard such an expression or such a request. I knew that if I told about this, he would only put some indignant interpretation on what he had said. Going home, my mother spoke for a long time about her disappointment with my manners. I thought I ought not to add any further load to her already weighed-down opinion of her relatives.

My grandmother Allan, the elder sister of that man, was always spoken of with references to 'dignity': she was stiff-backed, impassive, unwavering in her gaze. But as I grew older I realised  her reserve was because she had nothing to say, in most adult company. Tutored by her family in its self-regard, and with native cunning, she did not condescend to reveal that. Beneath the self-contained demeanour, she was lost and all but overwhelmed; uneducated, unsure, jealous of her husband's greater access to the world. She had been unusually tall in her younger days, built like an Athena, with strong, handsome features, and she could easily assume stateliness, and that must suffice for everything. In her wedding photograph, she stands behind her husband's chair, and rises up like a deer, with seemingly something of its physical prowess; with a wonderful stance and clear watchful eyes. Her hand lies on his arm, but only formally, it does not rest there. Later in life, her look would harden, in most of her dealings, and give her the appearance of someone inspecting incompetent troops. 'A hard case,' my father called her. He was uncomfortable in her presence, because it was difficult to manipulate someone so immediately imperious and so disciplined in opacity. When they met, inadvertently, they were like two feral beasts that skirted each other and went their way, with grumbling from a distance.

My father, at one time, used to hear the rest of the family discussing Grandma. We children would often be 'telling on her', to our mother, because in her seventies she was going through a series of cerebral haemorrhages, and after recovering from each was forbidden exertion. We would be reporting that we had seen her in the town, unaccompanied, stiff as a colours sergeant, tall as a cathedral, treating with a withering self-assurance someone behind a counter. Or we would describe how, while we were visiting her, she had suddenly gone out and chopped off a chook's head, plucked, singed and scalded it, and stuck her arm up inside it, through the bum, at which stage she sent us home, and we had gone, having had enough already, with the smell of singed and wet feathers. Or our story was that she had split kindling and boiled the outdoor copper, set propped up like a barbecue on bricks, to do the wash, refusing to let any of us near the axe, despite our agitation, and our threats to 'tattle', as she called it. She disdained to ask 'favours' of her husband, but waited until he went to shop, and then did herself anything she wanted done. This attitude was supposedly caused by some misdemeanour he had committed years before, which was only an unwarranted suspicion of hers, my mother said, but which she had taken hold of like a staff, to maintain her remarkable dignity.

When we talked of her at home, my father would usually be sitting at the dining room table, making slow work of his evening meal, and sometimes he facetiously drew the sign of the cross before him, as she was named. I remember him burbling on in the background, quoting bits of the old Scottish ballad 'Barbara Allan', as I now realise, which was her name. We caught theatrically delivered phrases, in the pauses of our story, such as 'Hard-hearted Barbara Allan', and 'Cried woe to Barbara Allan', all intoned with the pleasure of someone who idly picks at a piano. My mother would turn away from us suddenly, saying 'Can't you stop that, for God's sake, you fool of a man? If we're going to mock people's mothers, I know an old demon you might not like to remember.'

My father referred to the drawn-out history of Grandma's illness, with its throes of madness, in a callous way: with a reference to Seutonius, and exaggeration, he called her affliction 'The Twelve Seizures'.

Only around her grandchildren did Barbara Allan relent (and perhaps with our mother, late in life). With us, she loved enquiring about our lessons, asking the most naïve questions – 'What do you mean, a.m. and p.m.?' 'Is the premier or the prime minister the real boss?' 'Do they know how big the world is?' 'Are there high walls between the different countries?' I never saw her read anything, but she listened to the radio through the morning. She loved stories, and spoke with wonder and nostalgia of 'The Man in the Iron Mask' and 'East Lynne', which had been serials. When my mother read to her from the Bible, my grandmother sat looking into space, even though my mother followed the words for her with a finger on the fine-printed page. I feel sure, now, that she was illiterate, although my mother never gave any hint of it. She said that the only time my grandfather's business ever really made money was when he discussed everything with my grandmother and she made him keep proper records.

When she asked you questions, quietly and alone, you felt her soul become pliant and anxious, like that of a young girl – even though she had by then grey frizzed hair, tired grey eyes, and a mouth like a vacuole, because of her false teeth hurting and her preferring to leave them out. And when any of us children met her in town or went to her house, she was never curt with us, but her whole body relaxed, and she reached into her purse or her biscuit tin, although we wanted nothing.

'You know, she probably had some musical talent,' my mother mused, with distance in her face, after her mother died. Grandma had won an accordion in a raffle, it seemed, and had left it unregarded for quite a while; then one day she picked it up and persisted with it, for hours, until she was able to play a basic tune, at the first session, although she had no musical knowledge. So my mother claimed. My mother was amazed at the unexpected patience, and the canniness, with what she heard called 'tomfoolery'; and my grandmother herself was surprised, and pleased with her success, although she tried to hide that feeling. Others of her family had overheard my grandmother playing, where they were working on the trucks, and in the evening they praised her, asking for the tune once more; but because they had mentioned it, she put the instrument away and never touched it again. It was given to a neighbour's child.

My grandmother sometimes told me disturbing stories when I was young and we were alone: she would whisper them toward my ear. She overflowed with Celtic superstition. Once she saw I had cut my finger and she said a boy had cut his finger like that and had sucked the blood and developed a craving for it. He had been driven to kill his parents, to drink their blood. Having to hide the bodies, he cut a hole in the bedroom wall, put them inside, and replastered it; but as the bodies decomposed the wall shrank around them and their faces began gradually to re-emerge. Lying in bed in the dawn, the boy thought he was imagining the faces staring at him, and each day he saw them more and more clearly, until he was driven mad and confessed to the police. My grandmother told me this with all conviction, and with anxiety, as if compelled to share it with someone. There were numerous other stories. A little girl on a dairy farm, where the family had to work hard continually, was ill with TB. Her job was to stand in the cow yard in the early morning and at dusk with a switch, urging the cows into and out of the bails. While she was there she began to see a man, almost concealed in the edge of the bush, watching her, just his white, long face showing. No one else could see him, or after a while bothered to look where she pointed. She began to feel that he was the only one who noticed her. Then she saw among the shadows his white hand beckoning and he gave a smile. Perhaps it was just a branch in the distance; she couldn't be sure. The dog barked and fawned around her, anxiously...

It took nine cerebral haemorrhages, over years, each of which was like a flaring, smoking short circuit in a switchboard, to kill off my grandmother completely. Her humanity was burned out of her, a bit at a time. By the end, like some tortured dog, almost blinded, she loathed and distrusted anything that stirred on her periphery. In her charred but relatively lucid moments she knew that no one could help her and she seemed to despise them all: the doctor, but also her husband and daughter, so stricken and assiduous. In the detonations of one of her attacks, and while waiting for the town's sole ambulance to turn up, she would have to be held down on her bed – my mother and grandfather wrestling with her limbs, like sailors with a squid, as I saw when drawn by the noise and hovering in the door. Her obscenities then were so vile that you believed they must have risen out of some collective memory, some cesspool of consciousness, into which the hatred of galley slaves had drained, because they were surely not things that she herself could have heard or have dreamed.

My mother was terribly troubled by this language, much more than by being vomited over. She looked up in her concordance and then her Bible about demons, and spoke to her minister. The sect she belonged to had no practice of exorcism, apart from ordinary prayer, which was fortunate, or the torments my grandmother was going through would have been compounded.

I was barely a teenager then, and still under my mother's influence, but I could not for a moment believe in demons, and so not in any spirits – not in that small wooden house my grandparents had moved to, opposite ours, with its linoleum and its simple furniture; not with the antiseptic sun finding out every corner of the rooms, and the leaves along the front rail turning in the light, and the bright-lit dusty street. I could not believe in such things in that lazy small town, at the edge of the blue steppe of the ocean. From that time, I gave up all those indulgent fantasies of mine, and the world became for me completely physical. There was only this. Things were as they showed themselves to be. I never again believed anything else, although for years I hid my attitude. I saw the mind created more evil than otherwise existed in heaven and earth.

When my grandmother was in the hospital for the last time, she came back to the surface once while I was taking my turn at sitting through the visiting hour beside her. Her face rolled over and she opened her eyes and said, 'Who's that?' When I told her she said, with a weary disdain, 'No, you're not Bobby Gray. He's a little boy. I'd like to see him. Is he still here? He had a poor heart, you know.' (They never said I had a 'bad' heart.) Her face rolled upright on the pillows and seemed to be draining off the bones, as it soon would, into the earth. It was a slow afternoon, in the extended bungalow of the hospital, with its shiny floors, its blue hydrangeas at the windows, its canvas awnings fluttered.

My grandmother said to my mother, with me there, speaking as if almost under the waters of death, her pinched nose and her tightly draw-stringed mouth barely emerging there, that she was not to be buried in the cemetery, and her husband was not to be put beside her. She said, terribly, that her 'limbs' were to be 'scattered, as far as they can be, in every direction, ground up as small as small,' so that 'God won't try to find them.' She was far too exhausted to want the Paradise that my mother, with the Bible across her lap, had just 'witnessed' to her about.

She was buried in a cemetery that for most of the day is covered with shadows, from the trees as tall as cliffs around it. Barely a year later my grandfather was lowered there, too. In her last years she had shunned him, more and more, and had grown angry if he appeared at the hospital, and had refused to be fed by him. After she died, I said how dreadful it was she had behaved in that way, and my mother replied, 'She loved you children.'

My grandfather died after getting out of bed in the night and crashing to the kitchen floor, while trying to go barefoot to the outdoor lavatory. He had not wanted to wake me, sleeping in the next room: I was supposed to help with a chamber pot, if he called. I leapt out of bed at the noise and put on the light, and my mother must have been lying awake across the street – she was almost immediately there, in her nightgown. I was crouching over him, trying to turn him from off his face. She knew at once he was dead. A dog kept barking, somewhere near, probably at her barefooted, loose-haired flight. We sat on the floor with blankets around us until the ambulance came. She had pushed a small cushion under the side of his head.

My grandfather was buried alongside his wife, as he had been preoccupied he should be, to assert his solidarity with her in the sight of his family, of the hospital, of the town, of all that is. Cold concrete, set with a cheap bathroom's pale blue tiles, and a single headstone, bind them together.

7. Sisters of Limited Mercy

Far different from life at home were the visits I made to my aunts in Sydney, for part of the summer holidays each year, from nine years old until I was fourteen. I would see the doctors and then stay on in the city, as 'the girls'' contribution to my education. I came to realise that the lack of even-handedness with this privilege was not just a practicality, but was because of having been singled out from photographs as 'a Gray', a distinction I did not want.

Margaret, I would almost say, was fond of me. She was kind without being affectionate; which for a boy of my age was fine, but it made me unsure about the depth of my welcome. We never touched, not even in crossing a busy street. She would have said that she kept her 'place'. I imagined she had had enough of illness, having heard about her care of her mother, and so was diffident and subdued. She seemed, toward me, now that I can put words to it, both propitiating of bad luck and wary of catching some.

Throughout her life, Margaret had a passion not to know which must have been the equal of many an intellectual's ardour for knowledge. She did not want to be aware of anything unsettling to her. The television news would never have been put on, except that Olga insisted we watch the late programme, with our warm drinks. Olga was enlivened by disasters. Margaret would keep on jumping up, going in and out of the room, lamenting the state of the world, and irritating her sister. There was about Margaret a definite feminine warmth, which you felt was always kept under a shapeless overall.

After my father was banned by my aunts from bringing me to Sydney, it was Margaret who took me to the hospital. I was admitted there for examinations, and it was she, following the visiting hour, who waited around to question the specialists about my report. Hers was the last face I saw, on one occasion I remember, as I drifted into sedated sleep, before the anaesthetic. She seemed embarrassed at her involvement.

When Margaret, years before I knew her, returned to Sydney, with her small suitcase, after disappearing for a year, she had decided to take in gentlemen boarders, two at a time, in a larger flat she and Olga would rent. The one they found shared the top floor of an old, two-storey, dark brick building, still in Vaucluse. A few houses down the street was the main road, where the trams ran. The windows, all on one side of the flat, showed descending tile roofs and tree-tops and the harbour, a great drowned valley, deeper blue than the sky, or on some days grey and impassive as a glacier.

The flat had dark wooden skirting boards, doorframes and doors, ornamented picture rails, down its long hallway, and high ceilings of decorated plaster. All the lights, except those in the kitchen, were chandeliers. Margaret chose for her boarders athletic young men, usually bank clerks, from the country and well brought up, and among them were some she lightly flirted with and elusively doted upon. Over the next twenty-five years, one after another, her boys would invite her to their weddings, back in a wheat-growing or sheep-farming or irrigation district, which she never attended, and in due course they would send her pictures of their children. In old age she was burdened with Christmas cards, since they all had to be reciprocated.

Margaret, when I got to know her, was in her fifties and still youthful. She was tall and thin, and had spindly legs. Her face was narrow and pale, with a pointed chin. Her low forehead made her look good in hats. The eyes were grey, slightly squinted, under finely curved brows. I liked her nose, which was perfect, in its straight, geometrical elegance and its proportion to her face. Her thin, usually rather smudgy lips matched the fuchsia-coloured nail varnish that she painted on nearly every day, in dashing strokes. (She did her nails, I thought, rather in the way that she played patience, with impulsive gestures. A game was constantly going on, laid out again, after a virtuoso shuffling of the pack, in the sunroom, or by the telephone, or on the dining room table: any-where she passed. It was supposed to keep her calm.) Her hair was dark-chocolate brown, when I knew her first, and although wavy and thick was worn deeply sectioned through, cut off abruptly onto the back of her long, bowed neck. It was densely packed, like some sort of fine grain, fascinating to a boy. More than prettiness, her face had personality. Her manner was like a bright mist, diffuse, ingenuous, elusive. At times, she could seem as if about to faint on her feet. She was short-sighted but never wore her glasses; they were carried in her handbag and only brought out if they really had to be, for use as a lorgnette. Whenever she left the flat, even if she were only going to buy vegetables at the nearby shops, she would be immaculately dressed, in white gloves and usually with a little shell-like hat. She told me to keep up, as we walked: all the women in the street, who did not like their husbands talking with her, from their gardens, would be watching us, she believed.

Margaret's boarders were united in a tradition, picked up from one another, of rallying around her, with bluffness and bonhomie, to protect her from Olga's irritations – those of them who could overcome their dislike of the younger sister and stay. A number remarked that they were not to be driven from such cooking and such cheerfulness as Miss Margaret's by the rule of jackets and ties at dinner, or by Miss Olga's severe restrictions on the bathroom's use. (I remember Olga bellowing at a young accountant, through the bathroom door, her cheeks pinker than her bathrobe: 'What's keeping you, Johnson? You working out the depreciation on your toothbrush?')

One of Margaret's infatuated young boarders called Olga an 'evil woman', after he found Margaret sniffling in the kitchen, and heard the door slam, on Olga's way to work. He was told by the victim, gently, firmly, with his hand still resting on her back, that he must find another place to live by the end of the week.

At dinner, Margaret was always on stage. She had a story to tell every night, usually about some bafflement of hers that day, from which, inevitably, she had been rescued by a man. 'Such a lovely man...' she always said. The boarders would start to grin, in anticipation. She could never go out, it seemed, without an older man offering to help with her parcels, or in getting off a tram, or crossing the road. Or one of them would talk to her at the butcher's, perhaps, and urge her to put her money, she would tell us with excitement (although she had none, at the time), into – what was it? – Caesar. ('Caesar? Caesar? Are you sure? Could it be – CSR?') Or a man had told her a joke in the fruit shop, which she remembered, and it reminded her of others. Or one had walked with her around the old furniture and china markets where she loved to browse. (The sexes were more easily approachable by each other then, it seems, probably because they were more formal.) Margaret would refer to such a man, on coming home, as 'My boyfriend,' or 'My pin-up boy,' particularly if she had met him before. If one of these men asked her out, she always said that she had to spend the evenings with her 'guests'. She could hardly have left the boarders in Olga's care. But she made excuses for the weekends, also.

At one time, over a period of years, she had weekly engagements with an elegantly dressed older man, who had brushed-back silver hair and great blisters under his eyes, and whose wife was an invalid. These 'outings' were all to do with racing carnivals and drives and luncheons, as no one doubted. She seemed too unruffled by the friendship for it to have involved the bedroom.

Olga listened in exasperation to Margaret talking about her 'adventures' of an evening (which would go so far as her accepting a shandy in a beer garden). Olga referred to these stories, to me, as her sister's 'amateur theatricals', and disbelieved, outrightly, any anecdote about flirtation. Still, she saw Margaret's performances as part of a business, and business was something she respected, so she tried to keep quiet. She had the sense to take her dog for its walk as soon as possible after Margaret began amusing the table. When the door shut, the rest of us would change our postures, at once – we felt that we were now allowed to sprawl – and someone would agree to Margaret's suggestion of another drink.

'I must have such a cheap face,' Margaret would resume. 'Do you know, something else happened to me today...' The stories were trivial, but were told with a kind of warbling charm. The interest in them, like that of a comic strip in the newspaper, was strung out from week to week: would our heroine ever find the right man? I came to realise that she had no intention of doing so.

Margaret told me she was a snob. This was confusing, as my father had more than once remarked that snobbery was ill-mannered, and Margaret could do no wrong, for him. I did not quote him. I saw that she was always drawing distinctions; but these were not, basically, to do with family or money: her criteria were dress sense, looks, accent, and whether or not one was 'good value'. Many people have similar requirements; it was just that Margaret was so unhesitating in applying hers. She was dismissive, in a moment, of people she thought unworthy of her time. This action was always a surprise, when one's impression of her was, mostly, of a youthful hesitance. I could never get used to what I saw when shopping with her, while I was in short trousers – her sniffiness, her erasing wave of a gloved hand, barely acknowledging a greeting, her averted face. These responses might occur in dealings with a Greek fruiterer or an Anglo-Saxon butcher (she said to me once, leaving a shop, 'It used to be that butchers were interesting people'), or with some plain, self-important neighbourhood woman, passed in the street. Next minute, she would be easily responsive and chatty to the good-looking, bright young assistant at the newsagency. I was inwardly aghast at her progress down the shopping streets of the few suburbs we went to; I felt this particularly because I had come from a country town, where no one would have dared behave in such a way.

The scorecard Margaret judged people on was to a large degree one that was applied to her, by certain residents of Vaucluse. Her 'passing mark' meant that she was regularly invited to a 'girls' circle' for cards, and to their afternoon teas, and matinees, and lunches in town.

When I started noticing such things, I realised how hard Margaret worked to entertain her guests, during her turn to have the group home, and how she would not have missed the chance. I helped her to bring food into the sunroom, wearing my tie, answered the questions of the red-mouthed, carefully poised, suntanned women, and smiled, and was allowed to go. I listened to Penny and Poppy and Helen and Blondie idly, from another room, and noticed how Margaret directed the conversation with her wit, keeping it away from talk of possessions, where she could not compete. She had confided to me that was what she had to do, when we were in the kitchen, beforehand. I heard the others cavorting flat-footedly behind her, trying out their own jokes. They were also eager for the gossip that she picked up at the races, or from her male acquaintances, up and down the street. The women visitors all had husbands but were 'simply never told anything', they complained. Margaret was the one among the group who, in her words, was 'pale and interesting'. I could not understand why it was worth the effort.

Olga had needed to be highly efficient to advance in her job quickly, but her efficiency was carried inappropriately into every part of life. She continually interfered with others' independence, and was not dissuaded by the problems this caused. Having lived so much amid resistance, she had perhaps become inured to that response. It seemed that she was compelled to sort people out, to staple them in their logical order, and to dispatch them as she thought best. Olga judged everyone by how prodigiously they 'got things done'; by their effectiveness as a spindle, a pulley, a flywheel or a lever in the great productiveness of the world. This was a type of egotism most of us have succumbed to: extolling a quality in which we excel. Olga's version was held with unusual conviction.

Although she was a single working woman, when she comment-ed our way for us through the television news of an evening she would be particularly heckling of any liberalism or left-wing reform. Words such as 'commies', 'bludgers', 'pinkos', 'nancies', 'traitors' and 'foreigners' were flung at the screen, in a hobgoblin rage. Margaret never demurred from the politics, just from the expression of it. 'Olga, wherever do you hear such language?'

Olga had a fiancé, for a time, a soft-fleshed, middle-aged man, with flimsy red hair and a thin nose, like a proboscis, who lived with his mother. His manners were much too good, Margaret told me, because they made him hesitant, which was not appealing in a man. Margaret was rarely allowed to meet him. She remarked to the flat at large once, in Olga's hearing, that nothing would come of it, since he lived in fear of losing his trousers, judging from how high they were worn. Olga stomped on, unresponding, down the hall. Perhaps she had not 'caught on'. Olga used to talk with him every evening at a precise time, after dinner, on the big black telephone in the hall, sitting on a footstool, and doing all the talking, as I glimpsed through the double glass doors. On a later visit, I noticed these telephone calls were accompanied by vehement gestures and restlessness; then one night, after a slamming of doors in the flat, I heard from Margaret the whispered news, that 'lover boy' had decided to stay with mother.

Every Saturday, one or other of a small group of women came to pick Olga up, on the way to golf. All of them were similar to my aunt – all spinsters, dog lovers, 'in the commercial world', and of peculiar shape. Each wore a tweed or tartan skirt and a cardigan, and some had a little mannish hat. Unlike Olga, Margaret told me, they were 'churchy' and 'good'. After the game, they would sit together in the clubhouse, and over a ginger ale tactfully encourage Olga, who regularly had the worst score. Olga would not give up her golf: that would have meant efficiency had been thwarted. She had special, expensive clubs made, to suit her height, which improved her game, slightly. A couple of the women were friendly toward Margaret; they used to call in, on their way home from the game. 'Well, how did Madam go today?' Margaret would greet them, with a wink. Olga liked the visits, but wanted the women as her friends, and Margaret to stay in the background. There was no chance of that. Margaret would go into her bright act, Olga was cast into a sulk. If enquired about, she would say she was just a little tired, or was thinking about work, and she was then ignored, cheerily, by everyone ('Why don't you go and have a lie-down?'), until after a while, with a careful off-handedness, she again tried to join in the laughter and storytelling. Later she was angry at

Margaret, for 'taking over'. Margaret would say, 'I thought you wanted me to entertain your friends. You want them to come back again, don't you?' Or, 'I consider them my guests, too, in this flat. I can't just go off to my room...'

'You know what I mean,' her sister would say, with a long memory in her voice.

Olga formed a special friendship, from among her group of women, with the youngest, Shirley, who had a pretty face and a lumpish figure, and who dressed like her mother must have, the widow with whom she lived. They spoke to each other regularly in the evenings on the phone. As well as playing golf with the group, the two of them went out to shows, to shop, or to have 'supper'. They always had to have early evenings. Shirley was an easily dominated personality, whom we heard being continually advised about her extended family, by her enthusiastic 'best friend', or scolded again, the next day, over that second drink. Then after a few years she drifted away, becoming more and more busy with nieces and nephews, and I saw that Margaret was saddened for Olga because of it.

Olga became secretary to the harbour master for the port of Sydney. She told us that in this job, which she held for twenty years, until well after she could have retired, she took as much work as she could 'off the Captain's shoulders'. You were meant to under-stand, Margaret explained to me, that it was really Olga who was the director of shipping.

Like my father, Olga seemed unable to sit down to a meal with-out complaining about it. 'Really, Midge, these beans' – pushing them away with the back of her fork – 'they're soggy! And why are they so neon-coloured? It's that stuff I asked you not to use.' Or on a bad day, 'I simply can't take any more of this,' rising from the table with a napkin pressed to her mouth, while others were eating.

'But you've eaten it all,' Margaret could usually point out. There would only be a steak bone left on the plate.

'I simply can't eat meat that raw,' Olga would gasp (or that well done), tottering toward the kitchen, trailing her napkin in defeat. We would hear her clattering about in there, beginning ostentatiously to tidy up.

After Olga came home from work, if I was staying with my aunts she would soon come down the street looking for me, and make me stop playing tag (we called it 'whippy'), with the neighbouring kids, or cricket, along the pavement and the grass verge, in the dusk. She told them I was in Sydney for a medical check-up and was not well enough to run around – even though I was easily the quickest at the game. She made this announcement regularly, when I was with children. They became bored with it, too. The pretty Sutherland girl would glance at me regretfully and with pity. Margaret had no need of me indoors, as yet, but Olga demanded it; I was not to get 'overheated', she said. At home, my mother had long since given up trying to stop me running about: she remarked, 'A young boy should not be kept in a cage.'

But Olga was decent to me, a number of times. She sat with me through what she must have found a dreadful Dean Martin and Jerry Lewis film, without complaining, having given me my choice; and another time through a Western with Bob Hope in it that I myself was uncomfortable about. It was hard to tell; she may have enjoyed *Abbott and Costello Meet the Mummy*. She took me to a soccer match, at my request, knowing nothing of what she would see, and was inveigled into a conversation by some gentlemanly old Greeks there, who instructed her in the game, so that soon she was leaping up and shouting advice, in disagreement with theirs. Most gratefully of all, I remember that she rescued me the last time my father brought me to Sydney, when I was eight years old, from a pub doorstep in the next suburb, where I had waited for hour on hour, since before nightfall. Bored and forlorn, in the rain-filled dark, and subject to the concern of old ladies, thinking self-pityingly of *The Little Match Girl*, I saw with relief Olga appear out of a taxi, in which she had come looking for us. She clove her way straight to the bar, and dragged my father out, metaphorically, but almost literally, by the ear. Catcalls and jeering followed her, on what must have been a Friday night, it was so rowdy. Keeping the umbrella over herself and me, in the high-kicking rain, she manhandled my tottering father one-handedly across the street to the cab. He leaned against the car while she opened the back door, and I have the distinct impression that in pushing him into the back seat she was able to play a heavy runnel of water from one of her umbrella staves, directly down his collar.

8. A Jungle Boy

My mother was always formal with the neighbours: she did not approve of people 'running in and out of each other's doors', and after forty years in that street still insisted on the use of her surname. This was not snobbery with her; she would talk over the front fence with whoever came past, and greeted everyone when out walking. She must have been influenced by my father's mannerliness, but I think her reserve was mainly because, having had to take a menial job, she wanted to keep some dignity. The oldest woman in the street, only she went out to work.

At first, she cleaned people's houses and ironed for them, but then found a job mopping the junior school in the afternoons – the classrooms, corridors and stairs of a new two-storey building – and taking down the chairs from the desks of a morning. She did not have to walk far, for this; the playground voices and the bell could be heard in our yard.

Her only recreation was to chat with the neighbouring women, who were Betty and June and Maureen among themselves. She found that she particularly liked to talk with Mavis, on the lower side of us, who was a Jehovah's Witness and who spoke about the

Bible. Mavis told my mother that the dreadful conditions under which we lived on Earth would not last much longer: God had promised that. My mother was susceptible to the idea.

By then my mother had discovered she was not as reclusive as she had thought. She felt worn down by years of worrying, without the support of anyone, except her parents, from whom she tried to keep her anxieties. The Jehovah's Witnesses seemed a religion in which the congregation were friendly among themselves; they called each other 'brother' and 'sister', one or other of them was always visiting Mavis, and she was often seen going out with them by car. Also, most of them were women whose husbands were not interested in religion, so there would be no need to feel left out among them. When it was suggested that a 'minister' might call and study the Bible with my mother, she agreed.

She had been listless about religion for a long while before this, as shown by the way she was prepared to send my brother and me to the Sunday school and services of the Church of England, which was not a serious religion, she thought, by the Gospels' standard. 'Every man's hand shall be against you, and you shall be outcast for my name', was hardly a sign that pointed to the Anglicans. My father wanted us brought up in the Church of England, but of course did not take it seriously: I remember him remarking, in my youth, that Holy Communion for the Anglicans was a cucumber sandwich and a cup of tea.

I was uncomfortable with the Anglican minister, an archdeacon, who was full of self-importance because of having been a chaplain in the army. When he took us for religious classes at school, he used to snap off pieces of chalk and throw them hard, like a fast bowler delivering, at anyone whose attention wandered, or who got an answer wrong. He was distended in build, his face flushed and damp, the veins in his cheeks and nose the purple of his vest. The archdeacon described the Catholics, smirkingly, as the 'Italian'

Church, or sometimes as the 'Irish' Church. At mention of the 'English' Church he opened his chest. Other Christians he referred to as 'poor types', except for the Jehovah's Witnesses, whom he once included in one of his ideological clearings-of-the-board: they were 'very poor types'.

I thought this ridiculous. Mavis was clearly a good-hearted woman, even if she was, as my father said, 'stone ignorant'. She seemed to agree with that opinion, often referring to herself as 'muggins' or 'buggerlugs here'. She had almost colourless, frizzy hair, which seemed a direct expression of her nervousness, was small and freckly, and had the flat chest of a child. I used to steal a glance at her bosom, simply because it was not there. She wore cotton print dresses and often had a cardigan draped on her shoulders, with her arms folded about her. Her son, of my brother Max's age, was a particular sissy, but she seemed to approve of my brother and me, unexpectedly smiling when she remarked that we 'ran wild'. I would have liked her for that alone, but she was also kind to my mother. I was not worried by my mother changing her religion, although my father was disgusted – he complained that the 'JWs' were 'social outcasts'.

Ours was a street of boys, all about the same age: there was one girl, but none of us found her attractive in either temperament or looks and she was ignored. She might otherwise have been our Helen of Troy. The boys formed gangs and fought. For shields we had palings sawn off at about half our height, nailed onto two crosspieces, and a grip made of rope tacked to them, or else we stole metal garbage bin lids. Our weapons were clods of dry orange earth, from a bulldozed lot at the end of the street, carried in old school satchels.

Street was pitted against street, in our full-pitching battles. These swung in fear and exhilaration across some vacant lots, which were around a corner and down a gully from where we lived. Each team would try to drive the other into the bush at the cleared ground's perimeters. A small fortress of saplings had been left in the middle of the slope, within those couple of acres, and bulldozers had tumbled together a rampart of big logs beside it. The broken antlers of the torn-up tree roots, clotted with earth, would have made any child think of galleons grappled together, and we fought for possession of them. There were as many as ten or twelve who joined in our wars. The clods stung when they struck you, in a burst of fragments and smoke. We had one rule: no stones. If someone threw something that clanged or cracked on a shield, as they occasionally did, everything was called off at once, and that side was abused (while they angrily sought the culprit) and was considered to have lost. To relieve our feelings, we would then have wrestling matches, one-on-one, boys matched by size, or a game of cricket or tackle football, on the wide verge of our street, played with such vehemence that the neighbourhood women came out in their aprons, some with a child in arms, to supervise, and would end up barracking.

I was the only boy, or person, who wandered much in the bush behind our street, although my brother went with me sometimes. A dog belonging to an old neighbour of ours, across the road, would nearly always want to go with me. I only needed to set out in the direction of the bush for him to appear. He was a cattle dog, blue as shale, ageing, but canny and tough, and avid for young company. On our expeditions, during the extended season that could be called summer, my brother and I usually wore only shorts, and went barefooted or wore sandshoes, and we became very brown. My father said that we went about like savages, especially when we were seen carrying our 'spears', which were lengths of dowel curtain rod, scavenged from behind a joinery and sharpened in a long bevel. These could pierce a ten-gallon empty kerosene tin, through two sides, or the bole of a banana tree, but were never used against birds or animals, except for the occasional challenging frill-neck lizard or goanna. My father warned us against the black snakes and brown snakes he had come upon many times in working at the aerodrome, which was on one side of the heath we wandered through. We told him we beat the grass ahead of us as we went and made plenty of noise and that the dog was always out in front, pouncing on all fours, scrabbling, barking, unsuccessfully chasing anything that moved.

The dog's name was Blue, of course, but my father always called him Nikita, because he said that he had 'a wonderful smile, just like Mr Khrushchev's', a perverse opinion for that time. I discovered more about this sympathy later.

The bush grew thickly over the hill behind our house, and then there was heath, for a couple of miles, out to the long, empty beaches, scalloped headland by headland, up and down the coast, and to half a world of ocean.

Leaving our house, you went through the edge of the bush, beside the furthest fairways of an eighteen-hole golf course, then out in the open you passed the airport, at one end of its landing strip, seeing the windsock and hangars and control tower, on their mown plain. You could see at the far end of the strip a large paper-bark swamp – an escarpment, off-white, dreaming, melancholy, as though a long cloud seen when at sea. On the other margin of the heath were the backs of some low-slung houses, one edge of the town. Planes occasionally inclined closely above there, most of them small and old, one a biplane, from the aero club: they were like the winged insects that leapt from and floated back into the grass.

On that flatland, low bushes grew thickly together, out of purplish-grey sand – intricate embroideries of twigs, speckled with leaves or furry globules; feathery, upright fronds; tough grasses in clumps; stooks of reeds, all to waist height. In their season, brilliant orange and yellow 'Christmas bells' dangled all through the scrub. A great many small white flowers were there in spring and autumn, brilliant as if crustings of salt blown in from the sea. There were outbreaks of low trees, twisted smooth white angophoras, swamp oaks, and paperbarks, all keeping to their separate encampments. You crossed a polished railway track, on its oil-stained gravel, to get to the grassy-topped sandhills and to a beach, as curved and bold as a mainsail, almost always empty, maybe just a couple of fishermen there.

I remember drifting through that grassland until dusk, in what must have been winter, seeing across the brush a damp, cold-breathing, plaster ocean, in solid blue, beneath its 'strange, straight line'. High up was the daylight moon, a broken lump of salt. The isolated groups of trees threw their shadows far away. Finally, I would have to turn toward the broken yolk of the sunset, and start for home.

I only ever trod on a snake once, with my bare foot, and I knew immediately what it was and leapt onto the air and seemed to run there on nothing, like a cartoon character. By the time I came down, the snake had twitched and was a yard off, but I saw it was a black one, the poisonous kind, and crushed the small thing again and again under a big stone, unnecessarily. Then, perhaps a month or so later, I thought that vengeance had come for me, when I was hurrying home across the golf course in a humid dusk and a black snake reared up, just ahead, and stood on its tail for moments, like the Indian rope trick, taller than I was. The dog yelped and scuttled sideways, and I did the same, in the opposite direction, and ran like a threshing machine until I thought I could taste blood in my lungs, sure the snake was coming after me in running loops like the Loch Ness monster. My mother told me it would have just hatched its eggs. I went to find the dog the next day, and it was on its porch in the morning sun, and opened a lazy eyelid at me, as I stroked its head. Then I set off for a walk, and I heard the ticking of its nails, coming down the concrete path. We skirted the golf course, for a time. (My imaginary adventures gained so much by having the bush for their setting that there could be no thought of not returning there. This was before I had eschewed fantasy.)

In imitation of a film I had seen at a Saturday matinee, called *Big Sky*, about buckskin-clad hunters trekking through the American wilderness, I wandered deep into a swamp. I knew that whatever my imagination might tell me, there were no predators, no crocodiles, that far south, in New South Wales. I used to wear swimming trunks under my jeans when there was the likelihood of a diversion like this. Though I had a finicky dislike of feeling dirty – except that I often chose to go barefoot – I forced myself to enter the beer-coloured water, among the clay-white, shaggy forest of wading paperbarks. The dog came with me, swimming, and helped convince me that I was fearless.

The water was warm and aromatic at first, and seemed as if it might be medicinal. I waded on in sandshoes, going up to my waist, thinking to reach the other side of that place, or to find a secret island within it. The trees tightened about me, their naves grew narrower; it became dim and still, and the water was cold, away from the sunlight. I had a stick that I felt around with, to save me stepping out of my depth. I could feel the floor was thickly coated with leaves.

The swamp turned into a black infusion 'that a spoon could stand up in'. The dog was swimming with its nose at a steeper and steeper angle. I put my stick underneath its forepaws, but it turned around and went back, vanishing in a minute. The trees were even taller, sapling-thin, and grew closer together, in an endless

171

stockade. For some reason I felt compelled to go on. There must be a sanctuary in there. A heron flew heavily away, veering among the trees, but there was no sign of fish. There was the spacious chirruping of frogs, falling silent when I came near, occasional slow-breaking bubbles, and some abruptly sliding, veering dragon-flies. Wide spiderwebs, with twigs and leaves hung within them, along with the spider, were stretched above. The stillness and dimness settled more deeply. Then, when I thought I could allow myself to go back, and not feel cowardly, I found I had no idea of the way. I had thought that my wake, left on the dusty, still water, would show a winding course for me, like Theseus; but the light had changed and it was hard to tell which slightly brighter area was my path and which was the disturbance of fallen sticks or of the secretive breeze. I could not recognise any of the landmarks that I had deliberately noted – the strange-shaped branches or the trees leaning far askew. Panicky, I thought I might have to wade for days, and began to make promises. The story had now become 'The Escape from Devil's Island'. I knew I was going the wrong way when the water grew deeper, going up to my chest, and up to my chin. I backed quickly away from there, and laboured on, with my stick.

After what seemed hours of anxiety, I was led to freedom by momentarily glimpsing, far away to one side, through a chance alignment of the spaces between trees, a faint flicker of redness – which turned out to be the triangular red flag on the eighteenth hole of the golf course.

I returned to where my clothes were hidden. The dog was not there; he must have gone home for his dinner. I ran across the empty, long-shadowed golf course to a tap, to clean myself of the leaves, twigs and feathers that were stuck all over me. As I washed in the chill twilight I was drenched with a sense of exhilaration, at having escaped that place before night.

Wandering further off, one day, I found an abrupt, long hollow, in some stony bushland; a damp gully, the breadth of a small river. It was thick with rainforest. I climbed down, from the height of the tree-tops growing within it, into the shadowiness and stillness of a church. There was a trickling 'soak' at the bottom. After poking about for a short while, I became aware that big, portentous rain-drops had begun to drip through the dense leaves, onto the dark mulch there, and occasionally onto me. I looked idly for a heavier part of the canopy, to shelter beneath. Then I realised that those were leeches dropping. I was dressed only in rolled-up khaki shorts and a 'sacred thread', some dyed string, for my role as Mowgli, the jungle boy. The shadowy floor had begun to writhe everywhere with leeches – all blindly marching toward the warmth of my blood. With a rapid thumb-and-forefinger spanning movement, each bunched-up half-inch of gristle stretched two inches or more, as it lunged toward a rare meal. Each was a miniature black elephant's trunk, making a wild trumpeting gesture, voluptuously testing the air. I left that place in 'cat on hot bricks' style. Up in the sunlight, I tore and twisted the leeches from me. I was covered with them; finding more and unexpectedly more, on shoulders, legs, feet, hair, neck, legs, groin. I saw that they each left a fine slit in my skin, when wrenched off, wounds I at once thought of as from glancing knife blades, in close combat. Leeches have a chemical that prevents blood coagulating, but makes it run thinly and copiously, and soon I was sluiced in bright watery blood. They cause a relentless itch, too, which meant that my hands became 'dipped in gore'. Turning home, I was able to fantasise how the scout (I had become a Red Indian, on the side of the whites) might bleed to death, after his close escape from an ambush, before he could make it to the fort.

My mother would have seen someone as ensanguined as St Sebastian, after his quills had been pulled out, standing in the back door. She looked at me in horror.

I caused her many other shocks, the worst when she thought I had hanged myself. There was a tree I liked in the park near our house, some heavy kind, with a deep umbrella of spaciousness inside it. This was the largest tree among a stand left in our corner of the grounds; partly screened by the others, it shaded an area the size of a small house. I had an idea, from the Tarzan films, of swinging on a 'vine' through its high canopy. From somewhere I filched a coil of rope, and around the same time, in a second-hand shop, found a *Reader's Digest* issue which had an illustrated article on knots. I fastened the rope high in the tree, with plenty of clear space around it, and then, after much tugging and testing, climbed with the other end onto a branch, away over at one side, and launched out. I plunged down, through a deeply dredging swoop, rose fast into the tree's other limit, and just managed to fend off with my feet the branches there, before plunging back, facing about on the way. I gradually came to a dangling halt, and lowered myself, so as to climb into the tree again. Because it was hard for me to hang on the rope for long, I made a stirrup at the end, in which I could ride. Then I had the idea of tying a big, stable noose, to sit in, so that I could push away from the branches at the end of each swing with both feet, and keep up momentum. I made the noose, and on my first ride with it set off before getting properly seated, intending to haul myself into place while in flight. I was holding on with one hand just above the noose, and with the other high on the side of the loop, so as to haul myself up, the rope lying low across my back, but the knot suddenly closed on me. It caught me under an armpit and across the opposite side of my neck, pulling me askew. My left arm was forced out stiffly to the side, the other hand was unable to loosen the drawstring tightness of the rope. Luckily I was wearing a shirt with a collar. I dangled helplessly, neck pressed far over as if it were broken. My chest was constricted, making it hard to breathe and impossible to shout.

Wondering if I would have to hang there in pain for a long time, or if I would die like that, I glimpsed through the leaves, as if I were imagining it, my mother hurrying down the street towards me, without a basket or a handbag, and in her old, flat house shoes. She came straight into the trees and stood underneath me and I heard a horrified moan. She said I had seemed like a lifeless, black scarecrow. 'I'm all right. I'm all right,' I gasped to her, hoarsely. I was dangling fairly low, but well above her height, and she looked around for what to do, and grabbed a long stick; she pushed this up underneath my foot and said to brace on it and then she pushed me so that I swung sideways and could snatch hold of a leafy bit of branch. I pulled myself one-handedly, in snatches, along this, straddled a stronger branch, worked the noose off, and started to come down. She said to pull the rope up first, out of reach, and out of sight. Both of us were subdued, walking the hundred yards back to the house. I was made to promise I would never go into the tree again. (Before long it was sawn down, when that rough corner of the park was thinned.) My mother was pregnant at this time, with my sister. She told me that she had been in the kitchen when she heard my voice and felt an absolute conviction that I was in trouble. Going out at once, she had not hesitated, but had found herself compelled toward the trees in the park.

I spent my time when out of school running messages for my mother, or 'going for a walk' in the bush, or playing neighbourhood sport; but what people remembered of me was that my face was always in a book. A child of my age, from a poor family, in most other countries, would have had a job after school, but there was no culture of that among us, nor work to be had: we saw few tourists then, and there were adults who were unemployed. People in the towns looked down upon the 'cow cockies' on dairy farms who 'put their kids to work'. My mother was of the opinion that 'children should have a childhood'.

Sometimes I read in the garden, cross-legged under the shade of the backyard palings; sometimes on the front porch, with a cushion; sometimes inside a tree at the top of the lane that ran beside our house up onto the hill, my back against the trunk, seated on some boards I had put across two branches; and nearly always I read in the living room, by lamplight, when everyone else had gone to bed, until my mother came out blearily and told me to stop.

I had the school library to draw on, and also the School of Arts in the town; the newsagency sold a range of paperbacks, and I found some of the most interesting things I read in a second-hand furniture dealer's, among the wardrobes and kitchen dressers. The books were stacked in cardboard boxes, sharing a table-top with preserving jars, mangles, mixing bowls, piles of finely-crazed white dinner plates, colourful drinking tumblers that had been peanut butter jars, and old, pewter-grey cutlery, with the knife handles the yellow of horses' teeth. There I found 'Bulldog' Drummond and Fu Manchu, Dr Nicola and Deerfoot, albums of stories from the *Magnet* about Greyfriars school in England, and many paperbacks by Edgar Wallace. These books must have been the reading of some of the local farmers, or of retired men from the city, probably cleared away by their families after they had died. The fact that the books were already old-fashioned then, in the fifties, gave them the interest and authority of the past, I felt.

My favourite book, at that time, across all categories, was *Twenty Thousand Leagues under the Sea*, which was given me by my mother, after she came home from shopping one day. It had a coloured picture on the cover of men battling a giant squid, while waist-deep in water on a strange deck and armed with harpoons; she had bought it at a gift shop, having been assured it would be of interest to a boy. I loved it because of the character of Captain Nemo, whom I aspired to be like: an avenger of the world's wrongs, living secluded beneath the sea, self-sufficient, except for some shadowy crew. He had an immense library, and a magnificent pipe organ, on which he could commune with the depths, inside and outside himself. (I later realised he was an offspring of Lord Byron.)

When I was about fifteen, I discovered the only books from my youth that I can still read, a series of crime novels by Ross Macdonald. They are influenced by Raymond Chandler, who is better regarded, but I prefer them. Lew Archer, the central character, is from a fatherless, delinquent background, has been a policeman, and takes private cases, which become frenetic efforts to make the world a little more just, even if only momentarily, among the sun-bleached housing estates and the shady, beach-front avenues of Southern California. He is earnest, driven, humourless, his own life empty, but is not that cliché of the genre, an alcoholic. I liked him more than I did the facetious Philip Marlowe. Archer was not struck so often on the head and he never smoked a pipe. What I really liked was Ross Macdonald's copious use of similes; the books are a series of pictures. His comparisons, with their unlimited range of reference, give his stories density and dimensionality, open in passing the sense of a complex, surrounding life. Macdonald compares a sunrise in the California desert to the colours of a juke box; he says that people at pool tables, seen from outside a building, are like spearfishermen in a green light beneath the sea. There is a suggestion of the immeasurable plurality of things in his writing. I was far more interested in the imagery, the atmosphere, of his books, than in the story. If I had known it, I was already being drawn to poetry. 'Thou source of all my bliss and all my woe,/ That found me poor at first, and keeps me so.'

I cannot remember anything about my sister's arrival or much of her infancy. When she was less than two I was away from home for almost a year. I remember her as a sweet presence in the house who charmed my father as boys had never done – or perhaps it was just that he was older and around the house more. I see him walking in the garden with her in his arms in the morning, to soothe her, showing her flowers, tidying up things with one hand. I have few memories of my brothers. To paraphrase the poet Les Murray, the one in the family who is going to be a writer is always an only child.

There is one thing I recall, connected with my mother's pregnancy: her coming to me upset and trying to explain a guilt that she felt. She had eaten the last piece of fruit in the bowl and my father had said – knowing how affected she would be by such words – that she had 'taken food out of the children's mouths.' My mother tried to explain to me what it was like to have a craving when you are pregnant, and apologised if I had wanted to eat that pear.

I was much estranged from my father by this time, at the age of ten or eleven. His many complaints and disparagements, so obviously self-justifying, the constant cruelties in his remarks, wore on everyone's nerves, not least on mine. The household was always 'on edge' when he was around. I particularly could not see a need for his campaign of sneering about my mother's new religion, which had provided her with friends. I became all too ready to leap in and criticise him hotly, before he could begin upon us. Yet, although I was disrespectful to him, I was always quick to be reconciled, if he spoke amusingly, or with any generosity at all. I remember being charmed by a remark about manners that he made to me, on a relaxed occasion: 'When I ask you how you are, you should not say "good", you should say "well", to which I will respond "good". But if you say "good", my response can only be "Well..."'

On the evening of my mother's apology to me about the fruit, I told my father that it was 'stupid' of him not to realise that this food had actually gone to a child, the one who needed it most.

My mother was angry at the way I spoke. It was perhaps necessary, though ineffectual, for her to abuse him, but it was never right for the children to show disrespect. My father called me an 'upstart', but as usual he did nothing: he was always concerned, above all, with his dignity when he was drunk.

I had many such conflicts with my father, my part almost invariably reactive. His mockery fastened on my 'narcissism', as he called it, an air of self-involvement I had; on my 'laziness' (a favourite expression was that I 'wouldn't work in an iron lung'), on my 'vagueness' (I was 'only half there', in contrast to my brother Max, who had some 'go'), on my 'getting above myself'. My father said that he had seen me walking through the park, and that I stopped and stood staring down for a long time, and then started talking and making gestures. People would think I was 'touched', he said.

On Saturday mornings he often tried to get me to work in the garden with him, weeding, and moving stones about in a rockery, but I hated the feeling of dried dirt on my hands, and as soon as his back was turned I would vault the fence and be gone. I would head for the bush, with his shout following me up the lane. Going without lunch, I stayed away all day. When I came home after dark, I went in beneath the house, up to where I had to move on all fours, under the kitchen, and listened to find out what sort of reception I might expect. My mother was trying to be a disciplinarian, at this time: she thought that we 'ran wild', too, and disliked it, when she had time to think on the subject. What we needed was the attention of a father, she believed, and she hated the way I, in particular, was alienated from him. Under the floorboards, I hoped to hear my mother say, to one of the other children, 'I wonder where Robert is. He should be home by now. I hope he's all right, that he hasn't done anything silly.' Her voice, when she said something like this, on a few occasions, was distracted, which was better than that she should be worried. Usually, however, I would give up waiting for any mention of me at all, and appear on the back porch, in a casual but subdued manner. I hated being given a 'dressing-down' by her; I found it worse than being slapped.

When I had arguments with my father, and my mother sided with him, I saw that she liked their rare solidarity. Betrayed, I decided after a particularly hectic session to leave home; to stow away on one of the timber ships that came to load at the port. I took some clothes and a few books in a knapsack, and bought some chocolate on my walk to the harbour, like someone in an Enid Blyton story. This was another adventure that seemed incumbent on me. The timber ships delivered their cargo, I understood, to the South Pacific islands. After sitting on the sand beneath the pier, with my melancholy wound, waiting until it was dark and the crane had stopped working, I casually approached the only ship at the wharf, which looked like an elongated tramp steamer. There was a net of ropes hung under its narrow gangplank, I supposed because the sailors got drunk at the pub while in port. Everything seemed deserted. I crept around on the bolted plates of the deck, skirting the hold, in which the stripped logs were stacked, long and thin and bluish-white, like pilchards in a tin, under the misty arc light from the jetty. I slipped by below the lighted portholes, now as 'The Shadow'. Trying to find somewhere to hide, I was giving up on the whole idea when a man plunged out of a doorway beside

me, grabbed me by the shirt and swore in my face. He seemed
some sort of officer, and was already furious. He looked in my
bag. 'Stowing away!' he shouted, incredulously, in a thick-tongued
accent, as I was explaining I was just there out of curiosity. I would
learn about stowing away, I was told, through being locked under a
hatch, below, where it was hot and stank of diesel and I would have
to crouch, and where the Tongans wouldn't hear me shouting, if
I was lucky; otherwise they would cook me in steam. When we were
at sea, he would throw me overboard – making a contemptuous
backward gesture with one hand. I did not believe him: I thought
then that people were not so depraved as that. I felt such bluster
at the start of things ought to mean this was the worst of it. There
did not seem to be anyone else around; he had dragged me into
an empty, oily-coloured, oil-smelling small room, and he shouted,
while still holding a fistful of my shirt-front. In a sudden panic,
I shouted, too, for help, picturing the jetty, where people sometimes walked at night, and he threatened but did not hit me. A man
appeared briefly, outside, and was told something I did not understand – it must have been to go to the public phone box, under
the lone streetlight at the start of the jetty. Gradually I gathered
there had been vandalism, of the office and about the wharf; that
I had no matches or methylated spirits, no tomahawk, was what
had saved me, I was told. I sat in a corner of the small metal room
until I was ordered to go on deck. The police came, ambling along
the jetty; they said a few words to my captor, complained about the
gangway, and hardly looked at me. The one I remember, who sat
beside the driver, was bored, flaccid, humourless, unable even to
be bothered with much chastisement; they delivered me, briefly
portentous, at our front door. To my surprise, it was still early, and
I was in time for dinner; there was a plate for me on the table.

My mother kept her 'upset' about this from my father, for a
while; when she did let the story out, perhaps to shock him, it was

ardently taken up by him for mockery. He twisted it around, so that I had been running away to join the circus. 'One cliché is as good as another,' he told me, when I wanted him to at least be accurate. He set about deciding which job I would have been given there. The only one it could be, he more than once drunkenly remarked, was being fired out of a cannon: he said they would have aimed me right out of the tent, having discovered how 'useless' I was.

A few times my father made what was perhaps a reconciling effort, and took us all to the beach, on the bus. On one of these occasions, he wanted to teach me to swim, having watched me make a few head-upwards strokes, but I refused the offer. I was scared of him having me in his power, and kept out of his reach. He insisted; an argument began; I was rude to him, and I discovered that I could easily outrun him, along the shore.

I remember coming home late from the bush: I see myself trailing down through the tall trees on the hill, when lights had opened along our street and the lights of town were brokenly visible. I waded through deep ferns, dragging my stick, and saw my mother come out onto our back porch and raise her face toward the hill, blindly, and call my name. I returned a single shout, which immediately released her posture and felt like a vibrant plasm between us.

My father's garden in the front yard, ranged around the edges of the lawn, was as bright as a parade. I remember a frothy white crepe myrtle and a magnolia tree to one side, blue hydrangeas along the house front, and frangipani and hibiscus bushes at the other edge, by the lane. The pine tree's shadow reached out from its corner like a great sundial, lying across the house, with a rockery beneath it. There were azaleas and camellias inside the front fence. Outside the gate stood two coral trees, which soon grew large, their

blossom in clusters, each one the shape of a toucan's beak and as red as lipstick.

In the back garden we had papaya, mulberry and custard apple trees at one side, acacias and a jacaranda by the other fence, and a crowded row of banana palms along the back. Within the yard, beside lawn and clothesline, were cornstalks, tomatoes on stakes, pumpkin vines, rows of lettuce, and a few tall sunflowers. On the fence by the lane there hung passionfruit and chokos, the latter never eaten by anyone except my father, who made that slippery vegetable seem worse by having it served with white sauce. Chokos were so unpopular with children and so prolific on the palings that they were gathered by the boys for pelting at each other.

There were always flowers in the house. I have seen my father with what was obviously a bad hangover carefully arranging them in the living room, in the bright morning. He would change the water, bring in fresh blooms, take out what was withered, shuffle the remainder into a lesser vase, and begin some ambitious new creation. He was proud of his vases, which he must have bought when young: I remember him carefully wrapping and packing them when we moved into town. In the midst of a new arrangement, he would step back and consider, for minutes at a time, rapidly advance, make a few slight adjustments, back off, approach again, wincing all the while, as if at aesthetic misjudgements, more likely at the pain behind his eyes. Later in the day, if he was pleased, he would sometimes, more and more rarely, take a photograph of what he had made, for his sisters. He preferred black-and-white shots, which shows an unusual interest in form, a real aesthetic sense. His arrangements were the best things in the house. Taking photographs and having them developed must have cost him the price of a few beers, and he examined the negatives over and over, against the light, and usually had only one print made.

At dinner times we washed our faces and hands, combed our hair, and sat at the table in our places, with napkins, bread and butter plates, cut-glass butter dish and a butter knife, and refrained from speaking – unless spoken to. We waited for our father to begin the meal, and to begin his monologue, poisoning the air.

My mother told me to go and look again. There was a light in the porch and wet electricity wires. A face was rising among the stains on the moon.

My father's health was becoming worse, and he was behaving even less capably. On numerous nights he set his bed on fire, through falling asleep while smoking. My mother could not prevent it: he would insist on smoking, however drunk he was. He was sleeping fitfully, and so would light a cigarette in the night. Then all of the house, except him, would wake – to the stifling smell of kapok smouldering. If he had been alone, he would have suffocated. My mother once put the fire out by dumping a saucepan of water over the bed and him. I remember her beating on the mattress with her hands. Deep in the night, the house would be in uproar: the small children crying, my mother angry, my father blearily telling her to 'have some consideration for the neighbours.'

He used to sleep the rest of the night in a blanket on the cane lounge. In the morning, the mattress, manhandled by our mother and we two eldest boys onto the back porch, to get the smell out of the house, and spread on the railing, was a bedraggled sight, like some skinned, dried-out animal with a burst black stomach. My mother would have to patch it with an old blanket.

Much more often than setting his bed on fire, my father burned holes in the sheets, and he needed to endure my mother's anger for this, also.

Worse than a night when his bed was on fire was one in which his ulcers haemorrhaged and he vomited blood and groaned and clutched his stomach. The lights went on again, my mother knocked ice cubes from their tray onto a tea towel, pressed the bundle to his stomach, and held his head off the bed, so that he could bleed into a plastic bowl. My job was to get down the street, a few doors, in my pyjamas, to the neighbours who had a phone, knock on their door until they came, and ask them to ring the ambulance for him. After such an event, he was in the hospital for a week, and we slept peacefully.

9. In a Cold Haven

My father was granted the highest level of pension, 'totally and permanently incapacitated', by a medical tribunal in Sydney. His TB and ulcers were ruled to have been contracted in New Guinea, from drinking contaminated water. My mother remarked it was through drinking, sure enough, and that the local doctor, who had supported his case, would have known how much.

This doctor my father called a friend; they had been at the same school, the doctor later than him. He saw the doctor regularly, with a pleasurable sense of occasion: they spent most of their consultation speaking in Latin. The doctor was a bit rusty, we were told; he was called 'my patient'. For my father, this visit was the high point of his fortnight.

My mother was not ungrateful for such a pension; not, I think, by whatever means obtained. It was double the normal allowance, although was diminished for us, of course, by my father taking his considerable share.

Before that, and after my father had finished working at the aerodrome, we lived for a year on his unemployment cheques, child allowance, and what my mother could earn from ironing and cleaning, less the undiminished amount spent on drink. At that time, my mother was approached by a social worker, or made contact with one, who suggested she send her three boys to a home in Sydney, for limited stays, to ease the financial problem.

My mother said she was being 'driven to distraction', and numerous times made my father's nose bleed. I used to intervene with arms raised, and she would get a last blow in, in a style I particularly disliked, a stabbing gesture. There is a poem by D. H. Lawrence, 'Discord in Childhood', which speaks of his mother's 'she-delirious rage' and his father's bloodying response. My father never struck back, or even defended himself.

To go to a home, we would have to be classified as 'neglected children', which put my mother off the idea; but she was soothed by being told that it was merely a bureaucratic definition, based on nothing but income. This was in 1956, in the days when social work was a new hope for the world.

It was proposed that we boys be enrolled in the Far West Children's Scheme, a private charity, which had originated as a holiday camp in the city for inland children who might need medical attention and who had never seen the ocean. Later, all 'underprivileged' children were made eligible.

My brother Max was the first to go, to the Home at Manly, for a few months. When he was due back, it was my turn; it was planned I would be taken to the Children's Hospital while there. My mother took me to the railway station one night, troubled, and I was handed over to an older woman, who leaned out of a carriage window, amid the steam, holding a piece of cardboard with our name on it. I said goodbye quietly to my tearful mother, the guard blew his whistle almost at once, and I sank again within myself.

We picked up another boy, after a couple of hours, who was nine years old (I was eleven), brought to the train by his grand-mother, with whom he lived. As the train drove again into the darkness, groaning and rocking, making its roar, occasionally letting out a wail, the boy was at one moment panic-stricken and the next brightly tearful, so that he seemed abnormal. He talked very rapidly, as if his teeth were chattering, and then burst out crying, clinging to the agitated chaperone in an uproar of homesickness and fear. Suddenly, after enquiring if we minded, he sang us the 'Yellow Rose of Texas', in a sweet, high-pitched voice, his hands held together in his lap, sitting up straight, and asked if we would like an encore. Then he began crying again. After that he fell asleep, and the woman, too. We had a compartment to ourselves, in which the woman had drawn down the blinds. I lay awake, on a leather seat opposite them, in the almost complete darkness, struggling with a panicky sensation that the train was actually falling downwards – that it had just plunged off a high bridge or a cliff. I had to keep pulling up a corner of the blind to see that we were travelling over level ground, in weak moonlight. As soon as I stretched out on the seat, I would start awake, with that sensation of falling, and almost cry out.

I was kept for nearly a year at the Far West Home, much longer than was promised, and I hated every day. For one thing, I was always hungry; and then I was unsure of what was happening: I was told I was waiting for a bed at the hospital, where I would have a proper examination, but that the doctors were too busy, at present. I should appreciate that I was being examined free.

The Home looked like a high school: it had two big, three-storey brick buildings in an L-shape, and three demountable classrooms, around a concrete yard that was hidden from the street. There was no grass, and no park nearby. The concreted playing area had a plain brick wall at one end, with barbed wire along the top. A wide hurricane wire gate in this wall, set with spikes, showed a vacant lot, full of broken concrete paving, weeds, and the reverse side of plywood facades, which had been part of a funfair. Then there were corrugated iron hoardings, and the seething air above a busy street. We could see the pressed-metal, hollowed-out back view of a big clown's head, which looked out on the world with a faded guffaw from the street corner: through that grin people had once passed. Above the tin fence we glimpsed some of the pine trees on Manly's promenade, and heard at times the surf, and even smelled it.

We were never taken to the beach, to play on the sand or to swim; that must have been thought too risky for children who were mostly from far inland, with not enough staff to watch us. We walked in our shoes on the promenade above the beach, on our two outings for the week: on Saturdays to a matinee at the cinema, and on Sunday mornings to the Anglican or Catholic church.

As soon as I arrived, I was given my regular job, which was to scrub the chrome legs of the dining room tables with what smelled like vinegar, to remove the corrosion caused by salt air. This I did on several mornings a week before breakfast, ineffectually, crawling around beneath the furniture.

I remember my dismay at the food served in that room: porridge for breakfast, as grey as dirty washing-up water, with barely any milk and that already added; sandwiches for lunch, spread thinly with peanut butter or anchovy paste, and a piece of fruit; boiled wet vegetables for dinner, and always the same protein, reconstituted egg white, like shivery junket but flavourless; jelly or pale starchy custard, with two thin slices of banana, for pudding. The menu was always the same, except on Sundays, when the egg white was replaced by a boiled sausage. I ate far better at home.

I complained desperately in the weekly letter to my parents, which we 'big children' were sat down to write, each with a single sheet of paper. These were collected by the staff, along with an envelope we had addressed, but my letter and those of others were brought back each time, lines and whole paragraphs blacked out, and we were asked to write so as not to upset our families. Sometimes I had to revise more than once, as I tried to write in what I hoped were hints. The matron began to call me to her office, suspicious of phrases she did not completely understand. 'Explain this to me...' (I once wrote, 'Being here reminds me of the time we went for the picnic at Mooni.' We had gone there with one of my uncles and his family, by car, miles up the coast, and had forgotten to take the lunch basket. We went for a swim and then all declared ourselves ravenous and decided we had to go home.) 'Now, I think we can do much better than this,' she would say.

'If I can't complain, there's nothing for me to write about. Nothing happens.'

'You haven't mentioned what you learned in class this week. Just write that, if you're such an ungrateful boy.'

I had no need to play an imaginary game that I was a prisoner.

I was distracted from my unhappiness a little by my brother Billy arriving. He came shyly up to me in the playground one day, and from then on I stayed close by him, in solidarity against the bullies.

The yard seemed to me a sordid place: its cement was painted industrial green, which was worn off in ragged patches, and it always had big puddles across it, from hosing down, and wads of sodden paper and rag strewn about. Several acts of deliberated physical and mental cruelty would be going on, at any time, small children were blindly knocked over and left bawling, and the single female teacher on duty was ineffectual and ignored, despite clapping her hands and raising her voice – 'You boys! You boys! Excuse me...'

I had only my sharp tongue to hold the playground bullies at their watchful, calculating distance, and I knew it would be easy to go too far in using that, into the place where affront outweighed the fear of being mocked. The boy who had arrived with me was constantly taunted, and I often saw him in tears, and made to sing 'The Yellow Rose of Texas' for a jeering group (he was called 'Rosie'), or having his arm arbitrarily twisted, by someone who was passing by. Of course, I used to 'stick up for him', in my best boys' magazine manner, mocking and then cajoling his tormentors.

The attack on my brother and me came at night. We had been given a room together, and were in bed, just falling asleep, when suddenly there was a click of the door being closed and a flurry of crashes all around us, and someone began striking me through the blankets. I turned my head instinctively into the pillow and took a blow on the ear, which felt for days as if it had been scalded. Our chairs were thrown down, our clothes flung at the window, our cases knocked off the low wardrobe. I jumped out of bed and on some ridiculous impulse snatched my pillow and swung a hard blow against the head of a shadow in the room, and they had gone. After lights out the next night, as I came back from the bathroom, I was set upon again, in the dim corridor, by boys with pillows this time, who wielded them like clubs, and I was beaten to the floor. They scattered, hissing derision. But the choice of the pillow the previous evening had been lucky: the antagonism became symbolised, ritualised, and relatively harmless, as pillow fights. Within a few nights, the pillow fight had caught on like a stock market craze. It was enough to strike a few solid blows and then disappear back to one's room without being heard by the nurse, who was often downstairs. In a more sustained battle, a pillow was wrenched out of my hands and I plunged into a room and snatched another from under a small boy's head and continued the slaughter, swinging a double-handed sword. Feathers began floating around us and then less and less inhibited whoops and laughter. A warning was called. We scattered to our beds. It was the matron, striding with a nurse on either side, wearing her headdress, arms folded under her red half-cloak. She strode on her heels the length of the squeaking corridor, then came back, looking into each room, telling us to get up and to come into the long dormitory. We stood on parade: the little boys hysterically tittering; the bigger boys answering 'Dunno' to everything. As a big boy, I was singled out for punishment. 'There is only one way to get to the bottom of this,' the matron told the nurses, a line she had no doubt used before, and we culprits were made to drop our pyjama pants, bend over a bed, and were beaten. She used a wooden spoon for some, but for a few of us she asked for a sandshoe, and struck tennis court blows. Her exasperation with me I already knew. I saw later I had a bruise the colour of an eggplant, but felt no resentment: I understood all was fair in war.

As for love, it first glimmered before me when one night a boy who had been among the bullies came to me excitedly with a message that I was wanted at the fire-escape window. His group seemed to feel there was a solidarity between us now. Two or three boys were waiting there, whispering excitedly, and they pointed to a girl standing on a fire-escape across the drive, outside the girls' dormitory, and said that she was asking for me. I knew her, from some remarks we had exchanged in the yard. She was a little older than me, blonde and thin, and came from a farm somewhere far out in the state. Now she was wrapped in a blanket, like a Red Indian squaw. I could just make out a friend of hers in the window behind her, although the building was dark. The girl on the landing hissed that the others should go away, but I should stay. They withdrew against the walls, trying to peek, and then she opened out the blanket, in a gesture like a personification of the Dawn, and showed me she was naked. She already had small breasts and a shadow of pubic hair. The boys crowded the window. 'That girl!' came the yelp of an adult, from our building, and the girl flickered like a lizard, folded under the sash and was gone. Soon a nurse patrolled the corridor where my room was, with a torch, but all was quiet. The incident did much for my prestige, and meant that I was left unthreatened, as if I could lead others to a secret.

The girl, whose name I cannot remember, was not caught. She grinned proudly next day, and sat by me in the classroom. When I talked with her uncomfortably at recess, I asked her the reason she was at the home. She wore dressings on her elbows, and from the wrist to fingertips of her right hand, and her next intimacy was to unwrap the bandages and lift the padding off her hand. I saw that the flesh of all the knuckles hung open widely, dry and pink, to the white bone. This was curious to her and shocking to me, although I suppressed my reaction. I felt sympathetic toward her. We became friends, and played a game of trying to bounce a tennis ball past each other, off a brick wall, she using her tight bandages like a bat. She clearly felt no pain in this, but was skilful, competitive, and highly excitable, and was inclined to embrace her opponent whenever she scored a point, or even when he did. She was sweet-natured and pretty, with her hair in a constantly rearranged ponytail. She began tugging at my sleeve or pressing me in the back, to get me to leave the playground, so that we could 'explore' the main building. We knew a back door into the building, and went soft-toed a short way along the dim, out-of-bounds main corridor, and up some stairs, which were folded about a lift shaft, to the unused top floor. We found there, in a dusty grey light, not the mad children whom I said we might discover, but rooms used to store large cardboard boxes, plastic Christmas trees and their decorations, dark old furniture, most of it under dustsheets, suitcases, folded hospital screens, and clothes racks with hundreds of coathangers on them. We found dry bathrooms, full of lofty shadows like cobwebs. In one of these my companion had us lie down and embrace, at the bottom of a deep bathtub, where we lay whispering until we heard the far-off sound of the bell.

As we had arranged, I sneaked into that bathroom on the top floor, after lights out, and waited for my 'girlfriend' (which she was being called by some of the children, even small ones, to my embarrassment), until the small hours, sitting in my dressing-gown in a dark corner, hoping it would be she who pushed open the door. But her dormitory in the other building was securely locked at night, and I woke alone, cold and sore. I found that such an old trick as leaving a couple of pillows lengthwise in my bed had worked.

We hid together a few more times in the deep porcelain tub, the far-off voices of the world reaching us, in that dim white cave, while each of us drifted in our own sunlit landscape. I was too young and too puritanical to do other than whisper, exchange blunt kisses, hold her, and stroke the shape of her head, though I felt pleasurable tendrils stirring in my body. I had seen her disease and was afraid at what I might find with her other fissures. She readily bared her chest, for my curiosity. In hindsight I see her breasts as two small jellyfish, the shadowy blue veins in them as delicate as those of her wrist. Although her breasts were milky white, almost translucent, they had a resistant density. The nipples were the unripe pink of a succulent I had seen in a rock pool. Our bodies squirmed together at times, as though they heard a music we could not. She was timid, also, before the mystery we faced, but barely content to be affectionate. Her legs rolled restlessly around mine.

I think I was partly relieved when I heard I would soon be going into hospital for my check-up, and that the girl (whose name has now returned to me, in writing this sentence) was going some-where for treatment, too. I was driven off early in the morning, with just a glance at her for goodbye, as I was called out of the dining room. I never saw her again. Apart from my mother, she was the first of the generous-hearted women I have known, whose poetry, even if brief, has been the best thing I have found in life.

At the hospital I felt I was just a curiosity for the doctors. Nothing was going to be done. My little brother had been allowed to go home, before that friendship of mine, and he went with a message to rescue me, soon.

I remember of that children's ward a pallid girl, of ten or so, who regularly knelt up on her bed and prayed, with her palms together, and who tried to have the other children join her. She was asked gently by the sister not to call out this request to the children, as she was frightening some of them, with her intensity. She was in the bed next to mine. I was fascinated that she looked like a Rackham illustration, with blueness under her eyes and long fawn-coloured hair that she brushed straight down and a long nightgown. Her parents came every day for many hours. One morning early there was a disturbance in the air and I woke to see a screen around her bed, a light burning there, some nurses moving, urgently and quietly. The tall window opposite was just beginning to become navy blue, with immensely distant stars still within it. When I woke again, the screen was gone and the bed was flat and stripped. I asked the nurse who used the flannelette on me at morning wash where the girl was and was told she had gone home, but I thought no one left at that time of day. Other children sensed something was wrong, too, because all day the ward felt broken and anxious and was more than usually tearful.

When I was examined by the specialists, the chief of the group, taking off his stethoscope, and holding my charts, told me I needed to come only intermittently to Sydney for check-ups, now, and that I could go off the medicine, and should try to live a normal life. There was nothing that could be done about my condition, he said. He would write to my parents. In answer to questions, I had told the doctors I ran about a great deal, that I would consider myself 'very active', and they said this seemed not to have done me any harm, I could go ahead, but I ought not to overdo it. Come back in a few years time, or if I started to feel in any way strange, or became continually tired. The tenor of their advice was non-committal. I found running through my head a Biblical text I had heard, on Jesus' return: 'No man knows the day or the hour.'

Doctors seem not to have talked much in those days, or at least not to my parents or me, about advances in medical science, and about the possibility of a 'procedure' for my condition being found. My defect seems to have been considered unreachable.

I was taken back to the Far West Home, but they did not release me, as I had hoped. Margaret came to visit, which she sometimes did, even though it took 'a whole day's journey', and was distressed that I was listless. She went and asked when I would be leaving and was told my mother had been contacted about her circumstances but nothing had been heard back.

I decided to escape. I had pocket money Margaret had given me, which should have been handed in for safekeeping. My new room-mate wanted to come, too. We put on our clothes again, at night, packed our bags – we each had what we called a 'port', a compact bakelite suitcase – and went to a bathroom. I had noticed a close-branching creeper of ceramic pipes underneath a window that could be used as a ladder, in school-story fashion. I went down first and our bags were lowered to me on some sheets. Then we went along an alley, crawled beneath a lighted window, and had to go over some barbed wire on the top of a narrow iron gate, to get into a lane. It was difficult standing on top of the gate, on the balls of one's feet, shins braced against the stave of wires, between its metal burrs, crouched, holding the stanchions through which the wire was threaded, to keep one's balance while hauling up the two cases. It was done with much wobbling, and then I lowered them outside, one to a sheet.

'There are boys! There are two boys getting over the fence!' Someone had appeared on a balcony at the nurse's home.

We each dropped hard onto the bitumen beyond the gate, and ran doubled over behind parked cars, scraping our cases on the road and knocking them against an ankle, a shin, changing them from one hand to the other, or carrying them in our arms. 'In here!' 'No, in here, in here!' We went down a driveway, into the backyard of a block of flats, hid in a dark laundry, where there were cement tubs. We heard the slapping and clatter of feet going by, out in the street. After crouching behind the door for what seemed long enough, in the caustic smell of old soap and the smell of leaking gas, we set off again, going over a paling fence at the bottom of the yard, down a narrow passage beside another block, out into a quiet street, and from shadow to shadow there, circling towards the ferry wharf. The terminus was still busy, on a Friday night. We waited down on the beach, in the shadow of an embankment and the wharf, looking at the distant lights of the city, watching for the ferry to come from among them. I bought our tokens at the booth: I thought it best to ask for one child and one adult. Then we went on board, among other people, and sat right at the back. The great rope creaked and smarted around its pylon. Adults laughed and smoked. I thought I would go to my aunts: they surely would send me home. I would not care how flustered Margaret became or how Olga fumed. Or I thought I could stow away on a train, since there was not enough money for a ticket. I could move from toilet to toilet along the carriages, putting on the engaged sign in each one for a while. I could leave my case on a rack somewhere. Or I could say I was with my father, who had the tickets and had missed the train. They would have a list of names, though; but you could get on a train late, without booking. He had gone back for a newspaper...

The ferry men started taking the gangplank away, as the last couples came running. A man in an open gaberdine overcoat held his hat and made his shoes ring on the cement, calling out, and a heavy woman toddled her legs, moving them much more rapidly than his, but left behind him. They came on board gasping and looked about for somewhere to sit, but I knew better. I hoped he might walk past us; our heads were down. His hand fell on my shoulder, hard. 'Get up. Get off. Bring your bag. No fuss.' He had a weak face and a small moustache. The woman was talking at the deckhands, still short of breath. They kept the ferry churning by the wharf.

In the car, the woman sat in the back beside us, as if we were going to jump out. She talked to the driver about 'poor Matron', for us to hear. 'A nice mess you two have caused,' he said with spite over his shoulder. I never found out who he was: perhaps the husband of someone at the home or a local policeman. I think the woman looked after the nurses quarters; I had seen her in the office.

The matron came down the main corridor, dressed in uniform but without her veil. She was like a dark boil in need of lancing. 'Do you realise what danger you were in? Do you know what you could have done to many people's lives, if anything had happened to you?'

We were not talking, averting our faces. ('Look at me!') I said: 'I was told I was coming here for just a few months, like my brothers. You're keeping me here, making me a prisoner. I've seen the doctors, so I should be allowed to go.'

I was put in a bedroom with the usual wire grille on its window; the door was locked. Within the next day or so I saw the older woman, with the clumpy heels and the handbag as big as a shopping bag, who had brought me to the home. She was drinking a cup of tea, alone in the dining room. Later that day she appeared in the doorway of our class, knocking on the lintel. I had already begun to disentangle myself from the basketwork we were doing, as she spoke to the teacher.

She still called me dear, on the way home in the train, probably because she could not remember my name. She read magazines and slept, snoring and tutting. Her neck seemed very uncomfortable. All this travelling was no good for an older person, she told me; she would have to give it up. But it meant she could have a few days' break in Sydney, sometimes, and see her daughter and grandson. While she snuffled and groaned in her sleep, I held back a corner of the roller blind, to look out at the dark hills that slowly revolved around us, in the chemical moonlight. The air in the compartment was cold and sour with soot. I heard, as I vaguely drowsed, the metal hammer beating out its warning at dark railway crossings. I stayed sitting up, in discomfort and tedium. I remember a small black car, steaming alone at one of the crossings, waiting on a narrow dirt road behind its forked lights. Later there was a bedroom window, in a house on a hillside, still lit toward morning. I wondered if my mother was lying awake.

The first thing my mother said to me was how thin I looked. She had made me a late breakfast of savoury mince on toast: I told her it was the best meal I had ever eaten. She began to cry, standing in the kitchen and looking at me. She said it was 'they', the social workers, who had wanted to keep me longer in the home than arranged. Enquiries had been made about her financial situation and she was forced to admit it was not much improved. She guessed that the home wanted to keep its numbers up during the winter.

So I went back to my school at almost the end of the year, where the teacher welcomed me in front of the class and said that I must now put on some condition. The boys laughed. He said he expected me to be playing in the Rugby League team by next season. The next year I did play, although without any real distinction; but that year, when I was twelve, turned out to be the best of my life up to then. I organised, outside of school, a five-a-side soccer

competition, with four teams, introducing the sport into the town.
We played our games in the park, using the hockey club's goalposts. Unselfconscious in my enthusiasm, I proselytised at school,
rounded up players, coached them in the rules and techniques of
the game, using scrapbooks full of diagrams, photos and articles
I had cut from English magazines, persuaded the boys to get their
mothers to dye singlets in their team's colour, to be worn over a
shirt, had someone contribute a large clanking old golf trophy from
a family collection, conferred the title of referee on a boy who we
all thought was a sook, but who was transformed when in authority, had photographs of the players taken, led the championship
team, and awarded myself a scroll as the top goal-scorer. (There
were other scrolls conferred, which I lettered, including several for
most improved player.) I would be disquieted now at the thought
of persuading and organising any group of people.

All year I played cricket on the grass in front of the houses of
our street, with the neighbourhood boys. In summer, in the long-
stemmed afternoon light, we would still be playing when my father
was brought home by his mates: they stood him on the roadside,
staggering themselves, and got back into the car, amid wobbling
shouts of farewell, and he often fell down by the time they began
driving away. Sometimes he rested a hand on the back of the car
and it drove out from under him. I would leave the game as soon
as I saw him arrive. If the neighbourhood women were watching,
they used to say, 'Here's your old man now, son.' I helped my
father up, with the adult eyes on us, but the kids went on with
the match, unless I had been batting, when everyone would stand
around, the boys idly tossing the ball between them. I dusted my
father off; if there was gravel embedded in his hand I brushed it
away, and I told him to lean on me, to hold my arm.

'What's the matter with you? Don't act the fool. What do you
think you're doing?' he would say, grabbing hold of me, as he

lurched about. 'Nil desperandum,' he announced once, when he had pulled me to the ground and I was trying to get him up. 'That's "She'll be right", to you.'

My mother kept an eye out for him, or had a sense of his arrival. She used to walk to the front gate to meet us. 'Come on, Geoff,' she would say quietly, 'stand up, man. Stop making a spectacle of yourself.' He went down the front path, leaning heavily on my mother, gangly as drifting seaweed. In his elevated, quoting voice he instructed her, once: 'They also serve who only stand and wait.'

We would resume the game of cricket, matter-of-factly, without any comments about my father. Everyone accepted that was the way he was. I think some parents had told their boys my father's condition was the result of his war service, probably on my mother's word. The other men in the street had been too young for war. So there was a thin air of interest toward him, among the children, such as there might have been if he were badly scarred.

I was twelve when I had my great revelation. It was in the class-room, while the teacher was reading aloud, as he had been doing each Friday afternoon, from that wonderfully Keatsian book *The Wind in the Willows*. One day he read, quickly, a description of the Mole and the Water Rat at breakfast: Mole was eating hot toast, through which the butter was said to be dripping 'like honey out of the honeycomb'. The class was swept on with the story, but I remained, caught on that image, aware that I had just seen some-thing in my imagination more intensely, more sensuously, than I ever had in life. I saw, it literally seemed, what I must previously have only noticed, distractedly: the way butter comes welling through hot toast and hangs from it in slow globules; and how, if it is hot enough, the butter takes on the exact amber tone of honey. I realised we perceive in some ways most intently through words, when we are lifted out of the 'buzzing, blooming confusion of life'. Having been made aware of something, in our mind, we are able to notice similar things more fully in the world afterwards. I knew, all at once, that I wanted to write. I wanted, with my imagination, to pluck the things I valued off the river of time, as it went careening by; to save them, or at least the feeling of them.

10. 'The Church of the Midnight Cry'

I was relieved when my mother told us, about a year after we arrived in the town, that we children need not be Anglicans any longer. For me, the Church had been only rarefied incantations, entirely ineffective, it appeared, and an atmosphere of piety, which despite breathing deeply I could never inflate within myself.

Very soon, though, my mother expected us to go with her to the Jehovah's Witnesses' meetings, and I was willing to do this, because her new beliefs had clearly been 'a tonic' to her. But I never had any conviction about this religion, either. The private living quarters within me were firmly closed against it, although no one suspected.

The Jehovah's Witnesses held three meetings a week, as well as carrying out their door-to-door ministry, to which part of at least one day was given up, usually on weekends. There were about thirty people in our congregation, not counting children and the very old. The main service, of a Sunday, was held in the School of Arts hall, otherwise used for touring theatre and for dances. I remember a dog lying on the rounded bitumen of that side street, in front of the hall, on a sunny afternoon, and seeing it still there when we came out of the hollow wooden building, hours later. An ugly brick entrance had been added to the hall, long after it was built, where there were posters in glass cases, for the Amazing Carlos, a hypnotist, for the Memory Man, with his Amazing Mind-Power, for a dance, called a 'round-up', and for a country and western trio, whose performance had been held years earlier.

An embroidered cloth, sometimes a small vase of flowers, and a Bible, were displayed on a cane hall-table in front of the meeting. We sat on chrome chairs that the children unfolded and lined up in the middle of the dance floor – the women wearing nylon dresses and small hats, the men in stiff dark suits or in suit jackets and differing trousers, and with thick ties – and we sang in a way that must have embarrassed many of us, led by a man who played a quavering saxophone.

Then twice during the week we met on the glass-louvred back verandah at someone's house, where you could hear crickets out in the dark garden. Later we rented the town band's practice hall, in a park. There, louts sometimes threw stones onto the roof, whereas at the School of Arts they rode their bicycles up and down the side alley, yodelling and swearing, and rattled the locked double doors.

I sometimes became so bored at the meetings that I felt as though a pestle were being ground down hard onto a mortar inside my body; the herb being worked was a narcotic, and it licked me with its smoke-thick vapours, as I sat hidden behind heavily built working men. If I was unable to find the place in the 'study guide' when called upon, I would be ashamed, because of my mother's embarrassment. Yet I accepted my presence at the meetings as one of the many things that had to be endured. Children are often natural stoics, or they used to be: they do not know enough to pre-empt their futures, and realise they simply have to wait on life. This feeling was in me too passive to be resentful.

My mother seemed calmly resolved and purposeful now, because of what she and her new friends kept referring to as 'The Truth'. She had hope – to such an extent that she thought, unrealistically, she would speak to my father about it. Preaching at him, he immediately called it. He was embarrassed that people in the town should know his family had joined such an irritating group (as he was never ashamed of his drinking). In his opinion, also, the Witnesses were 'very poor types'. 'What a lot of no-hopers,' he used to say. 'Look at them: council workers, butcher shop employees, a truck driver, a telephone linesman, a hamburger cook, a few cow cockies, a barber. (He had enquired of us who came to our meetings.) And all of those dowdy women, trailing around from door to door. They're a laughing stock.'

My mother of course said, 'Look at yourself. What makes you think you're so much better than these people. They're the sort that Jesus chose.'

In my father's smile appeared a rare thing – the hard, blunt crockery of his teeth. 'No one in this town has any idea about the sort of person I am. No one is able to judge me. It's what goes on in here,' tapping his forehead, 'that matters.'

'There's not too much goes on in there. You're blotto most of the time. Anyway, judge not, if you don't want to be judged. I've got a duty to tell you what God's will is, and if you don't want to listen, that's your look-out.'

'How would you know what God's will is? You went to school at Korora for a couple of years, for crying out loud. There are professors of theology who can't agree on what God's will is – why would you know any better than they do? This is just some new-fangled, crazy, two-bit, Yankee, money-making racket. Do you know how many sects there are in America? There are thousands...'

'God's will is in the Bible, plainly written. We only need to be humble enough to see it, and to obey.'

'That's the trouble with Protestant Christianity: it fills non-entities with arrogance. At least the Catholic church kept people in their place. For centuries it did society the service of reminding the ignorant of how low they were.'

Jehovah's Witnesses, despite my father's suspicion, are a non-profit corporation. They are led, entirely without charisma, by a grey committee of older men, and have not been touched by financial or sexual scandal. They hold the Bible is the literal word of God, which means they believe that ever since man was misled into sin in the Garden of Eden, Satan has been influencing human history, 'walking up and down in the Earth…seeking whom he may devour.' Therefore, they try to keep themselves separate from 'the world', not contributing to it, associating with outsiders as little as they can – only prophesying humanity's approaching destruction, and 'calling forth' those who are to be saved. At the Second Coming, the archangel Michael, who is Christ in his heavenly form, will triumph over Satan (belatedly) at the battle of Armageddon, and the Earth will be restored as a paradise.

These beliefs are not different to those of other Protestant fundamentalists, but there is a little proudly displayed product differentiation. Jehovah's Witnesses use their own modernised translation of the Bible, in which for every mention of God the word Jehovah is substituted, an anglicised form of the name of the tribal deity YHWH (a name so holy it was not uttered among the Jews). They are notorious for refusing blood transfusions for themselves and their children, a belief based on the Jewish dietary laws given in the book of Leviticus, where there is an injunction against eating blood, 'which is the life'. (This is not followed up, among the Witnesses, with a proscription against eating meat or meat that has not been properly bled.) Other doctrinal eccentricities include refusing to celebrate Christmas (which is really the Roman festival Saturnalia), and not celebrating personal birthdays (which is vanity). Jehovah's Witnesses show an extreme Protestant distaste for the Catholic church – 'the triple-headed beast', 'the whore of Babylon', etc. – and of all its vain and corrupt ways, so that anything at all reminiscent of Catholic symbology has to be shunned. (The Roman church must have been a great tyranny, in its most powerful days, to have earned an enmity that persists so strongly in the traditions of its renegades.) The major distinction of the Witnesses is that everyone who can must proselytise, as the early Christians did, bringing the 'good news' of the Bible to the world – the good news that most people are going to be consumed in the fires of Armageddon, so that there can be a new world. Strangely, considering the blood-thirsty Biblical teachings they emphasise, and which they are not embarrassed by, the Witnesses themselves are the mildest of people – it is as though they had passed all their aggression over to God, who will see to it for them.

There is no indulgence of personality among them. Celebrity entertainers who in another organisation might have been flaunted as converts are never mentioned in the church's publications (and are exempted from ministering because of their vulnerability). There is actually embarrassment about them, as not always being 'good examples' for others. Their names are whispered. At present, there are about ten million Witnesses worldwide.

What strikes me now, looking back on my time in that sect, is how narrow an experience it was. The culture was very thin. There was no place for a celebration of 'the spirit', as in African-influenced Christianity, but nor was there the slightest risk of intellectualism. When later I read Milton's *Paradise Lost* I found almost the same theology as Jehovah's Witnesses held, but there was nowhere in the offices of their religion the slightest sense of grandeur, of density, of colour, of mystery, or of a tradition – not in their publications, their presentations, nor their consciousness. Everything was understood in an entirely pragmatic, business college way; under fluorescent lighting, as it were. They believed in evil spirits, but there was no discussion of them, and in Satan, but he was barely a shadowy presence, never illustrated, and the crucifixion of Jesus was never emotionally dwelt upon. Jesus was depicted in the publications of the Watch Tower Society (the sect's official name) as beardless and with shortish hair (another detail that removed him from Catholic theatrics); as healthy, smiling, dynamic, and extroverted. He looked to me like someone in an advertisement who had regularly break-fasted on bran flakes. The whole organisation strove to be as neat and spruce and positive in its thinking as a life assurance conference. Just as the Salvation Army was a stood-upon-its-head version of the British Empire's Imperial Forces, as Christian Science was a watery derivative of Transcendentalist philosophy, so this was an adapt-ation of the Fuller Brush salesman's door-to-door approach. (The illustrated brochures for the product, God's kingdom, made it look like a safari theme park, with all the animals tranquilised, and with the beaming human inhabitants in their national costumes – all of them fully clad, unlike the 'original couple'.) This was a religion as American as a clip-on necktie. The whole of history was going to be wiped clean by God, like a high-gloss formica kitchen.

Jehovah's Witnesses is a cult, in the sense that they manage the lives of their adherents. Having such numerous meetings constantly reinforces their teachings, and believers have no time for 'bad associations' with the world. There is much pressure to conform: time sheets have to be put in on ministry activity, personal counsel-ling with 'elders' is conducted, there are ardent, up-building talks, and a public method of study is used, in which a Bible-aid is read aloud, paragraph by paragraph, questions are asked, and the right answers elicited, and reiterated, before moving on.

All organised religions use fear as a means of maintaining

their believers' adherence, but with most it is fear of what will happen after one's death; this religion sees judgement as more imminent than that. The world will end 'in the life-time of the present generation' (a claim updated in almost every decade of the church's existence, since the late nineteenth century; their failures in prophecy presented as a part of the 'sifting out' of those of little faith). The Witnesses' magazines used regularly to feature drawings of tidal waves sweeping into city streets, as buildings toppled above, and earthquakes opened beneath the fleeing crowds. Panic-striken faces were pressed into the fore-ground of the illustrations. Off to one side, cocooned in a great nimbus, sequestered from retribution, were the faithful who had regularly met their monthly quota for starting Bible studies and for distributing magazines.

When I was a boy, we had to study a book called *From Paradise Lost to Paradise Regained,* which was intended for those with little knowledge of Christianity, and for young people. I have seen a copy again, recently; it contains passages like this one, on the battle of Armageddon:

Christ's angels will smite all the opposers of God's kingdom and his kingdom Witnesses with a terrible destruction. A flesh-eating plague will destroy many. Says Jehovah: 'Their flesh shall rot while they are still on their feet, their eyes shall rot in their sockets, and their tongues shall rot in their mouths' (Zechariah 14:12). Eaten up will be the tongues of those who scoffed and laughed at the warning of Armageddon! Eaten up will be the eyes of those who refused to see the sign of 'the time of the end'! Eaten up will be the flesh of those who would not learn that the living God is named Jehovah! Eaten up while they stand on their feet.

Others of Jehovah's Witnesses' publications, like *Babylon the Great Has Fallen,* describe a phantasmagoria of rampant monsters, in the last days, borrowed from the Biblical books of Daniel and Revelations, with the aim of coercing those innocents who can be affected by them. These are now mainly people in the Third World.

A moral pressure was brought by all upon each in 'the organisation'. Everyone had eyes that watched everyone. As a 'sign of the spirit', one was expected to demonstrate always an equitable manner, to be unfailingly friendly and polite, to dress modestly, not to form friendships or to marry outside the religion, not to smoke, to drink only very moderately, not to swear, not to follow worldly interests, like politics or sport, not to go to any but the most innocuous films, to be scrupulous in business practices. (Many of the Witnesses were successful in business, on a restrained scale. People respected their honesty and efficiency, aware they followed an austere morality.)

It was ironic that my mother should become involved with such an efficient organisation, in which none of the 'workers' were paid. She spent uncounted hours in its service, over the years, and I wonder whether her life would have been better if she had peddled tupperware, rather than salvation. Was hope, illusion, dreaming, better for her than some cash in hand?

I occupied myself, in my years as a Witness, from ten to fifteen, by giving most of my attention not to the study aids but to the Bible itself. Fortunately, their modern English translation appeared only toward the end of my time with the church, and I had the King James version. I read almost the entire Bible, and some of the separate books several times. In the quiz games we played on Sunday evenings, if we visited the children of a Witness house-hold (there were six or seven of us of about the same age), I knew what 2 Timothy was about, could trace on a map the travels of the apostle Paul (not 'saint' to us), knew which books come either side of Micah, who was 'a priest after the likeness of Melchizedek', the companions of Abednigo, what was written by the holy finger on the wall above Nebuchadnezzar's banquet, the prophecy of the witch of Endor, and the meaning of the phrase 'a time, and times, and half a time'.

In reading Paul's epistles I came on the phrase 'the church of the midnight cry', and I thought this was what the Jehovah's Witnesses were to my mother. I felt I was partly responsible for her having taken up the religion, because one day she had urged on me a particular article, with a well-known slogan of the church as its title: 'Millions Now Living Will Never Die.' I knew that she had drawn this piece to my attention with reassurance in mind.

So I went 'witnessing', for her, calling from door to door with 'the magazines', even though I was embarrassed and reluctant. I had performed well in the public speaking classes – my pride made me put some effort into the practice talks I gave – and was commended by the visiting inspectors from national head office as a Bible student, and so I was always given the difficult houses to call upon. The difficult ones were not considered those of gruff or irritable people, the young were protected from those, but the homes of the clergy. That was where real outrage was encountered, and threats to call the police. I replied to them, as taught, that we felt we must not neglect anyone, so that God's desire to give all people the chance to side with him, by name, could be fulfilled. There was then a fierce table tennis match of Biblical quotations, bandied back and forth, until I was ordered off the premises by someone I thought was a sore loser.

Once, in another town – we used to travel around the district by car – I and a younger boy, having just finished our 'service', found we were being followed by an irate clergyman, through the dusk. We were walking along a dirt road in a little valley, at the edge of the town, with sparse houses in the paddocks and a wooden church on the rise behind us. A flat sea lay in the end of the gulley

211

like grey water in a clear bowl, and frost and smoke hung in the violet air. The minister, in his collar, was thin and aged and wore black, like the Brontës' father, and he came hopping behind us, calling out like a crow. We decided to stop and let him catch up. He shouted that eighty per cent of the town were his parishioners and to leave them alone. I said that we were only trying to find the other twenty per cent; he could have no objection to that. I was sure his parishioners were satisfied and perfectly safe from us. He told me I had a cheeky mouth and to go to the Devil where I belonged, then flapped away crookedly, calling out, on his stick. He had introduced himself, and the name was the unusual one of a boy in my class at school, who I knew travelled to the main town on a bus. Then I saw that boy, up in the manse's front garden, shading his eyes in the last of the sunlight there, and watching us. I groaned to think how I would be ridiculed on Monday.

I went to school and tried to be as dull and unobtrusive as possible. The day went by and not a word was spoken to me in derision; no gossiping campaign had begun. And then enough days had passed for the expectation to be almost forgotten. I began to spend lunchtimes in the grounds again, instead of the library; I made a few jokes, which people laughed at; I sank some goals at basketball practice. That boy caught my eye accidentally, one day, a couple of weeks later, and considered me with an embarrassed look, for a moment, and I am sure that I looked embarrassed, too. There seemed to be a rapport between us, and I realised he must have been ashamed of those rantings of his father, as he had probably been before. My feelings changed: I was bothered by having troubled a man who seemed on reflection to have been tired and ill.

Almost all of my 'witnessing' was done to the outlying villages and farms: young people were often allowed this privilege, when they went around with their briefcases and Bibles, as an outing for them, and so that being in the church would not seem too hard and they lose heart. I was able to see much of the beautiful country that lay outside the town, in this way. I sat in the back seat of a car with the window open, on white roads, smelling the warm, dry grass, and occasionally the cows, and their dried dung. We went through the 'pillared forest' and among jute-coloured paddocks that had the roundness of tightly packed bales. I remember a sky-blue river, the glassy shafts of light within it, and pastures that gave me an idea of what the English meant by 'water meadows'. I longed to go on and on in the car.

We took turns to walk in pairs to the isolated farmhouses, with their backdrop of dark bush. Often there was no one at home; I have been told that people, seeing us coming, in our ties and pressed shirts, would hide in the house. Sometimes we were ordered away by snarling farmers, their own mastiffs; sometimes stringy, drained housewives, hushing children, or bristly-jowled, slow men, talked on and on, over every subject we raised, seemingly not wanting us to go, offering tea, telling us their own wisdom, which they must have found by looking into the strange Antarctic purity of the light.

Once, while going from door to door in the wealthier part of the main town, I called on a class-mate whom I would have particularly wanted to avoid. It was at a long white house on a hilltop, near the town reservoir; across the road was blown grass and then the bright wall of the sea. The door was opened by a girl with whom I had been exchanging carefully accidental glances at school, which contained some impending significance. We were both about fourteen. She came to the door in an apron, wearing a jumper that showed much more of her breasts than the school uni-form did. I quickly looked at her bare, painted toes, and asked to speak with her mother. The mother was brisk, uncomprehending, then impatient. Her hair was lacquered and she was putting on earrings as I spoke. What I said sounded to me utterly rote and hollow and unrelated to life on a hot, windy Saturday afternoon. I could hear a loud radio or a record playing.

'We have our own religion,' the woman told me, 'and I can't understand the purpose of these calls. We're perfectly happy with what we believe.'

The girl looked at me from behind her mother with huge, sympathetic eyes. She had a mixing bowl propped against her hip and licked delicately at a wooden spoon she was holding. The mother saw my gaze had wandered and told her daughter to check the timer on the stove. She thanked me for calling but suggested I tell 'my people' that they could save themselves the time.

At school, the girl was angry with me. She stood near me in morning assembly and made hissed comments to her girlfriend. Had anyone noticed how I never saluted the flag, nor even pretended to sing the anthem? Jehovah's Witnesses were people who wouldn't fight for their country...She was only mollified and became flirtatious again when I won the school essay competition, probably months later, and had to read my piece aloud to the assembly, and there was laughter at its jokes. She said to her girlfriend, one lunchtime, while looking at me, that people should be prepared to break from their family and to think for themselves.

I did break with Jehovah's Witnesses at fifteen, but not because of the girl, who I had decided was not nearly as attractive as Audrey Hepburn (she also having the advantage of being unattainable). What it took to make me detach myself completely was the 'disfellowshipping', or shunning, of a boy younger than me, one evening at a meeting in the band hall. This boy was the nephew of our local 'overseer', a butcher, and no doubt he was disobedient toward his mother, and ran around on his bicycle with wild boys, and swore, and mocked his uncle, and threatened to go and find his father, but I liked him, and had been exploring the creek with him. We once stole a rowing boat together and poled it around for a few hours, then returned it to the wrong place, with muddy footprints all over the seats. My father wanted to know if I had had anything to do with this, as a man enquiring at the pub had told him that some 'white-headed kid' was often seen at the creek. I denied all knowledge.

When I heard that Colin was in trouble, again, I certainly could not accept that it was anything for which he deserved to be cast into 'outer darkness'; that he had forfeited his 'hope of life', and should be pronounced anathema to the rest of us. I could not accept that God was going to be called on in support of such a petty exclusion, in that sordid little fibro shed. I was so repelled by the whole special proceeding that I refused to attend, or to go to any more meetings, even though my mother became tallow-faced on the spot and wept.

It was difficult to be allowed to break with Jehovah's Witnesses: in the town's main street, the women of the church, whom I met by chance, were melancholy and spoke kindly to me; the men were bluff and embarrassed. My mother had one of those men call to see me on a Saturday, in an otherwise empty house – he was a German  immigrant, who had been an officer at the battle of Stalingrad. His children were called Siegfried and Brunhilde (my brother Max later married the daughter). This man accosted me bluffly, and my mother left the room at once.

'I had always like you. You seem fine boy. Vot's all dis nonsense that your poor mother tell me? Your head got big?'

I could see that the only way to make the Witnesses relent was for me to appear higher up on the moral slope than they were, so I flared up at once, criticising their beliefs – their acceptance of capital punishment; their failure to alleviate immediate suffering, through any sort of social work; their joining in what I had decided was the holocaust of animals that humans engaged in every day.

Hans blustered, ignoring my ideas. 'Dis world rotten. Nussing in it. You vant to go into dat? You silly boy. I seen things you not believe. Dead kids, bodies everywhere. Slippery on der guts. Tell me somesing: Do you acknowledge sacred name of Gott?'

I grew more impatient. 'How can you believe in this primitive stuff? It's just a fetish; it's a form of magic, don't you see...?'

That put an end to the conversation. 'I give up you for der Vorld!'

I found my mother was outside the door. 'Please don't be unhappy,' I said. 'Just think that I'm one of the honest searchers the Bible talks about. I'll live properly...'

From then on, I often used to feel when my mother and I were together that she was like that figure in William Blake, 'Calling the lapsed soul/ And weeping in the evening dew'. Only gradually did I come to realise how much I had been cut out of her confidence, how subtly she had distanced me.

When I was in my twenties, and living in Sydney, not having been home for years, I was a passenger in a car accident. I was taken by ambulance to hospital, conscious, and told that I would need an operation for internal bleeding and for broken bones. Although sedated, I remembered to refuse a blood transfusion. My mother's visceral revulsion at the thought of someone taking blood hung before me. The doctors were surprised and irritated.

'It says on your form that you have no religion. What's going on here?' one asked me, on the way to the theatre. I found it hard to explain that since my mother would be informed of the details if I died, I did not want her thinking I was cowardly or unclean. I was simply adamant: I would only accept a saline solution. I said I was not arguing and the nurse intervened. After the operation I was given too much aspirin, and during the night my stomach haemorrhaged. I woke to a nurse slapping me and shouting; my head was glued to the pillow with blood. More saline, and again it was sufficient. But I felt I was not popular in the hospital.

When I broke with Jehovah's Witnesses, I happened to notice in the newsagency a paperback copy of *On the Origin of Species*. Standing and browsing in this, a little each day, I was charmed by the clear, calm, observational approach of Darwin to questions about nature, and by his personal integrity, as summarised in the book's introduction. Darwin, I had been taught, was the anti-Christ, whose features showed him to be what he claimed each of the rest of us were – a brute. (This was a Jehovah's Witnesses' joke.) Buying his book was a celebration of my liberty. The world lay all before me...

Some weeks later, my father saw me reading *On the Origin of Species* at the kitchen table, late at night. He had come out for a glass of water, and was sober.

'Show me what you're reading. Huh. You'll get little comfort out of that. The survival of the fittest. You understand who the fittest are, I take it? They're merely the ones who have the most children; who reproduce their genes. And you know the reality of that, nowadays? It means that some diabetic, scabious, overweight moron, living on social security in a caravan park, who has ten children, is the paragon of nature. That's all the meaning there is in evolution. Go to bed, save on the electricity. Goodnight.'

I could not ignore Darwin's insight, however, because all the evidence was clearly on the side of some refinement of his approach. I made a joke to another curious-minded boy at school, saying that the most impressive book I had read was 'Heart of Darkness' by Charles Darwin.

I was attracted to Buddhism, which claimed it had no problem with science. The doctrine was recommended to me by what I thought some sublime words of its founder: 'Knowing the nature of the world, the wise do not grieve.' My father had in our living room a seated figure of the Buddha in white soapstone, from Thailand, which had always fascinated me. To him, it was decorative. My mother called it an 'idol' and was not sorry when it was accidentally broken. The figure had an expression that was aloof, slightly insolent; it seemed to say, I am liberated from what distresses other humans; find out how this can be, for yourself. But over years, through reading introductions to the subject I bought in Sydney, I became disillusioned with at least the original form of Buddhism, for its nihilism. Nirvana, liberation, which was detachment in life, was extinction at death, escaping the inevitable, endless dissatisfactions of being reborn. Buddhism certainly held, despite the evasions of Western interpreters, that what is best of all for us is not to exist. It seemed too early, on an already chill morning, for such a cold meal.

I knew no one who was curious about such ideas, then; but the overripe fruit of the sixties was soon to fall thunderously from the trees. Like raindrops blown ahead of the storm, I found two books by Alan Watts, within the one year, a single copy of each in the revolving wire stand at the dim-lit newsagency, in that sleepy town: *The Way of Zen* (six and sixpence) and *Psychotherapy East and West* (eight shillings). These were about a 'critical' Buddhism that originated in China and was positive toward nature: its aim was to achieve absorption, like a craftsman or an artist, in all one's dealings with the world. It was about self-forgetfulness through intense involvement. I was at once an enthusiast for the austere aesthetics of Zen poetry, ink drawing, calligraphy, raku pottery, sliding screens, tatami matting. This involvement continued to grow over many years, and led me to Japan in my forties. (Only then did a certain disillusion set in, witnessing Japanese society, and Zen's implication in it.)

My father said to me, 'I gather you've been dropped by the Jehovah's witless. What are you going to do with yourself now?'

'I'm going to read a book, go for a walk, go to school. That all happened a year ago. Did you only just notice?'

'Nobody tells me anything. I hope you won't end up like your mother, jumping from one crazy idea to another. What are these loony-looking books you're reading?'

'I'm just curious. I've got the choice of loony on the one hand and stultifying on the other, I suppose.'

'The trouble is you've got no stability – no breeding. That's your mother's fault. I at least had an upbringing...'

I used to go 'training' in the early mornings – running for miles, before high school, across the frosty golf course and along a bush lane that was heavily laced-up with shadows. I had read about Percy Cerutty, the eccentric coach of the Australian runners who were gold-medallists at the 1956 Melbourne Olympics, a few years before – he had been told he was dying at the age of forty, but through exercise and diet recovered his health, won marathons, although much the oldest competitor, and began to teach his method. He had his athletes train barefooted, running up sand-hills near his isolated camp, then all throwing themselves into the surf. In the evenings he gave talks on Greek philosophy. So at weekends, I jogged for miles down the long beaches beyond the town, crossing an estuary on the railway trestle, after listening, as they did in films, with my ear to the line. In the evenings I read Heraclitus. 'This world, which is the same for all, no one of gods or men has made, but it was, is, and shall be, an ever living Fire, with portions of it kindling and portions going out.'

On those mornings, I ran until it seemed I tasted blood from my lungs, until my heart rose up and beat its drum in my ears. Vulnerability makes the senses tender. Resting by the lane, I saw the golden wall of the day, along which a rickety cantilever of ash-white smoke hung, from a single farmhouse. Before that, the crop was viridian; behind it, a solid mass of lavender-coloured forest was smeared with steam.

On my way home, I crossed the golf course, over the lit dew in its myriads, as though walking the tips of candle flames. I was living on nothing; just the heat of life in a package of dust. Exultance welled up within my temporary, disbelieving heart.

11. Off the Bitumen

In high school, I balanced always coming top in English and History with never doing better than last in Maths and the crafts, and being low-marked in most other subjects. I specialised, working on nothing for school but what I found of interest, and was able not to think about the reason behind such an attitude. My teenage incommunication was mainly with myself.

Our school had almost a thousand pupils, a good proportion brought in by bus and train from small towns across the district. Classes could have more than forty students. The buildings were dark brick, the grounds mainly cement, but the school was set on a rise near the harbour, so that the upstairs rooms looked across iron roofs, railway station, jetty, fishing fleet, breakwater, island, to the precise horizon. Clouds performed out there, through the days, a slow, mysterious narrative, which drew everyone's eye, intermittently, including the teachers'.

By doing practically no homework in Geography, Economics, Biology, Chemistry, Physics, French, and the rest, I could write all my creative essays to unheard-of length. This situation was encouraged, unintentionally, by my English teacher, who welcomed whatever I showed him. I heard that he defended leniency toward me, among the other teachers, but when we were speaking privately he would sometimes remember to be critical of my general performance. I made desultory promises, but nothing changed. He had no idea of my medical history.

This English teacher, whom I continued to be allocated in my later years at school, was an occasional drinking companion of my father, and became something of a friend to me. A class with him was likely to drift into a personal exchange between us, over the text. If someone asked the meaning of a word, or of a line in Shakespeare, he would often deflect the enquiry in my direction, although I found this hotly embarrassing. None of the other students resented it: I was allowed to have my elevation, because I walked so much upon the ground in other classes.

After the half-yearly and yearly examinations, there would be vast hilarity in the mathematics class when my marks were read out. Fourteen per cent, I remember, and nine per cent, for stapling the pages together properly. Only once did I put up my hand in a maths class, and the teacher hushed everyone for my answer. I wanted to tell him that he had spelled 'coefficient' wrongly on the blackboard.

I admired my English teacher, for his enthusiasm about the subject and because he was a former amateur boxing champion. A flyweight, he taught on the balls of his feet, verbally feinting and sparring with the class. In the honours group, he would go into a clinch – saying risqué things, to make the girls chortle. He used dramatic gestures, often laid hands on a pupil, and spoke rapidly in a stream of consciousness style, firing many synonyms into a thought, looking for the blow that told. He had thickly brushed-back brown hair, which he ran a hand over, tightening it, one of his nostrils was almost blocked with scar tissue, and the opposite eyebrow was permanently displaced, a little way up his forehead.

I though he had the strained good looks of a Battle of Britain pilot.

Once my father came home from the pub and said that this teacher had mentioned I had won a prize, for having come top of the year in his subject three times in a row. My father wanted to know why I had overlooked reporting this at home. 'No need for modesty,' he advised me; 'you're not that great.'

Then, just as I began my last year at school, I became ill: I had fevers and night sweats and crippling pains in the limbs, which were diagnosed as symptoms of rheumatic fever. Because this illness can affect the heart, there was a sense of suppressed panic about my mother. The present had become so much where I lived that I was unable to worry.

I had brought the illness on myself, my mother believed, through all the running I did, and through having taken long bike rides out of town. On occasions, I went to where my father's first plantation was still being worked, by strangers, because I was interested in the view from there. Riding outward or back, I was twice caught in heavy rainstorms, but pedalled on, into a sweltering sun. My mother believed this had done me harm.

Going to the plantation, I turned off the highway after about five miles, onto a shadow-dampened dirt road, and went gradually uphill, a few miles further, to a place where I hid my bike among trees. Unnoticed at weekends, I climbed between the banana palms, on the most prominent ridge, to just beneath the forest line. That ridge seemed to stride forward like a thigh beneath a gown, from the closely planted folds on either side. Below, the country-side unfurled its green banner horizontally on the wind, and the bright sea beat at the shore like a curtain hem out of a window.

I used to eat my lunch in the long grass there, above the vast drapery of the plantation, and the dark tree-lined creeks, the few silver roofs of houses, the powerful black flex of the highway. I looked across bare green headlands to the islands Captain Cook had seen, when creeping past that place in his small wooden ship. His voyage seemed more isolated than a satellite's orbiting of the planet. There were three bald, grassy islands widely scattered before me, and Cook had named each of them Solitary – South, Middle and North – so the word, one felt, had been much on his mind.

I could think of nothing better than living isolated in the place where my father had been, with his books and his income, and was puzzled that for him it had not been enough.

In my attacks of fever, I seemed to be scorching to the touch, like oven-heated porcelain, and I would be ground with pain, in the hips, legs and shoulders, so that there was no way I could lie still. The available painkiller, at least in our house, was an aspirin, maybe two in a real emergency. I used to groan in my sleep, disturbing everyone except my father, who took sleeping pills.

When I was getting better, it was decided, on the doctor's advice, that I should not hurry back to school but take my lessons by correspondence, for a while: this was a government provision to isolated or bedridden children. I was supposed to continue resting, most of the time.

I dealt with the forms involved in this arrangement, for my mother, and informed the correspondence school, after a few dreary lessons, that I was going back to high school, and the high school that I would be continuing with the correspondence course. I signed her name. So I was left free, with my own interests, for six months.

A lot of mail came to the house for me at this time, catalogues and newsletters I had sent for, and my mother never noticed that what I was reading and scribbling had only to do with my personal thoughts. Advertising arrived on every sort of utopian, fantastic, self-improving idea that touched my curiosity, but I was unable to feel conviction about any of it: information came on the Rosicrucians and hatha yoga and body building and Theosophy and the Communist Party, as well as on buying real estate in the Whitsunday Islands and appreciating classical music, and there were endless catalogues from booksellers and second-hand book dealers in England and Australia. I had money from my aunt Dorothy, who had set up a trust account so that I could continue at school past the minimum age, but from all of that smudged or glossy information surrounding me, the only subscriptions I took were for a record club, from which I accepted a few records, and for a magazine about ballet dancing, a sudden interest. While sick, I got out of bed and 'rugging myself up' insisted on taking my mother and sister to a performance by a touring company of *Swan Lake*, at the School of Arts.

After a few months into my illness, the English teacher used sometimes to call, and sit by the bed. His visits were made following a late afternoon spent in the pub and before my father came home. I think he did not get along with my father: he may have found him too opinionated. The teacher would come into my room reeking of beer, as in the classroom in the mornings he often smelled like methylated spirits. He must have been about forty years old then. The conversations between us were always strained, at first. I thought he believed his voice was like that of the actor Richard Burton, which it was (he had loaned me a record of Burton reading), and he would growl his first few remarks as if on stage, listening to himself in a strange house. He often seemed melancholy when he arrived, as he was not in class, where he played the cynic energetically; but after a little he would revive, and perhaps quote from Dylan Thomas, our favourite poet, and I would finish the verse, or sometimes correct him: I had been loaned his copy of Thomas's poems. Then we would begin to talk.

My mother kept flowers in my room, and I was collecting reproductions of paintings, from a series of small art books that I could afford, and from *Life* magazine. Pasted around the walls were a portrait by Modigliani, a Cézanne still life, Matisse's *Dance*, a landscape by Kokoschka, a print of a Giacometti head, and others; it would change. My teacher liked the flowers and disliked the pictures: he disavowed any interest in modern art. He also seemed bemused by the many photographs from ballet magazines, pinned up on a big noticeboard my grandfather had made, as everyone in the house was. This was around the time when Nureyev had leapt the fence at Paris airport, claiming asylum. I had a collection of pictures of him with Margot Fonteyn, or floating alone. It was athleticism, to me, like the newspaper photos of acrobatic soccer players I also had on the board. Still, my parents seemed disconcerted by these pictures, although I could not imagine the reason.

Every time my teacher visited, he brought me a book – *Riceyman Steps*, *Crime and Punishment* – and the next time he would expect me to say something about it. I disappointed him by hating Dostoyevsky and refusing to finish his work. Instead, I enthused about Rider Haggard and Joseph Conrad, indiscriminately. *Middlemarch* was beyond me; but on *Wuthering Heights* we were in agreement. I much preferred poetry to any novel: we did best talking about Shakespeare. My father scoffed to me when I mentioned this, although he looked alarmed.

My mother did not approve of my English teacher, and although she was polite to him for my sake, she was distant. I never knew if he noticed this. The coolness was not just because of his drinking, but because of rumours about a girl in his amateur theatrical group. The girl had been in my class but had dropped out of school; he drove her home after rehearsals of an evening to a street around the corner from us, and they were reported to sit for a long time in his parked car, in darkness, under some trees near where she lived. What gave credence to the story for many, I would think, was the girl herself, who was almost ideally endowed with primary sexual characteristics, while none too bright. Her nickname among the pupils had been 'Marilyn', because of her looks and her ambition to be famous. She had gone to work in a fashion store in the town, until her younger sister grew up a little, and then she was going to leave her widowed mother and go to Sydney and 'make it'. My teacher encouraged her by giving her the part of a housemaid, or something similar, in the plays by the town's theatre group, which he directed and acted in (Rattigan, Shaw and Priestley, and so on). I was rather scornful of my mother when she told me about his reputation, for having listened to those who would stand in a darkened room, the venetian blinds dilated by forefinger and thumb, timing people in a parked car – who may have been engrossed in the subject of Ibsen, as far as anyone knew. My mother was offended at having been counted among gossips. 'A lot you know,' she said.

When I was almost better, I used to call by invitation at my teacher's house on Saturday afternoons, while his wife was playing golf. He would be drinking, and I would accept a beer, so as not to put him off his conversation. In the right mood, he could 'tire the sun with talking/ And send him down the sky'. My gratitude to him is as ardent now as it was then, although I did not express it at the time. The relationship between pupil and teacher can be among the deepest one has; every writer I have talked with at length has mentioned the decisive importance of an English teacher in his or her past. My teacher once remarked, also, what a good thing it was for him to have an eager student. He hoped that I would come top of the state in English; a colleague of his at school had taught a pupil a few years previously who had achieved that position, and my teacher was sure I could. I repaid his interest in me with disappointment.

We played a word game on the sun-deck of his house, while he drank: he would think of a word and define it and I would use it in a sentence, which was expected to be bizarre or amusing or at least memorable. I remember 'ululate', 'rebarbative', 'couchant', 'antinomy', 'infrangible', 'besom' were some words I learned in that way. (I remember that he defined 'uxorious' as referring to a man who was deluded.) We would revise with him reading rapidly from a list of the words he had given me. After one of our sessions, he remarked that words stuck to me 'like flies to fly-paper'. He regretted, and I did, that our school no longer had Latin on the syllabus.

When I went back to school, feeling that I must get it over with, I realised I could not catch up in my other subjects: I would have to repeat the year. But I was seventeen and another year at home would be interminable. My English teacher insisted I repeat, and that this time I do some work, instead of simply indulging myself. Still, he indulged me. He set me the same personalised homework every few weeks, on top of his ordinary essays, and without regard for my other workload. 'Read this,' he would say after class, handing me a paperback from his library. 'Write a few pages explaining what it was that you learned from it.' The books he chose included *Dubliners*, *The Waste Land and Other Poems*, *A Portrait of the Artist as a Young Man*, *The Waves* (the most effete thing I had ever read), *Bend Sinister*, *Sons and Lovers*, Ernest Hemingway's stories, and plays by Ibsen and Shaw. I went on making my own discoveries, as well, which secretly I liked just as much as his books: Somerset Maugham, Katherine Mansfield, Raymond Chandler.

The teacher wanted to see one of my pieces of fiction, which flaunted O. Henry's technique of the trick ending, typed up and sent to a literary magazine in Sydney. That made me feel I needed to make more revisions, but while working on it I became dis-illusioned, because I read in a book on how to write short stories that the 'twist' ending had been discounted, for modern taste; it was seen as glib. What was self-evidently more impressive, the book said, was the resonant, unresolved ending of a Chekhov story, which was truer to life. I took out from the school library a book by Chekhov, and felt elevated onto a new level, into an encounter with absolute quality. My own story was dismissed.

At this time, also, I heard on the radio by chance, one Saturday afternoon, while I had the house to myself, Bach's *Concerto for Two Violins in D Major*. Although I had no knowledge of music, nor an urgent interest in it, I knew this must be one of the great experiences that someone could have.

I still went to Sydney in my school holidays, once a year, using some of Aunt Dorothy's money, but I never saw the doctors now, nor did I visit Margaret and Olga. I stayed in the cheapest hotels, near Central Station, and spent a week or so wandering the streets and parks, browsing from bookshop to bookshop, drifting in the state art gallery, going to films, not speaking to anyone but shop assistants and waitresses.

I realised when on these trips, in my mid-teens, how closed-off the future felt, for me. All at once, arriving in the city on an early morning train, I could sense possibilities. I stood in the rocking corridor of a carriage as we arrived, and looked out on streets freshly washed by council trucks, unfamiliar billboards, cramped backyards, plastery terrace houses painted in pastel colours, faces crowded on the platforms, and was carried past them and released, into aimlessness.

The sordid hotel was necessary, if I was to maintain the feeling of openness for as long as possible. I usually stayed in the ironically named 'People's Palace', run by the Salvation Army. A room there was like a cell in a termite's tenement. It was just a narrow plaster slot, with an iron bedstead, some folded blankets, a wooden chair, and a small wardrobe that screeched open and that always had curlicues of fluff in the bottom of it. I asked the clerk if there was a room with a sink, on one visit, but he said, 'We don't have sinks. People would only urinate in them.' The bathroom had a concrete floor where puddles of glutinous water lay, overflowed from the blocked-up shower cubicles.

I read in the bookstores until my legs ached, and sometimes I bought, but only those books that were beyond hesitation. I liked best the old Angus and Robertson store in Castlereagh Street; its long polished floorboards and solid wooden bookcases with wooden ladders propped against them. My mother had taken me there when I was much younger, on a wet, wrapped-up, wonderfully idle afternoon. The traffic sizzled in the narrow street outside, the yellow lamps were lit indoors; I watched the polite condescension of the staff, and saw the books being calmly examined, taken from their stacks on tables, as colourful as jewellery. I had looked up at my mother and said, 'When I grow up, I want to work in a bookshop.' She patted me on the head: 'You'll do much better than that.' I felt determined I would not.

In Sydney, I followed up everything I wanted to know about, from Aldous Huxley's *The Perennial Philosophy* to the biologist Jacques Monod's *Chance and Necessity*, out of a list I kept in a notebook. I found a little art bookshop in a lane from which I collected postcards and small posters: 'View of Toledo', 'Bacchus and Ariadne', 'Primavera', the landscapes of Morandi and Paul Nash. I discovered the Theosophical Society's library and bookshop and sat all day in the cloying smell of incense and the carpeted hush, looked down upon by Madame Blavatsky in her headshawl, who leaned on one meaty fist, her pouched gaze as sombre as a moonlit marshland. She resonated fraudulence, I thought. But I was smiled on by the dowagers who presided there, and I browsed *The Secret Doctrine* and *The Gospel of Ramakrishna* with fascinated disbelief. What interested me was the psychology of those books – the inventiveness of our imaginations in trying to deny an implacable reality. From that shop I bought *170 Chinese Poems*, translated by Arthur Waley, and it has lasted the best of all I discovered then.

For a while I had a fascination with Jacob Boehme, the seventeenth-century German shoemaker and mystic who experienced a vision while looking at sunlight on a pewter dish. I loved the concepts in his writings – the 'Ungrund', or Abyss; the 'Thirst', out of which God is born (an impulse that begins 'as thin as nothing'); the 'Wrath', or divided nature of God; the 'Blitz'; the 'Mysterium Magnum'; the 'Signature of All Things'. At the same time I was interested in the Quakers, and the early Buddhist scriptures, the *Dhammapadha*. But from all of this I withheld a final assent. There were no grounds for deciding which was right, and therefore none of it could be right. I did not believe in the Theosophists' motto, that all paths lead to truth. One had to find one's way out of the labyrinth by a golden hair. But where was it?

While in Sydney, I looked in the telephone book and found the address of a ballet school. I chose one at the Rocks, the original Georgian village of the colony, now below the giant stone pylons at the city end of the Harbour Bridge. I leant on the chisel-marked sandstone wall of a quiet alley, in wintry sun, opposite the school's entrance, and heard the piano's notes floating and the thump of bandaged feet. A girl in leg warmers was stretched along the sill of a large, arched window, in profile, above the few people who passed up and down the lane. She seemed a sylph or a luxuriant animal, with her small head and her furred limbs. I could hear a woman's high voice and clapped hands. Some adults came and waited at the doorway of the building and I joined them, peering in.

I took sketching book and pencils to the school and presented myself as an art student, and was allowed to sit on the periphery and draw. I was afraid someone might look over my shoulder and see the gaucheness of my work. When the girls began to leave, scarves over their shoulders, they were shrill and undignified, or some were sarcastic and superior to the younger ones. They walked like geese. The girl I had thought the most beautiful turned out to have a pinched, goat-like face, when glimpsed close up. I had no wish to speak to any of them: it would be awkward and pointless.

On one visit to Sydney, I had enough money to go to a performance of the Australian Ballet's *The Display*, by Sir Robert Helpmann, which is about a girl who is raped at a picnic. The villainous dancer, with large biceps in his rolled-up plaid shirt, drank from and threw down imaginary beer cans in a stylised and petulant way that was irritating and unconvincing. The falsity of the gesture rankled with me. After the attack, the girl fled into the bush, where she was courted and consummated by a giant bower bird, engulfed in his wings. I decided that dance was too stylised and too limited a medium; that my interest in it was simply because it represented 'Art', with which I felt I ought to affirm solidarity, and my belief in it fell away, there in the theatre. A love of poetry and of paintings was enough 'artiness' for someone from the North Coast to have to carry.

(Many years later, although I saw only rare performances, I learned to enjoy ballet again, led back to it by Degas' paintings of dancers. It was the imperfection of the ballet I responded to then, instructed by him; I was moved by the way nature denies fantasy, when we are close to the spectacle, having sat there once by chance. The failures of technique, the sweat, the grunting, the thump and slither of feet, the concentration in faces, the coagulated make-up, the strain of lifts, the smudging footlights, the glimpse into the wings – these things were in poignant contrast to the world the dance sought to evoke, and offered something ineluctably real, although set to music.)

At school, I had no particularly close friends, and yet I was not unpopular. I played basketball in the lunchtime competition and scored a respectable share of goals. A few of the others invited me to their houses at weekends and I sometimes went, in my younger high school years, but I found it an unsatisfactory experience. Their mothers laid on the charm watchfully, the way they spread jam or peanut butter on rounds of bread, while asking me questions about my parents and home life, which could only be answered with lies.

We had no family tradition of people visiting us and I only ever agreed to someone calling once, as I remember. That boy, the son of a well-off car dealer, walked through our house, while he and I were there alone, insolently opening cupboard doors and seeing what was behind them, even looking into the bathroom cabinet. I was too amazed and embarrassed to protest. The next day at school he ignored me.

I felt I could not maintain a close relationship with outsiders because of Jehovah's Witnesses, even after I was no longer associated with them. Their atmosphere seemed everywhere in our house, contending with my father's.

I hardly ever went out in the mixed groups into which I was sometimes invited, but claimed to spend the weekends with my uncle on his farm; I had no conversation about cars, fashion, or pop songs, and I was embarrassed to be among the girls in their shorts. I remember us riding our bikes around, arguing over where to have a picnic, and later the girls dancing to a transistor radio under a tent of trees, and then sitting on somebody's front fence, near a general store, with my arm dutifully around a girl's waist, as instructed by her, until the owner of the house came and told the group of us to get away from his property.

My father and I entered the lowest region of our relationship when I was fifteen, a state brought about by the appearance of a stranger in the town. Whenever I went into the shopping street after school, a man would be there, watching us all. He stood outside the milk bar, talking to young labourers and apprentices, or near the taxi rank, with the older men who gathered in that spot, and gazed around, taller than the others. He was often near the newsagency. He smiled and nodded to me, and would approach, to say something, but as though oblivious of this I always hurried on. Almost any afternoon I was in the shopping street, this man would appear beside me. I was always polite, but rushed. He was tall, and was distended, yet not sluggish or flabby-looking: he looked taut. He was similar in shape to a fisherman's float, and with its brisk, buoyant movements. He folded a newspaper and flicked it under his arm; then he shook it out, refolded it, and slotted it beneath the other arm. Fastidious and fast; able to pounce. His skin was swarthy, as if tea-leaf stained, and his hair was oily and sleek and close-cropped. He had large eyebrows, lips and cheeks, and a curved nose. His voice was soft, complicit. He smiled, looked around, was easygoing. 'Of course; of course you must hurry. We can speak again, on another occasion.' The eyes were very dark, and searching; insinuating. He wore tailored shorts and long socks a lot of times, and always cheerfully coloured shirts.

One night he sat in the same row as me at the pictures, where no one else was sitting. Then he moved along, as if to get a better view of the screen, and spoke to me across some empty seats. I made brief replies and said, apologetically, that I had to move further back. He suggested he come and talk with me; but I said 'No, I like to see a picture alone.' I sat near a group of people, and went and stood by the door to see the last of the film, keeping an eye on him; then I left instantly it was over, and set off at a jog. Halfway home, in a blue-lit empty street, a car came out of a cross-road and pulled onto the verge, facing me, and sat there, obscured behind its spiny headlights. No one and no other traffic were about. The door opened and that large figure stood up, in silhouette; he called out something. I opened the nearest front gate and ducked along the side of a house, through their backyard and over a fence, into someone else's place. I ran across a road, to the park, and went out onto the dark football oval there, where a car could not follow. Watching the lights passing on the perimeter of the grounds, I ran down the length of the playing field, and then raced among the trees in the park, avoiding their shadows, and made it home, my back creeping with fear, as I opened the front gate. As soon as I was inside I began to recriminate with myself for being so scared.

I was at home on a Saturday afternoon, everyone else was out. I went to answer a knock on the door, and it was him. I felt drenched with horror. He was talking about raffle tickets, showing me a roll of them. Was my mother at home? No? He had a car, perhaps we could go out for fish and chips at the beach. Could he come in? He unlatched the screen door, through which we had been speaking. I slammed the wooden door on him, and ran and locked the back one. There was no phone. I watched him obliquely from a bedroom window, along the curtains, where he stood on our porch, facing outwards, seeming to enjoy the sun, taking his time. Then he slowly walked up the path and looked back at the house. He took a gardenia from a tree in our garden, and held it up to himself, with a modest, courtly gesture. His forefinger, braced against the flower's woody stem, had the shape of a teapot spout. He strolled along, out of sight, toward the next place.

Not long after, late in the evening, two policemen came to our door. They told my parents that I had been seen talking with a man who was known as a 'child molester', and that he had called at our house. I said he was selling raffle tickets, door-to-door, but the police told us that no one else was called on. His car had been noticed sitting for a long time in our street. I assured everyone I had not been 'interfered with'. Why had I talked with him, when I was at the shops? I had never wanted to speak with him, I said, and had got away as quickly as I could, without being rude. The police told us they were moving him on, which was all they could do, since they could find no one to testify against him. They seemed disappointed I had nothing to report. Word would be passed from town to town about him, and about his twin brother, who was travelling with him. This seemed a nightmarish touch. No wonder he had appeared to be everywhere. I was instructed by the police not to talk to strangers in future, as if I were a child.

Both my parents were disturbed by the news the police brought; but I realised, in the following weeks, that my father held me some-how implicated. When he came home drunk, he would say in my presence, 'I was never that way myself; I can't understand it.' He began telling my mother that she had made too much fuss of me. My mother was guilt-ridden and had no rejoinder. My father said, on several occasions, that I was too 'ethereal'. He began to mention homosexuals with disdain, as people who were interested in each other's 'drainage system'. He called them 'coprophiliacs'. ('Look it up.') He said that he himself had seen me 'loitering' in the news-agency. My mother and I were aghast at the drift of his talk. I guess now that he must have been trying to practise aversion therapy on me, against something he feared might become the case. But the 'proclivity', as he called it, had never occurred to me. My father had introduced a tainted atmosphere into the house, while my fantasies about girls were still ending in ellipses...

Those years were a particularly cold trek for my father: he seemed to be wading through a sandy, fog-bound landscape, whenever he was not relieved by alcohol. He had his secure pension, half of which he took for his drinking, but the drink appeared to be steadily poisoning him, making him either more irritable or more subdued. He still made jokes, occasionally. When my mother suppressed a heavily impending sneeze, in the kitchen, into a lady-like titter, he remarked, sonorously, 'Ah, deep calls to deep'; and he referred to a puffy-faced woman neighbour of ours, I understood, as being 'dough-eyed'.

We were told that he sat in the Returned Soldiers Club from early afternoon into the evening, getting drunk alone, while the men he preferred to know were at work. When they arrived, his time was out of joint with theirs. He would be driven home by someone among them, at about eight or eight-thirty, the hour at which the otherwise more sober men left, and we would wait until then for dinner. If we heard him stagger and fall on the path at the back of the house, one of us went to help him up the steps, onto the porch. Then he had to go through the ritual cleaning of his shoes, before he would come inside. We sat and heard him crash in through the laundry door, lurch against a wall, find his equipment, wobble out and position himself in a corner of the balustrade, get his foot up on the lowest rail, while grasping the top one, and at the first swipe let the brush go reeling out of his hand and clatter across the boards. Someone would pick it up for him, and try to give his shoes a cursory dusting, perhaps, but he would insist on dabbing at his feet himself.

At dinner, he began his monologue, straight off. 'You'll never amount to anything, you lot. You're good for nothing. What are you looking at? I'll get to you in a moment. The little girl will be all right. She's going to be a beauty. But as for you boys: you take after your mother. No background. Max might get into the navy.

237

He'd look good in the navy. But you,' he would turn to me, 'I hear from your teacher that you can't get two and two right. Cosines, geometry, algebra, I was always head of the class.' My mother would say that I had missed a lot of school and had never been helped to catch up; I should have had coaching, if it could have been afforded. He refused to listen. 'You think you're smart, with your head in a book,' he told me. 'You're about as deep as paint.'

Another theme of his was that we were not good at sport. Why wasn't I playing Rugby Union, a real game. It was no use explaining that there was no Rugby Union played in the district; we were letting him down. Who was the swimming champion of the school? Was it one of us? No. He had to listen while other men...

My mother agreed to let me escape some of these evenings, since as the eldest I took most of the criticism. I ate an early dinner on my own, then would take myself off to the picture theatre, several nights a week, with two shillings. She had no idea of homework.

We used to stage boxing matches in the back garden: my brothers, some neighbourhood kids, and myself, wearing cartoon-sized, heavyweight gloves that a man who lived up the street had given us. The rule was that we were not allowed deliberately to hurt each other. One Saturday afternoon my father came home early, with the bad-tempered look that his close fortnightly haircut always gave him, and saw us playing about, hurling our punches onto each other's guard. He was tipsy and he stepped at once onto the lawn and challenged me to a match. My mother, leaning on the window-sill above us, told me not to have anything to do with it. My father said don't be ridiculous, he only wanted to teach me a few moves. His hat and jacket were laid aside on the grass, someone tied the gloves onto him, and he came at me at once with a mean warp to his face. I danced backward from his wild, heavy swings, and kept on eluding him, taunting him by lowering my gloves and ducking and weaving, and by beginning a mocking commentary, with him as 'Max Schmelling'. He stumbled in pursuit, all about the yard, grunting at me to fight. My mother kept calling out to him to stop it: she could see how much his blows were in earnest. His guard was down, he was sweating, I could smell the beer. It would have been easy to have rammed my fist against his broken nose and have bloodied it. I looked at him, wallowing around, a grass stain on the knee of his good trousers, where he had slipped. He had needed to be helped up, holding the clothes prop. I felt disgusted at my impulse. I dragged off the gloves and threw them at him, and walked away. He was bent over, globular fists braced on his knees, coughing, trying to shout something after me.

When my father was pompous about his taste, his education or his family background, my mother knew it was mostly 'the drink talking', but she still grew irritated and would make rejoinders, such as telling him that he was 'just a big style of nothing'. You could see from the effect of such remarks on his face that his self-assurance was not perfect.

At this time, my father came up with a belief of his own: he began bringing home large-format, colourful magazines from the Soviet Union, given to him at the pub by a man who he said was a 'commo'. These magazines had poster-like covers; on one a stone-jawed young proletarian, with great muscular forearms, and a wheat-coloured, shining young woman, each drew behind them a banner that was like a red stallion on a halter. Behind the rolling flags, marching in columns, were beaming workers of all races, brandishing spanners, sledgehammers, rakes and scythes. It was like the Jehovah's Witnesses' style of illustration. On inside pages, there were pictures of dramatic oratory by Lenin, straining from the podium, above an exultant crowd; of Marx, Engels and Lenin together, in low-relief profile; of combine harvesters, with groups of women in headscarves, surrounded by blossoming branches. The headlines on the articles always had the words 'Smash' and 'Crush' in them.

My father said this system was the future, the only hope. There was no other way that the life of the ordinary 'battler', worried sick, always struggling, could become better. I hated the idea of marching in a column and thinking the same thoughts as everyone else; but when I suggested this, my father said that such people as me were 'bourgeois' and the future was going to roll right over us. Then he said one night, that he was one of the expendable, too. Before long he gave up his talk of communism and went back to drowsing over library books. Still, if politics was mentioned, he defended the communists. 'The commos are right. You've got to be prepared to fight, literally, if there's ever going to be any improvement. The strike has the power of an arsenal.'

Yet my father was maintained, for no contribution, by a system whose ethos he claimed was merely 'Bugger you, Jack, I'm all right.' He seemed unaware that he, also, exploited the worker, and not least the one closest to home.

Just as books had not been able to rescue my father, his love of my sister was unable to change his course. He always spoke differently to her, although admittedly she was a young girl, nine years old when I left home at seventeen. She helped my mother a lot around the house, fore-ordained a materfamilias. One Sunday, hurrying the preparation of lunch (my father already dressed to go out), not realising the danger, she started to undo the lid of a pressure cooker while it was still boiling on the stove. The lid blew out of her hands and all the scalding food struck the ceiling and fell back onto her bare arms and legs. While she screamed, my father grabbed the butter dish and went to rub grease on her burns; I snatched her away and ran outside with her in my arms to a tap, and held her under its rushing water, which immediately eased the pain. My father stood at the top of the steps bellowing at me: 'You fool! You fool!' I told my mother to tear up old sheets for cold compresses. My sister was completely relieved by this treatment, could sleep peacefully, and ended up without scars. Right after the accident, I explained to my father that butter and oil had been discounted for treating burns; cold water was the method: I had just been reading about it. He listened grimly, with a look of not knowing where to turn.

My father's middle sister, Dorothy, or 'Bill', kept in a sort of contact with me. I remember first meeting her in Sydney, at ten years old, when she was told that I was a reader. Every year from then on, while I was at school, several books arrived for my birthday, in hard covers, always including the latest adventure of Biggles, the 'air ace', with just a printed card and her signature. We had no other acknowledgement from her. (Perhaps at Christmas a card came, but my mother never displayed those.)

Bill stayed clear of my father all her life, after she had married into money. She came to our house once, when touring in the district with her husband, for afternoon tea. I suppose it was to confirm my father's fecklessness. My poor mother was blush-coloured from the moment she was told of the visit; she was particularly embarrassed that not all her china matched, and by its thickness, and was angry she should have to feel like that.

Stories of Bill's extravagance were legendary with her sisters, and these irresistibly found their way to my father. Their setting was her house in the country, to which 'Margo' alone was invited (and was therefore unable to go), and the great hotels in Europe at which Bill and Ronald stayed – anecdotes about both kinds of residence would get loose and drift along the air.

My parents knew that Bill helped out her sisters with money because I had mentioned it, in answer to questions: during her visits to the city, she left a generous 'something', a cheque, in the kitchen when she took away the cups and plates. Nothing like that happened on her visit to us. My mother, after her guests had gone, began a tirade against them, angry she said at the way they had sat as if unable to admit the support of her chairs. My father was too wilted, at the failure of any sign of a settlement, to defend his family, until he heard Margaret's name mentioned.

On one of Bill's travels, while I was in high school, she went to Stoke Poges churchyard, near London, where Thomas Gray's 'Elegy Written in a Country Churchyard' is supposedly set, and where the poet is buried, and she collected some earth from his grave in a jar, and sent it to me. I wrote and thanked her, but did not mention I had read that Thomas Gray was probably homosexual, had no offspring, and was no direct connection of ours, as her note showed she liked to believe. One day my mother dug this earth into her pot plants. She told me about it with a brusque but guilty air. It was done, she said, because she did not want me becoming morbid.

I was conscious of Thomas Gray's poem through my father intoning passages of it. He would say this was the best poem in the language and that it was written by an ancestor of his. Sometimes he seemed to run his hand over the marmorial cool perfection of its craft, but often he was more concerned to make its content apply to him. He knew most of the poem by heart, but I remember him lingering theatrically on 'Full many a gem of purest ray serene,/ The dark unfathomed caves of ocean bear:/ Full many a flower is born to blush unseen,/ And waste its sweetness on the desert air', and also on, 'Here rests his head upon the lap of Earth,/ A youth to Fortune and to Fame unknown...' When I think of this now, the joke redeems the self-pity, and the self-pity spoils the joke.

The books Bill sent me provoked my parents in different ways. It was urged by my mother that my father write and put an end to such 'favouritism'; although I pleaded that was illogical, because anyone in the family could read them. My father, I should have realised, was not going to cut off even such attenuated contact with his sister, and so he always checked that in writing my letter of thanks I included his personal good wishes, the exact tone of which he dictated.

When I was fifteen and Bill provided money so that I could stay on at school, it was because she was prompted to do this by my other aunts. The money was paid into a bank account that she instructed we open in my mother's and my name only. The atmosphere at home, after my father learned by what means I was remaining at school, grew more sullen and more than ever sharp-tongued toward me.

I spent the first instalment of the money as intended, but then, well into my final year, when I was seventeen, my mother agreed that I should use the remaining funds to get away from my father. Not only did I worsen his irritability, I now had a positive dislike for him, which she could see me struggling to suppress. I said I would find a job and send money to her.

I did not feel an obligation to repay the money to Dorothy, perhaps because it was so impersonally received. I interpreted liberally my aunt's instruction – 'for expenses incurred in your education'. Besides, halfway through the year, there was little enough money remaining.

Before I left home, we had relied for years on credit at the corner store. Always, as dinner was being made, I would have to run there for things we needed: a quarter mile each way in the twilight, beneath a strata of woodsmoke. The shopkeeper was particularly decent to us: I remember him allowing me to take even one egg on credit. I wonder how my mother managed to catch up

on her bill with him; I think she used all of her holiday pay, when it came due.

My brothers and sister each left school eagerly, at their first opportunity, took apprentice-ships and jobs locally, and stayed at home for a time, until they married early. My sister had the best academic record of any of us, coming top of her final year, and it was considered a tragedy by her teachers that she did not want to continue her education. She was typical of Jehovah's Witnesses in that.

My mother may have been prepared to let me leave home early just in case my apostasy spread among her other children, but it would have been hard for her, I think. Later, when I lived in Sydney, she wrote to me every week, until she entered the nursing home: hundreds upon hundreds of letters, in my adulthood, all of them affectionate, all quoting a Biblical text, for my guidance and persuasion. (I have kept many of her letters. Even in writing this book, I have been unable to bring myself to open them.)

My schoolwork was so far behind, I told my mother, that it was not worth worrying over, any longer. She did not blame me for this, but my recent illness. She thought that because I did so well at English I must be clever and that I would be all right in life. However, far from being smart, I had decided to go North, to the tropics, to become a 'beachcomber', driven by a need to get away from people.

A year earlier, in 1962, while visiting Sydney, I read a news-paper review of a reclusive artist, Ian Fairweather, who had lived for years on an island off the Queensland coast, on almost no money.

The article announced that he was Australia's greatest modern painter. I went to the exhibition, and the pictures I saw remain my favourite Australian art, although the ones I like are often scenes of China. His style, loose and calligraphic, is influenced by batik patterns and by Chinese ideograms, and often depicts schematised figures. The colours are Aboriginal earth tones, the medium usually gouache, on pieces of salvaged cardboard. His later paintings, like *Monastery* and *Monsoon*, are essentially abstract art, and are the greatest I know of in that genre.

At first I was as much interested in the painter's life as in his painting. Fairweather had built himself on his island a tent-like shelter that he could walk around in, of roped-together poles, bark, corrugated iron and hessian. He worked in the evenings by hurricane lamp or candlelight, and by day translated with a dictionary Chinese Buddhist and Taoist texts, for his own interest. He had been caretaker of a public park in Beijing, and had lived in poverty in the Philippines and Bali. Born in Scotland, he was a survivor of the trenches of the Great War.

Fairweather, I read, was interested in the process of painting, as a meditation, rather than in the finished object, which was just as well, because of the poor materials he had had to use. (Later I heard of a Sydney socialite who would scream when anyone closed a door too heavily in her house, knowing another piece of her Fairweather had fallen to the carpet. She collected them with tweezers.)

Fairweather at once become a hero to me. The possibility of living almost as a hermit in tropical Queensland was my ambition.

I disappeared from school with no hint that I was leaving. After a couple of weeks I sent my English teacher, with unintentional callousness, a postcard of a tropical sunset and palm trees, from the Great Barrier Reef.

12. The Reeking Sun

I took the train north to Brisbane, two hundred miles, and found the city was without associations or interest for me; I had intended to earn some money there, but decided at once to go on, and to hitch-hike, as I saw some Germans and Americans doing then, at the start of the sixties. I had a portable typewriter and in my haversack a copy of Walt Whitman ('Afoot and light-hearted I take to the open road,/ Healthy, free, the world before me') and a selection of Van Gogh's letters.

I travelled a thousand miles, towards Cooktown, the end of the road, thinking I would be sure to find work, and able to forget that I had not one practical skill. There was no trouble getting lifts, and no one bothered me, in my innocence, although some people said that I looked as if I should be in school.

I remember being picked up by a father and grown son and how they argued in the front seat over every topic they mentioned and asked me to adjudicate on each. I kept trying to balance the score, but they became irritated at too many tied results. I remember a lift with a newly married couple: she sat almost on top of him as he drove, kissed his ear, stroked his neck, and they whispered together, ignoring me for a hundred miles.

I remember the landscape, as it grew more tropical: it became loose savannah, and yet had a feeling of closeness, because of the boiler-room, dripping heat. Every day the sky was the blue of a swimming pool, a colour stripped of any nuance. When it rained, the long traceries of thick water were as shiny as syrup and drenched me immediately, before I could take shelter by the road. A storm was suddenly enclosing, overwhelming, immense, the sky erased in great sweeps of greyness, as though someone were roughly cleaning a blackboard.

Along the narrow highway the coarse, twisted trees, with splintered foliage, stood in dry, coarse grass. The highway rushed on and on, down a sparsely occupied peninsula, leading us off the planet, out of the world.

The intestines of many animals were discarded on the bitumen – kangaroos, goannas, birds, snakes, possums, rabbits, dogs, and a Brahmin cow. All through the bush the red, thick stalagmites, bigger than a man, were termite nests. They, and any cut in the earth, had the rawness of meat.

Sugar cane, a lacquered green, covered great tracts of land, back to the hills. The cane was burned-off at night, ready for harvesting, and it seemed that streams of lava were trickling everywhere through the dark.

A town made you feel the isolation. Some of the houses had an art nouveau wooden elegance, with their verandahs and stilts and fretted decorations, and some were like chicken sheds. There was often a fusillade of blossoms over a front fence. A huge impassivity hung everywhere. At the coast, in the end of the bitumen streets with their small white houses, lay a steam-ironed, flat, polyester sea. The marinas were full of white porcelain hulls, far more costly than the houses. In these towns, I found new orange-brick shops, plate glass windows daubed with zinc-white signs, the smell of fish and chips and of coconut oil sun-lotion, plastic flags clattering, and popsicle-coloured sails sliding by.

Stopping in such places, I slept on the beach, beneath upturned boats, or in hotels by the railway yards. The smell of coal and rust blew into those rooms, where every wood or formica surface had cigarette burns. The corridors sagged and creaked, and cigarette smoke hung in them like a swamp mist all night. The showers at the end of the hall dripped endlessly, their floors cement; hair clogged the gratings. When I passed a bar of an evening, coming back with something to eat, it was in uproar, like a fire.

The most interesting man I met on the road was a short, round Indian who had elaborate good manners, even though he wore the typical outfit of singlet, shorts and rubber scuffs. He took me to his house for a meal; a place on high poles, beside a cane field. His wife and an elusive number of children came onto the verandah and hovered about me. Before we ate, he wanted to show me something that would be of interest. I went, a small boy holding my hand, beneath the house, which was lattice-enclosed, into a padlocked, dark section, and waited there until the man put on the light. I had been told not to touch anything. I stood in a darkness that seemed strangely heavy and present, the small boy unusually still. When the lights opened we were in an alley made of boxes, stacked to head-height, all of them of glass within a wooden framework, and all of them filled with snakes. Ugly snakes, dark and thick, like black long animal droppings, were draped over each other, some just stirring, some watching us intently. To be bold, I looked more closely at one cold head, and it myopically struck at the glass, fast as a pistol-hammer, and left a soapy streak there. Taipans, I was told, 'most deadly', caught by this man in travels around Queensland, using only a forked stick and a bag, or else donated to him. A bite caused all of one's blood vessels to collapse, beginning almost immediately. The snakes were kept by my host to be milked; the venom, sold to the Queensland government, as his sole income, was used in making an antivenine.

The man's name was Ram Chandra: he was famous throughout the state, and had been honoured by the Queen. He had begun his 'vocation', he told me, after having been a cane-cutter, 'dreadful work', for many years. One day he had seen the daughter of his boss, 'a blonde child', who had brought her father morning tea, die horribly, within minutes, from a taipan's bite. Mr Chandra's own life had been saved by the serum he helped produce, after he was rushed in an ambulance to hospital, in agony, the poison becoming 'hard metal' inside him.

Upstairs again, the dining room table was lifted back and I sat among the family on a rug, eating chapattis and dahl and a delicious chicken curry. 'Now even a bee sting will kill me,' Mr Chandra announced proudly, and all of his family swayed involuntarily towards him. I felt like saying something ridiculously Kiplingesque.

I was picked up by a woman in a jeep; she had long, kinked grey hair and wore overalls and loose rubber boots. I remember she said her name was Char because I thought that she looked charred. She soon drove off the highway, up a packed-earth road, through a forest, saying she had something to do before going on. We stopped all of a sudden on a corner and with the motor still running she pulled out of her boot a long hatpin, a bauble at one end of it, and pressed the sharp tip against my throat. 'Don't move. Now, you see how easy it is? I've got something to tell you.' It was a story about hitch-hiking in France and in North Africa, with a girlfriend: they were so short of money in Morocco that they had slept in a cemetery, on top of a grave. In the morning the girlfriend was gone. Char waited, went to the police, went to the Embassy, searched, enquired of everyone, sat in a room by a phone, collapsed, and had to be shipped home. To that day, she said, she lived every hour waiting for a phone call. 'So. You see how easy it is?' She took the pin away from my jugular vein, wrenched at the gear-stick, drove me back to the highway without looking at me, and said, 'Get out.' As she was driving off, she waved a long arm wildly above her head, once, without looking back.

I stayed in Townsville for a day, beside the light-threaded waters of the Great Barrier Reef, and then went out and waited at the edge of town again, in the late afternoon, the slightly cooler time. A timber truck I had not hailed pulled over. It was driven by someone sun-scarred, middle-aged, with greasy black crewcut and stiff, grease-blackened hands. His son, twelve years old, was beside him – flabby, friendly, and retarded. After I had climbed up into the high cabin, the father chatted a little, over the top of the boy, and then asked if I could read. He could not. He wanted me to help with some legal papers, in return for which he would give me dinner and, if I wanted to stay on, use of a house he was building a little way up the coast, which had a completed room in it. The house, I was told, was on a headland, facing the sea, and just a walk along the beach from a general store.

The man did not want people from Townsville knowing he was unable to read, because some might take advantage of him. He was worth money, he said. The only time he stopped for hitch-hikers was when he needed help with business that could be done without a solicitor.

It seemed a safe thing to go home with them, since the boy was talking about his mother and sister in an obviously unrehearsed and affectionate way. Shortly we turned off the highway and went along a hard, sandy road, between ragged trees, on which the drooping leaves might have been blue mistletoe. It was dusk when we came into a big clearing where the house was, with swamp oaks scattered between us and the sea. The low house stood in a copse of these thin trees; their dried brown needles covered it with thatch and padded the ground so deeply that it was spongy underfoot. I could see old trucks lying around in the gloom. There was lamplight in the oil-blackened, wooden house, a place that appeared to have grown horizontally, by accretion, over many years. Its disjointed silhouette was halfway settled into the earth; just 'a swelling of the ground', as Emily Dickinson says of the house that she imagines Death bringing her to in his carriage.

When I stepped down inside the house, things were all right. The wife slipped in her teeth, at the kitchen sink, and came to greet me, warmly, hobbled by her weight. The daughter was partly vacant, although not so much as the son; she was a teen-ager, already beginning to struggle with a baggage of breasts and hips. An older son was like the father, crop-headed, balding in his twenties, big-framed, watchful and quiet. The dim interior of the house seemed medieval. There were floors on slightly different levels, in the large, open living area, and the furniture looked homemade, in dark, heavy wood. The creosote-treated timbers of the house were as dark as soot. We gathered for our drinks at a table which deserved to be called a 'board'.

After dinner, papers were carefully served up, a lamp was positioned for me, the father leaned on his thick forearms across the table, intent. I spent the next couple of hours reading and re-reading to him, plucking the small berries of meaning from a rebarbative language. There were several issues, but the main one was to do with a building company contesting that it owed the amount of money he had invoiced; they claimed incomplete delivery. Even while I was reading silently, he kept up his watchfulness. The elder son was in the background; resentful, I thought, and embarrassed when I caught him watching. Eventually, the father seemed satisfied with my work. He then raised another matter, the main one. He wanted me to write a letter to the young man who was the sole teacher at the local school, saying he had 'evidence' that the teacher had been 'playing with' his daughter, and asking 'what he was going to do about it'. What did he mean, I said. Did he mean, marry her, or what? It sounded like money was being demanded. What they should do was see the police. Was the girl still going to the school? She was. And she had to wait around the school until she could be picked up. The father grinned. 'He's a randy young dog, that Mr Cheney.' I told them it would be crazy to write such a letter: they would lose all their standing before the law. The mother said anxiously, 'We just want him to do the right thing.' The daughter stamped out of the room, wailing. I said, 'See the police, and don't leave your daughter around the school by herself.' 'We have a witness,' the father said. 'That Cheney's been here at my house for a meal. He said she's a bit slow, my girl. He's a bit fast, I reckon. I'll have a talk with him. You reckon not write? He'll want to keep it quiet, I say.'

While tea was served, I went outside to clear my head of woodsmoke. I saw that the place was built near the banks of what appeared to be a lagoon, with mangroves on the further shore. There were cattle nearby; I could hear an irritable bellow; and down by the water's edge there were the red eyes of dogs. I turned towards the moonlit plain of the sea, through the tree trunks, moving tentatively on the dark ground; but then the father came up and suggested that I come back inside: the bellowing and the red eyes belonged to crocodiles, which came out of the water at night and lay on the bank.

I slept somewhere in the house, in a heavy, hewn bunk, and early the next morning the father drove me, through a big hairpin shape, for what turned out to be just a short way along the coast, to the new house he was building. It stood in the open, at the root of a bare headland, looking directly on the sea, with one over-reaching crude fig tree for shade.

The place was large, but almost all scaffolding; it had some tin roofing at the front, and beneath this was a roughly completed big room, still raw. There was a water tank on a raised wooden stand attached to it. When you went around to the front, you saw there were double glass doors closing off this living area, locked with a chain, beyond a completed sundeck, and an awning. Inside, the room had masonite walls, rough diagrams and numerals pencilled on them. It had a narrow iron bedstead, for my sleeping bag, a broom, buckets, a plastic wash dish, plates in a draining stand, lanterns, a metal boiler, and an electric jug and hotplate, fed by a single strand of cable that went looping back through the trees beside the dirt road. I could see the roofs of a few shops and houses from the front deck, above the tree-tops, along the bay. The place had not been vandalised, although, by the colour of its timber, it must have been standing there for years. I said I would like to stay a few weeks.

Of a day, I walked along the shore, or spent my time on the deck. A wide rattan blind was slung there, to be lowered against the light, its fibrous shadow on planks and canvas chairs. I ate under the awning, meals of fruit and cheese, sardines or baked beans with bread and salad, dates and milk. It was never unbearably hot, because it was winter in other parts of the southern world.

I watched the dilated yachts, drifting bubbles that had disappeared into the vaporous light the next time I looked, the schooners with segmented canvas, the cruisers and fishing boats. On the beach, the sand had the whiteness of salt. The water was lime-coloured and blue in swathes, like a cocktail. There was just a sluice of waves on the shore, no surf. Pandanus palms were propped on their stilted roots at the edge of the sand, the driest wood that lives. From the rocks going out from shore, you could look in on the coral of the Reef: it seemed a New Year's explosion of fireworks, hung within a sky. I had been warned not to go into the water without something on my feet, because of the paralysing stone fish that lay shallow in the sand.

I wondered what I could do for work, as I read the local papers or listened to a portable radio I had brought. I wrote assiduously in my notebook. I thought I might go further north and find a job at a resort, or else work on the newspaper in Townsville, the biggest town nearby, for a couple of days a week. I tried ringing the editor from a phonebox at the general store, but each time he was busy and his secretary asked for my number.

I washed and pegged out all my clothes and the sheet from my sleeping bag and came back to myself standing under the clothes line, shading my eyes and gazing at the blackened shapes of the islands, in pointillist water. I felt adrift, between heaven and earth.

Sometimes I walked up the dirt track, leading off the headland, into a close, shadowy forest, as a relief at midday. Coming back, I saw the empty shapes made by the house's framework, its rectangles, triangles, stripes, coloured in halfway up their height by the sea. At night, moonlight spread across the ocean, like the sheen on a black fuselage.

For days, there was a bushfire somewhere behind me. It was a vast acridity of burning leaves and an oxygen-depleting additional heat. The sky became filled, high up, with heavily swagged, rolling clouds, that were glary, bright apricot in colour during daylight and in the long dusks an earthy brown. The night sky seemed gauze, of luminous dark grey, with the reddish glow of a city somewhere near. Black ash fell like drifting snow, and at times whole blackened leaves, which were perfect fossils, but they crumbled when picked up. No one came from the store to tell me to move, so I remained as blasé as they were. I thought I could put my bag on a plank and paddle into the sea, if I had to.

People talked to me when I went to the store; old men suggested we sit on a bench beneath the trees. If I asked about work, they said maybe I could be a tour guide or a hotel porter – anything was better than cutting cane, eh? That wouldn't be my line, or theirs. I sent postcards home, from the store, as I had done at every opportunity on the way up the highway. They were addressed 'Dear Mum and Kids', or 'Mum, Dad and Kids'. I was unable to bring myself to write 'Dear Dad'; it sounded somehow ridiculous.

I met a woman of about seventy, walking on the beach; I had seen her most days: she used to wade through the water in shorts and sandshoes and gaze into it with goggles, while holding her canvas hat. She was lean and preoccupied and always alone. Her thighs and bare arms were so deeply tanned they looked smoked, and were as lined as old timber. We stopped and spoke a couple of times, and then she invited me to dinner. She was a marine biologist, retired from the University of Melbourne, who lived by herself in a caravan, just off the beach, and who moved about Queensland. We made a fire on the sand, between stones, over which to cook in a frying pan. She had a beaked nose, hair that was ringleted, salty-looking, still partly black, a cultivated voice, a peremptory manner. She told me I should be in school, that I may be seventeen but was totally unrealistic, living without forethought. Her suggestion that we do an interview, she said, was only because it might start me earning money. Already, in those days, she spoke about the pollution and coming destruction of the Reef; she was ahead of her time, also, in the way that she emphasised 'men' had done this. Power boats, plastic and oil disgusted her. After dinner, sitting on the sand, she introduced me to a treat of hers, because the night breeze had an edge to it: she heated milk in a can on the fire, into which pieces of a chocolate bar were broken and dissolved. She liked her drink thick, finishing it with a spoon.

After another meal together, she brought out an old paperback and asked me to read some poems to her. Her sight wasn't good enough for that, at night. One she asked for was 'Dover Beach', which, when I finished, left her sitting in a glassy-eyed silence for a long while, gazing into the dark. 'Very fine,' she said. 'That's it, isn't it:

And we are here as on a darkling plain
Swept with confused alarms of struggle and flight,
Where ignorant armies clash by night.'

One evening, just over two weeks after I had arrived at the headland, someone tried to break into the room where I was staying, when I was half asleep. I heard a brief stumbling and a grunt outside and was awake in an instant. Then nothing more. After a while, I drowsed. There was a single window to one side of the locked glass doors, propped up on an insect screen which could be removed, and because it was a dark night I only gradually became aware that a silhouetted figure was squeezing in under the sash – a leg had already been lowered inside. My friend at the beach had leant me, that evening, a torch to show my way home. I aimed the beam, onto someone crouched there and still – I saw a bare, thick male leg in shorts, doubled-up like a praying mantis leg. 'Get out of here,' I yelled. The torch wavered over a person shielding his face, outside the glass, with an arm. I had a weapon by the bed because I was aware of my isolation – a piece of rusty steel rod, left over from among similar ones cemented into the foundations of the house and standing like the rough beginnings of basketwork. I had picked it up because it was the length of a spear and had a broken-off sharp end. The torch was in my left hand, in my right

I had the weapon. Swinging out of bed, legs in the sleeping bag, yelling again, I drew back and hurled my spear toward the figure, who was seemingly stuck in that horribly doubled-over position. I flung with all my boyhood practice behind my hand; but even as I aimed, I flinched momentarily from propelling the piece of steel into a person. I aimed a little to the side of that powerful, black-haired leg, involuntarily. The spear drove through the fibreboard and waggled there, and almost in the same instant the leg flailed like a scalded snake and was gone. The window crashed shut.

I stepped over and screeched the length of metal out of the wall, and then sat up for the rest of the night, wrapped in my sleeping bag, nodding off, weapon in hand. What worried me was that I understood, from observation, how people who are mainly physical take badly to being bettered in their one means of expression. I decided that I should move on, further north; I was sure, without having exactly recognised him, that the person who had tried to break in was the elder son of the owner of the place.

In the morning, keeping an eye over my shoulder, I packed up and ate breakfast, then returned the torch. There was no one at the van, but I found my friend on the shore. She said she had never been bothered by anyone; naturally enough, she thought, because she was old; but she had a weapon; in fact, several of them, hidden around her van. She was quite detached about me going: she thought it the only thing to do.

I went out to the road and walked on northwards, with some anxiety about who might come along. All at once, I felt weary of being prey, from all directions. I had for some while been conscious that this was ultimately what each of us was: prey to nature's chances, and to others of our kind; we, the sick cousins of the apes. I realised things were worse if one were a straggler on the edge of the group. It could only be through work that I might belong to something; through a craft. In those days it was possible to think of journalism in such a way. I would take it seriously, as though it might be a long-term career. One could live unknown, just as well, in the city; not isolated, as here, beneath the sun's magnifying glass.

With this thought, I crossed the road and stood on the side leading back towards the south's more temperate valley.

13. With Cords of Water

As I remember, I dropped back through Queensland as if I were abseiling. I caught naps in the cars that stopped for me and washed at the tap behind a garage. Outside Brisbane, I waited by a road that ran through pineapple fields, and noticed a metal-frame telephone box on the close horizon, near a few houses. The telephonist gave me the number of a neighbour of ours, and I rang to leave a message for my mother; but the neighbour said she could see my mother in our front garden and would call her. The woman seemed excited. I had enough change left to tell my mother I was on my way home, and to hear her say that she was relieved.

When I crossed into New South Wales, rain was falling as though something were broken, and was said to have settled in all down the coast. I waited for my next lift under the awning at a service station a long while, the highway almost empty. I was wet and shivering. Rain smoked off the big concrete driveway. I spoke to people who pulled up. A man and woman were going to try to get to Sydney before the rivers flooded and agreed to take me. I used not to tell drivers my exact destination, in case boredom or bad driving made me want to get down sooner.

The trip became nothing but scalding rain, headlights looming by day. The people in the front seat were agog, having some
urgent reason to make the journey, trying to listen to the radio for
news. In one town, where we stopped for a meal, we were advised
not to go on.

Lights burned in the towns and along the highway. When trucks
wailed by above, surf fell on us. I remember thinking excitedly that
we were getting near my stop, but there was not enough oxygen in
the back of the car and I was exhausted; I fell asleep. When I woke,
it was night. I made out the broken shapes of a forest outside, and
the slowing machinery of rain. I asked where we were, and was
horrified to hear that we had just passed through a town about
sixty miles beyond my unspoken destination. I had slept for hours.
The driver said they had been told theirs was the last car the police
would allow through.

They let me out at a truck drivers' café, and I picked up a lift
almost immediately, which would take me a short way back: this
from 'a family man' (so he told me) who had come to see his girlfriend in the carpark there. He was stocking up on cigarettes, as an
excuse. He offered to put me up at his house, but I said no.

The man went past his turn-off and took me as far as he could,
to where a large bridge was barricaded. The rain had paused. The
river was vast and shapeless and we could hear it roaring like a
continuous landslide, in the dark. He drove up a side road onto
an empty hillside and we had a view across the massively driven,
rotating water, lit up by the bridge lights. The river was passing
just under the causeway, mud-coloured and breaking into foam. It
seemed to be tumbling out of a hydro-electricity dam. Beyond the
far end of the bridge, which was fully lit as usual, along its opened-
out concertina frame, water had spread through the town, to the
level of the shop awnings. In the river, trees plunged by, torn out
by the roots. My companion grew more than ever excited when we

saw, carried out from beneath the bridge, a horse – the chess piece of a horse, and its fore-feet – swimming bravely amid that great surge, and headed out to sea.

That man took me a little way back along the highway, just over a rise, to a service station with a '24 Hours' sign, among a few houses, and he dropped me there. When I went into the shop, the attendant said he could not see much point in staying open; he was going home. I could sleep, he reluctantly supposed, on the shop floor: it had never flooded there. He was doing me a favour, he said, that could cause him trouble. I had seen, on the rising ground opposite, above the road, an old cemetery, and in it a picnic shelter, a pitched tin roof over a wooden table and benches; I would be more comfortable there, I told him, than on cement.

I laid my haversack and shoes on one of the seats, under the shelter, climbed into my sleeping bag on the table top, and curled up. I woke to hear that the rain had come on again. By a streetlight near the grounds, I saw a cage of rain all around me, with its bars endlessly compounding. The noise grew stronger, and stronger, as if the rain were raising the stakes against itself, but under that low roof I remained completely dry. I hung there, exalted.

In the morning, the rain had stopped, although there were still low clouds, and I discovered where I was: the graveyard (an empty grey auditorium), the garage, and four houses in fibro and timber, were completely cut off, by water that was the colour of cold, milky tea. A few other small islands, with trees on them, lay around, and everywhere, vastly, there was slowly moving water, stretching away through the tree-tops. The trees were the sort of ragged, non-descript eucalypts with hang-dog leaves and bark that look forlorn at any time.

Children waved to me excitedly from a front window, down the slope, across a chopped-off section of highway. I shaved by touch, washed my face and torso under a tap, and used the public lavatory at the garage. No one was around.

I had just got back to my shelter when a stocky woman in rubber boots came walking up to me. She carried an umbrella and a dinner plate covered with a saucepan lid. 'Here's somethin' t' keep y' goin'. Where y' from?'

After we had chatted a bit, she invited me to have a bath, later in the day, though I would have to bring my own towel; all of hers were damp.

'Y' mother know where y' are?' She said I could ask to use the phone at the garage, when it opened.

The breakfast was fried eggs and tomatoes and buttered toast. She had no thermos, but I could get a cup of tea when I brought the plate back.

I had rinsed the plate and taken it back, gratefully, and was starting off to explore the other end of the ridge on which I was isolated when a rowboat came out of the tree-tops, with two girls in it, who called out to me. They sat 'offshore' and I saw they were about my age. It was the thin, dark-haired one who did the talking; the tall one with long brown hair sat with her head lowered a little, playing with her hair like a harpist.

'You have a séance here last night?' asked the thin girl, who said her name was Valerie; the other was called Sue. 'I've had a séance here,' she said. 'It was creepy. The glass was completely out of control. This is a very haunted graveyard, you know.'

I told her I hadn't been bothered by any ghosts. Didn't she know that ghosts hate getting their bedsheets wet?

'Have you heard a weather forecast,' I asked. 'When's it going to go down? I'm just wondering about food. I don't want the people around here having to feed me – they've probably all got kids.'

'It's stopped raining up-stream. It'll take a few days, maybe a week. So, you're a traveller in distress. Do you want to be rescued?

We've come to get some milk for Sue's little brother, from the service station. We have to go straight back. Come for the row, if you like.'

The shop at the service station was unlocked. They told me it was always kept like that at flood time. We left money for two bottles of milk on the counter. They worried whether taking two was all right. 'That lazy bugger, Brian,' they decided, could go and get some more; the road was open, further along, leading to the next town south. I bought them each a chocolate bar.

We rowed off, through the trees, taking it in turns, someone sitting in the front and saying, 'Pull on the right, more on the right. Look out for the branch.' There was a drowned road nearby, marked by the tops of telephone poles, along which the girls lived. We took a short cut, veering away among many big trees, their powerful branches spreading straight off the water, like chopped-off broccoli.

Sue got out barefooted in a soggy paddock, after we had poled in as far as we could. It was curious to see the still perfectly formed short grass looking upwards through the water. A hundred yards away was the back fence and the back of Sue's house, with smoke. She had sat braiding and unbraiding her hair for most of the ride. She wished me good luck, and said she would see her friend in a couple of days, when the witch let her out again. Then she said, not looking at me, 'I just want you to know that she's a virgin. So don't try anything.' She started to run off, with splashing high steps.

'Huh. Listen to you,' Valerie called after her. 'You're certainly not one.'

'I am so.'

'What about Reggie?'

'It was just his finger.'

'That's what he told you it was.'

They waved with the whole arm to each other, and I pulled

away, looking over my shoulder, although we were in the clear.

'Don't worry about her. You're not scared, are you? Let's go and see what it's like at the sawmill.'

Valerie was what we used to call 'peppy': talkative, vivacious. She told me that she lived with her father, who had a small dairy farm, just over there. Her mother and father were separated. The mother lived in Sydney with Valerie's elder sister, and Valerie was staying on with the father until she finished high school, then she would join them. She wanted to go to university and to wear black stockings and sit in coffee shops smoking cigarettes. The mother worked in a factory, now; she was quite a few years younger than Valerie's dad, and she deserved some life. She was good-looking; she would probably meet a rich man. Her dad was hopeless; he had had an accident in 'the timber industry' and had put the compensation he received into dairy cattle, which brought in nothing, for all the work that you did. She cut her hair herself, nearly every day, making tiny adjustments, with two mirrors: what did I think? Her black hair was in a meticulous fringe and bob, a shiny helmet. I admired it. I said she could get a job as a hairdresser. No, I was told, her sister was doing that.

What remained above water at the sawmill was a long tin roof, slightly sagging, and an incinerator chimney. Several piles of timber rose out of the flood: thick beams stacked in squares, built with a crane. The overlapping of the wood at the cornices provided easy hand-holds and footing. We climbed up and sat on top of one of the stacks that was about half the size of a boxing ring and ate oranges that Valerie had brought in her backpack. She had been going to stay out rowing. After a while, I went down to get an umbrella from the boat, and we sat together beneath that, amongst the fine blowing grey hair of the rain. The boat had left a wake, slowly softening, because the water around the mill was thickly coated with sawdust. Also afloat were a great many sawn pieces of timber, off-cuts, and sheets of plywood. There was so much debris, a ship might have gone down. All of it was beginning to be dragged slowly in one direction, towards the distant attraction of the river.

Valerie's face was wide-eyed and broad-mouthed, with a strong short nose, slightly tilted at the end. Her eyes were a remarkable deep brown. Except for them, and her pointed chin, she looked like a cat. She was wiry and flat-chested. Like a cat, her manner was at one moment independent and self-willed and the next caressing.

She took me home so that she could make her father lunch. This meant heating a tin of soup and buttering some toast. We were to have the same. When he came in, taking off his boots before walking on the worn lino, dressed in floppy shorts and a pullover, she said to him, 'Look what I found.'

Her father, bone and sinew, weathered, dark-haired, his hair like short, rough grass on the top of a bank, with painful-looking, protrudent cheekbones, was diffident and, you could sense, depressed. He said grace for us. Then he tore the bread with a hand that had only the thumb and a stump of little finger left on it, and was still purple. His daughter was obviously attached to him, for all her ordering him about. She made him take off his wet socks and draped them before a radiator, though he hopelessly protested about her using it in the day.

Mr Morris heard my story and said at once that I was welcome to stay with them. He might get me to help a little bit, in the next few days, before the water went down: he was working on his tractor. Valerie said I could pull up all the beetroot and cut the cabbages, because they would rot. She had school work she had to do; it was her last year.

I was given her sister's room, and was told I could ring up and leave a message for my mother, but was not allowed to pay. We rowed back and picked up my haversack and the towel I had spread to dry in the rafters of the shelter, and I told the woman who had given me breakfast that I had been taken in. Going back to the Morris's plank and fibro house, we scraped ashore on the bitumen road, not far from where they lived. The boat was usually kept in a creek, nearby. At the house, I chopped a pile of wood, under a canvas awning, by the kitchen. I went to the shed and talked to Mr Morris, passing him tools, adjusting wrenches for him, holding wires together. I lay on the carpet in their living room with Valerie and listened to some records. Before dinner, I went and had a shower, and she pushed open the door a little and watched me from the doorway, not trying to hide, wiping her hands on a tea towel. 'Don't take too long,' she said. 'Food's almost ready.'

The next morning, we went out rowing again. I plucked a spray of the topmost leaves from a sapling gum tree, as we drifted by, and chose two, curved like drawn eyebrows, dampened them and stuck them, close together, over her own brows. She looked like a gypsy dancer, I told her. She leapt up and snapped her fingers and stamped, happily rocking us about. Then I remembered a bottle of sun lotion in the pocket of my jacket, and I moistened some leaves from this and made myself sideburns and a drooping moustache – 'The Magician'. I carefully tore out Native American markings and arranged them on her face. We found some beautiful long gum leaves and I put eye-holes in them with a pencil and we wore them as cat-eyed masks. When those fell off, small feathery leaves were arranged across her forehead, to make a coronet. All of this was, of course, an excuse for touching.

We rowed around, laughing and idle, through a labyrinth of trees, into a place that she said was a state forest. The complicated smooth branches, among which we hung, strangely elevated, ran with wobbly rings of light. Even high on the boles of the trees, their coarse fur was fire-blackened. Sunlight came in and made every alcove, under the closely overarching branches, a grotto, with its wavering phosphorescence.

'"There is nothing, absolutely nothing, half so worth doing as simply messing about in boats,"' I told her, in a quoting manner.

'Who said that? Lord Nelson?'

'No, that's the Water Rat, speaking to the Mole.'

'Really. Well, you're the burrowing animal, so I must be the Water Rat.'

She laughed at my startled look. I was sitting with my legs together, stretched out between her legs, as she rowed. She raised the oars, lifted herself forward on them, and kissed me, glancingly.

When we got home, she wanted to do some homework; she put on a record of the 'Moonlight Sonata', and the 'Rhapsody on a Theme of Paganini' and other selections, and I helped with an essay, stretched out on the carpet beside her. Before dinner, 'tea' as we called it, I went to have my shower, as the water had reheated by then, and she came and watched me from the door, again. I thought I should say, 'Do you want to come in?', while I was dry-ing. She said, 'You come out here.' I pulled my jeans and shirt on; she drew me into the living room and told me to sit on a chair, with my back to the main window. She opened the venetian blinds a little, so she could see out into the yard, over my shoulder. Then she pulled down my jeans to my thighs, and gathering up her dress in one hand, straddled my lap, leaning her free arm heavily on my shoulder and kissing me. She rubbed herself on me, and lowered her hips gradually, as someone lowers carefully, backwards, off a parapet, withdrawing and then gathering courage again; biting her lip, smiling, and sighing. I held up her dress for her. Neither of us spoke. When she had finally sunk right down, she kissed me deeply, and began smoothly to roll her hips, less and less carefully, on my groin. When she stood up, there was a butterfly of watery blood across her thighs, and I was shocked, but she only laughed. She told me that she had read a recommendation for doing things the first time in this way, in a book her sister owned, which she had kept for herself.

During the next few days, we went out in the boat and moored among one or another dense group of trees and performed variations on our enlightenment. We took the book she had mentioned, hidden under my jacket. It was an old paperback, illustrated with clinical-looking drawings of what might have been tailor's dummies, the theme of which seemed to be how someone should go about getting pregnant.

Valerie had retroussé small breasts and a high, hard bottom. I remember that I made some jokes, about the aft-position at the bow and the fore-position at the stern, and about sitting athwart a thwart, and that she told me to shut up and get on with it.

Against the side of the boat there collected a wide matting of leaves, twigs and straw, and we saw this drawn off along the clay-coloured water, caught in a strengthening traction.

Neither of us knew anything about contraceptives, nor seems to have cared, taking as enough reassurance her belief that it was near the time for her period. We slept separately, on the three nights I was there after our confusing sense of trespass, although I could hear her father snoring – a sound like furniture being moved on bare floorboards. She crept in and kissed me goodnight briefly, with the faintest of whispering.

At mealtimes, and during the evenings, we talked with her father warmly, ungrudgingly, and listened to the radio with him. We only brushed against each other, lightly, going in and out of doors. Her father thought I had said I was reading a book on poultry, a practical hobby he commended me for. He gave me advice about Rhode Island Reds and Orpingtons and laying mash and how to get a good-coloured shell. Valerie would leave the room to make tea at these times, clenching her stomach, I thought.

After a few days, the floodwater had gone. The air, in the sunlight, became Vaseline on glass. At times, it was a wobbling jelly. Everything steamed like breakfast. There was long matted grass hung from the forks of the trees, and mudbanks in the middle of the road.

I quietly left the last money that I had on the sideboard, in the morning, went to the bales and spoke to Mr Morris, and then Valerie and I walked to the junction of their road and the highway. She pushed her bike, wearing a box-pleated school uniform. I crossed the highway and she waited on the other side, so as not to confuse drivers about my intention. We shouted back and forth. 'I'll write.' 'Don't lose that address.' 'Thank your father again.' 'Say hullo to your mother. Do you think I could visit?' 'Don't stay. You'll be late.' A lift came suddenly. A truck stopped, blocking our view of each other; and when I tried to wave out of the back window there was a canopy in the way.

A letter came to my parents' house within a couple of days. She had told her father she wanted me to come back and stay at weekends, and that she wanted to visit me, and he had said he knew very well what would happen, if she was feeling like that. He wasn't having it. In an argument that followed she defiantly said it already had happened, and so he forbad my return or her to have any contact with me.

I found a job almost immediately on my return home, with the local newspaper, thanks to a reference from my English teacher. He insisted that the way to be taken on by a big city paper, which I said was my intention, was through experience in the country. I wrote to Valerie, who could intercept their mail at a post office box, with this news, and on the first Saturday after I was in work, I took the morning train to her town. She met me at the station, with her bike, very nervous in case her father or someone he knew saw us. I doubled her on the bike to the edge of town and we sat in an empty football grandstand, an arm around each other. It was a cold day; a row of poplars had their leaves turned silvery side out, and washing flew horizontal in backyards. Some children came and idly threw stones on the roof above us, which trickled down its incline. I went and bought lunch. There was no chance of making love: the toilets were too dank. Valerie said her father was a 'fanatic'; he had struck her mother more than once and she was afraid of him. She had blamed her mother but now she could see the other side. She was shivering and her arms had broken out in a rash, within the last two weeks. Then she had to leave, to be home on time. We parted at the railway station, she in tears; so changed from the boisterous girl she had been.

I had to wait four hours for a train, staying out of sight, on the platform, as I had promised. I watched a tethered cow grazing on the far side of the tracks, a few swallows making long, low runs among the weeds of the railway yard, and had only a newspaper to read. My mother was worried when I got home late, with my claim to have been 'just walking', along the coast; she could see I was exhausted.

We continued to write, Valerie using pages of a school exercise book. She said her eczema was bothering her. She was unable to study. Then her mother wanted her to go to Sydney, after her father had written complaining of her. He wanted her to leave, too: he said that Valerie had been disloyal, like her mother. He kept saying she was like her mother. He was not really the subdued man I had known when I was there, she told me; that was just a good face for a visitor. His real nature was hard and suspicious.

Then she wrote to me from the city: she was going to fail her exams and wanted to repeat the year. Her mother was furious. She had been told that she would have to get a job in a shop. Perhaps I could come to Sydney and marry her.

I was horrified at the thought: I had always assured myself, from when I was a small boy, that I would never be married. Not enough had happened to change my mind. Besides, I was a person who lived in a cul-de-sac, with an ending to it that was fog-bound but perhaps somewhere near. Such an understanding might be pushed aside by me; it was not something I wanted to tell her about.

As soon as I was back in my parents' house, I felt taken over again by a spirit of endurance and fatalism. I was embarrassed at a romantic relationship, when there. At the same time, I was aware of a new confidence. My mother said I had grown up; even my father minimised his jibes, now that I was in work. I could feel Valerie being drawn away, to the edges of my mind, and felt ashamed; I wrote fervently to her, against that feeling.

My letters – sent *post restante* to a suburb of Sydney I had never heard of – grew sparser, and more and more contained 'news' and evasions. And then, after angry words from her in writing, and a couple of constrained, embarrassing phone calls at my work, which I had asked her not to make, I realised one day that I would never hear from her again.

14. By Craft Alone

Although employed by the local newspaper as a cadet, I had to write the lead stories almost at once. These were sub-edited under my gaze, which often meant under my protests. Standing behind the editor's shoulder, watching him cross out and rewrite, I believed painfully in my own judgements, and thought that practical writing need not be so neglectful of rhythm.

By defending my articles, I could have phrases and whole paragraphs reinstated. At other times, unsuccessful in saving what I had written, but anxious to do so, since there would be a by-line, I delivered my marked-up copy to the workshop via the lavatory, where I had forged the word 'stet' at places in the margins.

My guess, that the editor, who was old and always busy, would not bother to read his newspaper again the next day, or would glance only at his own stories, proved right, on those numerous occasions.

But I was aware of learning through being edited, and felt grateful. I was also taught, with more submission on my part, to lay out pages, using an ems rule, to report sporting events, to design advertisements, to proofread, and (late at night) to insert the last hot aluminium 'slugs', the lines of corrected type from the linotype machine, into the metal forms – back to front and upside down – and how to lock those up and lay them, weightily, on the press bed.

I wore an apron in the back room and washed the ink from my hands and forearms at a filthy handbasin, with sandsoap. In the news room, I put on my jacket, ran up my tie again, and sat trying to make sense of someone's letter to the editor, or of the notes from the ladies bowling club (by 'Without Bias', our correspondent), consulting the writers and rewording their submissions on the phone.

I went to Council meetings, Lions Club meetings, meetings of the Country Women's Association, watched football games and horse racing, telephoned every day to the ambulance station, the hospital and the police, became the court reporter, attended political speeches and school prize-givings, and wrote my stories with two fingers on a black Remington typewriter which looked like an upright piano and made the sound of a sten gun.

The newspaper office, a low, industrial-design brick building, had a sawtoothed profile, its ranks of dirty skylights. It stood between a vacant lot, of tall grass, on which a listless horse made little progress, and a fibro house with a bank of frosted louvre windows facing the world and pink hydrangeas above a low brick fence. Across the potholed, bitumen street stood a bakery, the brick side wall of which, at certain places, could scorch your hand. In winter, the printers ate their lunch with backs leaned against carefully chosen parts of the wall – for which they scuffled – and looked into a used-car yard.

The bakery had a regular advertisement in the paper and the printers used this to play a joke on me, as my initiation. I was meant to proofread the day's advertising, which I did last thing, but on this occasion I had to deal first with additions to a story of mine. It was getting late when I read the proofs, in a hurry. Pleased with the story I had just finished, I skimmed confidently through the more simple ads, including the bakery's, and let them go. Only one compositor was left at work, who was supposed to save me at the last minute, while pretending that the advertisement had gone to press, but somehow the others had forgotten to warn him that the back room would be running its immemorial trick on newcomers that night. The paper came out the next morning with the joke advertisement in place. Headed 'O'Riley's Bakery', as usual, below that was a line of seductively wriggling italics saying 'Freshly Made', and then in megaphonic sixty-point condensed black capitals, one letter substituted, the offer of HOT PISS.

The ad filled almost a quarter of the front page, with a decorative border. The whole town was said to be laughing. My father's amusement, that evening, took the form of mocking at my 'rag of a paper'. I argued it was nothing to do with me, it was the proofreaders, but he said that he had heard I did 'all the menial jobs'.

The printers and I had to cross the street and apologise to a man who we agreed, on our way back, well deserved the embarrassment we had caused him. He was given free advertising for six months. The editor, when he calmed down, said that at least I had been taught the first lesson of newspaper work, which was 'Check the obvious, especially the obvious, and what you're not interested in.' He said I might notice I was saved from his real anger; this was because of my 'fine general contribution' to his 'journal', and because I was probably being overworked.

Apart from the editor, the paper employed a part-time senior journalist, retired from the city, who seemed mainly interested in his pipe (he usually wrote the sport and would not report meetings), an advertising salesman, doubling as our photo-grapher, two office girls, two linotype operators, a pair of lank, slow apprentices, a senior compositor, a man who attended to and ran the immaculate press ('the Beast we worship', the editor said), who also did job printing in the day, and me.

The editor and I got on well, despite my occasional recalcitrance. I learned from him about 'Checking for Clarity' and about 'How to Achieve Speed of Syntax'. When we first met, he had said, 'What's beyond a glowing recommendation? A radiant one? That's what we have here, my boy, from your school teacher.' He seemed pleased on my behalf, and I was surprised at his generosity. He never, thereafter, tried to mortify my gangling ego, perhaps because he could see that beneath it I was eager to learn; or perhaps because I had had the sense to acknowledge, in my interview, that I knew the teacher's praise was only relative to my age.

The editor seemed always to be writing, and always in biro. One big, flour-white hand, stiff as a flipper, continued to work while he spoke to me, scrawling paragraphs on short pieces of copy paper and thumping them face-down for his secretary to take. She gathered a little bundle at a time, knowing the rate at which he worked, and spiked it beside a linotype operator. The editor continued to write while he answered the phone – his pen hovered a moment as he listened, then crossed a 't', dotted an 'i', scored out a word, and went on again, through his conversation.

On the wall behind his desk hung a tweed jacket and felt hat, above his cow-licked white hair, his overgrown eyebrows, like snow-bowed grass, his scalloped jawline and long nose, his humped back in a starched white shirt, and his deep upper body, almost prostrate on the wide desk. When he spoke he rolled his eyes up to you, without much raising his head. He was like a big, white, mild walrus, come ashore. Between us, we ground out four issues of the paper a week.

I was taught about writing by being given Hazlitt's essays. '"On Gusto",' the editor announced, passing me a selection of his favourite author's work. '"Gusto in art is passion defining a subject".' Then he remembered himself. 'But that's for your own writing, of course. Here we must be Dispassionate. That's our first rule. From Hazlitt you can learn, for your work here, Immediacy. He has wonderful Immediacy. And notice his Compression, without there being any loss of Clarity.' He told me I needed to adjust my style quickly, to what was appropriate for a news story: he didn't have time to edit my work. It was not appropriate for me to say that the football players left the field, in the wintry dusk, steaming like steers in a cattleyard after rain. Not for a newspaper. He understood I was trying to appeal to the local mentality, but it didn't work like that. Just say that So-and-so picked up Thingamajig and slammed him upside down into the ground, on the twenty-five yard line. Don't worry about clichés. The reader would miss them, if you didn't put them in. Clichés are an important part of sports writing. Don't let Hercules and Antaeus even cross your mind, at such a time. (I had not.) He talked me down to earth, without a bump.

And then, overnight, he was gone from the job – a gentle, cultivated man, treated crudely. The company had a new board member, who wanted a more aggressive editor, someone he knew from Sydney. One day, without warning, a little curly-haired, baggy-eyed man, with sleeve links and a bow tie, and a vicious, squinted style of smoking, was among us. He seemed to be constantly moving in and out of the press room and the printing shop, alternating between a scuttle and a strut. We were called together, to what was now this man's office. 'I've done it the hard way,' he told us. 'My whole life's been spent in the gutter – the gutter press. I wouldn't have had it any different. Now that means I am used to making stories, not waiting for them. It means we're going to excite this town, get it talking…'

One of the first jobs he assigned me was to interview the family of a woman who had committed suicide. We would never have touched anything like that, before. She had filled her child's school satchel with bricks, late at night, wound the strap around her neck, and jumped off the end of the jetty. I was meant to go to the family house, obtain a photograph of her, and talk to the husband and the older daughters, whom I knew slightly. Did the fact that a supermarket had opened, just down the street from their general store, have anything to do with the tragedy? Find out. No, I said, I couldn't do such a thing. It was that or my job, the editor told me, waving me away. But it was too ill-mannered, I argued. People wouldn't like it. I knew what people would like, better than he did? Besides, he had found I had been skipping shorthand classes, at the tech college, when he checked on me. So I had to win his confidence. Now, did I have the stuff...? It would have to be my job, I told him.

I had been there over a year, and had enjoyed it. There was nothing for me now but a precipitate move to Sydney. The former editor must have heard the news: he invited me to his house for afternoon tea, and offered me a reference. We sat alone, his wife somewhere in the house, bedridden. (I heard he had been forced to give up the nurse he formerly employed.) He told me not to be put off by my experience (which I was actually not worried by): journalism was a wonderful and worthwhile profession, and he wished me well in it. He would watch for my by-line.

While I was working and living at home I noticed a further change in my father. He had become, when sober, more taciturn and more bitter-looking. There was the same ominous skull, but it was brooding rather than vindictively aware. His tongue was curt but constrained. He was noticeably more weary: on staggering inside of an evening, he wanted to go straight to bed.

Sober, he still had some playful moments. He remarked, after my mother had scolded him, that she must have been reading 'a cross word dictionary', and referred to receiving 'a dressing-down in a dressing-gown'. He showed me a news story in the Sydney press about a man with a German name who was before the courts and said that here we had an Ur-lout and an umlaut, not an unusual conjunction, as we had found. And he made a pun to a neighbouring woman and my mother, which I chanced to hear, when they were talking over the front fence on a Sunday morning. It was about the milk teeth of the child who was holding the woman's hand: she had fine, pre-carious teeth, my father said, emphasising for the sake of his meanings. I doubt that he was understood.

By this time, he was far less a presence in our lives. My mother and the others had their religious meetings, and their 'door to door ministry', and more sociality with the Witnesses; and I had withdrawn to my room or was working late. He had become for his children merely a threadbare curtain against which we enacted our own interests, past which we brushed. Our purpose, I see now, was intimidating to him.

In the near future, after I had left home, my brother Max would marry, at eighteen; he had by then completed an apprentice-

ship as a motor mechanic and was sought after for his work. Already he was spoken of, in the way that he would be through the years, as 'the salt of the earth'. His looks were admired.

My brother Billy would leave school and become the local postman, on a motor scooter. He developed a nerve disorder, and while he managed to keep up his job he lived at home for years. He thought he would never marry, but he underestimated the attractiveness of his warm nature. He married a Jehovah's Witness, of course, and moved to Melbourne to work in the office of a chemical company. Their only child was to be killed in a car accident, at nineteen. He was the last of the family with our name.

My sister Alicia, as soon as she had settled into work, bought a car and drove every day to the club to pick up my father, at seven o'clock, and bring him home. She had him paged, and he came with a quavering walk into the foyer, helped by a barman. Every day my father said to that man, or to the woman at the desk, with the tedium of a drunkard, 'Have you met my beautiful daughter?'

My sister married young, too. My mother opposed it: she was losing her best companionship, so soon, when my sister was barely eighteen. I received a letter in Sydney from my mother, telling me to come home and intervene, but I wrote back to ask what arguments I could possibly use. If the marriage didn't work, my sister could get divorced: it had been made easy enough, and people should be prepared to use that hygienic provision. Could I have meant that? my mother wrote. Did I really believe that my father should have been left alone by her?

My sister married a surfing champion, who had started a business making surfboards in fiberglass. He used to come to our house, I was told, on a motorbike, riding up to the gate on his back wheel. My father would panic when he heard the bike's approach, on weekend mornings: 'Nina, get that fellow out of here. Don't let him in the house.' My mother would never have made a scene, although she said to me that she felt like throwing a bucket of water over the suitor. She stayed inside. When the young man appeared as a large shadow on the screen door, my father would say, 'Oh, hullo John, it's you; Alicia will be with you presently...' leaving the visitor outside. But he would hiss to Alicia, 'You're not to go out there; he's a hooligan...' John was bronzed and confident, with his helmet carried under his arm in a swaggering Sir Galahad style. He had sleek black hair reaching below his shoulders and a Pancho Villa moustache.

My mother was partly reconciled to John by his conversion to her religion. He claimed to have experienced a spiritual conviction while out on the waves at daybreak, and to have decided immediately to give up drugs. He used to watch my sister going into the Jehovah's Witnesses' meetings, seated on his parked motorcycle in the street, and one day, taking his crash helmet with him, he went in and sat at the back of the congregation.

My sister and he have been married for more than thirty years, and have four children, in as good a relationship as I have seen.

While I was working for the newspaper there began my longest and most involving friendships, with a painter and his wife, and later with a friend of theirs, another artist. The man I met first, ten years older than me, had newly arrived on the coast and was teaching freelance art classes in our town, and at a few others along the highway. He lived, with wife and child, short of money, on a back road in a rented farmhouse. His wife taught science part-time for the Catholic school, but had some financial prospects, I gathered, which kept up their morale, while he struggled with a critically unfashionable style.

Often my new friend would drive me twenty miles in a rattling Volkswagen to his house, where we filled an afternoon and evening with talk. I think he wanted to give me a change from where I lived; he had seen my mother's formality, suspicion and discomfort toward a visitor and that atmosphere he thought destructive for someone wanting to write.

Ted occasionally waited outside our house in his car, if I had not been at the office when he called there. He remembers me appearing among trees in the park, walking through the rain in a gabardine overcoat and carrying a briefcase, a habit from my Jehovah's Witnesses days. I am supposed to have come up to him, soaking, and to have said, 'You see the smoke hanging from the chimneys in this street? I was just thinking how like ectoplasm it is. This is a poor street, lots of problems, and domestic smoke's thought of as comforting, but this is not. There's something ghoulish about it – the way it lies there so flaccid and inert, and so flimsy. You can see any hope that it offers is a sham...'

Ted thought at the time that underlying the apparent enthusiasm of my nature there must be depression. It was hard to tell my state of mind in those days, he says, since I was often in my own world, as if in a diver's suit. But far from being depressed, I recall feeling entirely caught up with that image. No matter how melancholy a subject I might chance upon, the things that I valued about writing, clarity and vividness, made it always a pleasure.

I first met Ted deliberately, after I overheard part of a conversation he was having, although it was with one of the town 'socialites'. On Saturday afternoons I often lay in the long grass of a hillside, up the road from where we lived. This slope, twenty paces from the roadside, through trees, was suddenly so steep that anyone who stretched out upon it remained all but upright, prevented from sliding by its deep grass. When there, you were lying down, leaning and standing, all at once. No one else seemed to try it. From that position, which was more secure if you were spread-eagled a little, there was a view across the golf course, the heath, and the aerodrome, and out to sea. One Saturday, hearing voices nearby, I rolled over carefully and parted handfuls of fronds to look uphill. I saw on the crest of the slope a loose-limbed man of middle height, so thin that his shirt seemed almost hollow, with thick brown hair combed forward, a narrow, triangular face, a somewhat broad but

aquiline nose, and heavy lines between nose and mouth. Later I would be able to describe him more fully: although asthmatic he was wiry and energetic; he had a rumpled face yet looked boyish; his eyebrows were heavy and low-slung, above alert, unusually blue eyes; and he often hummed passages of classical music beneath his breath, as if they were an incantation. Angular, all ganglion, he might have been painted by Soutine.

That day he was commenting to a stylish older woman, who stepped carefully among the fallen sticks, on the view, in an unusually appreciative, detailed way. He then began talking about composers. What was immediately apparent was his charm and, despite the subjects, his unpretentiousness. They remained unaware of me. I realised this must be the artist who placed a small advertisement in our newspaper each week.

On the date of the next class, I took some drawings of mine and a poem or two and called at the shed where he taught, in a back lane of the town. There was a still life set up inside and he had his ladies working at their easels, so we stepped out into the sunlight to talk. He borrowed the poems, to look at more closely, but the drawings he said at once were 'too uninformed by considerations of design'. This was stated with such impersonal conviction that it did not prevent us becoming friends, at once. Ted says, though, that I persisted in addressing him formally for a surprising length of time.

The next week, when we met at the studio, he gave me a small paper-covered edition of Rilke's *New Poems*, which was influenced by the objectivity and the close attention of visual artists. A work of art, however fine its feelings, and it certainly ought to be informed with a humane response, was judged by craft alone. As for drawing, he returned to the importance of the underlying design, but said that I should never take lessons. One simply drew with sincerity, in search of something that made an impact.

My friend had hardly ever sold a picture and seemed in no hurry to do so, even if it meant living precariously. He was determined to develop a personal manner. The Australian bush was so broken and scattered, so casual-seeming, that it was an impossible subject 'for a painter with a classical temperament'; but perhaps there was an opportunity for originality in just that problem, he thought.

This was at a time, in the sixties, when anything but abstract painting was treated with condescension by the art world. It was the noon of Clement Greenberg, the internationally-known New York critic. Greenberg isolated the aesthetic response. Painting was about paint laid on a flat surface and ought not to try to be anything else. Ted said that such 'isolation' held no interest for him, whatever the consequences for his career. He believed, with Pierre Bonnard (who was then much underrated), that if you turned away from nature all that was left was the self, and oneself was not enough. I felt I had encountered integrity.

Ted's friend, Joe, a thirty-year-old former merchant sailor, an English immigrant, stockily built, red-haired, with whom he had been at art college in Sydney, held a similar attitude, but was much more theoretical, keeping copious journals on his ideas about art. Joe looked like a sea-captain, with his short beard and staunch demeanour. In manner he was quiet, intense, judgemental, taking readings of every situation and making entries in his log-book; but also suddenly humorous, a wonderful raconteur, and able to dance like a tom-tom, in his lone performances to the radio.

At that time Joe was living isolated in an army tent, on a coastal headland, about ten miles from Ted's place. He lasted there a year, even though he had a beautiful girlfriend, who was an archeology student and artist, in Sydney. He would be pestered by skin cancers for the rest of his life. His idea was to experience the 'intensity' of nature, drawing and painting the twisted gum tree forest and the fretted banksia scrub, above the sea. He was like Gauguin going off to Brittany, I remarked, but Joe was inclined to dismiss Gauguin. Too reductive. Anyway, he pointed out, in his situation there were no hangers-on and no pub life in the evenings. He rode ten miles on an old bicycle to a general store for supplies, and Ted brought him his booze twice a week.

I sat with them on the rocks above the shore at twilight, and to be polite sipped from a bottle of beer. Looking out to sea, I listened while they talked obsessively about art. For all their reverence of it, they treated the subject matter-of-factly. Soon, out of my enthusiasm for ideas, I was joining in, asking questions and trying out summaries of their position. Most people barely noticed what was around them, but these two were constantly perceptive. There seemed more in life for them. Even as they reclined on the animal warmth of the boulders, relaxed and ruminating and condemning the art world, one or other would draw our attention to a change in tone among the bands of light on the sea, or to the shapes of the darkening headland – keeping in practice, like a footballer who has found a tennis ball. I had always been observant, even while lost in my imaginings, and that tendency seemed now a calling.

I remember seeing from Joe's camp at twilight that the spattered, pale lights of my hometown had come on, beyond the shorter headlands, and that the beam of the lighthouse, from its island opposite there, was being swung around on the distant clouds like a stopwatch's hand.

Stendhal wrote somewhere that when the arts are in trouble they return to realism. Ted and Joe thought that art could avoid a good deal of shallowness by not departing from realism so much. In realism, the known and agreed appearance of the world was plainly seen. Such a work could still be identified by the artist's style; there was room in the approach for idiosyncrasy. The objective world was always changing and was endlessly complex, so realism was a mode that could be constantly renewed. Revealing the process of painting and design might be part of a realist attitude. A work of art that referred to nature gained in emotional resonance.

I have retained this attitude. Realism is the foundation of art; whatever forays we make from that, and we certainly need to experiment, they are minor forms. Realism always needs its old ally classicism, with its refinement, to save it from drifting, at one extreme, into a merely gross reportage. Realism in art is innately satisfying – it bites down hard into our experience. It is not just style, but is morality – a respect for what is outside ourselves. To feel we have before us an effort at the truth adds another dimension to a work of art.

Joe's work, in what I think the most successful of several manners he has used, was a little reminiscent of Dürer – of the exact attention to detail in a picture like *The Piece of Turf*. He made oils and large pencil drawings of the leaf litter and twigs of the forest floor, of weathered stumps, long grasses, undergrowth, and of the tattered heights of the forest against moonlit clouds. These had a rare clarity which was enhanced by their earth or bleached colours. In his pictures one felt the strangeness of the world.

Ted was more of a colourist. Early on, he chose to paint in a naïve style, seeing this as ahistorical, removed altogether from the fashions of mainstream art. He used exaggeratedly fertile shapes in bold patterns. Later he became, at times, like an Edward Hopper of small-town Australia, and made something monumental from motifs of his own – from fibro houses and caravans by the sea, kids with beach towels and surfboards, railway yards, fishing boats, breakwaters. Rather than loneliness, as in the American's work, his pictures suggested nature's 'generosity'.

Joe, after a year in his tent, went off to Italy to work at an archaeological site, pursuing his girlfriend there, whom he would marry, and intending to study in particular Piero della Francesca. He was away for years. Before he left, he took me aside and told me that Picasso had got it all wrong about Cézanne. Cézanne didn't imply Cubism, with its lack of colour and its obscurantist attitude to the world; rather, Cézanne had been concerned with the revelation of forms entirely by means of colour. His paintings made original and brilliant use of an optical fact, the advance of warm tones and the recession of cool ones, to create a real space, in which his objects existed with unusual presence. It was the presence of the world that Cézanne was interested in. Morandi, more than the Cubists, was his real heir. I should remember that.

Ted's house was at the end of wheel-tracks that ran across a paddock, among a stand of trees on an open ridge. It looked along a river and a valley to the mountains. Below it, in the olive-green

pastures, there were poplars. The broken-off or rounded shapes of the mountain range changed colour through the day, from navy to mauve to cerulean, and then back again.

Out of the weathered, rusty-roofed farmhouse, which was either subsiding or supported in its net of vines, would come an endearing young woman, waving an arm to greet us and leading a child (there was soon to be another). Inside were lacquered black floorboards, a large brick fireplace, a piano, and double glass-paned doors onto the verandah, where I sometimes had a bed, behind the vines. Floorboards creaked and a primus stove burned blue in the dim kitchen. The couch and chairs were draped in broad-patterned fabrics. Kathy played the piano, Ted sang lieder, the child slept on my lap, and the house was aromatic with fresh oil paint, linseed oil, and turpentine. We talked until the distended, burnt-orange moon, among the coarse-ground stars, had become a pale membrane, low on the far side of the ridge.

There were pictures everywhere through the house, raised on the walls or leaned against them; some originals, some reproductions, a number of them copies, from the modern period. The tutelary spirits of the studio (which was in an old cow bales, nearby) were Cézanne, above all, for his balance of realist and formalist intentions; Seurat, in his oil sketches and marines; Van Gogh, except for the disturbed psychedelic works; Bonnard; Marquet, who seemed the object of a secret cult among us, he was so neglected elsewhere; Matisse, the more depictive phases; and Morandi. (Since then, there have appeared in the 'canon' some suggestions of mine, Edward Hopper and Max Beckmann; although there has been no room, I think, for Paul Nash.)

An Australian artist, Elioth Gruner, who preceded my friends in that valley, on visits in the forties, was respected by them and idolised by me. I had prints of his work framed for my parents' house years before I met with painters, because they were so accurate about the shapes and the light of our landscape. I understood Eliot's words, 'And the end of all our exploring/ Will be to arrive where we started/ And know the place for the first time.'

I spent many evenings at a cleared-off dining table being taken through a minute, reverent analysis of French or early Italian paintings, on the pages of books; or in a similar way, listening to Romantic symphonies, German and English 'nature' music, or to New Orleans jazz.

I was left by Joe from his library novels by Lawrence and collections of poems by Pound and Yeats, but was suspicious of the stridency of these 'life affirmers', of the underlying sympathy with brutality I thought I detected in them. I was much more taken with my discovery of the poetry of Hardy and Owen and Edward Thomas, those fine-tuned pessimists. Luckily for me, the copy of Lawrence's novel *Kangaroo* I was given had the remarkable parts of it, all the passages descriptive of the Australian bush, identified with long scratches of charcoal in the margins.

On days when I visited his place, Ted drove us around the back roads, looking for subjects he could paint. We went among the torrential white saplings in the state forest, through paddocks the colour of weathered canvas, close under navy-blue, dented mountains, and along the coast, a speckled ocean behind the constant rearrangement of trees. Later, we strolled on the haunches of the home paddocks, knee-deep in orange whisky grass, out in front of the misty blue façade of a forest, above which the early stars appeared.

Ted was considered eccentric by the local small crop and dairy farmers, but was befriended by them. After many hippies had quickly settled in the valley, he became entirely respectable. The farmers' lives were of interest to him. He recounted to me conversations he had with them. One man had said something like, 'I was brung up in that stony country up at Uralla. We tried growin' everythin', up there at Uralla. Beans, peas, friggin' cucumbers,

lettuces, carrots, don't forget y'r carrots, pertaters, an' bloody corn (no money in that).' The frosts were always destroying their crops, so they came down to Milestone, on the Coast, 'to grow fuckin' termarters.' Then it was dry: in the thirties and forties 'there was not a drop' of rain, for years. After that, in the next ten years, there were five frosts with hail storms. They lost their entire crops. 'Didn't wear boots in them days an' once there I walked out in the paddock an' the hail was up t' me bloody knees. Took days t' melt. It breaks y'r friggin' heart, coz y' gotta leave off every other fuckin' thing t' look after termarters, for months, an' y'r jist about t' get somethin' back an' it's all gone in a few fuckin' minutes.'

This farmer, who after his parents died had lived on alone in the house, was told he had prostate cancer. 'Could have three years, he reckons. Takes me an hour now to drink a fuckin' bottle o' beer. I've gone two years an' I'm still at work, same as before, buildin' fences, ploughin'. I reckon I might get more 'n me time. The dawgs'd miss me, o' course, an' the cows might notice. I'd miss the fishin'. A year. Might jus' show 'em. Did I tell y' me granddad grew a third set o'teeth? Must a' been fuckin eighty. An' Mum, she stopped wearin' glasses when she was – Jesus I dunno, in her seventies. Could read anythin', 'cept the phone book indoors. I come from a line that's got somethin' goin' for it. Eh? Fuck me if I don't.'

With Ted and Joe, I regained the intensity of a sect. I have been going back to visit them for more than forty years (since his return, Joe lives there again): innumerable journeys on the train, overnight when there were sleeping compartments, and more recently by day; but either way, looking out for almost the entire trip on the marvellous country of the coast.

'Into many a green valley/ Drifts the appalling snow' Auden says; and there has come among my friends serious illness, and Joe's divorce, and a fire through his studio which destroyed almost all his paintings (except those he had sold), along with the sketchbooks and notebooks, and disappointment about exhibitions, and debt, and creeping red-brick housing estates, but no weariness with nature, and nor with art. In his essay *On the Pleasures of Painting*, William Hazlitt says, 'There is a pleasure in painting which none but painters know'; and a pleasure in the world which is known best to them.

15. Walking after Dark

I was nineteen when I went to Sydney to find work. Having bought the clothing I would need there, I left the train on a wintry morning with enough money for a week in the cheapest hotel and for just an apple, a sandwich and a milkshake each day. I had to find a job at once, and one that paid weekly.

After shaving at the public lavatory in Central Station, and leaving my bag, I presented myself at the desk in both of the big newspaper offices, but they each expected written applications. I tried the bookshops around the inner city, and all of them wanted experience or were fully staffed. It was four o'clock before I had some luck: a young clerk at the government employment agency remembered an unusual offer, searched for a card, and sent me to the Reader's Digest's national office, which wanted to train an editor. That kind of job would not be available these days to a person from an unemployment queue. The address was a short walk, across the city's main park, from where I stayed, so if successful I would not have fares.

I was interviewed among oak panels and leather by the general manager, who reminded me of Mr Gutman in *The Maltese Falcon*, but with a much more expensive suit. He had a soft American accent, like someone leisurely spreading mayonnaise on bread, and seemed entirely uninterested in this chore with me. All the while we spoke, he lay semi-recumbent in a padded chair. After talking about the Reader's Digest as if it were a religion, mentioning modestly what a wealthy organisation it was, asking a few bland questions, he decided he had fulfilled his time and said I should meet the production manager.

That man, short and powerfully built, arrived in the room like a tennis service, calling instructions over his shoulder. He spoke rapidly, American style, but with a nasal Australian accent. Pacing before the boss's desk, gesturing, talking, talking, about concerns of their own, he was so tightly muscled and restless that I thought then of a golf ball being sprung off cement. The general manager clearly found him reassuring. I was introduced (with enthusiasm now) as 'a good type of young man', although it seemed to me the production manager would be irritated by that description. He glanced me over, flicked among my newspaper cuttings, and was drawn to read some, one buttock on the edge of the desk, a thigh straining his slacks. His mouth chopped at his gum; the jaw muscle had the twisted fibres of a rope, under his tanned, razor-polished skin. 'The real thing.' He leapt upright. 'You did these? Yeah, the by-line. They're good. This is the real stuff – what we're looking for. Editor? Nah, we need you to write. Have a look at this,' he told his boss, tossing my package toward him.

The production manager wore, as he did every day, a short-sleeved style of white shirt that was like a tourniquet around his biceps. His tight black and grey curls made his skull seem as hard as a ram's. He would spend the weekends, I thought, with a young woman taller than himself, eating and watching television in his underpants, in a penthouse above the sea. As I shook a hand that was as heavy as stone, but self-consciously restrained, he mentioned, with what I learned was his usual acuteness, that the Reader's Digest paid fortnightly. I must have looked alarmed, because he said that something could be done about that, for the present. The pay would be the basic rate.

My immediate assignment was to write articles that might be used in local issues of the magazine. I researched at the library and wrote many short pieces, on chance topics that I thought would be considered interesting, from the battles of Scotland to Captain Cook discovering surfing in the South Seas. These were enthusiastically received by the production manager, with embarrassing loudness, in the open-plan office. I was congratulated again on them if he saw me at the tea wagon. Someone in the editorial department told me, coolly, that no articles were ever published which originated outside the home office in America, but the production manager continued to request that I write them.

I noticed with the weeks that there settled in, rather than lifted, a stiff, incurious politeness among the writing staff toward me. There were three others in the department, middle-aged, middle-class, who talked among themselves about dinner parties and school fees. I realised this constrained person, thrust among them, from some outlandish place, with not even halfway-decent schooling, who was being ridiculously over-praised, was the production manager's instrument for provoking them; probably just the latest one. Now I noticed something insolent about the 'PM's' broad accent, and saw a rowdy working-class assertion and self-confidence in his walk. He would lay a hand on my shoulder, in passing. Was I meant to feel complicity?

The production manager wore a large gold tie-clip every day, as if to distinguish himself as group leader, but he had no need of that. He led entirely through involvement, and invariably was found up-stage. I saw him always moving fast, jaw always rolling, his attention competed for with his first name by all of those in his team. I heard the word 'brilliant' from the younger designers after his meetings, which I did not attend. He seemed to be throwing a jazz party on a double-decker bus and they all wanted to be on board, except for the 'old guard', the telephonist, the secretaries, and me. Working with him had 'real cachet', I was told by an illustrator; you could get a job anywhere after that.

The PM flung his admirers away with rigorous gestures toward their offices and his face averted, telling them to surprise him. He wrote and scored all over the artists' work; carved up the editorial copy with a carpenter's pencil. His tight hair seethed on his head. He had books scheduled for years to come.

I began to feel as sterile as a worker bee, and was repelled at the thought of being patronised, although he denied, when I spoke of it, that my work was simply being put on a shelf. 'Give it time. Do me another story like that last one. What's the hurry?' I had been collected for his team, but he had no idea of where to use me.

I went for an interview at the *Sydney Morning Herald*. The grey-faced, grey-shirted old journalist behind the desk said, 'These references are all about bloody "style". This stuff of yours is too full of nicely turned phrases. That's not journalism. We don't have time for that in the city. Journalism's not art. Journalism's about breaking news. You're not so much interested in that, I'd say. We get them all the time: these kids who want to write. They're always frustrated here.'

'Where are your glasses?' an attractive woman said to me, as we passed in a corridor at work.

'I don't wear glasses.'

'But whenever I see you, you always look so in-turned, like

someone short-sighted who's mislaid his glasses...' She gave me a catty smile.

'Oh, that's called thinking. It's rather interesting. You'd find it strange, but why not give it a try?'

I was told to apologise, by the PM, as if it were an afterthought. She remained hostile.

The production manager said to me, 'I saw you last night, flitting among the trees in Hyde Park, in the spitting rain. It was freezing. You were like someone out of Dickens. What were you doing, walking around there, at that hour?'

'I like to walk,' I said.

He asked why it couldn't be done in a more populated place. I shrugged. 'That would be less interesting, for me.'

Then he wanted to know where I was living, and I was evasive. He said, 'All I mean is: if you had an iron there, you wouldn't need to wear your jacket all the time in the office. I'll give you a raise; make sure you get all your shirts pressed.'

The walks, until late, kept me from being encapsulated in my hostel room of an evening. They always led into the older, more deserted parts of town. I went around the harbour foreshores; onto wharves where men were darkly fishing; through parks and public gardens; along peninsulas of terraced houses, with their windows in bronze; down industrial streets and lanes; across the Harbour Bridge; into bus and ferry sheds, out of the rain; always back to water on stone, always skirting anyone I saw.

I loved the look of the city after dark, probably influenced in this by Kenneth Slessor, the poet of Sydney Harbour and of its evenings. 'Darkness comes down, the Harbour shakes its mane/ Glazed with a leaf of amber...' I had seen that.

So night, like earth, receives this poisoned city,

Charging its air with beauty, coasting its lanterns

With mains of darkness, till the leprous clay

Dissolves, and pavements drift away,

And there is only the quiet noise of planets feeding.

I found myself, at times, in high-walled passages, near the docks, where my footsteps echoed like dripping water and roused me from reverie, and I hurried on. I was often shouted after and sworn at by drunkards, during these wanderings, but that was all.

At work, I became part of a real project, at last; helping to write a home handyman's manual, which was intended to be encyclopaedic. The PM challenged that this was beneath me; I said it must be better than the lay-outs and paste-ups I had been diverting myself with recently.

Teachers from technical colleges came to the office and described in conversation and with rough drawings how some home-maintenance job was done. I asked questions, wrote notes, and produced paragraphs on each stage of the process, which the informant approved, for accuracy. An artist was present, who roughly sketched what was being diagrammed and said, and I wrote the captions for his illustrations. The work was cleared as we went along, with another expert and with an editor. The completed book, large portions of which were until recently still in print, had instructions on everything from furniture repairs to bricklaying to what seemed to me the higher mathematics of bathroom tiling. Two teams worked on the project. When we began, I would have known, of practical things, the look of a mortise and tenon joint and how to change a washer, with no interest in anything more, yet I found myself engrossed in the emergence of precision with each day's work. I learned more about writing from this process than by any other means. I was not, however, to see the project's completion.

I had moved from the hostel into a room in the suburbs, found through visiting the Theosophical Bookshop. One of the middle-aged women there, with whom I used to speak, saw me reading about the room on their noticeboard and urged that I ring for it, using the shop phone. She was a rarefied Hungarian, with a voice and gestures like wafting scarves. I would get on so well, she told me, with her friend Lotte, the landlady. The rent had been reduced, for 'a spiritual person with references', and she was 'pleasantly prepared' to vouch for me.

I was drawn to Buddhism, still, because although it was atheistic it encouraged morality with the urgency of a religion. At the time, I was worried about whether we could rely on a natural morality. The young, when serious, are more serious than the old.

I found that, despite trying, I could not accept orthodox Buddhism, because it was built around the belief that we are reborn, even though we have no unchanging soul, and must continue to be, always suffering, while motivated by desire. Buddhism required the separateness of mind and body, since something was passed from life to life, but the evidence of research showed that any mental phenomena – volitions, memories – coexist exactly with activities of the brain.

Letting chance lead me, I found myself with a room among Theosophists, in a brick bungalow, in a brick suburb. The room, at the front of their Federation-style house, looked across a short, steep lawn, out of which grew just one exceptionally tall palm tree, onto a main road, usually flooded with traffic.

Indoors there was a cloying Theosophical piety. This was partly because of the incense fumes that sidled through the house. The other rooms that I saw were ponderous, darkly furnished; mine, fortunately, had mostly cane furniture and a faded Persian rug. On a wall of the twilit hallway were heavily framed large photographic portraits of important Theosophists, in Edwardian clothing, and a Hindu *sadhu*, almost naked, all in a sepia tone. Many smaller black-and-white snapshots, framed in groups, were ranged on the opposite side; they showed outdoor gatherings of a Theosophical order called 'The Star in the East', held in the thirties in India, Switzerland and Australia. Their centre of interest, among the overdressed bourgeoisie, was the New Messiah, who spoke at those gatherings, the young Krishnamurti. He was almost always posed in profile and looked like a star of silent films.

The house belonged to a statuesque elderly woman who had magnificently bouffant white hair and a grand manner of mystical distraction. It was shared and kept up by her middle-aged daughter, with repressed impatience, beholden to a high-minded, one-woman bureaucracy. There were sometimes female guests, drifting in long frocks in a way I took to be spiritual, and a man, with the white, square beard of Orthodoxy, who seemed always in deep consideration. The daughter I saw as a lean, chronically irritable French school mistress, on parents' day.

I had the use of the kitchen in the mornings, but felt I could never leave it tidy enough; certainly, I could never make my bed properly, but would come home to find it had been tightened, straightened, and the pillows plumped more and set at a better angle. The chair had been realigned, my pyjamas refolded, and there was a large crockery chamber pot on offer, appearing from under the draped side of the bed, although I shoved it far beneath, again.

I let myself quietly into the house after dinner, which I often had at a Chinese café near the railway station, and during the evening went in socks along the hall to the bathroom, past the living room with its door almost drawn. In there the television gestured obliquely, a blue light in a far corner. If they were without visitors and she caught sight of me, the mother would call me in and switch off the programme ('so unprofitable'), and the daughter would go to make herbal tea. The elder woman liked to chat about Theosophist doctrine. Did I have any inkling of a previous life? No? Most unusual, for someone who had shown my knowledge of the Path. Never mind, that experience would come. And I was right: we must live with our attention here. We ought to fulfill our duties at this karmic level; that was the lesson of Lord Krishna. Now, what was my astrological sign, again. Ah, Pisces: very expectably so. She knew it was something sympathetic, from our first meeting. At what hour of the day had I been born? At dawn! That explained my spiritual propensity. The Lord Gautama, in whom she understood I was interested, represented a very special manifestation of the Divine. He was one of the highest Vehicles: otherwise, only Christ was on that level. Her own path was not as demanding as the Buddha's way: it was *bhakti*, worship. Her guru had been living for thousands of years in meditative bliss among the Himalayas, and appeared to her in dreams, with spiritual encouragement. She hoped to be reborn into a higher sphere, where her late husband was, as she had been glimpsing over many years. He had now a far more refined, etheric form. Gradually, we would all be absorbed back into the One Source, which had given us the experience of individual existence. Our minds would be reabsorbed into Mind. (Talk about Mind always made me think of a brain wired up and kept conscious in a jar.)

While I was living at this house, people came a number of times for séances. I declined to join in, despite Lotte's urging, but glimpsed the small gatherings of mostly older women. Looking back, those visitors remind me of novice concert-goers, with their dark clothes and handbags, chatting a little, subdued, anxious about whether consolation or an ordeal awaited them. Lotte led the meetings, for which a homemade ouija board was used. I lay on top of my bed to listen, the door ajar, but usually drifted off, rising and dipping along the coast of sleep, murmurous sounds coming off-shore.

I dreamt once that spirits had clustered above the house and were hung upside down on the darkness like pale bats. They were compact, the size of small children, although they seemed mostly aged, and it was hard to guess how numerous they were, since the ones further off were hidden against the smoky stars. I saw, in those closest, that although they were head-down no blood suffused their tightly-moulded faces and gravity did not distort them. Now and then, one, as if realising it was in the wrong place, would suddenly drop toward the suburban roofs, becoming a syrupy pale streak, and in mid-plunge go out. A spirit tried to speak to me, with blind, tight lips, and when it did its mouth became, incongruously, the normal way up, with a wrenching, mechanical movement, showing how difficult it was for them to communicate. Although the heavy eyeballs were sealed, I realised they could feel us within themselves. Only one seemed available for interview at a time, in any location. Those 'dead souls' that were not involved reminded me of tramps drowsing on park benches. They roused themselves, regularly, to argue about their common misfortune, or about what their heavy protocol required next, with rancorous, almost inaudible shrillness.

When I lay awake, lengthy stretches of subdued humming came past me from the sitting room, until Lotte's voice was heard again, in elevated tones. Once, as I was adrift, there flew out of that room a shout, from what I instantly saw as a heavily powdered, dewlapped throat. It was shocking, as though someone old and naked had leapt in among them. I listened, like a dog pointing. There were passionate tears.

Of a morning, from the street outside, the orange-tiled roofs looked packed together, laid like plating to the smeared horizon (although many were on quarter-acre blocks, with a few trees among them). The suburbs seemed as though being drawn outwards, onwards, to fill a vacuum. Then in the long twilights, walking home from the station among the dark-brick houses, I was reminded by their colour of the lines from *Hamlet* about 'the funeral baked meats' that 'coldly furnished forth the wedding feast'. I told myself I must not let my usual escape, into reading, allow me to tolerate this place, so lacking in sensuousness.

'The greatest gift is the passion for reading,' Elizabeth Hardwick has said. 'It is cheap, it consoles, it distracts, it excites, it gives knowledge of the world and experience of a wide kind. It is a moral illumination.' (From my experience, the last sentence seemed dubious.)

I read on the train to and from work every day, in parks and on ferries of a weekend, while lingering in cafés, and at night in my room, where the sound of the traffic might almost have been rain.

I needed to save the bond for a flat, but I was drawn inevitably into bookshops and spent to my limit on films and eating out. It was unthinkable that I would share a place and have a closer association with strangers than I already did. I could go for a week, where I was, on just a few words, because my novelty had worn off and my opaqueness about past lives had been accepted. It was only after a year at work, when I received holiday pay, that I was finally able to move from there. I had grown more than ever to detest the 'inner light', that light of crypts, and wanted 'the clear, calm daylight' of the rational mind.

Sometimes I went to a club where there was folk music, which had an underground following then, because a friend I had made in the state art gallery, who was my age and a painter, invited me. I listened to songs about whisky in the jar and girls who laid themselves down and the treachery of the English and drank a few ciders, but boredom soon drifted across me as thickly as the cigarette smoke. Invariably, instead of sitting for long at the booted feet of the singers, I told my friend that I thought I might walk home.

A small, blonde girl, a new employee in a little art bookshop where I used to browse, was friendly, and we went for a drink together. She asked me, as soon as we were seated, for money toward her abortion, and in surprise and confusion, and because she said (inaccurately) that she was sixteen, I gave her what I had, a good part of a week's pay. When I saw her a few weeks later she wanted to come home with me, but I told her it was not possible, where I lived. She smoked continually. She was then sleeping in the bathtub at someone's flat, and I introduced her to my friend at the folk music club, in case she would go home with him, and she did. She and I continued to meet, regularly at that time, and then sporadically, over the years, to talk about books. Our tastes overlapped sufficiently for that to be possible, although she was as hectic about life as I was quiet. I disliked library books, but she needed them because of reading so quickly. She was the first writer I knew, and I was always fascinated that her work came to her as copiously and as naturally as rain, whereas everything I wrote, for myself, was in some way dissatisfying and needed continuing effort.

I could feel a need for extremity in her that I found disturbing and tiresome. It was something inert, it seemed, which needed to be cranked up mechanically, so that she could come alive. She must have life in high-gloss red or it was nothing. Any method of getting high would do, even horror movies, just as long as there was stimulus. At some stage she had a child that was so badly deformed it died. Over the years, she lived in a long series of dives, with 'poets' and musicians, some of whom abused her, one of whom, in his stupor and rage, deliberately set fire to the dress she was wearing and threw kerosene onto her. She saved herself by instantly roll-ing all around the floor. I saw her with her Nordic hair cropped and her eyebrows gone, and her face peeling, although it would end up unmarked. She refused to talk to the police about what had happened, despite her suffering and the large welts that were left on her body and arms (they looked like the plastic of melted dolls). When she was with that vicious man, she told me, they lived by stealing from charity clothes bins. Their lives had 'intensity'. Whomever she was with, though, we met every fortnight or so, in the early years, and went critically through each other's work, find-ing things to praise and blame. I wanted her opinion because she was so easily bored: she was my gauge of Impact. She could seek out at once in any piece of unresolved writing the emotional core. After about three years, when we each thought we were ready, we had our first acceptances from magazines. She went on to publish several books of poems and stories, and some of those pieces I still think are vivid and excellent. All of her books are out of print, but ageing admirers of her work (other writers or hip academics) remind publishers about her. 'Too sixties,' they are told.

The last time I saw her was thirty years after we first met, and after a long lapse. She had lived in India for years, where she had always felt she belonged. It was the sacramental use of drugs that interested her most, I thought. She had been repatriated home by the Australian government, after becoming penniless, then a prostitute, then jaundiced and cared for by the Salvation Army. We met by chance in the street, I cannot remember how soon after her return, and she asked me frankly for money for 'smack', say-ing she was in pain, and I gave it to her. A few weeks later, she was dead, alone in a dark, pokey room, and not discovered for several days. She had beautiful hands, and into her face would come one of the sweetest expressions I have seen. The last time we spoke was early in the morning, on a dirty street at the Cross, both of us squinting because of the glare. She was sitting on a doorstep, bedraggled and dazed. 'Hullo, Vicki,' I said ruefully, going over to her. 'Hullo there,' she said, shielding her eyes with the gesture of a Cambodian dancer, and with the same old slow luxuriant smile. I am not sure that she knew who I was.

'O, for a life of sensations rather than of thoughts,' said Keats. Goethe said, 'Classicism is health; Romanticism, disease.'

Both my mother and Ted wrote to me every week, for many years, but the one letter I received from my father came after I had moved into my first flat. Could the idea of me living alone in a bohemian area of Sydney have stimulated my father to write, out of nostalgia for his youth? Whatever lay behind it, the letter turned out to be entirely impersonal; it was all but completely taken up with mockery of the planned visit of Queen Elizabeth and Prince Philip to our town. He imagined the sycophancy and the solecisms of the local councillors and their 'ladies' in detail, and the boredom of the 'Regal Pair' under a flapping canvas awning on the beach, squinting at the surf carnival being staged for them – 'easing the sweaty elastic and squirming at the inquisitive grit'. He saw their sunglasses embedded in the zinc cream on their 'high-drawn' noses, which would be replenished by the local beautician, Miss Maisie Beamish (a name he was delighted with, for someone who he said appeared to be from photographs an 'ample' young woman). As an afterthought, there was a paragraph of facetiousness devoted to my sister-in-law, Max's wife, of whom I was fond. I could not understand why he had written, since there was no personal element, and I was unable to think of a tone or a content with which to reply.

I turned twenty-one and was notified that I must register for military service in Vietnam: there would be some large chance of one's birthdate being drawn in a ballot. When the time of that event came, mine was.

I knew I would not go to Vietnam; I thought it a bully's war. The North Vietnamese had no navy and no air force, so it was difficult to feel they were a threat to Australia. I admired them as underdogs and for what I read of their tenacity, and did not want to kill them. I envisioned a terrified small peasant in a singlet being flung backwards from my machine gun, an old, jammed rifle falling out of his hands. (I was invulnerable in these imaginings; to be shot was not my destiny.)

We opponents of the war had our dishonesties: we thought, without saying so, that although we would not want to live under communism, such a regime was good enough for the backward Vietnamese. We noticed only austerity and what seemed idealism in the North, and corruption in the South. Now I think, better a corrupt democracy than a virtuous police state; and I think that bourgeois freedom is the supreme political good and worth fighting for. But this does not retrospectively change my attitude about the opportunity I had for killing Vietnamese: there were other possible strategies for the West, rather than the frenzied destruction of a country. The South Vietnamese opponents of forced unity might have been encouraged to emigrate; it would have been less costly for the Americans and their allies. When the war was lost to the North, the earth did not subside under the region's democracies, and it would not have taken impossible foresight to have projected that, only a less bellicose attitude.

I had been going to anti-war demonstrations, although too self-conscious to shout slogans, and had folded pamphlets and licked envelopes in the back room of a grimy socialist bookshop. When asked at the Reader's Digest if I was registered for war service, and told they would keep my job for me, proudly, I explained it would not be necessary, I was going to court. My immediate boss was an Englishman who had been a war correspondent and then a prisoner of the Japanese during World War II; he seemed to want every young male to experience something of the hardships he had been through. Until my announcement, he was remote and polite toward me, but then he began soliloquising loudly in the corridors, after his long lunches, about courage and duty. My face looked sunburned at these times I was told by an amused woman. 'Windburned would be more like it,' I said to her.

One day, on the way to work, I decided not to go in again. I wrote a letter of resignation at the post office, to the production manager, saying I was a disruptive presence and it was best that I left the job. (Most of the staff had been constrained about the situation, eyeing me as a curious object, remaining pleasant enough. Some would not have been convinced about the war, either, I imagined; but they kept quiet, with such a conservative employer.) I thanked the production manager for employing me, but not warmly: I felt I had wasted time because of his 'puppeteer complex', because he was a collector, a manipulator of people. This was perhaps unfair. He would have thought I was settling into a career, and that he had been generous in taking me off the street.

I might have told the management there was no chance of me being inducted, since I would never pass the medical, but I could not use that excuse, or perhaps could not acknowledge my condition aloud. I might have waited for the medical examination and not registered as a conscientious objector at all, but I thought it too easy to take that way. As assurance to myself that I was not a coward, I wanted to do something I would find difficult and that was a witness against the war.

As it turned out, I merely caused annoyance in the court. Enquiries had been made about my background and it was thought

I was a Jehovah's Witness. I said, from the dock, that I was not at all dependent on the Bible, but was arguing out of conscience, which left the prosecutor unprepared and embarrassed and the judge impatient. I said my argument was on the grounds of just and unjust wars, and that my ethical sense was opposed to this one. In feeling that way, I was not eccentric or merely subjective, since a great many people, almost half the population, agreed. I thought the war against Hitler had been a just war; but this one was undeclared because it could not be morally supported. A considerable amount of quotation was thrown in, from such stand-bys as Lao Tzu, Aldous Huxley and Bertrand Russell, about the possibility of over-extending and undermining the enemy through 'passive' means.

The judge ruled that I did not have a conscientious objection to war as such and that what was a just or unjust war was for the government to decide (ignoring the Nuremberg War Crimes Tribunal's ruling on individual responsibility). I was ordered to report for service. That meant a medical examination, so I was not too bothered by the verdict.

The doctor who examined me, as I stood in a line of naked young men, each with stomach muscles clenched and chest squared, because of a youthful nurse who was present, was a rheumy-eyed, ratty-looking older man, wearing a white coat. 'This one looks as if he hits the grog,' whispered the boy next to me. 'D'ya reckon we could bribe him with some turps?'

The doctor drew on a cigarette, squinting, and laid it on the edge of a table, before listening to my chest. We were on an unfurnished, echoing floor of some government building, among a few trestles and screens, in the downtown city at night.

'You'll notice it sounds a bit strange,' I remarked, in a reassuring way to the doctor.

'What do you mean?'

'My heart. It's got a hole in the inner wall, the septum.'

'There's nothing wrong with your heart, son. You're under-weight, but you can build up. How are your feet? You got flat feet?'

I realised it was the intention of the government to pass every-one they could. I did not have asthma, or a limp, or look obviously diseased, and that was enough. So it was going to be jail. I was at once worried I would be put in among rapists and sadists. I had heard that conscientious objectors went usually into low security farming work, and were mostly kept to themselves, for their protection. I hoped so.

I waited for the next letter from the Department of Defence and in the meantime took a job as a filing clerk, in another govern-ment bureaucracy. I earned barely enough, at the lowest level of qualification, for rent on the bed-sitter and for necessities, so I stopped going to films, joined the Public Library, and walked to and from work every day, along ugly, sun-blasted streets. Then the letter came: it said I had been found unfit for military service for medical reasons, but could be called on again, and to inform my employer of that. What a malicious old bastard the doctor was, I thought, encouraging me to worry; he knew I had been to court and he obviously detested 'conchies'.

I worked as a labourer in the Botanical Gardens, for a couple of months, during which time it rained almost continually, so that I had to clean terracotta pots and shovel humus into bags; then in the chinaware section of a department store, although I had applied for the bookshop; and in a bookshop; and another bookstore (the one I had admired as a child, but in its Education Department, in the basement); and as a shelver at a university library. Only my writing made me feel I was not merely drifting. Unpublished as yet, I used to revise a poem until there was no room in the margins, and then type a clean copy, and gradually transform that, until each page looked like a shattered windscreen.

About six months after being told I was not immediately wanted in the army, I took some time off work with the flu, and because
a medical certificate was necessary to receive sick pay from the
bookshop where I worked, saw a doctor. He gave me a complete
physical check-up. I asked how my heart sounded, and told him
about it briefly, and he said I had better see a specialist. Many
innovations had occurred in surgery in this field, during the almost
ten years since I had been under care. He happened to know a
world-famous pulmonary expert in the city, working in Macquarie
Street, the street of doctors. This man was bound to be interested
in a case such as mine.

I had seen Dr Gaston Bauer, the heart specialist, written up
in the newspaper. The article was about what should be done to
keep one's heart healthy. He was photographed standing astride a
bicycle, in white shorts, a sailor's top and a beret, tweaking one end
of his moustache.

I did go to see Dr Bauer, since urged to so seriously by the local
doctor. He listened intently, questioned me, rang up the Children's
Hospital and had them read at length from a report, and put me
through a long series of tests, with what he said was innovatory
equipment. This included an enlarged electro-cardiogram, and a
radiation machine, for which I stood secured by the arms and forehead, my back against an almost door-sized lead plate, and during
the running of which he left the room. Finally, I sat before his desk
again, whether on that or another visit I cannot remember. 'I have
to tell you,' he said, 'there is nothing wrong with your heart, at all.'

'Really! I can't believe that. What about all the tests, the tubes
up through the arms, the X-rays, the groups of specialists, the years
of visits to Sydney, the medicine, which cost my parents money?
What was all that for? What about the hole, the size of…?'

'What can I say? Either you never had a lesion in the heart,
and people found what they expected to find, given your mother's

condition when she was pregnant, and given there perhaps was a benign murmur, or else the lesion has completely healed, as you've grown. It very rarely happens. Your active childhood would have helped. You did exactly the right thing, if this healing has occurred, by not being an invalid. All I can tell you is that the tests you have just undergone are very accurate. You have no sign of any heart disorder. I think you never did have. Your debility when young? Neurasthenia, perhaps. Did your parents go through a divorce? Anyway, I advocate activity for the heart, so I would like to think that you helped cure yourself. Whatever, I congratulate you. Your heart is strong. In fact, as far as I can see, the only thing you need worry about is being hit by a bus.'

I came out onto the pavement and stood there, I remember, with no idea of who I was. I felt – resentment. Some distinction that was intimately mine had been taken away, far too lightly. Something in my life that had been concentrated now had gone slack. Suddenly the future was a long space, unfolding ahead of me in mechanical perspective. What was I to do with myself?

I realised the hack doctor at the medical had been right. So, why was I exempted from military service? Obviously the government had not wanted too many people publicised as conscientious objectors – there were hectic news reports at the time about a TV entertainer being dragged off to jail – and it had been quietly dropping cases, allowing the subjects to think themselves unfit.

When I told my mother about this, in person, not too long afterwards, she chose to believe something actual had healed up, but seemed confused, as if it all belonged to another life. I never knew my father's reaction, if there was any.

For month on month after seeing the specialist I felt entangled in boredom and confusion, and could make only the most habitual choices. I was fired from my bookshop job, found another the same day, and before long was fired from that. In the street, sometimes,

I was hardly able to walk. I would find myself standing at the curb, unable to recall what I had just been thinking. Then something happened that helped me regain myself. It seemed to show prescience on the specialist's part. I stepped in front of a bus.

I had been trying to keep up a practice of observation, and as I walked off the pavement, toward disaster, was looking into the distance at magnificent clouds, which might have been an African mountain range. It was probably autumn, when the clouds around Sydney are their most imposing. I had been reading Walter Pater's essays on Aestheticism at about this time – perhaps I was discriminating 'some tone that was choicer than the rest'. All at once, I found myself with a hand pushed hard into a chrome grille, while around me there burst out harsh smoke and a deep bay like a wounded bloodhound's. I was aware of the heat and grit underneath my palm, momentarily. The bus, just launched away from the traffic lights, had braked, but slid forward, and it threw me down: I lay with my legs lengthwise underneath it, a filthy tyre pinching my shirt to the road. I was up again in an instant. The driver had his forehead on the steering wheel; he lifted himself and simply shook his head. I mouthed 'Thank you,' and smiled as warmly as I could. No, no, I conveyed with a level gesture, I was fine, and disappeared. As I hurried off, tapping lightly on my leg with a rolled newspaper, for the bystanders, my new heart was vibrating like a punching ball.

'We are all *condamnés*,' Victor Hugo says, quoted by Pater in his essay *The Renaissance*. That was the point. Why not live as though still under sentence, but permitted a short reprieve? We cannot control what we experience. Our daily efforts deny this, but perhaps it was possible to avoid complacency by holding onto that realisation. Then the days might have again their strange interest.

16. A Vacant Possession

I lived alone in flats near the inner city for the next eleven years. The girlfriend I had at any time might visit on weekends, but was not encouraged to stay the night. We ate out, and I saw her home to the suburbs in a cab or by train, rather than have anything like domesticity between us. Sometimes, late in the evening, I had to rouse us both from sleep. If I missed the last train back, I would have to sit in a waiting room at the station until almost daybreak.

I remember shiftworkers appearing on the platform in the dark, on cold or wet Saturdays, in the years when I knew a girl who lived near the city's outskirts. At her station, in winter, the trees along the embankment were like fishes' skeletons, and the waiting room was as stark as an empty refrigerator. Finally, the train would come, sliding along the platform's edge, out of drizzle or fog, and with their collars about them the workers shuffled on board. There was never a glance or greeting among us, but I felt at times an inkling of a strange emotion, solidarity.

When I look back on my relations with women then, I see them as shallow. The interest I had in my girlfriends was partly truth but mainly friction. It was something to do with the era, as much as with me: that was the high season of psychoanalytical culture, when everyone read utopians such as Wilhelm Reich and it was possible to believe one was virtuously ridding oneself of neuroses and of fascistic 'character armour' through light sexual encounters.

Still, some of my relationships continued for years, when they should have ended much earlier. That they did not was because of an egotistical image I had of myself as not causing hurt. Of course one causes hurt: if people actually want involvement and one has no intention of allowing it, one is using them.

My criterion for partners, apart from looks, was that they be working-class. I had a distaste for the self-satisfaction I thought I sensed in attractive young middle-class women I met – for their easy familiarity with art, or whatever culture their families had, which made it seem like a dress-accessory.

Fired from somewhere, for lack of application (no one young seemed to take their employment seriously then), I heard a

job was available just across the street, as a copywriter in the advertising department of a chain store. I applied, and ended up employed there for five years, because of the manager's indulgence toward me and a facile ability I had for the work.

That was the late sixties, and every male who was allowed to, or who could, had grown his hair long, and had become more decorative in his clothing; and this included me.

The advertising manager had hair piled up at a slant, in a shiny Elvis Presley style; tall and plump, he wore double-breasted chocolate or burgundy suits, paisley ties, rings, and under his sleeve silver bracelets from North Africa. He ran a 'fun crew', he assured me when I applied and said that he could tell I was 'switched on'. I thought of my appearance as a rather half-hearted conformism, so as not to stand out among those of my age. 'Do you have a girl-friend?' was the last question of the interview. My answer pleased him. 'Let's keep it that way. Well, I think we'll get along wonder-fully, wonderfully well.' He even patted my knee.

At the end of the week, all the staff went drinking after work. For my welcome, the boss took some of us to an Italian restaurant. He must have put too little orange juice in the champagne he poured me, and I had accepted too much of it: I found myself leaning at a urinal, in a basement under the road, near what seemed an iron cage at feeding time. Through the noise I heard him say, 'There you are, my dear. We've been so worried about you.' I zipped up and lurched around to see him approaching with both fat, jewelled hands extended and the quiver of solicitude on his jowls. Perfectly cued, I vomited at his feet, and was aware that he had vanished, as if edited from a film.

I became conscious of lurching about in a loud, brightly lit street, trying to escape. I was getting nowhere, in deep, slipping sand. I blacked out again, and came to floundering in another unknown place, with people looming before me and separating to let me by. Oblivion once more, followed by the sense of crossing a road in danger, blaring lights all about me. And so on. Moments of desperate lucidity kept clattering up like white, startled birds from out of the darkness.

I discovered myself staggering in a park. There was a row of Moreton Bay fig trees and between the high-sided roots of one I saw a drift of big, dried leaves, piled deeply. I climbed in among the leaves, heaped them completely over me, and breathed from under a broad, curved leaf that I poked into place. I felt myself spinning, going down a vortex and grasped at handfuls of the leaves, crushing them ineffectually. I wondered if that could have been what my father felt, on the occasions when he staggered by the roadside, and fell down. How could it not have created an aversion?

On Saturday morning, soon after I arrived home, the boss rang me. 'Are you all right? We looked everywhere. You left a book. I can drop it in, later. What happened to you?' I told him I had woken up in the bottom of a cornflakes packet. He was a sensitive man and was soon embarrassed by my obstructive flippancies and rang off. From then on he was uncomfortable with me, or with an attitude that he saw might be undermining of leadership. All so easily, I was no longer a favourite, but was given, for a while, the dreariest work.

I counted the characters and spaces in what I wrote, and measured with an ems rule, fitting my words to the visual designs of our newspaper ads. The copy had some factual content, but was mainly puns, exhortation and excitement – it was meant to be 'fun'. This was urged upon us as the store's image. We were to be 'very sixties'. I am sure that no one read what we three or four copywriters turned out, or not more than a line or so, except for others in the office, the lay-out artists, secretaries, publicity people: they giggled over it, and quoted a line or a phrase to each other, usually contributing a pose as they did so. There was competition among the copywriters to see who could best amuse the staff. Gradually, I exonerated myself, and was given some of the better jobs. It was all absurd, I thought, and acted as though I were comfortable with it.

I used to work on my own writing in the office of a morning, which was a reason for staying in the job, along with a disinterest in anything else I might have done; the pay was average. The boss knew of this distraction of mine, through turning up in my cubicle and looking over my shoulder. 'And what, my dear, has this to do with our whitegoods sale?'

'I'm afraid you've caught me getting off with the Muse.'

'Well get on with it and get it done. I was never a voyeur – of that sort of thing. I want your copy on my desk by lunchtime. And if what you're writing ever appears in a book, I expect it to be dedicated to me.'

He was a kind man, to all his 'kids'. I put such a dedication in my first pamphlet, acknowledging it was written on his time.

Though I began by thinking of them as a disguise, I later took an interest in fashionable clothing; I remember wearing embroidered shirts and Indian *dhoti*, flared trousers, a long corduroy coat with a coachman's collar and tight waist, silver bangles and necklaces, and Cuban-heel boots. When the staff went out together, the girls wore tiny skirts, which made me think of lit-up lampshades. They admired a black, crushed velvet jacket I had found, worn clasped with pieces of silver jewellery. Some of them wanted to make up my eyes, but I resisted. I was warned by an irritated male that I was only saved from femininity by my long-boned jaw.

It seemed that if one were thin and fashionable then, and even slightly reminiscent of someone famous who sang, sexual favours were likely to be readily won, from the female votaries of Dionysius. For almost a decade, there was a matriarchy among the young: it was a time of feminine triumph, when women sexually persuaded young men of a similar generation into their self-affirming image. With ensured contraception, women were independent, decisive and adventurous, were no longer patronised, nor vaguely contemptible, as they had very often been, one could guess, for men. As well, which had hardly been admitted before, they were felt to

have a broader human nature, not so reductionist as the male. They were the human creatures of grace, as de Beauvoir wrote: what had men to offer any-where near so fine as what they took. Because of which, a certain androgyny became a positive attribute of young men, for a time, with those who were not bisexual. It was my good luck, given my temperament and physique, to have come of age in a decade in which a more. nuanced type of male was the most acceptable to women, or fashionable with them.

My experience of drugs was minimal, for that time. I realise now how much I hated the 'drug culture' atmosphere: I was put off from the start by the ugly wet joints that people were always passing you, in the sixties. It felt to me that because they were mechanical, drugs turned you into an object for yourself; more than ever divided, wrenched about like a gear-stick. My idea of satisfaction was always making something, or appreciating something, through judgement; but with drugs, one had no such discrimination. The only drugs I was really curious about were hallucinogens. The idea of 'cleansing the doors of perception' interested me greatly; I had a desire for the 'visionary experi-ence', after reading Thomas Traherne – 'The corn was orient and immortal wheat, which never should be reaped nor was ever sown...' At first my experiences looked like Maxfield Parrish posters, which were popular then; everything high-keyed, like a sunset in an autumn landscape, which was rather expectable.

LSD only briefly accomplished that: after the novelty of the first few outward-looking trips, it spilled a previously subliminal, now lurid jumble of indiscriminate associations, mostly from pop culture, onto one's flaccid consciousness; something similar to seeing silly profiles in clouds, everywhere. Endlessly maundering, I found myself force-fed with Daliesque or Disney-like clichés. LSD showed the subconscious to be as banal as the conscious, when not continually transcended through criticism.

I had a particularly grotesque experience with 'acid' while lying on a crowded beach. Everyone suddenly took on the appearance of those engravings of human anatomy by Vesalius: they were stripped of their skin, to reveal themselves as overlapping straps and fans of striated muscle. They still had their hair. All over each person's surface, chemical signals or perhaps platelets in the blood were performing frenetically; with more urgency than ants have in pouring out of a broken nest. I left the beach and went to a café, and could see, in cross-section, flayed people revolving cuds of food in their mouths. The experience went on and on; it was not edifying. After that, in a different sense to Keats's, I 'emptied my dull (hallucinogens) to the drains'.

I lived in a series of two-room flats, all needing perseverance to discover, but with something to be seen from all of them. After Paddington, at the top of a three-storey terrace, with its glimpses of sails sleepwalking on the harbour, I moved to Balmain, then a working-class suburb, to the last house on a street that drooped above the abandoned wharfs and warehouses of one of Sydney's innumerable bays. In the ground-floor windows of my flat there, a morning glory vine was like a Chinese ceremonial dragon, carried on the palings of a staggering fence; beyond that, down an entirely vine-covered, flowering slope, stood the wreckage of the old buildings; and then the high, rusty walls of chained-up tankers, gulls drifting across them. Next, I had a place near Centennial Park, from which, looking over heavy traffic, I saw vistas like those of a golf course, groves of fir trees and pines, and people riding horses. Then I lived, as if in secret, behind one of the big white houses of Woollahra, among the plane trees, in a flat that had a small, private backyard underneath camphor laurel branches; these stirred or tumbled like the edge of the sea, and their dry leaves piled up in corners, deeply. Once I was mugged in the street near there, by someone I never saw, and although nothing much showed, my split mouth became infected inside. I was unable to eat, but did not go to a doctor. Leaving home to meet a friend in the afternoon, a few days later, I locked the back door and must have passed out; I awoke lying on my back, sunk in a drift of leaves, the pale lichen of the stars beyond the guttering. I stayed there, in the dark, drifting in and out of sleep, watching the new moon passing over, calm and deeply happy. I wondered what could ever make me get up. If one were falling, I thought, there was always the Earth; one need fall no further than that. Sometime around dawn I found myself inside, eating honey.

Those flats were kept orderly enough to suit my father. I took from one unfurnished place to another a broad-angled, black-and-white African rug, a futon and base, with a red cotton bedspread, a few jute-coloured canvas chairs, a worn, pale blue, narrow wooden table, a typewriter, a small television, and a collection of books, stacked against one wall as if they were modelling the city sky-line. There was a blue enamel jug I crammed with flowers, and on the wall, at one time, a print of a geometrical abstraction in lyrical colour by Ben Nicholson. Abstract art has a beauty that is intensified by its meaning nothing else – it is freed from psycho-logising and expression, as at times we want art to be – but it is not finally satisfying, because it cannot be a precise, fully engaged language. It leaves a vacancy. After a while I replaced it with Edward Hopper's *Rooms by the Sea*. That picture was of a bare room with an opened door on its right-hand side, cut off by the top of the canvas, in which, seemingly with little transition, a deep blue sea was standing, reaching from close below the room, away to the horizon, halfway up the door-frame. In another room, to the side of that empty one in the foreground, there was a bureau and a lounge chair, partly glimpsed. The picture did not have a surrealist harshness; rather, it seemed to say, in its calm, that the ordinary world, the way we find it, was marvellous, and strange enough. As always with Hopper, there was an extraordinary sense of the massiveness of things. Light entered the room as a lighter-toned, large, geometrical shape, on the blue-grey wall, an asymmetrical chevron, lying on wall and bent onto floor. The persistent interest a still image can have is a mystery, something to do with its proportions, among other things. This large poster created a captured, extra sunlight on the wall of my room, that was always there, like a Parsee's flame.

I was married at twenty-five, but lived only briefly with my wife. She, I had thought, on first seeing her, among a group at a bar, standing calmly within herself, was 'an archangel, slightly damaged'. Unusually, I went over and spoke, fascinated by her sculptural features, alongside the stringy, roughly pinned-up, drab-blonde hair, and touched by her baggy dress and clumpy shoes. Although she smiled, there was already something hooded and remote about her; a twilight quality, at nineteen. Knowing the unhappiness that she was being brought, I see myself approaching her with a plummet of remorse.

Her father was almost blind, a jazz drummer, who made himself completely 'blind' at the parties he held in his house, over three evenings of practically every weekend. Her mother was heavy, raucous, and boozy, but generous, warm, hugely warm, to her five children, two of them adopted.

I used to call for the daughter on a Saturday and Sunday morning and would find the house, in Paddington, littered with empty wine casks, bottles, beer cans, and with comatose bodies, in various states of undress. The father came reeling through the chaos, holding onto the smeared walls, stepping into puddles, to greet me like a friend, still mumbling the obscene songs he composed for their group. His voice rose in a chorus: '... AN' NIGEL'S A DROP-KICKING PUNT!' His daughter would depart the house, directing mocking rejoinders over her shoulder at its bleary, rousing inhabitants, seemingly unembarrassed.

When she became pregnant, through miscalculation, she was reluctant to have an abortion, because she said she had fairly recently had one. So we went to the Registry Office to be married, along with just her family and their closest friends, a homosexual pimp and a vastly overweight prostitute. All the usual crowd turned up for the party at the parents' house.

After a few days holiday at a cabin on the coast, we lived in my flat. Then, at the hospital, she seemed to be suffering terrible, unusual pain; they thought that she was behaving badly, and I was sent away. The child was stillborn. Early in the morning the doctor showed me a boy, perfectly formed, nothing detectably wrong, and I filled in a form and gave him a name. They asked what I wanted done and I chose to have the child cremated at once, without ceremony. I thought this would be best for my wife, but now I understand it was utterly wrong.

The marriage continued for only a couple of months; I did not want another child, which the doctor said my wife should have. Having been so closely missed by a situation I had faced with secret trepidation, domesticity as I imagined it, I then over-reacted. By the time my wife moved back to her parents, who were unrecriminating, completely decent, brimmed with care, I already had a new girlfriend. It was eleven years before my wife thought of marrying again and applied to me for a divorce. She has never had a child.

I moved to a new job, as a copywriter in an agency. I soon had a bank balance but was unhappy about the obtuseness of my clients, who always chose the least interesting of the campaigns I designed. To judge by my rejection rate, I was not a particularly good copy-writer. I have kept no scrapbook of my acceptances, but can still feel disappointment about what was not used. Asked to name a new beer, which was to have a particularly masculine image, what I suggested was 'Crowbar' ('Busts any thirst'), but some-thing by another writer, which in my colleagues' opinion was far less effective, won. Then when I was working on the account of a pearl farming and retailing company, and none of the campaigns I designed was used. For the ad that was my favourite, I envisaged a pearly black-and-white photograph of a young native woman kneeling in a thatched hut, a magnificent pearl on one hand, beneath her gaze, a subtle look in her face, the caption simply 'The Diver's Widow', and the dealer's name. I thought of it in *The New Yorker*. I also proposed a series of tonal photographs, each of a woman's throat and a low-cut black dress, a man's hands doing up her necklace of phosphorescent pearls; beneath this, various captions. Two I remember were 'Tender is the Light' and 'Her Price is Above Rubies (Proverbs 17, 39)', which refers to 'a good woman' in that way. These went from my desk into a meeting with the client and straight to oblivion. I did have at least one success with that company: again a black-and-white close-up shot, of a couple obviously dancing, she with a luminous pearl earring beside the softness of her cheek, and the caption 'The Light Fantastic'. There were, of course, more acceptable campaigns that I wrote for other clients, but none I remember with pride; although, I enjoyed writing the lyrics to some Jerry Lee Lewis type rock and roll, as jingles for a used car dealership.

After a year in the job, I gave what money I had saved to my wife, who wanted to train as a schoolteacher, and went to work at the central Mail Exchange, sorting letters. I chose the shift from four until midnight so that I could do my own writing in the mornings, the best time. I lived at Woollahra then and often wrote by hand on the back steps in leaf-filtered sunlight.

Of an evening, I was one of many hundreds of employees in a kind of factory – on a polished vinyl floor, as big as a football field, were crowded running belts, long sorting tables, vats, wheeled bins, and ranks of coding machines, with their steady clamour, beneath banked fluorescent lights. Packed canvas bags constantly arrived, thumping out of the overhead chutes into wooden sorting trays, which were trap-sprung; the bags were quickly shaken out and their content roughly culled for size. Letters and packages were carried away, chaotically, within a wooden trough, running like an irrigation channel across the floor; workers gathered and aligned these, again hurriedly, making neat selections on the sliding belt of their bench-tops, pecking among the mail like battery hens. The squared-up letters were stacked into bins, pushed away, parked, snatched up in handfuls, and fired from equipment like mounted machine guns, between thin horizontal tapes, to women typing, reading postcodes, at rows of letter-distributing machines, in a great chittering noise. Occasionally someone came back drunk from the locker room and in a mood to throw the mails about, which would raise a cheer and a rush of overseers. The work was stultifying. Everywhere workers argued, teased, or fell into intense conversations, out of boredom, despite the overseers urging them on. The air conditioning rumbled and the public address system crackled like cellophane, with exhortations and instructions.

This was a place where the mildly unemployable were taken in, as a policy: the businessmen recovering from breakdowns, the burned-out taxi-drivers, the immigrants whose professional qualifications were not recognised, the long-haired drop-outs, and the moonlighting housewives, some amazing proportion of whom were rumoured to have succumbed to a man known as 'Fiddler on the Roof'.

A nervous, fussy man, in middle age, whom I will call Barry Fitzgerald, was constantly being asked how Gerald was, etc., and continually having his wig flicked from behind, so that it fell over his eyes; this despite the protests of a few people. One afternoon when everyone was clocking on, he appeared with a shotgun and fired directly at a group of his tormentors. People were lying on the floor everywhere, in the reverberating explosion, but the gun was loaded only with blanks, and the gunman was led away in tears, and never appeared again. Nothing else was done about it.

As I came to understand that place, I felt as though the cleaners, who mopped continually among us, were its emblem – they appeared to be always puddling in the same grimy water. There were the drug deals, meant to be unobtrusive but noticeably self-conscious; the many drop-outs drifting stoned and passive among the workers who were medicated (often hard to make the distinction); the girls, mainly single mothers, who went to the car park with certain supervisors, or accepted lifts from them, as their overtime; the person who owed the bookmaker suddenly trapped by a group in a corner, struggling, gagged, and his head shoved into a toilet bowl, or he was thrown fully-clothed under the hot hand-washing fountain, caustic soap in his mouth; the young men constantly solicited for sex, by overseers and workers; the people who were treated as idle amusement because of their nervous rituals (touching fixtures around the place in a certain order, at regular times, while others tried to frustrate them, disingenuously piling bags and bins in their way); the ones who with a furtive casualness examined certain letters and parcels, and were later found to have lockers full of other people's mail; and always the petty obstruction and confrontation between workers and management. No one, except thieves, for whom the police had to be brought, could be sacked, because the union would have called us out. The mails were more crucial then and the postal department was conciliatory and feared for its reputation. These days, there has been a decentralisation and contracting-out of the service, and the culture has entirely changed; the building itself no longer exists.

The union rep, a man who waddled around in shorts and long socks, collecting dues and awarding everyone a quip, who wore a badge with the message 'Post Marx', had a large banner put up in the locker room – 'Nothing's Too Good For The Workers'.

During most of the three years that I worked at the Mail Exchange, I went on my two days off, mid-week and on Sunday, to visit my father in a psychiatric ward, there in Sydney, where he was being kept heavily sedated. I will come to that.

At the time I was fascinated, more deeply than ever, by Rilke, who seemed to me the best poet of the twentieth century. I particularly liked his more objective work, in the *New Poems* and in the 'uncollected' writing done at the end of his life, between 1919 and 1926. I owned numerous versions of his work, translated *en face*, and a German-English dictionary, and I carried the rough drafts of my own translations with me to my job, or on the bus to the hospital, to occupy myself. I sat sorting mail, for part of every night, among the more taciturn, older workers, making occasional swift notes. Then I was more sociable again, joining in the banter of my friends. Rilke got me through the evenings best of all. This is his most famous poem, though I would not say his best, in the form I came up with then:

The Panther

(Jardin des Plantes, Paris)

From having gazed too often on the bars,
he seems to find a thousand bars, unfurled.
His sight's so weary that although he stares
among the bars, they are the only world.

All of his supple, soft, powerful paces
are tightly wound about themselves; that stride
is like an encircling dance of forces
in which a great will finds itself denied.

And yet, the lens of his pupil sometimes
dilates, in silence; an image can start
inwards, amid the tense, suspended limbs,
quickly to its destruction, on the heart.

I rode home sometimes after the late shift on the back of a friend's motorcycle, along the freeway, our hair streaming like comets. He usually affected a stoned manner, but was witty and droll, and so I thought nothing of going with him. He agreed to teach me to ride, and after a little practice, one evening, let me take the bike at speed, on a detour down long, blue-lit, empty roads, winding beneath warehouses. I recall a hurricane wire fence beside us, hung with silver rain, like scales, and sheet-lightning across the sky. He shouted beside my ear, 'I thought you'd lost it, in that corner,' his voice filled with hilarity, and I realised he really was 'off his face', as he had joked, and that I must keep the bike in my hands. I opened the throttle further, and felt a mindless exultation. Gripping my shirt, crouched above me, he urged me on, the road crackling like a running fuse.

17. The Sufficient Place

Then I went to live in the country for a year, in the house
of my friends Joseph and Diana, who were teaching art at
a remote Aboriginal settlement. I could afford to stay there
because of having given up most social life to the night shift.

The house was small, on a ridge in the forest; influenced
by a Japanese style, it had an isosceles steepness to the tin roof,
extended eaves, and further extended rafters. It was in dark, oiled
wood, except for the sliding glass doors, like screens, which made
up two walls. Close by, on either side, long narrow tree trunks rose
out of the gullies as smoothly as pipes, and released a steam of
leaves, high in the sunlight.

Uphill and down, the close-set trees were long stripes of widely
varying thickness; beneath them was leaf litter, old logs, shadows,
bracken, and floating scraps of undergrowth; above, the foliage
rose, shelf upon shelf, eternally green. All day, there was the sound
of a sea among the trees, and of sticks and gumnuts thrown down
hard on the metal roof. Sometimes, if I was lucky, a downpour of
rain came at night, extinguishing the radio with its overwhelming
presence.

I stayed at 'The Clearing', on and off, through the year, working in Joe's vegetable garden, writing under a tarpaulin that was strung among saplings, going to Ted and Kathy's, half a mile away, on certain evenings. Coming home from those visits, I had to find my way through the winding gravel verge underfoot: the forested nights, often overcast, were completely opaque in the road's damp hollow. The vertiginous small watery torch beam was about as helpful to me as his instincts are to a drunkard, and I several times fell into the undergrowth, though having had only a few drinks.

Of a day, I took long walks in the forest, on deserted fire trails, and sometimes made an excursion to the highest peak in the ridges above the house. Having ascended there, I climbed further, on an unused fire-watching tower, going up through level after level of ladders, to a high, small crow's nest, just a platform, at the pinnacle. I sat with legs dangling either side of a thin post in the one-beam railing, looking over an immense vista of forest, pastures, and distant ocean – a glider pilot hung on the travelling air. Red eagles drifted far out, below me, and all of the widespread country stirred beneath cloud-shadows, or lay with a dream of sunlight in its face.

Sometimes visitors came to the house for a short while, mainly a young woman I had met on the train. I remember she drove us to a creek where there was a pebbled bank and a deep swimming hole, and how her strong, white body rose from the water, against the dark trees, in the humid dusk.

When not at Joe's I stayed in Sydney at the house of Geoffrey Lehmann, a solicitor, who was also, for those who knew about such things, one of the country's best poets. I had admired him from my high school days, after finding some work of his in a weekly news magazine. I see myself coming to a stop in the school grounds, the magazine folded tightly in my hand, to finish reading the poem and to read it again. I cannot remember how we met, but I was invited to dinner by him a few years after my arrival in Sydney. He was five years older than me and well established as a writer. We became friends, amazingly, his generosity allowing him to indulge my then rather extreme political opinions, which were far from his. We have never argued.

It was he, I think, who introduced me to our mutual admiration, Kenneth Slessor, at the hard-drinking Journalist's Club, above Central Station railway yards. The eminent poet, famously no longer writing, was president there, and we came across him sitting with a whisky among the poker machines, acknowledging his constituency as it began to arrive. He was portly, sparse-haired, gingery-coloured, immaculate, wearing a bow tie and a gingery expression. His haemorrhoids must have been giving him hell (as they were rumoured to), because when made aware of me he immediately instructed, 'Get your hair cut!' But then we talked, unbothered by the racket of the place, about Tennyson and the supremacy of his music. Later he gave me a remarkably good review, for my first book, in the tabloid newspaper of which he had been editor. I was told his notices were almost invariably kind, but I thought, after many re-readings of my two paragraphs, that I could detect an air of conviction.

From Geoff I learned to admire a classical style of writing ('cool water refreshes best'). I tried to substitute for my heavily freighted Romanticism the swiftness and lightness, the cleanliness and severity, I found in his work and in his Greek and Roman influences.

His house was large and dilapidated, in a wealthy suburb, with a wild scrawl for a garden. Inside, it was bohemian: faded Oriental rugs, old divans, lacquered sideboards, mismatched silver, eccentric vases, no two second-hand chairs alike, and paintings everywhere, mostly bought from friends. Although he has since become a partner in an international accountancy firm, an advisor to government on taxation, has made a second marriage and raised and released five children, and is paid 'megabucks', he has not changed the youthful atmosphere of his house.

Geoff has remained of normal build, with face tending toward roundness, symmetrical features, white skin, black hair, often a flag of it on his forehead, a slightly aquiline, intellectual nose, a stiff posture, a slight stoop. In manner, he is often constrained, even awkward, and is neglectful of tact when enthusiastic. There is about him still something of the precociously clever boy who passed his university entrance exams when he was fifteen. He is a reader of science, a disbeliever in other than pragmatic knowledge, and unfailingly the most decent of people.

He is also an obsessive collector of certain types of recorded music, having an urge to experience 'something different', after thorough familiarity with nineteenth-century Romanticism. He has turned to blues, minimalism, *a cappella* masses, the undervalued composers from Alkan to Zelenka, Broadway musicals, Ethiopian jazz, and the cruel and unusual Morton Feldman (whose String Quartet no. 2, of six and a half hours, he listened to at home 'with only two toilet breaks'). Among all of this, he returns to comparing performances of Bach.

He has written about a collector's life as being 'solitary and courageous, meaningful only to himself...'

Arriving home at night
with my newspaper neatly
folded under my arm,
I'm bailed up by my son
at the top of the stairs:
'Mum, he's hiding more CDs
in his Financial Review!'

During one of my visits to the city, from Joe's house, someone called to me out of the rush on a late afternoon pavement. It was a young woman with a two-year-old child in arms. We had been introduced, years before, and soon after our first, glancing encounter, I had met her again, on a downtown street one night. Loping alone among drifting people, impressively thin, with a wonderful stride in her clinging cotton dress, she immediately had distinction and dignity. We stopped to talk, on that earlier occasion, and went to a film I was on my way to see. Afterwards, I found her a cab, since I was then involved with someone. She was German, a few years younger than me, with swept-back, buoyant blonde hair, a marvellously rounded forehead, smoky-blue eyes, skin flawless as fresh snow, and a face shaped as boldly as a shield, though with a gentle expression.

Then, there she was, years later, coming up to speak to me on the street, a large-eyed spider monkey wrapped about her, glaring. Within a few blocks I drew from her that she was married, worked long hours as a hairdresser, her child was anxious, her husband had found work was beneath him (he would spend his life waiting for an inheritance, like someone in Dickens), and they were separating. At her bus stop we arranged to meet in a few days.

After our lunch, I left for the country, but we each wrote the other a letter, and she flew up to stay for one night the next weekend. About a week after her return to the city, I learned she was now alone, and I went back there because a divorce had begun and her child was being kept from her. I met with her briefly, but stayed out of the way, as I was asked. She returned to the old relationship, in a new flat, tried to settle, and then left again. It was agreed, after a tense couple of weeks, that the husband would give up their daughter and in return be relieved of financial responsibility for her. (Yet he saw her devotedly, all through her childhood. He was a man, I found, in his too-brief lifetime, who even when penurious had  style and charm.) So at thirty I entered on a fully grown domestic life. We had had, when I moved in, knowing it required serious-ness, the equivalent of three days with each other.

Dee was brought to Australia a few years after the War, when she was two, her parents refugees who had asked to go to Argentina. After starting school, she and her two sisters taught their parents in the evening the English they had learned that day. There was no support for immigrants, then. It was expected that she leave school at fifteen, and since she had found an after-school job in a hairdressing salon, that was the sort of work she took. Inexplicably, she wanted to go to art school. She moved out of the heat-flattened suburbs to the city, completing an apprenticeship, and then was asked one day in the street to work as a catwalk model. When she married, she went back to hairdressing to support her husband, who was recurrently out of work.

The new life was immediately accessible to me through Dee's gift for creating, on a small income, flats that were by general agreement both aesthetic and livable. Her taste had been influenced by her former husband's, who had worked as an interior designer, and whose principle was that in such matters limited income was not entirely a disadvantage, since less money imposed restraint. Gradually, with judicious pieces of furniture, rugs, objects, paintings, she transformed the interiors of a series of places we lived in by the harbour. Eventually, not through any virtue of mine, but due to good fortune, we owned an apartment there.

We have both worked part-time, she with designer clothing, I with books, to supply, through the considerable discounts available to us, our 'non-essential', major needs. Again, we have been lucky, avoiding a major expense because Dee's daughter, Harriet, was clever and was accepted into a government 'selective' school.

Later, when we travelled in older, more artistically endowed countries, in connection with my writing, I noticed Dee's intent response to sculpture, and joked it was because she was used to 'thinking in the round'. In middle age she began making figurative modelled pieces, ignoring modernist strictures about what could now be done, fulfilling her temperament. The works are made without thought of an audience; getting her to sell, someone said, is 'harder than making it for yourself'.

Soon after Dee and I met, I received a fellowship from the government's arts funding organisation, the Australia Council, and over the decades, as my work became known, was awarded many of these. As my writing stands, I am entirely a creature of its Literature Board.

While receiving grants, I was allowed to work two or three days a week, and I found a job in a bookshop in Paddington as a sales clerk and buyer. The owner was the grandson of Lady Gregory, the poet W. B. Yeats's patron, and in an appropriately far lesser way, he became something of a patron to me. During years when I had no grant (it was always something of a lottery), William de Winton arranged I have extra work at the shop; then, when I won prizes, scholarships or writer-in-residencies, I was given time off to go travelling, with Dee and Harriet. We made numerous trips through Europe, Britain, Asia and America, and I always found there was work at the bookshop when we returned. Her mother and I took Harriet everywhere with us: not only on our travels, but to films, restaurants, studios, and even hiking through the bush, with me doing much carrying. The painter Tom Carment, with whom we often went out on drawing expeditions, when he was young, was always ready to take a turn at piggy-backing, while we scrambled over rocks and down narrow pathways, with drawing books and knapsacks.

In those days, people I barely knew often looked askance at me for not having more ambition. Some of them, when they called into the shop, patronised me by saying it must be wonderful to be able to work part-time in a bookshop. I would usually reply, 'The books are always interesting.'

That shop was highly fashionable, for years. It was long and narrow and easily became crammed with people, but they continued to push in; they would queue in the street, not only at Christmas but on weekends and holidays. There was a tea room next door, belonging to the shop, and entered through it, which had something to do with its popularity, but there were also unusual books to be found, defiantly imported from America against restrictions protective of British publishing, at that time. The staff sometimes had to swim boisterously to keep their heads above 'the chafing tides'.

I acquired, at last, something of an education through the store, in the fifteen years I worked there, because William, although he

335

had an attitude of *noblesse* disoblige toward many, allowed me to borrow books, to buy at cost, and to follow up on my interests, when ordering.

Many famous writers and actors came in, Australians and visitors, the most interesting of whom, I thought, was Bruce Chatwin. He and I were introduced by Werner Herzog, whose films *Aguirre, the Wrath of God* and *Nosferatu* I particularly admired. I met Herzog when he arrived at the shop hung-over, early one Saturday morning, while I was still vacuuming. He knocked on the glass door. 'I am in urchent need of der Proteins,' he told me, a hand in his tangled hair, 'I hear is good in there.' I arranged for him to be served eggs and toast before the tea rooms opened. He came to me on his way out, told me who he was, and we talked about the director Fritz Lang, an admiration of mine, on whom he had written. Then he said, 'Now I vill show you someding.' From his leather bag he took a long, barbed, wooden spearhead with some of the shaft attached. 'You see dis spear – it has been through der human flesch.' This was said with great solemnity. He had been filming *Fitzcarraldo* in South America, and on his way home was checking up about the possibility of an Australian film. One of his cameramen had been attacked with the spear, among many other disasters while filming. 'I am going to give dis spear to my son, for his room,' he said, ardently. 'I am going to tell him: Dis spear has been through der human flesch...'

Herzog came in with Bruce Chatwin; they were talking about filming *The Viceroy of Ouidah*. Chatwin was in Australia to research a travel book, which became *The Songlines*. He returned to the shop several times and then we met for a drink. Beautiful-looking, he told beautifully paced and eloquent stories, one of them about travelling in Afghanistan. He had come on horseback with some guides to a remote village, and as soon as he dismounted the local people mobbed him, in strange excitement. He was urged down an alley of waving hands and ogling faces, to a tent. Then everyone stepped back. The flap lifted and out stepped a blond young man, the image of himself; it might have been his twin. The hubbub resumed. The young man took Chatwin by the hand and led him inside. 'Tea and scones?' I asked. Chatwin smiled demurely.

He explained that person's appearance as an inheritance from Alexander the Great's expedition. He was evidently of the same opinion as my father, who for no reason once instructed me, in the main street at home, 'You understand, of course, that these people who own milk bars are not Homer's Greeks...'

Chatwin and I talked about Ernst Jünger, on whom he had written an article I had read, and a copy of whose rare book *Storm of Steel* I had eventually found, in the days before the internet. Jünger was the most decorated German soldier of the First World War and at the same time an aesthete, in the fastidious, cold mode of the Goncourt brothers: someone drawn to 'curious sensation'. Chatwin had visited Jünger in Germany, when writing his article. He spoke in an admiring tone of Jünger's remarkable blue eyes, and might have been referring to himself, as we simultaneously realised. He smiled, and made a depreciating, comfortable gesture.

I was told other stories about his travels by Chatwin, and was surprised later to hear these repeated word-perfectly at a dinner party, with even the same pauses and emphases. I mentioned this, amused, to David Malouf, the novelist, who said that while Australians might disdain anything so studied, this was how it was, socially, for the intelligentsia of other Western countries: it was competitive, and there was preparation. Australians expected their social life to be relaxed; the only time they were other than casual was in discussing matters involving a ball and moving the limbs quickly.

When Chatwin returned from travelling through north-western Australia by bus or with a hired driver, he told me that he had cut the tour short and was giving up his effort to make a factual

account of the Aboriginals' trans-lingual 'songlines'. He would have
to fictionalise the subject, to finish the book. He had been disturbed
by the emptiness of the Outback, as by nowhere else in his travels.
It was an experience of 'nihilism'.

Chatwin asked me to dinner where he was also to be a guest,
at the home of a businessman in Elizabeth Bay, and my friend
Alex, another employee of the bookshop, was to join me. The
house where we went, a three-storey Georgian terrace, was like a
Roman villa inside: it had been opened out, and there were marble
floors, archways, and pillars. It had titian-coloured dining table
and chairs, footed with golden claws, long divans, bright cushions,
urns, vast green leaves, and Pompeiian red walls. The owner was
reclining with a drink, among other older men who impressed me
as wealthy and coarse. Chatwin was anomalous there, a figure of
rare quality, supervising the preparation of dinner – rather than
an adventurer, he was now the hedonist. A number of young men,
who looked as if they had been picked up off the streets, given a
bath and haircut, and put into expensive, ill-fitting, fashionable
clothes, shared the role of Ganymede. They smirked slyly at Alex
and me. Chatwin had two of them working in the kitchen with
him, preparing a seafood risotto and various meats; he seemed like
a boy, with his childishly large head, and he was the domineering
one, hectic, imperious, loudly ordering his helpers about. They
seemed timid and very young. Those who served the drinks were
shouted at, also. Without consulting, Alex and I knew we would
not be staying for a meal, and one of us explained that we had only
called briefly. The cold, sleazy streets of nearby Kings Cross seemed
strangely refreshing, as we went in search of a restaurant. What
lingered with me was the sight of the young men's thin necks, in
their ill-fitting, expensive shirts.

Soon after, Chatwin came into the shop, with his charming
smile, a little hesitant, and said that he wanted to meet an

Australian writer of whom he had been hearing in Britain, the poet Les Murray. I acknowledged I was friendly with Les and could probably arrange something.

Les agreed to a dinner, if I would come; and Alex wanted to try arranging an interview with Chatwin. We met at a restaurant in the city: Chatwin with his summer-blue eyes, feathery blond hair, slim and confident build, and Les, five foot ten and twenty-two stone, almost bald, with teeth broken, a snub nose, and mounded, often 'gleeful' cheeks. He looked like a lighter-weight sumo wrestler, and I have seen him take up the sumo stance and heave the back of his small van sideways, into a tight parking place.

Les Murray, as a poet, is overwhelmingly inventive, the master of a baroque style – he constructs Heath Robinson machines, all pulleys and belts, sprockets and trip hammers, steam whistles, vats and vast organ pipes, up in the top paddock, from which there floats a marvellous sound. He is a baobab tree in an Anglicised garden; a transport truck hurled along the highway, dragging a great mass of cyclists in its wake.

Les's mother died when he was twelve, his father was depressed for years, they lived in a rancid shack, on a rented dairy farm, and threw the tins they opened for dinner onto a great pile in the yard. He did not own shoes or a toothbrush for a long while. At school, he showed that he was gifted, but was mocked at by the girls for his weight. He dropped out of university and became a vagrant, while teaching himself a string of languages in the stacks of the library at his alma mater. Valerie Morelli, a young Swiss immigrant, a linguist, a radiant person, married him, no doubt impressed by the immediate and immense accomplishment of his poetry. By the end of the last century he had become for many, on the range and profuseness of his talent, the best poet in the English-speaking world, winner of the Queen's medal for poetry and persistently shortlisted for the Nobel prize.

Les has been begrudged his achievement in Australia, among the leftist literati, on the philistine grounds of their disapproval of his conservative, Catholic politics. His strongest political emotion, though, arose out of loyalty to the Murray clan who were settled in his home district: his defence of country 'rednecks' and their values against city 'intellectuals'. Despite having been raised 'up a hollow log' (in the idiom of the coast), with no mentor and no social skills, with only his gift and his conversation, he has accomplished a journey almost as prodigious as the fabled one of the nineteenth century, 'from log cabin to White House'.

On the night of our dinner, Les was occupied with the buffet-style meal for a while, but I noticed his nods and cackles and one-line comments became fewer, as Chatwin's perfectly tuned performance reached its highest altitude and settled into cruising speed. The stories were about Chatwin's background, which biographers and journalists have since made famous, and tales of South America, 'the North-West Territories', and West Africa. Les finally had a chance, and he told a story about a trip in Borneo, which I am unable accurately to recall, but which Chatwin became eager about and said was extraordinary. 'Do you mind if I...Where did you hear this?' Les raised a calming hand. 'I got it in the same place you found your stuff, mate – in an old collection of the Boys' Own Paper.' He smiled blandly.

Chatwin turned to me and began talking about Ivan Bunin, a writer I thought he overvalued; we had discussed him before. Les spoke with Alex. We soon dispersed. Les had a hard satisfaction in his eye, as he commended the meal. Chatwin went off quickly, with a cursory politeness, a knapsack on one shoulder, the only figure walking in the early Sunday evening street. I felt discomforted, shaking his hand, that we Australians had been so unaccommodating of style. He seemed the embodiment of imaginative flair, and Les an unlikely upholder of the verification principle.

'Creativity,' Les has said, 'is the wound you receive in child-hood that never heals.' But that makes it resentment, and ties it to a perception that is immature. Much of Les's work, particularly the earlier, had a different motive: it was produced out of appreciation, rather than retaliation and anger. Recently, he has often been far from a remembrance of the 'uses of adversity', in his work; from Emily Dickinson's insight that 'Water is taught by thirst'.

Alex saw Chatwin in England, a year or so later. He rang a number he had been given at their last meeting, and was invited by Chatwin's wife, after a noticeable absence from the phone, to come to the countryside and visit them. He found Chatwin in bed, looking terribly ill: clearly, he was dying. But Chatwin spent his time with Alex reiterating that he had a rare blood disorder, picked up 'in a remote part of Mongolia', for which there was a cure. Alex guessed it was AIDS. (It seems likely that rather than somewhere exotic, Chatwin's disease was contracted in Sydney, after being in Oxford Street or Kings Cross.) Chatwin asked Alex to carry him out to a bed that was made up in the garden, and there he held Alex's hand and drowsed in the sun, or reminisced, with his flawlessly structured stories. There was still within him Nietzsche's 'dancing star'.

I knew Les to be amiable and generous, even if he had a country-man's short forbearance with anyone he thought was 'putting on side' (his defence to me on the evening of the Chatwin dinner, when I accused him of bad faith toward an ego under a white flag). Les bore with my annoyance as he did with my irreligion; we soon dropped the subject, but I think he considered my attitude, on both counts, a bit self-indulgent, produced by an overdose of Protestantism.

Les read his work at the Adelaide Arts Festival, appearing after Adrian Mitchell, the English 'protest poet'. The audience loved Mitchell, who played up to all of 'sophistication's' approved opinions. Then Les ambled on stage, in his famous hand-knitted, hoop-striped pullover, and introduced himself to the large crowd by saying, 'Now that's what I call lickin' arse.' When I heard of this, I thought, 'There's a man you've got to admire.' Often asked his opinion on political topics, in interviews, Les would take the opportunity to offend most other writers, who were left-wing, or 'self-righteous'. I liked his belief in the literary quality of his work – that his poetry would last, no matter what was thought of his ideas.

Les and I have disagreed on almost everything, except his genius. An aspect of his gift I have had to take on faith: he is supposed to speak thirteen, or sixteen, languages, but no one has assembled a committee to test him. His German, Dutch, French, and Italian are particularly good, I have been told in Europe. Once his wife remarked to me that in her opinion it was impossible to pick up the correct accent of a language after one had reached puberty. 'I don't know about that, Valerie Gina,' said Les thoughtfully, playing with some breadcrumbs, in the wreckage of a meal. 'Always excepting you, Leslie,' his wife told him. 'You come under the heading of a genuine "Pentacostalist".'

Les is not above playing to his legend. I was talking with him in his study one afternoon when his wife looked in, saying she was off to the shops. Raising a characteristic forefinger, where he lolled behind his desk, Les enquired, 'Will you be going near the library, Valerie Gina? See if you could pick up an Urdu grammar, would you? I've nothing to read this evening.' Smiling wanly at me, Valerie said goodbye.

After Les had recovered from years of severe depression, about which he has written, he was one day repeating his attack on the

Enlightenment and its values, to me. I became impatient and said, 'Les, the pharmacopeia has done more for you than the wafer ever has.' He said, 'Yes. Yes, that's true. But it won't always be able to.'

To me, it is not a matter for regret, but rather the contrary, that our limitations will not be perpetuated forever. A personality is something partial and therefore inadequate, but in a future life we could not depart far from it, particularly with a changed body, if we wanted to remain ourselves. And if we stayed as we are, we must again become entangled in our fate. All that we regret about our lives would find the way to occur again.

Meanwhile, how many times does a pleasure have to be repeated, to assure us that we have experienced pleasure? For some people, it seems, only the idea of eternity will suffice. Do they have a stronger, more primitive, hold on life?

When they lived in the city, I visited Valerie and Les occasionally for Sunday lunch. Once, after a long and hilarious afternoon, as I repeated that I must be going, Valerie told Les, 'Walk with Bob to the station; you need the exercise. Get up with you!'

Les and I went down his front path, and turned right outside the gate, into the abruptly tilted street. We walked a few paces, until we were behind a paling fence. 'Stop and talk with me a bit longer, mate,' he said, 'while I smoke one of these small cigars.' We leaned on the fence in the afternoon sun. After a while he remarked, 'I'd better be getting home, Valerie will be worried about me.' As he always does, he said, 'Keep well.' I see him smile his strangely contained smile, who is loaded with talent like a dog is with water, come in from the rain, and who flourishes in obduracy.

I sometimes imagine I have lived the sort of life that my father might have wanted, although his love of evocation with words and of precision in language was not nearly as strong as mine. I usually end up admitting he would not have had the resolve for such a life; in particular, would not have liked to be solitary, as a writer must be – in which case, I cannot imagine anything he would have believed in enough to have done.

Rather, I realise I have been as self-absorbed as he was, as indifferent to other people's opinion, in the pursuit of my enthusiasm, and almost equally as irresponsible, in some eyes. There has been, though, no self-destructiveness.

I have tried to be, as the incomparable David Hume said that he was, a person 'of great moderation in all my appetites' ('a turn of mind,' he remarked, 'which it is more happy to possess than to be born to an estate of ten thousand a year'). My ambition has been, like Hume's, for literary success, but while he was disappointed with the public response to his major work, I have never reached the stage of being much concerned with that: pre-empting such a complaint has been dissatisfaction at my own limitations. To see a work of mine in a bookshop filled me with remorse; those parts I have come to think of as failures usurping in my attention all the rest. My relative obscurity was then some relief. Not that I have, for a moment, thought of abandoning the effort to write: instead, I have gone on working at things that have already been published, believing them to have been broken with prematurely, by the need to prove to my government sponsor that I can produce. 'There was never a talent less spontaneous than mine' was Degas' claim, and it is one I could make.

I have buoyed myself as a writer by having sometimes glimpsed a state, 'as excellent as it is rare', where all things work together; where the revelation one would never otherwise have had, but for writing, has become as refined as a theorem, and has contributed its power to a passage of 'golden eloquence'.

The poem 'Ithaka' by Cavafy could be interpreted as an account of a writer's experience:

When you set out for Ithaka

hope that your way is long,

full of adventure, full of discovery...

May there be many summer mornings when,

with what pleasure, what joy,

you enter harbours you're seeing for the first time;

may you stop at Phoenician trading stations

to buy fine things,

mother of pearl and coral, amber and ebony,

sensual perfume of every kind –

as many sensual perfumes as you can...

And if you find Ithaka poor, she won't have fooled you.

Wise as you will have become, full of experience,

you will have understood what these Ithakas mean.

While living in Rome, awarded residency of a studio, Dee and I explored parts of Italy, and spent days travelling through Umbria and Tuscany by bus, smaller and smaller ones, passing hill towns, on the way to see what Aldous Huxley called 'the greatest picture in the world'. This was the title of an essay of his that I read when a boy; it sounds like something from the *Reader's Digest*.

Over the years, I have tried to fulfil an ambition to see, in actuality, all of what might rank as the greatest paintings, a project not too onerous nowadays even for an Australian. The picture we were going to find was the *Resurrection* by Piero Della Francesca, still in the small village of Sansepolcro where the artist had lived.

Arriving in the town at dusk, I thought we were too late. It was not going to be financially possible for us to stay in a hotel overnight; we must catch a bus that evening. We hurried along cobbled alleys to a building like a town hall, and it was still open. Inside, we entered a large, high room, with no one there, except an attendant, who dreamed in a corner. There was a couch, good lighting, and on an end wall, in a moderate size, just the one fresco. It did not flap and disappear, as I almost expected it would. No one was about, yet the place was open late; we sat down. It was perfection.

That probably is the finest picture in the world, but there are others of similar quality: in Chicago I saw *View of Toledo* by El Greco; in the Frick Museum in New York, *St Francis in Ecstasy*; and there is *The Housemaid* by Vermeer, of the woman pouring milk; Titian's *Bacchus and Ariadne* and his *Bacchanale*; *Las Meninas* by Velazquez, in Madrid. I have not seen Rembrandt's picture of his wife wading into dark water, in her drawn-up shift, nor his self-portrait with the great circle on the wall behind him, like infinity. I would include Tiepolo's ceiling for the palace called the Residence in Würzburg. There must also be counted *The Birth of Venus* and the *Primavera*, and opposite them, in the same room of the Uffizi, *The Nativity* by Hugo van der Goes.

In that room, the crowd cleared, and I stood in front of *The Birth of Venus*, with only a little French girl of about ten close by me, whom I had noticed earlier; an extraordinarily intelligent-looking, intense child, in thick glasses and with crinkled, full hair, who I thought must grow up to be Simone Weil. She was there with her father – his hair stuck out as if he were a brilliant mathematician – and a younger brother, and those two had left the room. The young art-lover stood beside me in silence, glaring ahead, one foot advanced, neither of us moving. After a little while she suddenly hissed 'Formidable!' and reached up and took my hand, and continued her scrutiny; of what she was up against, perhaps. When she realised I was not her father, she seemed unembarrassed, and even unsurprised, but apologised very gravely, for needing the 'support' of my hand. That was perfection, also.

Piero's painting of Christ standing up in his sarcophagus is a great masterpiece of the imagination. One foot is planted on the edge of the grave, like the foot with which it is prophesied he will crush the Serpent's head on the final day, and overcome death for all. Christ's face is sombre, immensely dignified; the eyes have seen and understood the infinity of nothing beneath all things. His wounded body is chalky white, half-draped with a robe, in a tender, visceral pink. His figure is dominant, in a mainly blue-grey landscape (appropriately damaged), among which some of the trees are like bronchia. Beyond them is a white-lit, dawn archipelago of clouds. Christ holds a conquering flag, planted in the tomb; before him lie the thick-throated soldiers, struck down in awkward sleep. The geometrically satisfying proportions of the picture (Piero wrote a treatise on mathematics) give it a sense of solidity, of accomplished fact. The light is subdued, like creation holding its breath.

When travelling, I have enjoyed Scotland most, where I feel a genetic string plucked and vibrate. Stevenson said Edinburgh was what Paris ought to have been, which is my opinion, too. In Scotland, the coarseness of many of the people is alleviated by their charming naivety. I said this to the poet Douglas Dunn, at St Andrews University, who replied, 'Ustralians, o' curse, are knuwn f'r thur delacacy.'

Among the happiest days of my life have been those spent drifting northwards, in the bare, surging Scottish landscape, canvas-coloured, or russet, or purple, empty and seemingly vast.

I remember the level sleep of the lochs; the up-ended black pine forests; the undulant outline binding the flow of the mountains; the secretive lanes among mossy trees, opening onto a light-struck water; the broken castle sleeping in the Sound, and a few white cottages at the head of the tide; the black thunderheads of stone over Glencoe,

with a stream trembling in the floor of the valley; an open fire, whisky and a plate glass window before a wide lavender estuary; the scallops in Oban at a restaurant by the ocean; and the drive back across the whole country by night, in two hours, down tunnels through the forest, in an open sports car, low-slung and fast as an Olympic toboggan with headlights – these are images from travelling with my friend Hilary Armstrong, whose place I have often stayed at, above the crushed and smoothed-out foil of the river Tay in its broad estuary. How fortunate that I once lingered to talk with her, many years ago, because of her wit and the warmth of her nature, when she was a young backpacker in Sydney and working at a café.

In Edinburgh, I made a pilgrimage to the house where the philosopher David Hume lived in the eighteenth century. He more than anyone had saved me from 'a philosophical melancholy' that came on me for a time in my forties. This disquiet involved 'the terrible doubt of appearances', as Walt Whitman calls it; the surmise that the world we perceive might be all a 'sham'.

The feeling was brought about through paddling in philosophy and science, and getting caught by what felt like quicksand – by the prevalent tendency, since Descartes, to treat perception as merely 'representation', and things as not really knowable by us.

The idea that sensuous qualities were illusions, that the true nature of the world was colourless and simple, and as thin as mathematics, I felt as smothering to any fresh access of life. It devalued all I had experienced and written. I took the idea seriously because it was so commonly proposed, in some form or another.

To escape this mire, I had to go on treading steadily in the one place (which is how it is literally done, I believe) – I had to keep on obsessively with philosophy, scribbling in notebooks, when I should have been doing other things.

There was something spontaneous and never repeated about the world, I believed, and it was far greater than us; but many philosophers had the unspoken intention, it seemed, of showing the mind as superior to nature.

I realised it was David Hume who could save the integrity of sensuous objects for me. I took over just his fundamental approach, disagreed about some things in his work. It is permissible to stand on the shoulders of giants.

Hume was influenced by the ancient Greek sceptics. He was mainly sceptical of reason. Analysis isolates and generalises, and then cannot explain how the world fits together. Everything is fragmented and set in opposition. Reason undermines itself.

Hume's positive position is empiricism – nature forces us to accept as ultimate the evidence of the senses. Whatever our theories, we cannot do other than live by common sense. He said he 'rejoiced to think with the vulgar' on this matter, although he was the most devastating critic of that popular institution, religion, then or since. 'Nature has...esteemed [our apprehension of things] an affair of too great importance to be trusted to our uncertain reasoning and speculations.'

The world is reliably as it appears.

It should be added that the senses correct and support each other (illusions are usually the work of one sense isolated). Memory among them, and movement. We can be mistaken in our perceptual beliefs, but this only shows they are usually accurate. Experience is corrected by experience.

That the senses can be depended upon we now understand is due to Darwinian natural selection. The extent of the world that we experience is clearly a real aspect of the world. We find in nature many examples of an exquisite coherence between organism and environment, and this must be the case with our perception, also. We are possessed by the world.

I became grateful for my forced involvement with philosophy – certain of its arguments brought the world up onto my senses in something like the way that art has done. Or at times I felt I was sailing, beneath snow-capped mountains in a Greek light.

The senses show us that things are at once inseparable and distinct. The interaction of things depends on them having parts and qualities. There cannot be something ultimately simple; it would be essentially unchanging, and so without presence or effect. Complexity is fundamental. (This is from another Scotsman, John Anderson.)

Only physical things exist. No qualities are found apart from mass (and no mass apart from qualities). Mass distinguishes what is physical from the thinness of sensation or thought. The nature of a physical thing is independent of what we think about it.

Just as we never find in our minds anything but a particular perception, so there is no essence in the world, isolated, funda-mental, unchanging. We should accept phenomena just as they are, as the particular nature that each thing has. Each is something ultimate. The commonplace is the sublime.

Since many things exist, as many things exist as possibly can. What things are made of is Existence itself. This could hardly be called God: it is utterly indifferent and brutal. But thinking of Existence returns us to a religious feeling – we are winged with awe. There is nothing other than itself to limit Existence. We can infer that it is infinite in all directions.

A light snowfall
and within that
a billion worlds arise
and within that
a light snowfall.

RYOKAN

A mountain is not large and a grain of sand is not small.

Rather than qualitative experience being a mirage, qualities are the whole of existence. 'The realm of immediate qualities contains everything of worth and significance,' as John Dewey has said.

It is possible to look with detachment on this marvellous and terrible river of things, as David Hume did in his entirely good-natured life and in the scandalous calm of his deathbed. He believed, rarely among Westerners then, that he was going to be entirely extinguished, and confounded with his equanimity James Boswell, who had come to spy on 'Mr Hume, just a-dying'.

In a world of chance and flux, one sees the futility of making demands on life. We can act without expectations and without insistence, doing things for their own sake – living the life of an artist. The wise are unmoved by things beyond their control. I do not think this an unwarranted belief, just because I will never be able to realise it fully.

18. White Continent

Towards the end of my father's life, I grew to know the novelist Patrick White, as famous for his irascibility as for his work, and we kept up what on my part was an elusive friendship, in his last fifteen years. My scepticism about the connection was because of a similarity I found between my father and him.

I only took an interest in Patrick's work after it was too late to draw out and gather his comments on it, which I might have done. When I did allow myself an absorption in his writing, I found a stylistic quality I thought was great: its charge of neurotic energy.

'And so...I have something to expiate, a pettiness,' as D. H. Lawrence says in that poem about his untrusting encounter in Italy with a snake, which he saw, at the same time, as 'like a king in exile' from the Underworld. The reference is not quite apt: to be fair to myself, Patrick, however great his gifts, could by no means have been called, as Lawrence might call his golden, venomous creature, 'one of the lords of life'.

The difference between Patrick and my father was, of course, extreme: that of a Nobel prize winner on one side, an all-round failure on the other. Their likeness I found in the practised way both did sadistic things to people with words, out of what Patrick identified, for himself, as 'self-loathing'. (My father's cutting remarks could not compare in animus but were far more inventive than any I heard of by the famous writer.)

The 'despised fault' in Patrick, I think, which animated so much of his discomfort, and which was a valuation prompted by his family, and by the society of his earlier days, was homosexuality.

Patrick told me that he was an alcoholic, and said he preferred vodka because it was the least detectable drink, but whatever he may have been when young, in the years I knew him he showed no signs of such a problem, which one has when one falls down. I found him self-dramatising.

He also boasted of the suffering he went through for his novels: they caused him severe asthma attacks, some of them putting him into hospital. He said this like a superstitious person who imagines he has colleted spiritual merit through mortification, or with the unpleasant air of a masochist.

During his young manhood, in London, Patrick had been part of the circle around Francis Bacon, the expressionist painter, and seems to have made that notorious 'sacred monster' his licence for how the great artist can behave. The artist, as egotist, imposes outrageously on others, with a high theatricality, and yet demands to be taken seriously. From what I have read of Bacon, the continuity of Patrick's behaviour with his is apparent; but Patrick had none of the master's lubricant, if treacherous, charm.

Even in Patrick's old age, he was struck by Bacon's personality, although they had not met for decades. His house was furnished in Bacon's taste, in a fifties style derived from the Bauhaus, which was the mode the artist had adopted, when young, as an interior designer, and the décor in his paintings.

I once mentioned that I liked the earlier pictures of Bacon's friend Lucian Freud best of all his work, and Patrick was indignant

I should like him at all. Freud was 'a DREADFUL man!' He railed on, with only the slightest content to his remarks, growing more furious to convince me as he watched my reserve. There had apparently been a falling-out between Freud and Bacon, and Patrick retained a bitter loyalty to 'Franny' – no matter that the main protagonists in the quarrel, as I later read, had long reconciled.

If the conversation at his dinner table seemed to Patrick sluggish, he would do as Bacon is described as doing: throw in some vicious remarks, to stir up the occasion. This might be attributed to boredom, but in Patrick's case, I think, was mainly a fear of being thought boring.

Patrick was not an intellectual; he was uncomfortable with abstract ideas, did not maintain his part in conversations about them, and would explosively sabotage any road that seemed to be slipping into that country.

There are reports in David Marr's biography of White of times when all the women at his dinners were in tears and all the men on their feet raging, while he sat unmoved, like an idol at its festival. Patrick once said to me wryly that his house had been known as 'Monkey Hill'.

Although he lived nearby, he rarely appeared in fashionable Paddington, and it was not at the bookshop we met, but backstage at one of his plays.

Experienced readers are divided over White's novels, especially it seems in unimpressible Australia, but it is now widely thought that the plays fail. They combine a ponderous mysticism with mis-anthropy, and their people are caricatures. They are like the novels in this, some might say, but that fails to appreciate the intensity of his descriptive prose. The febrile vulnerability and responsiveness he attributes to his characters, in the novels, are fully present in their style.

The play I saw, before meeting the author, was *A Cheery Soul* (its epiphany involves the realisation that God is dog spelled backwards), at the Sydney Opera House in 1975. The director was Jim Sharman, known for the stage and film versions of *The Rocky Horror Show*, and for other musicals, such as *Hair* and *Jesus Christ Superstar*, in their Australian and London productions. He was devoted to Patrick, who rewarded his loyalty in the theatre by writing the later plays for him. Jim gave me a ticket to the opening night of this one. After the curtain, he invited me backstage. I thought I was going to be shown the mechanisms supporting the director's craft, but as we were struggling through the crush in a corridor, I realised I was being led toward a tall figure whom I recognised from photographs. Patrick was loaded with flowers and receiving tributes, and I was told was pleased with the performances, but he looked grim. We came face to face and were introduced. His mouth was like a folded warrant for someone's arrest.

The voice, from his Oxford education and his years in England, in affected company, had intonations that reminded me of Sir John Gielgud's fruitiest manner – similar quaverings and lingering emphases. It was a voice that could easily be pitched into indignation, and outrage, and even hysteria.

'Do you go to the THEATRE orphan?' he asked, as his gaze took a mining-scan of my face.

'I don't,' I told him, remembering that honesty is the best policy. More was clearly expected. 'The people in plays are always shouting at each other: I find it embarrassing...(What was this effete nonsense I was talking?) I prefer to go to the movies. (That was all I could afford.) There's more likelihood you'll find something to enjoy there, on the whole. There'll be at least a pretty face, which you can see properly, or a landscape...'

'Movies? MOVIES! Surely you mean the PICTURES, or the CINE-mah? And what about SHAKESpeare?'

'Well, yes...But I hate the way directors feel they have to get creative with the plays, and they set *Julius Caesar* in the stock exchange, or *Macbeth* during the Vietnam War. The anomalies begin to preoccupy...'

'I couldn't agree MORE. SomeONE'S going to do that sort of thing to ME, one of these days, when I'm safely OUT OF THE WAY. Some new GENIUS from CoonaBARRABRAN...Come to DINNER, some time, if you would LIKE to. Jim has the NUMBER.'

But I was not anxious to try my luck again. And Patrick, I thought, would immediately forget his invitation. Indeed, I was on the same bus as him, soon afterwards, which was sparsely occupied, and he seemed not to recognise me. He was, however, distracted at the time.

On that occasion, I became aware of Patrick while I was at the bus stop, because of shouting which started within an open-fronted greengrocer's, just behind me. I saw Patrick inside, dressed in trench coat and beret, as if he were shopping in Paris, arguing with the slovenly-looking Greek owner, who kept putting aside what was being said to him with the backs of his stubby fingers. Patrick had taken from a string carryall a large brown paper bag of tomatoes and seemed to be demanding his money back. The Greek maintained his insouciance.

A man passing the bus stop became interested in this conflict, too. He was youngish, with unwashed hair, a tie hanging outside his jacket, beaky features, and a slight stoop. He stopped, on apparently recognising the unusual voice, gazed into the shop, and grew dithering and agitated. Watching this man's reaction, I was unaware of how, or whether, Patrick had resolved his problem; but there he was, coming into the street, his mouth compressed as if his teeth had been left out. The bus was approaching now, and I turned to hail it. Patrick pushed past me and climbed on board. Then the young man, his fingers twitching at the air like a praying mantis, followed. Patrick dropped into the first seat, blindly, and the young man sat across the aisle from him, skewed his way, seeming to finger the strings of a double bass and forming words silently. I passed to the back. It was easy to see what would happen.

At some point, the young man began unctuously to introduce himself, but he got no further than the first mention of his admiration. Patrick turned to him a face as set as a bullfrog's. Then his mouth erupted. 'GET STUFFED,' he ordered, in a voice high above the grinding of the bus and the traffic. Everyone shrank from that madman.

Patrick must have been reminded of me, somehow, because a summons came to the White House, in writing. I groaned and went around the flat saying 'Let this cup pass from me,' but I soon decided it would be too recessive not to accept; and of course I was curious, and flattered.

I regretted my decision when I presented myself on his doorstep and heard that I was to be the only guest, or the sole object of interrogation, for the evening.

Patrick's wooden, gabled, two-storey house faced the copses and grassy acres of Centennial Park, in the Eastern Suburbs. He lived with a companion, Manoly Lascaris, who was said by interviewers to be 'saintly' and 'long-suffering'. The night I arrived, the house stood in what appeared to be darkness, on its hillock, rising out of draped lawns and plots of lilies. A path wound through stringybark tree trunks, to where there was just an asterisk of light above a side entrance.

That house has been described as looking at night like the set for a Hammer Studios horror film; and Patrick was not unused to the effect of his glaring, German Expressionist appearance at the door. (In a letter quoted in David Marr's biography, White remarked that he had in the dining room, at a previous house of his, an ancient map of Crete, 'to which the timid cling desperately on making their first entrance.')

The first time I came into seemingly comatose Martin Road, by night, I had trudged there from an ill-chosen bus stop on the far side of the park. Although I was about thirty, I was in manner much younger, and I was late. Patrick demanded from me, almost immediately, my opinion of dentists. I had hoped we might begin with David Malouf, who had just published a novel I admired, and on whom I had some lines prepared, but I said for dentists, glibly, that in my case all of sexual attraction was dependent on their skills and their teachings.

Patrick cut in, denouncing such frivolity by intoning that he had WITHERING GUMS. His dentures would become useless to him. There was nothing that could be done. 'I shall be an old man DRINKING SOUP,' he almost yelled, and involuntarily, it seemed, crooked his back and made his hands tremble feebly before him. 'No one can help me. NO ONE,' he barked, looking at me with metaphysical disgust. I saw the evening was not going to be easy.

Abstracted for a moment, in what I hoped looked like helpless sympathy, I confronted my inflationary panic, then looked up again and into his gaze. He was inclined toward me aggressively, with the demeanour of a buzzard whose appetite was about to return. But something stirred in the back of his eyes, like a fleeting stagehand rearranging a set. Surely he knew how ludicrous this was. If he did not, I decided, it was better to be thrown out now. Taking that slightest hint, I began to laugh, and at once his face allowed itself a look of sly, almost smug pleasure. There was a twitch of the lips, and then a smile, as bleak as moonlight on a drought-stricken paddock.

Patrick complained to me, at a later time, of how people hardly ever realised when he was acting, because he was not able to signal that he was: he thought he looked 'ridiculous' if he smiled.

Manoly Lascaris, whom Patrick met in Alexandria during the War, a relative of the former Greek royal family, was employed in that city as a bank clerk. (He knew the great poet Cavafy through his work: all the young tellers were warned by the management against accepting an invitation from that notorious old man, who wore his hair 'combed up' and had soup stains on his clothing.) Patrick had come to Alexandria on leave from British intelligence in the Middle East and was in uniform when he and Manoly met, one Saturday afternoon at a salon. Manoly told me that after he and Patrick noticed each other, Patrick watched him unwaveringly. As the other guests moved into an adjoining room for lunch, Manoly hesitated in front of a large, gilded mirror; and Patrick, lingering too, approached him in the glass, and put his arms about him, without a word – 'desire looking into desire.'

Manoly, in age, was small and fine, with a neat potbelly and sloping shoulders, like a marsupial. He had a slim, mild face and oiled black hair, brushed back. A long, sensitive, aquiline nose supported Nana Mouskouri-style glasses, in which his sherry-coloured eyes were remarkably gentle. He shuffled about in slippers because of arthritis in his feet. For some reason, his accented, very fastidiously spoken English made me think him secretly lubricious. The more apparent side of his nature, though, was a feminine piety, devoted to Orthodoxy. It was an assurance Patrick did not share.

On an early visit to Patrick and Manoly, I was shown the house: we looked at the many art works (none any good I thought, they all seemed chosen for their anecdotal content), sidling around the living room, through Patrick's study, along the corridors, and upstairs to the bedrooms, where I was made witness to the sleeping arrangements, as they were then. Patrick's room was in tones of beige and fawn, had middle-height bookshelves on one wall and was as meticulous and impersonal as a hotel suite. The bed was vast. 'You'd think it would only be queen size, wouldn't you?' he remarked, in a deadpan voice. What had previously been the dressing-room was now Manoly's narrow quarters, with a child's iron bedstead, a thin mattress strapped tightly in blankets, and above the pillow a large icon. The lavatory was at the opposite end of the main bedroom; Manoly would have had to creep to it in the night, past the dark island on which Patrick lay marooned.

Patrick found promiscuity distasteful, and particularly so in the dominant sexual culture. He scoffed at people's 'dog-like behaviour'. One evening, while he spoke in this way, Manoly was sitting neatly on the couch with his hands folded. Then he interrupted. 'Patrick was unfaithful once,' he said, with a composed smile.

'WHAT!' said Patrick.

'Yes, Patrick, you remember. With Bill Dobell.'

William Dobell was, during the fifties, at the time Patrick and Manoly knew him, the most famous artist in Australia.

'WHAT!' Patrick said. 'That doesn't COUNT, Manoly. He was NO GOOD. Bill Dobell was NO GOOD at it. It DOESN'T COUNT. So you can DROP IT.'

Manoly sat with fingers interlaced, head downwards, sniggering, and Patrick struggled, but then had to grin, too, like the last squeeze in the toothpaste tube.

Patrick's closest friends, when I knew him, were all women, middle-aged or more. The men whom he had regularly to his house were younger, came at other times, and were homosexuals, mainly from the theatre. I was almost always invited alone, after having been given a trial at a dinner party, where my discomfort with groups was revealed. I was sceptical of the friendship with Patrick as soon as it occurred: judging from the record, a falling-out must surely happen. One of Patrick's hobbies seemed to be culling his friends, on the most casuistical grounds. So I remained detached, and left it for him to contact me.

Those rows for which Patrick was known were actually most often with people of similar prominence to himself, who had disappointed him morally – that is, his quarrels were with middle-aged artists or politicians who had divorced their wives for younger women, or had been flagrantly neglectful of them, or who had revealed some taint in their politics.

The chronic, righteous anger in Patrick had an obvious cause: it arose because he, a White, of the vast Belltrees property and the Lulworth mansion in Sydney, of a family famed as philanthropists, saw in many a parvenu socialite and her money-grubbing husband their secret condescension of him; their secret sneer, at his queerness. The pretentious class in Australia has always been desperate about respectability, and uncomfortable with even successful and heterosexual artists. When Patrick came back to live in Australia and brought Manoly here, in the fifties, this was the air they had to breathe. In their reception was the origin of his sensitivity to every nuance of hypocrisy, complacency or self-promotion. Such a situation and his irritable, asthmatic nature, made him combustible. (I think it is Aristotle who says that anger, every time it is indulged, takes a stronger hold upon us. It becomes our habitual response.)

Patrick was derogatory of 'good society', and yet was drawn to it because of his upbringing, his relatives' place in it, and through a novelist's interest. Knowing the response of his family and of their social circle to his sexuality – as in one of the short stories, the mother's shrill 'I cannot believe there isn't some lovely girl...it just isn't natural' – knowing this, Patrick himself became disgusted and moralistic, on political grounds, where none of those people could follow.

His father's and his uncle's cattle property had been so extensive, he told me, that at one time a horseman might have ridden from Victoria, across inland New South Wales, into Queensland, without leaving the Whites' land. But their enterprise was damaged by the chances of the seasons and of the export market, outsiders had to be invited to invest in and share the family wealth, and Patrick found himself often reprimanded by the trustees, for overdrawing his funds.

Nevertheless, he was the most generous person I have met, and the man of most principle. He was also highly conscious of his virtue. La Rochefoucauld says that all our virtues are really vanity in disguise. 'It is not possible to enumerate all the kinds of vanity,' he observes. One can believe that Patrick was moral because he was so vain; but it is difficult to be sure that we have not traduced something which may lie beyond vanity.

Patrick was 'by far' the largest individual contributor to the essential charities in Sydney, as was only fully revealed after his death, although he was by no means the city's wealthiest citizen. He also took down a fortune from his walls, in his best paintings, Nolans, de Maistres, a Fairweather, and gave them to the Art Gallery of New South Wales. He bought whole exhibitions by young artists and distributed their work; and he gave his money, name and time to any new leaves of talent that he saw, in young poets, novelists, dancers, musicians, actors, and to Aboriginal cultural groups: not always with enough eye to quality, I thought.

It has been complained that he was interested in many people only for the sake of his novels: that he wanted anecdotes from them and when they were of no further use, dismissed them. They were confused and hurt by his change of attitude, and he became extremely rude if they clung. I find his behaviour justifiable (though it might have been more tactful) – he was not beholden to swear a loyalty oath to everyone he invited, even a number of times, for dinner.

One of the few radical causes that Patrick did not support was Gay Liberation. He once recounted to me how he had been walking past a gay rights demonstration, that day, on a city street, and a young man involved there had come up to him: 'Mr White, Mr White, you should be here with us.' Patrick said that he replied (with his dignity showing in the re-enactment), 'I MAY be homosexual, but I am CERTAINLY not GAY!'

I often felt I was Patrick's guest under a pretence, because at the time I knew him I had not read any of his books. Their pace seemed too ponderous, for my self-indulgent taste. Working in a bookshop, I had so much else that was more immediately attractive to me, clamouring to be read. I did not make an effort with his work because I hardly believed we would know each other for long.

Patrick was not the sort of person to raise the topic of his own work with a guest. We talked continually of other people's books: he would cross-examine me on my dishevelled reading, then would insist on certain books I had missed, and say why they were good. When a book was mentioned that we both had read, we compared opinions. He liked prejudice, no matter how impressionistic and uncharitable – as his often was – so long as there was readiness to change one's mind. I read *Tom Jones* at his insistence, starting out sceptically, on one of the 'damned big books', and loved it, for its verve and its warmth. To my surprise, he said Tom Jones, that delight of women, was his favourite character in fiction; Fielding's book was his favourite novel; Tom was even his favourite name. He also encouraged me to persevere with late Henry James, for which I was grateful; and under his influence I read George Eliot. But I continued in what I thought a dangerous game, one that might lead me into a slip-up: my reluctance toward his own work.

I remember saying to him, at this time, that Henry James's short stories were all really moral fables, and that while I admired many of them, they seemed to me intrinsically inferior to Chekhov's stories, which had no such air of artificiality about them. Chekhov was my criterion for everything, whose only fault seemed to me the repetitiveness of his themes, through the thirteen-volume collected stories that I owned and continually read. Patrick never thought as much of him as I did.

Once we found ourselves cornered in a conversation, where the obvious next question was for him to ask what I thought the best Australian novel, and he did so, with a gesture of apology. He was not at all put out when I chose, conventionally enough, *The Fortunes of Richard Mahony*. He had never read it. He thought that one of Christina Stead's books, probably *Cotter's England*, must be the best, from his experience.

Although they were strongly recommended by Patrick, I refused to persevere with certain books – I remember particularly *Doctor Faustus*, and everything by Dostoyevsky, the 'festering atmosphere' of whose work I detested. (I defended myself by mentioning Chekhov's similar distaste.) Tolstoy I really only skimmed. He seemed to me a 'psychic cannibal', who was able to possess completely and know everything about his characters. I felt he sucked out their souls entire and put those on display, leaving them no autonomy, no essential arbitrariness. His treatment of people was as indecent and overwhelmingly egotistical as Picasso's (except in the latter's neo-classical pictures). Patrick accused me of not taking the novel seriously as an art form, of judging it by poetry, and I said that, after all, it was a new-fangled medium, and probably not here to last. 'You're no doubt ABSOLUTELY RIGHT,' he sighed, choosing to ignore that my remark was a joke.

I seem to have reversed the natural order of things, with my reading, and to have read more fiction as I have grown older. Earlier, I kept clear of it, as much as I could, because it appeared not to have done anything for my father. (I realise now that books did as much for him as could be expected of them: his only real comfort, as far as I can see, was found in reading.)

I used to turn those conversations with Patrick toward the short story and the novella; I favoured these because my main interest was in an author's style, which was at its best, I thought, over a short distance. Finding that he had not gone far with the shorter works of Joseph Conrad, who was one of my favourites, I bought him *The Secret Sharer*. With its close atmosphere and dense prose, and its homoerotic undertone, this was a foregone success. I also introduced him to Alice Munro, V. S. Pritchett, and William Maxwell, who was almost unknown then, all of whom impressed him; and to numerous other writers I cannot now remember; maybe to William Trevor.

I admitted to Patrick, early on, that I preferred to read my favourite poems over and over, rather than novels. (For some reason, I never recommended poetry to him; I kept that to myself; and reading it was not an obsession of his.) I read thrillers, but he would not hear of those, no matter how naïvely I wanted to talk about the merits of Raymond Chandler and John le Carré. He had read Graham Greene, whom he insisted on speaking of as merely a writer of 'entertainments', and about whom he was touchy. When his Nobel prize had been announced, many British commentators protested about him receiving it over Greene. Patrick thought I would like Greene's thrillers, and as he brought the subject up I saw in his eyes the silos open and the missiles rise into place. I was able honestly to say that I did not: I found them too thin in characterisation, in the texture of their language, and visually. As for Greene's Catholic novels, I said that the tawdry, ideological atmosphere of these always brought to mind the paraphernalia in the windows of specialty shops owned by Pelligrini or O'Dwyer. Patrick was pleased.

I read biographies, particularly of artists, and this was a taste we shared. I recommended Ellman's book on Oscar Wilde to Patrick, but to my surprise he said Wilde was a 'terrible' man and he couldn't BEAR to read about him.

Often during this time, I began to sit by the harbour, among trees, through whole afternoons, without opening a book at all. To justify merely looking, I would draw. I had always been dissatisfied with myself when I felt 'too much in the head', as could readily happen, and my interest in drawing and painting became more and more something I practised, as an antidote to that. I liked the idea that painting was, as an artist had told me, 'a dumb, intuitive process'. While in high school, I read T.S. Eliot's remark about Milton, that 'too much book-learning had withered his sensuous nature', and when later I was surrounded by books at work and at home – reading 'as if for life', like David Copperfield – I would experience at times an exaggerated fear of such a fate happening to me. The secret about reading, I used to say, at such times, was to know when to refrain. I would be told I had never mastered it; but that was probably because poetry, which I read slowly and only a little at a time, but almost every day, carried along on the rhythm, was not counted as difficult reading by me.

I made daytrips into the bush around Sydney, by train, to draw the landscape, going with Tom, my young artist friend. We climbed on the densely forested hillsides above the Hawkesbury River, north of the city; or to the south, looked out at the ocean from among sandstone boulders that lay on a wide, continuing rock platform. We saw the sea again, having climbed higher up, through the branching screens of eucalyptus trees.

Deer had been imported into the national park there and lived wild, and I once found the entire skeleton of a deer, lying

awkwardly below a cliff, on a shore of smooth stones. Going close to examine it, in the drifting sea smoke, I was moved to see that inside the rib cage there was hung, just then, a small black butterfly, fluttering where the pulse of life had been, as black and urgent as blood.

Perhaps Patrick and I never argued with any animosity simply because I met him late in his life, when age had worn down much of his hauteur. I admit that I had broadly similar political views to his, at the time, and these, though not lingered over, were all-important between us; our few weary comments on the news were the brief signals of our freemasonry. I no longer hold that America is the source of all evil, however blundering it might be, particularly under some regimes; it is a self-critical society, which is better than the alternatives. It is something preferable, also, to the 'last men', comfort-seeking somnolence of Europe. To me it is wonderful that there exists in all of its barbaric splendour the Great Babylon, New York. I am not envious that such luxury has been, for a while, in human history. But it saddens me, in writing this, to realise that now Patrick and I would most likely not be friends.

The radio and the newspapers filled Patrick with disgust. There was a child molester active in Melbourne, choosing little girls, and Patrick swore this person would be found to be a 'respectable businessman', with wife and children, and he fulminated on and on against this imaginary figure. I thought at the very least he would write a short story about him. In the end Manoly had to say, with exasperation, 'You don't know, Patrick, you don't know.'

Television was not allowed in their house, although Manoly would have liked it – television was 'insupportable'. Patrick could not have borne, he said, the 'tensions' of it. What did I think of television? I said I always seemed to be coming in on documentary programmes about wild animals, and I found them extremely depressing, in the relentless violence and competition they revealed. I thought they ought to be X-rated. 'THERE you are, Manoly. THERE YOU ARE.' But I thought we had to see such things, I said, to know the truth of our situation. These programmes were philosophically important. And the television news, because it was more graphic than the newspapers, was therefore better at what it was meant to do: reveal things as they are. 'Wait till you get older,' Patrick said bitterly. 'You won't be able to stand it, either. Contrary to what you might think, people grow more sensitive as they get older.'

Patrick began coming into the bookshop early on a Saturday morning, when I was opening up. My stepdaughter, Harriet, then aged about six, sometimes used to be with me, for half the day, playing around my feet behind the desk. On his arrival, he would proclaim something like, 'Did you HEAR what happened at REX IRWIN'S last night?' (He sought out and relayed gossip with a novelist's enthusiasm, but I had no interest, at all. Despite my lacklustre responses, Patrick invariably greeted me in the same sort of way. When he rang me at home, he used immediately to begin,

'ANY GOSSIP?' and I would have to say, 'Patrick, it's me you're talking with; I don't even remember people's names.') There would sometimes be a few early browsers in the shop when he arrived, listlessly pawing over the books (as my father would have punned), and while he was there, not one of them passed the desk, or raised his head, or turned a page. He was aware of it. 'Just a MOMENT, though – ' he used to pause precipitously, a little way into his story, 'is that CHILD with us today? Then we must be CAREFUL what we say...INNOCENCE is among us...Better come over for a drink, later, if you've got time – I'll tell you something SCANDALOUS.'

That was not what I would feel like doing, after a day at work, and I never considered such offers something I need take up. My relationship with Patrick, over the years, was as much one of avoidance and excuse, as of accepted invitations, the apologies apparently convincing. The atmosphere at his house I often found uncomfortable, in its blend of salacious interest and puritanism.

Patrick was in the shop while I was busy with customers, but I was unaware of him. He had his face in a book, his back turned, and was being left alone. I was trying to identify what a man was talking to me about – it was one of those requests for a particular book that had 'a green cover' – when a large, expensively jewelled, middle-aged woman surged in, and interposed herself, volubly. I was working alone, and there were other people waiting, who grew immediately murmurous, and so I allowed myself a little reprimand. It was a point of principle with me, at work, not to be subjected to Victorian notions of service.

'Madam,' I said, 'I suggest you go to the back of the shop, until you see yourself in the mirror, then quickly avert your eyes to the left. You will find what you want.'

She went with nose up, complaining.

Patrick's turn came at the counter and he immediately rebuked me, quietly. 'You should NOT speak to menopausal women IN THAT WAY. You could be the only SOCIAL CONTACT she has today, for all you know.'

'That was not social contact. We may have some when she comes back.'

'Well, you'd better go and help her. She has double-parked some sort of juggernaut outside and there's going to be CHAOS. I'll hold things here on the battlements.'

When I came back, having been accosted by other customers, Patrick was at the head of a patient, orderly queue, his back radiating authority.

I had a sudden opportunity to go 'up the coast' for a short while, to do some writing, and I missed an arrangement with Patrick and Manoly for dinner. I wanted to send them a postcard in apology, from there, but could find nothing suitable. Most of the cards at the newsagency were of girls on the beach, with their breasts or buttocks bared and oiled and standing out whitely from their tan. I decided on a picture of a local tourist trap, the 'Big Banana', a walk-in giant concrete effigy by the roadside, which led into a souvenir shop. A postcard of the Big Banana, in its lurid yellow and green, seemed kitsch enough to be amusing, and I thought it would affirm my broad-mindedness.

I wrote a brief apology on the back of the 'Big Banana' and sent it off. An answer came very directly, to my mother's place: a postcard of the giant beaming face at Luna Park, and on its reverse, in mock excitement, were hand-printed the words, 'I GOT YOUR MESSAGE!!!'

After Dee, Harriet and I travelled by train through America, Dee had a nostalgia for a place we had visited, the Zen Centre monastery in San Francisco. I remarked that her often tiresome experiences

as a hairdresser must have made the shaven-headed initiates particularly appealing. The monks and nuns sat cross-legged for many hours, in black robes, in the dim light of the meditation hall, where their heads looked like rain-wet gravel. I was attracted to the monastery, also – dailiness was lifted to one's attention there, ritualised and treated as significant, as if it were all part of a tea ceremony. When I enquired about staying on, I was told I would have to give up my writing to do so; but Dee's wanting to go back was completely understandable to me. She had seen me practise meditation at home, over the years; I had tried to explain what Zen was, and now I felt I must encourage her interest. I telephoned the centre from Australia and made enquiries; they remembered our stopover. We wrote a letter, and were told that work could be arranged for her in the kitchen (their food was excellent; Zen Centre ran the famous Greens restaurant and had published two best-selling cookbooks); Harriet would be welcome. I paid the fares, and Dee thought they would stay on according to their feelings. I could join them when I wished.

I mentioned the plan to Patrick and to my surprise he was agitated by it. 'Americans are very charming. You must not allow this. You will regret it.' My only answer was to quote what I called my motto: 'Everything that can be shaken, let it be shaken.' 'Nonsense,' said Patrick. 'Good things are easily destroyed.'

Patrick had met Dee, had invited her to dinner on an occasion or two; but after that, he understood her declining invitations, since she was a shy and unliterary person. They talked on the phone sometimes, exchanging recipes. He was fond of her. Now he rang her, when I was at work, and talked for over an hour, trying to dissuade her from this adventure. He was unsuccessful, but left her touched by his manner.

Dee was away for a year, as it turned out. Some months into her absence, Patrick asked after her; had she seduced a Zen monk yet, and I said perhaps so; there was someone she mentioned as a friend. He was shocked, and I explained that the Buddhist precept about avoiding 'sexual misconduct' meant, in its modern Western interpretation, not entering into a relationship where sex created a problem. I said, 'I don't need to go comfortless,' and he dismissed the whole business with a wave of his hand, gloomily. Sex almost always did create a problem, he said, even when there were, or should have been, just two people involved. Even living with someone created problems.

Dee sent Harriet, who was ten, home to her father and me, for a visit, and the child lived happily for some days of the week with each of us. When it was time for her to go back to America, her father decided there had been 'enough nonsense' and refused to sign the papers. So her mother had to come home. Just off the plane, she and I sat in a café for breakfast and 'a talk', which revealed that nothing prevented us being together again. I noticed letters came that were never opened.

Dee's time at the monastery, exploratory yet structured, had been one of the happiest of her life. Everything was taught by example; and by hours a day of the uniquely Buddhist *zazen* meditation. In this, awareness was continually returned to the body, to the posture and the breathing, while letting go of the mind, not being caught up with thoughts. There was nothing to be attained in this practice, apart from attention to the moment, which was an unimaginably great amount. Dee discovered that a large number of people at the centre were Jewish, and were educated as doctors, lawyers, business people, academics, but no one ever mentioned it. There was a freshness about the experience, which she identified as its lack of egotism.

Occasionally, Patrick, Manoly and I went out for dinner. Each time, on suggesting such an excursion, Patrick would ask, in all seriousness, 'Now, do you mind being seen with a couple of old queens?' Every time I had to reassure him. We always went to one of the currently popular restaurants, and when people I knew slightly saw me in his company, their faces would light up with intelligence.

A couple of times at dinner, Patrick put on a scene, which caused silence in the room. Once he made loud, supposedly impersonal comments while being seated that carried to a former friend, and were followed by a curt shouting match, with each party deprecating the other's manners. Once a woman came up and asked him to sign, during the meal, a copy of a book of his she happened to have with her. She had just come from an adult education class. 'Oh, dear, dear Mr White, would you sign this copy of your wonderful book, pleeaaase?' Patrick laid down his cutlery, wiped his mouth, and looked with soaring dark heat at what was being held under his nose. 'I HATE *VOSS*!' he bellowed. The life of the restaurant jammed, followed by a few careful titterings, like glass falling, and the Thai waiters came rushing from every direction. 'Oh, oh, oh...' The poor woman turned to me. 'Why is he like this, young man? How can you bear to be with him? We all want so much to respect him, and look what he does...'

I said, 'You would have to understand the history of his disappointments with *Voss*. It's not your fault.'

'Of COURSE it was HER FAULT,' Patrick said to me calmly, as the woman went off, clasping a wilted autograph.

The trouble with *Voss* began when Patrick was persuaded to let Harry M. Miller, an energetic show business promoter, be his producer, in a plan to film the novel. I follow David Marr here. Miller is said by Marr to have 'come out of the New Zealand rag trade' and to have 'talked his way into society'. Patrick agreed to Miller raising the money for *Voss*, so long as he himself could choose the director. It was decided $2.6 million would be needed, and that the American Joseph Losey should spend it. However, Miller's part of the project dragged on for years. Patrick's patience was worn sore.

In 1977 the aged Losey and his scriptwriter David Mercer arrived in Australia, with technicians, to begin a production survey. David Marr says, 'After a couple of days out in Central Australia looking at locations, Losey collapsed and was brought back to a Sydney hospital.' Patrick told a correspondent of his, about this time, that 'David Mercer lapsed into a kind of alcoholic melancholy while here. He started ringing ex-wives on the other side of the world, who proceeded to heap shit on him.' Patrick liked Mercer, even following one of the screenwriter's drinking bouts, when 'the crew had to heave him into a bath to rehydrate his collapsed body'. Finally a dinner was arranged for all the principals at Miller's 'villa', and it was witnessing this place that brought an end to the affair for Patrick. 'Terrible,' he wrote of the night, 'in the ox-blood dining room with suits of armour from *Conduct Unbecoming* and family portraits from the auction rooms. Everybody got a bit drunk, I shouted a little.' Marr says, 'White *raged*...Losey described the outburst as the most remarkable thing he had ever seen.' The project was dropped. Miller sold off his rights to *Voss*, and they came into the hands of Patrick's one-time friend, and by then vindictive enemy, the painter Sir Sidney Nolan. Patrick had a veto on the director, and Nolan had the property...

Patrick told me of how, after that evening, when he used to walk in the park near his house, he sometimes saw Miller out riding, in full hacking regalia, and that the businessman on noticing him would urge his horse away, 'until he was clear of danger.' One can visualise the performance – Patrick no doubt restrained the gestures of his stick, but he could shout, and his jaws would have been as phosphorescent as those on the hound of the Baskervilles.

I fell out of favour with Patrick. In an interview I said that I disliked the idea of being a poet and would never call myself one; to be self-consciously a poet seemed to me too sequestered from the mainstream of life, 'like being a deacon or a homosexual.' Perhaps I had in mind just the affected wearing of an identity, in this glib remark. Patrick must have read it. When I met him, after its publication, standing in a group at a reading for a political cause, he ignored me. Then if our eyes met, while we were moving around the hall, he severed his gaze at once. I had thought nothing of the comment, after uttering it, but I saw with sudden clarity it must be the problem. During my reading, he glared at me once or twice, and I noticed refrained from applause. I felt afterwards that I would not attempt an excuse, but left without speaking to him.

I did not hear from him on the phone for I suppose a year after that. Then one day a languid voice asked, 'ANY GOSSIP?' I was invited to dinner, and I went. Nothing was said about the hiatus in our conversations; he had just been busy, time goes by. I had never been the one to phone, so there was no reprimand about that. I thought he appreciated that I did not try to cling to and cultivate his company.

Patrick liked conversations with working-class people: he would stop the cleaning women who came into his street, on the pavement, and the young mothers or the grandmothers, in the park, to talk about their children, or about making a stew, or getting the washing done in wet weather. He was continually delighted by the attitudes and remarks of these people. His own domestic help at this time was a Spanish woman, and he took such an interest in the details, developments and dramas of her life he might have been following a soap opera.

This respect for the ordinary person was not always reciprocated. He told me that when their car, which only Manoly drove, had recently been out of order, the two of them went into the city on the bus and came home laden with shopping, among a peak-hour crowd. They were separated, Manoly forced to the back of the bus. Patrick had called out, through the crowd, 'Is this the stop, Manoly?' His voice in such anxious moments was a stentorian bleat. One can see him, wearing his knitted beanie, or his beret, his trench coat buttoned over his troublesome chest, carrying his knobbly string bags, and working his jaws. Again, 'Is THIS the one, Manoly?' He would have been imperious, quavering, irritable – and yet not failing to camp it up. 'No, Patrick,' Manoly called, 'not yet, Patrick,' with his beautiful Greek enunciation. Then: 'This is it, Patrick. This is the one. Get ready. The next one.' Patrick, standing over everyone's head, in his military bearing, with 'crater eyes' and pommy voice, had excitedly shouted, 'COME ON then, Manoly. Come ON. Hurry up, then.' The commuters had loved it, writhing on their seats in their glee and embarrassment. This would have to be a couple of poofters. They took up Patrick's imperatives as a chant. 'Come on, Manoly. Come on, Manoly,' as if at a football game. They passed Manoly to the front, from hand to hand, with all of his shopping. 'There you are, Manoly. You'll be all right, mate.' Much back-patting. One big workman, beside Patrick, had slowly turned to him and said, 'Now, you sure this is the stop you want, mate? I reckon what you might actually be lookin' for is the Gap' (a place famous for its suicides). As Patrick and Manoly clutched at each other, anxiously waiting their turn to get down, this man said, ''Ave you ever had the thought: Life, with all this gettin' off the bus, with yer lovely shoppin', is such a struggle. Does it haf t' go on...? Organ music, mates. I hear organ music.'

Patrick told me all about it, doing the voices – delighted. Manoly slowly shook his head, at the memory.

I noticed, after not seeing him for a while, that Patrick had become frail: he was high-shouldered with asthma, was wearing his 'teapot warmer' inside the house, kept the radiators on, and was constantly chewing. When he was rude to Manoly and stomped off to the bathroom on a stick, Manoly whispered, with a tear, 'He used to be such a wonderful man, so handsome, and look at him now – ugly, and angry all the time.' Manoly was the same age as Patrick, but was slimmer and his hair was still naturally black. He had a light touch.

Some people, it seems, can age with a calm compassion towards themselves, an almost amused tolerance. They look on the injuries of age with pride, as honourably earned. That was not Patrick. He was awkward, all the way. His emphysema made him seem to be tearing roughly at his late small handfuls of life.

After Patrick died, it was announced in the newspapers that I had received the last Patrick White Award he himself chose. (The awards are funded from interest on his Nobel prize money, and given annually to an older writer who has been 'neglected'. The year I received the prize, it was worth $32,000.) The award to me was controversial. It was pointed out in the papers that I was too young, at forty-five, and as one columnist said 'already over-exposed'.

The meetings of the Patrick White Award committee, from accounts by its members, seem to have been conducted with the three appointees proposing names and arguing for them, and Patrick, most of the time, knocking down their suggestions – screwing up his face, it was said, in simulated thick-witted horror and proclaiming 'Nah, no woy!'

Years later, one of the judges wrote a newspaper article on his time with the committee and mentioned that year, 1990. 'White was too sick to meet, and so the decision was made by phone. The winner was to be the poet Robert Gray – I recall the tremulous but definite tone of his pronouncement. In my time most of the winners had been over eighty. "Could this not wait a few years?" I asked. This provoked the blackest rage I encountered in Patrick White; obscenities poured down the phone. I realised how sick he was, and withdrew.'

I heard from Manoly that Patrick had years before decided I should have his last award; and in his final days, believing for some reason that as soon as he was dead the committee would ignore his wishes, he rose in his bed to denounce them.

Wanting to thank him, I found myself standing before an infinite silence, more adamant than any matter. I saw that my wariness had not been able to detract from the generosity of his nature. I realised the inadequate friend I had been, how misplaced all my suspicion and caution were. Thinking of him, I had overwhelmingly a sense of our loneliness.

After he died, I was prepared to read Patrick's books. Without any longer the readiness to react away from him and all his work, I realised what I had missed, standing off the coastline of an island that was full of strange presences, which induce admiration and 'hurt not'. I think of *The Aunt's Story*, and *A Fringe of Leaves*, and *Voss* particularly, which must be among the great twentieth-century novels.

The main influences on Patrick's work – after Dostoyevsky, no doubt – seem to me D. H. Lawrence and Virginia Woolf. His ultimate subject, like theirs, is Nerves – the nerves of the author. His are works of expressionistic distortion, but they have an underlying, convincing realistic detail. He provides such a rarefication of feeling that we love our own sensibilities, in perceiving his. And his prose is beautifully rhythmical: *Voss* is like a great poem.

In death, Patrick avoided the condescension of the living, and particularly a state funeral; the world was merely told that his ashes had been scattered in private, with only Manoly and his literary agent present.

I went to visit Manoly, in my appointed turn, along with the photographer William Yang. We sat at the kitchen table with him, and Manoly told us of Patrick's struggle to breathe, which had seemed to be driving the house onwards and onwards, through the days. Exhausted with listening, Manoly tried to sleep, in his neighbouring room. A nurse came and woke him towards morning.

'You had better come now,' he was told. Patrick lay very still, sunken into the bed. While Manoly stood there, Patrick opened his eyes and looked at him. He raised his forearm a little, and the two men, who had been together fifty years, shook hands. Then Patrick died, without speaking.

This was how Manoly recounted it, in his gentle way. Except for the part about the labour of Patrick's death, none of it was true.

When I reviewed David Marr's book for the *Times Literary Supplement*, I complained, in passing, at his curt treatment of Patrick's death, thinking he had been avoiding the impression of rising music in that scene, and had skimped on the issue. David Marr met me in the street after my article came out and patiently explained that his elided version of those events had been done for Manoly's benefit. Actually, Patrick had died in the same way as Mrs Hunter, the chief character in *The Eye of the Storm*, and as the model for Mrs Hunter, Patrick's mother, had done, and as many old people did: while being held in place on the lavatory. Manoly, with his long-absorbed distrust of the press, saw himself, unreasonably, as having to protect Patrick from them, in this matter. The facts need never have arisen, but he told everyone his idealised story. It is clear that he, at least, was not the unacknowledged talent behind his partner's pen.

I went to visit Manoly again, but realised my presence was not helpful. He thought of me as Patrick's friend and that was now his only interest in me. There was nothing distracting that we could say to each other. I sat on the couch and he came and sat beside me, interlaced his fingers over his little paunch, like the Dormouse, and cried. I went away quite soon, that first time, but on the next occasion I tried to talk, saying inept, reminiscing things. The two pugs were locked out, but the Jack Russell was in the house, and at the tears it began barking, braced on the floor before us. This upset Manoly more, who wagged a finger at it, while sniffling. I tried to

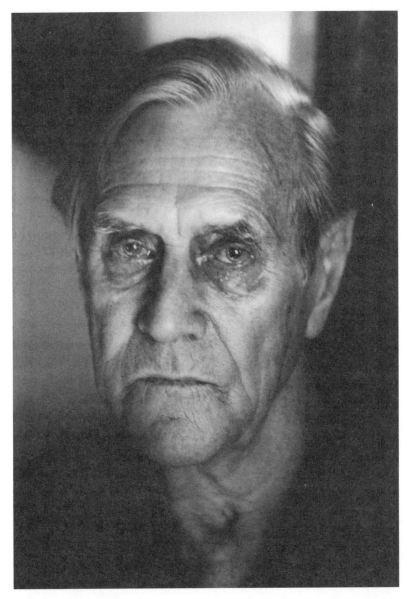

calm the dog and it leapt up on the couch and bit through the side of my hand. Manoly spilled the medicine chest, and his freshly cut tears spilled down, also.

The next time I called, we went for a walk, in the late afternoon, leaving the dogs at home, which meant he would have to come out again. On this visit, the subject he tried to keep to was his housekeeper and her unsatisfactory cooking and ways. I realised he would much rather talk about this to his women friends. We rummaged around for other topics, apart from Patrick, and found very little. Manoly said he was going to buy a television set. 'Good,' I replied. End of that. We were walking in the park, just at dusk. 'Patrick loved you, Robert,' he said.

'Oh, no, no, no, he loved you, Manoly.'

'Not like that. I don't mean like that.'

He seemed to be taking a direction across the lawns he knew well, diverging abruptly at a certain point into longish grass, at the unkempt end of the grounds. We came to a large pond, darkened by black low pine trees ranged on its other side. Manoly walked right to the edge of the water and stood silently there. Time passed and he stood and said nothing, his way barred. I realised this was where Patrick's ashes were scattered. Manoly would come here every day and bring the dogs. Years before, in response to an interviewer, Patrick had listed his likes and dislikes; I remembered his chief dislike was, 'The overgrown school prefects who think they are our masters'; and among his likes, the one that stayed in my mind was, 'The thought of my ashes floating on the lake.' This must have been what he meant by the lake: not as I had visualised it, at all. Stuck in the oil-black water, picked out because of their whiteness, were a slanted polystyrene milkshake container, some pasted-down sheets of newspaper, a lot of ducks' feathers, a scrunched-up sandwich bag, and a flat galaxy of coarse dust.

It grew chilly. Car lights surged back and forth, beyond the railings. Manoly roused. 'We had better go back,' he said. 'Nelly will be getting worried.'

Manoly lived on for thirteen years, to be ninety-one, the house kept like a museum around him: he saw himself merely as its caretaker, for the organisational inheritors, at his death. He was looked after, finally, by a band of nurses and carers. Arthritis kept him indoors; the last of the dogs died; he became lost in himself.

I never visited him again, after our walk to the pond. I remembered that place whenever I thought of Patrick or of him. I saw Patrick's face, looming large and transparently before it – his flashing eyes, his ashen hair. I found the choice of place too wilfully severe; rebarbative. It seemed a final stricture against the living, and it depressed me.

I preferred to think of Patrick as he was in certain photographs that William Yang took. Patrick was notoriously unphotogenic, but William had exceptional talent as a portraitist. He was a Taoist in his approach: yielding, deferring, unassertive, he enabled people to give themselves unguardedly. Asking, listening, always about to begin, he had finished. When Patrick wrote his novel *Memoirs of Many in One*, a book about his sense of a feminine other self, he trusted William to take photographs of him dressed as that woman. The pictures have not been shown.

Later, in one of their last portrait sessions, when Patrick was in his early seventies (he died at seventy-eight), William discovered or produced in him, an extraordinary loss of defensiveness. Patrick was steadfast, dispassionate, elevated above the anxieties of his usual self; as if he had cast off the burden of justification. He looked like the same man, but in a different life.

19. Extreme People

'Now the leaves are falling fast.'

At a certain stage in our lives, the people we know who are older than we are all begin to die, with an insistent, staccato rhythm. I thought for a while that I ought to call this book *Gray's Elegies*.

My aunt Bill died of cancer at seventy, a few years after my father had died, who was frustrated in his hopes of money from her to the end. Once she received the diagnosis, she saw no one she knew, apart from her husband. She told her friends and her sisters, by telephone, that she was going to have treatment and that her chances were good, but that was not the case. Suddenly, they were all cut off; and never saw her again. Her husband took their calls and temporised. There was no use in therapy and the hollowing-out of her body was accomplished in months. She had seen her mother die of this disease and knew what it does to one's appearance, and that seems to have been her final concern.

I met Bill numerous times when I was a boy, while visiting Sydney. This was in the days before she became, as Margaret confided to me, 'too grand' to stay with them. (The remark was unjust: the flat had four bedrooms, and a sunroom, where I was put, but with the two boarders it would have been crowded, unnecessarily.) Bill had an appealingly Pekinese face, which even in childhood photographs looked jowled, hyperthyroidal eyes, and a bosom that echoed her protrudent gaze, greatly amplified. Her hair was dyed blue-black and teased fully off her face, rolled back, and folded in a hairnet about her neck, to make that look narrower, I now understand. Her upper lip was painted in two exaggerated art deco bows, hiding the lip line; the lower was exactly as thick, but drawn in a perfect meniscus. The eyebrows lifted toward their outer, curved extent, and were so fine they might have been put there by a draughtsman. Her voice was husky, her demeanour impassive, her rings were admired.

Bill always seemed to me a bit strangled, a little breathless. If you caught a glimpse into her eyes, something embarrassingly naked and startled quickly withdrew. Children discomforted her. She would never have touched one. She remained immaculate throughout the evenings, wearing high heels in the living room, keeping her earrings on, and her fingernails on display, while we listened to the radio. After a show, she was always lightly dismissive of it, getting up from the sofa and smoothing her skirt.

Once I made the social mistake of seeing her in the hallway, of an early morning, when she was going to the bathroom in her dressing-gown. I had slipped into the bathroom out of turn, to relieve myself quickly. Bill saw me come around a corner, darting back to my room; she turned to the wall, pulling up her collar with a gasp. I was ten years old. I saw that she was wearing some sort of tight black cap over all her hair and that her eyes were waxen, almost closed, and looked like cowry shells.

Margaret reiterated afterwards that I was not to go to the bathroom until I heard Bill was back in her room and the door had closed. As usual, Bill was the last to come to breakfast, with her solid hair and her make-up set in place. She sat dabbing lipstick immediately off her teacup with a little handkerchief and ignored me.

Bill was waited on by her husband, a gentleman with fine silver hair, cravats and a pipe that he smoked out of doors, who stayed during these visits at his club and came in the car when telephoned. He was soothing of all anxieties, unblinking at any imperiousness. It turned out that he wrote to Margaret in secret, needing a confidante – although with complete propriety, I can believe. So we learned, some of us only much later, about life with Bill. One story involved her having their house redecorated, while she and her husband stayed at a hotel in the town. It was her turn to have friends for cards, however, and so she must have them to that less than satisfactory place. She was only able to do this after calling in her decorator, with the hotel manager's permission, handing him one of her powder compacts, and instructing him to repaint the suite in that shade. While this was being done and aired, they paid for extra rooms.

We learned that periodically her husband would come home and find Bill incoherently drunk. She had not left her bed all day and the sheets were drenched. Or she had wedged herself into the smallest possible space, in the bottom of a wardrobe or beside the toilet bowl. He would find, at times, that her most expensive dresses had been shredded with scissors and strewn about the room. She was inconsolable about this.

Soon after Bill's death, her husband, though seemingly active, bought himself a place in a retirement home, and began to decline there. But he kept up his letters to Margaret, until the end, talking on about Bill in worried tones as though she were alive. 'O good and faithful servant,' I trust there was some reward in all of that for you.

Margaret and Olga stayed together to the end of their lives, the last few years in adjoining rooms at a retirement home. Olga, who had seemed still robust, died under a hot shower, her head exploding within, in a massive haemorrhage. A nurse found her, after noticing that all the windows of the apartment had steamed up. Olga lay curled up under the running water, clutching her head with both hands.

I sat with Margaret in the front pew of the crematorium chapel for Olga's service. I was about forty. Many more people had come than expected, out of respect for my surviving aunt, I thought. All the minister knew of Olga was what he had been told by family friends. His eulogy described a person none of us could recognise. 'This much loved and popular woman…respected by…her kindness…responsibility…with Christian charity' he intoned, in a fine, rented-out voice. Margaret, almost ninety, sitting rigid and flushed and dry-eyed beside me, suddenly stamped her stick and snapped, by no means *sotto voce*, 'Oh, for God's sake, get on with it, man. What nonsense. What nonsense.' The minister startled away from looking in her direction. He continued, and she did, also. 'What sentimentality,' she confided loudly to me. 'Oh, really! Can you credit this? This is not what we expected.' The priest's mouth rotated on his stock of phrases, as doggedly as a herbivore's. Snorts and mutterings and angular, imperious restiveness continued from the chief mourner. Someone sitting behind prodded me sharply in the back, but I did not look around, nor did I lay a restraining hand on Margaret's arm. I thought she had a right.

Even a fictional character, encountered at length, is not credible without some redeeming trait, but I have trouble remembering what Olga's was. I would like to speak well of my aunt, yet she remains in memory, as she was in life, a skirted, uncomfortable presence. She was eminently employable, so she must have been more tactful at work than at home. Socially and domestically, she was always ready to challenge, and was tolerated by people, I think, mostly out of good manners and because of her size. She never gave any sign of having a moment's doubt about her rightness against the world, which she faced up to, responsibly. One can only guess to what degree she felt alone, as she would never have spoken of such a thing. I see now her good quality – that she was brave.

As an adult, I saw the 'Gray girls' irregularly, over the years. Sometimes I would fail to visit them for dinner between one Christmas and the next, at other periods I saw them every few months; but my neglect was never for want of invitation, particularly as they grew older. I spoke to Margaret on the phone, perhaps once a month. Never, in all of that time, thirty years, did she enquire about her sister-in-law, even when my mother was widowed, nor about my brothers and sister. She did not want to be reminded, either, of whether I was currently married or unmarried, or what unprofessional, part-time job I was holding. Were I to touch on these subjects, unthinkingly, she would immediately pass them over. Her interest was in our two selves alone, apart from any problems. We spoke easily, with jokes, of films we had seen, detective stories we could recommend (she liked Margery Allingham and P. D. James), of my travels out of the country, of our favourite television programmes, and of innocuous memories we shared, just as a way of keeping in contact, since we were family. I was expected always to be well. When a book of mine was reviewed in the papers, and mentioned to her by someone, she congratulated me, pleased, but neither of us talked about it; and certainly she would not have wanted a copy: it might contain who knew what revelations.

Margaret gradually came into family money, towards the end of her life, since she outlived all her relatives. Her uncle Percy, the 'ladies' man', left his money to a woman he married in his old age, with instructions that what remained at her death should go to Margaret. (I remember Olga, during one of my visits, coming home flushed and literally stamping her feet: 'They tell me that damned Maude is taking another world trip!') Margaret was always Percy's favourite, among other things for the way she had looked after her mother. She liked him, too: she showed me photographs of him in pyjamas and billowing dressing-gown, riding his motorcycle through a country paddock, the sidecar attached, in which he used to take his ladies for a spin; and of him, wearing a cloth cap and a leather overcoat, pretending to struggle with a Jack Russell,

over a chop, on a bare table; and of him at a ball, in tie and tails, surrounded by heavily fleshed women with fans and tiaras. (As with Casanova, looks were evidently not his first concern.) He had a beaked nose, sleek black hair, a great dislocated-looking jaw, and wire-rimmed spectacles, through which his eyes were humorous.

Percy's widow died suddenly, with most of the money still in the bank; and then Bill's husband died, and remembered Margaret and Olga. Suddenly, they possessed what was, for the early 1980s, 'a small fortune'.

With this security, Margaret set herself and Olga up in a rather luxurious retirement village (where a number of titled women were in residence, always referred to by the management with lowered voice). How my father would have writhed, how sinister he would have seemed, as he set about pursuing his case with Margaret, over some of the legacy. Luckily, it came too late for that, and she was spared his inflamed performance.

In her old age, even before Olga died, Margaret began to remark on the way that she and I had always 'clicked'. I was the closest person to her, she said. She became rather demanding about seeing me, and was relatively demonstrative, laying a hand on my arm, and holding onto my hand, as Browning says, just a 'very little longer', when we said goodbye. I was her 'pin-up boy', she would sometimes mention. But she was still very much of the formal school. I felt a certain affection for her, too.

Then, in her eighties and alone, Margaret began to insist on coming into 'town' once a fortnight, on the bus, to meet me for lunch. The alternative week, I would visit her. She discouraged other visitors, claiming they wanted to talk about money. My half-sister was allowed to call and they went for drives. (My half-brother lived in Queensland somewhere, and never appeared.) For other social contact, Margaret made do with the common room at the 'village'. There, I was told, she had a circle, who shared her dining table. Once, when I was on my way through the grounds to visit her, I was stopped by one of the other 'inmates', as she called them. This woman said that my aunt was 'a trick', and asked, with an air of tittle-tattle, if I knew how she embarrassed the local bus drivers. It seemed that when she was coming back from shopping in the suburb, Margaret would call out to the driver, between stops, and have him set her down at a place convenient for her. 'Young man,' she would say, rising from her seat at the front, and clinging to a pole, 'I am as old as the Queen Mother. You would stop for her; you can stop for me.' She must have often done this, because one day, my informant told me, a driver had slowed down, when approaching the 'village', and had called into the bus, 'Is that woman on, who thinks she's the Queen Mother?'

When I took Margaret for lunch in the city, she was not much interested in food, and often ate only oysters, but more and more she was eager that we go to a 'dive' and have some drinks. A glass of wine at lunch was all very well, but she preferred to be in the dim, dedicated atmosphere of our favourite bar. She loved to drink beer, belching decorously into a lacy handkerchief and patting her chest. As thin as a rag, with a slight stoop, she looked twenty years younger than her age. She only picked at food because she was worried drinking would make her fat, and she kept a check on her weight by whether her suits would still do up. Many years earlier my mother had said to me, with a sombre look, that Margaret 'liked a drink', but I had only seen her foolish once, at some gathering in the days of the flat. Out in the kitchen, Olga had been tearful and frightened-looking, and so there may have been burbling, tottering scenes like that before.

On her bamboo stool in 'The Jungle Bar', leaning at the counter in a fur, her long thin legs crossed at the ankle, Margaret would talk to anyone who wandered up, and was served low alcohol beers, without realising that she was being 'short-changed'. (She had never heard of such a brewing innovation.) 'Beer seems to have lost a lot of its flavour, these days. Get me a different one this time, dear.' The regular barman knew, from my having talked to him at other times, to bring a different light ale. He also knew that if one for the road should be a cocktail, it was to be long on flavour and have little else. 'I always had a good head,' Margaret would tell me, when it was time to go. 'I'll be fine. And you're sensible, too. Still, I'm glad that you're not shy of a drink.' She would pat me on the arm, approvingly, and kiss the air, as I put her into a cab.

For my visits to her, I was instructed to bring something 'interesting'. I used to take only one bottle of good wine, which I would share out meticulously between us. She had a housemaid, however, who would buy regularly for her the liquor 'specials' at a nearby supermarket, and towards the end Margaret must have been tipsy almost every evening. She lacked the capacity to drink beyond that degree. No one had any complaints about her, including her broad-minded doctor. ('I don't think anything can hurt her, now.') There was only the worry of a fall, but she was safe in her armchair with the television, until the nurses came to see her to bed.

She was adamant that she liked the bus into town, and that she could make her way alone from the bus stop to the restaurant where we ate. I decided to wait in a park by the bus stop and to follow her, to see how she was managing. I sauntered behind her, among the crowd, and hung back when she stood at the pedestrian lights. I found that at a busy crossing she hesitated beside a shop window, watching the passers-by, and letting the lights change several times, before going to the kerb. I saw that she then positioned herself next to some polished-looking older man. She would make a casual remark to him, begin conversing, and when the walk sign came on, he would usually offer his arm, if she had chosen well (or if she prompted him, perhaps). With her face turned up, she crossed over, smiling and chatting. On the other side, they paused to speak for a few moments, or minutes, and then she waved to him lightly, and he laughed, and raised a hand. I saw that her little adventures of the old days continued; that she was still 'picking up men' as she used to say. I realised why she was sometimes reluctant to take a cab home, even though I paid for it. She was rather addicted to her game: that half-minute it took for her to amble across the road on the arm of a silver-haired stranger, and the way he would linger, solicitous and charmed. (Or was it patient and amused? Or, perhaps, secretly impatient and bemused?) Then elusively, as she imagined, she would be gone.

Margaret used to arrive at lunch with an age-denying spright-
liness to her, with a satisfied air, and would take an interest in the
couples at the other tables. She particularly liked to see an older
man and a pretty young woman dining out. And she might touch
the back of my hand, briefly, where it lay on the cloth.

We talked about the same subjects we always had. She never
mentioned Olga, except in passing, and then quite dry-eyed. These
days, she liked to be told in detail the plots of films I had been to,
which she said it was too tiring for her to see. I was reminded by her
on the phone to bring to our lunches any scenes from these films,
or portraits of the actors, I could find in newspapers or magazines,
and the fliers from the cinema. Also interesting to her was talk of
other countries: descriptions, as vivid as I could make them, of the
people's idiosyncrasies, and of their landscape. She, in turn, liked
to describe for me the parties and friends of her youth, and to
remember old absurdities. When the arch of the Harbour Bridge
had gone up, before the roadway was put in, she claimed that Olga
had said, in wonder, to their father: 'What gear will you have to be
in, Dad, to get over that?' Sometimes Margaret brought me family
photos. On one late occasion she pulled from her handbag a small
photographic portrait, wrapped in withered tissue paper. 'Keep
this for me, will you dear? It's someone from my past – I'll tell you
about him later. I don't trust those nurses to look after my things.
This is Harry; put him with the other pictures I've given you.' She
unwrapped the photograph, for a moment. He was fresh-faced,
strong-jawed, curly-haired, still with the gloss upon him, no doubt
painfully handsome to women.

Almost everything Margaret had was left to me, including what
had come to her from Olga, except for small bequests to family and
friends. But then, between her death and probate being approved,
more than half of her investments were lost. She had gathered

together the majority of her money and had invested it – as one might have guessed, given her late-flowering enthusiasm – in a brewery. I had had no idea what she owned, nor what she was doing with it, and had not sought any advice for her. It turned out that her solicitor was a man of her age, who years ago had bought into her uncle's firm, and had known Margaret when they were young. She was one of the last of his clients. He used to come to see her at the 'village', I remembered her telling me, and want to hold her hand. Perhaps she had tried to simplify her dealings with him, as much as possible. The brewery, although large and famous, was only part of a much larger holding, which all at once revealed that it was bankrupt. I received enough money to buy the large 1930s apartment I live in now.

At Margaret's funeral, a distant relative told me, outside the crematorium, that my aunt had been engaged to a young doctor at Sydney Hospital, who had made a nurse pregnant and so had married her. Then I was told, within minutes, by another sympathiser, that Margaret had been in love with a promising athlete, a Rugby player and sprinter – it was well known they were a couple – but that he had died of TB. Neither of these people could recall if the man's name was Harry. One of them believed that it might have been Frank.

Could those men, with their different fates, have been the cause of so much distrust?

Margaret died at ninety-one, smiling at a joke she had made, as she crossed her room in the morning sun. A nurse, who had made the bed and was turning towards her, told me that my aunt 'went out like a light', between one footstep and the next. 'She was telling a funny story. You know what Miss Gray was like.' Although the nurse tried when I went to see her at work, and when I phoned her at home, and again weeks later, she could not remember what the joke had been.

20. How It Is Night

When he was in his late sixties, my father decided to make what he probably thought a valedictory visit to his sisters. That is, he wanted to see Margaret, and felt that he could put up with Olga to do so. It was three years before he returned home.

Although he knew how much it would upset one sister and infuriate the other, he was unable to stop himself going back to them drunk, on his second night in town. He lowered himself off a double-decker bus, opposite their building, and wavered out from behind it, to cross the road. A truck jerked to avoid him, but struck him glancingly with its mudguard, on the hip. A sound like a pistol shot, mentioned by witnesses, was the explosion of a whisky bottle in his coat pocket.

My father was taken by ambulance to a nearby hospital, and almost at once transferred across the city to the Repatriation Hospital, when it was found he was a TPI pensioner. He was operated on and pins put into his pelvis and his leg. Margaret rang me, so I was at the hospital late at night when he came around after surgery. He lay unspeaking, although he had been woken by the nurses, with his head turned away, looking as if in a driving storm.

While he was recovering, I visited him several days of the week. I was working at the Mail Exchange, during all the time that he was hospitalised. My aunts each visited once a week. They acted, in my presence, as though they were being persecuted by him. Margaret eventually settled into stoicism, underneath all her palpitations, but Olga maintained an intense exasperation, which was no doubt visible to the patient.

In the next few months, although he was recovering and doing exercises, I could see my father being drawn off into depression: he looked at me with bleary, coated eyes, seemed to cower from my banal questions, began not to answer.

One day, after a few months, I came to visit him and he was not in his bed: he had been moved to a ward for psychiatric patients. I went there, to an annexe at the edge of a river, down by the mangroves, walking on the running shadows of smoke from the chimneys of the boiler room. The ward was locked. I had to identify myself to part of a face through an opened grille. Inside, on that first day, a man was wandering off along the corridor without his pyjama pants. There was a coil of excrement on the polished vinyl floor, hung in the chute of light beneath a high-placed window. At other times, there would be puddles of urine along the hall, or was it orange juice? The staff seemed to move about mechanically, trying to respond to the screams and the bellows.

My father was in this ward for more than two years; I visited him there on Wednesday evenings and Sunday afternoons. For all of that time he never spoke, neither to me nor to anyone else. When I first came in, he would give me, perhaps, a watery smile. He had become wolfish-looking, grey-faced, hollow. The white hairs on his chest seemed suddenly overgrown, in the neck of his pyjamas, and his jaw was always badly shaven. I talked to the side of his face, while he sat hunched on a squeaky-surfaced vinyl lounge chair, his dressing-gown skewed, before a barred window in the sitting room. No matter how urgently or exasperatedly he was spoken to, there was no answer.

On the long Sunday afternoons we looked at a mown, grassy slope, with a footpath curving across it, and at a blank brick wall above, on which the day gradually sank. Sometimes the reduced-scale figure of a nurse hurried along a path and around the edge of that wall, with its immense number of bricks; or a few seagulls planed silently across it, on what I remember as always hot, over-cast days.

I read the newspaper to my father, while he looked away, uninterested, and then I wandered about in a monologue – kicking stones along the roadside, as it were. There was never any more than the slightest teetering toward a response. I thought, more than once, of the lines from Emily Dickinson, about how the soul makes its choice and then 'closes the Valves of her attention/ Like Stone'. Within his tortoiseshell eyes, sometimes, there was perhaps a flicker of guilt.

In my accustomed way, I simply accepted what had to be done, without even private complaint, and fell into the imposed routine. I was content on the buses and the trains, or waiting for them, so long as I had something to read.

A few times, on a Sunday, a girlfriend of mine insisted on coming along while I made my visit, and waited on the lawn. She sat on the grassy bank where I could see her, reading a magazine that she folded narrowly against the breeze, or hugged her knees, while smoking cigarettes, or sometimes stretched out in the sun, with the untucked end of her blouse flickering above her tight stomach. She wore a small straw hat down to her eyebrows, on those days, which made her look less intelligent and more sensuous. A couple of times, an intern in a white uniform (it may have been the same person each time) came and sat by her and ate his sandwiches and they talked. I saw her shifting about, assuming the poses of an art deco figurine.

My mother never visited Sydney in the years of his detainment; she worked at her cleaning job, looked after her younger children, and wrote regularly to thank me for the news, and with messages for my father, to read to him. Occasionally she sent some practical gift: warm singlets, nail-clippers, a soap case, a toothbrush and toothpaste.

Then, after almost two years in that ward, someone thought to transfer my father to a clinic the hospital had use of, in bushland, at the edge of the city. Margaret had regularly laid her gloved finger-tips on one or another doctor's arm, on weekdays, asking about what was being done for her brother: 'getting on side', 'getting on their wavelength', as she claimed it was necessary to do. This I was told I must leave to her; and perhaps she had been effective.

The new place took much longer to travel to, but was far better for the patient. I made a bus trip, caught a train to the city's outskirts, and then had an hour's bus ride, past market gardens and stranded, shabby bungalows, in bleached paddocks. I and a few other passengers got down at a white clinic, standing by itself, among rows of poplars, a few desultory horses nearby. There were gum trees, their long leaves dangling against the large windows. My father, I noticed, as I approached him one day, soon after his arrival, was smoking again; and then the next minute I found he was speaking. I said, 'Well, welcome back.' He ignored it.

He had much more physiotherapy there, and during my visits was made to hobble with a stick and with me holding his arm, while he bleated complaint, over the twigs and leaf litter of the paths. At this place there was an attractive, middle-aged matron, who had a sense of humour and who bantered with him. One day, while I was visiting, she said to my father, mockingly surprised, that some behaviour or other was unworthy of him: he had such an intelligent face and was an educated man. From that moment, it seemed, out of simple flattery, he enhanced his grip on the days.

After about six months at the clinic he went home. We had never thought to see him leave the hospital alive. When I thanked the matron for her kindness, she was modest and said that most of his trouble, she believed, had been caused by over-medication. (No one of our social standing would have thought to make something out of such an admission, in those days.)

Back in his own house, my father seems to have assumed he was a hero returned, and expected attention. He was seventy; my mother in her sixties. She had found his absence a relief, and it was difficult for her to readapt to him. She soon became tired of his demands. My father was not in pain, and was mobile enough to take a taxi into town to see his doctor, each week. He would go to the club most days, where he had just a drink or two: his bad scare meant that he was now prepared to follow my mother in her wisdom and have his liquor doled out at home. This put my mother under strain. He constantly complained to be allowed another drink, expecting to finish a bottle of wine at a meal, and then to move on to something else. If he grew impatient, he struggled up on his stick, pegged his way into the kitchen, and snatched up a bottle for himself. His taste in alcohol had changed: my sister was asked to pick up muscat, sauterne and sweet sherry. And my mother swore that he had drunk from the methylated spirits bottle she kept in a kitchen cupboard, when she was out. He drank a bottle of brandy, brought home in his newspaper, while sitting with his bad leg up on the new lounge (bought with the extra money his absence provided), and wet himself there. My mother said that he constantly smuggled rum into the house, drinking at night again, keeping the 'empties' under his mattress until he went out. This was an old game, and she was tired of it. She no longer went searching after 'contraband'; but she did find that some bottles, emptied of spirits, were the cause of the dripping in the cistern of her new indoor lavatory.

My father needed help to go to bed and to rise, to bathe and to dress, to sit and to stand, although he could walk with his stick. He wanted his lunch brought to him on a tray, at a certain time, and he ate it on the porch, just out of the sun, his leg made comfortable on cushions. He was still grudging about her meals, even though my mother tried to serve what he ordered. With his extra pension, he thought he should have oysters (which she would only provide from a jar, to his annoyance), avocados, fresh asparagus, crepes, and fish mornay. He never remarked on the way she presented his food, on a tray, with a starched napkin and some frangipani laid beside the plate. If he wanted something, he whooped as though he were in trouble, and made my mother and sister run. No visitors called and none were invited. He complained about the library books my sister brought him and about the programmes on the radio. Music was of little interest to him, except for the occasional Bing Crosby song, like 'Danny Boy' or 'Galway Bay'. He was bored. One Sunday afternoon my sister came home from the church meeting, without lingering there, to get changed for a swim, and found my father unconscious, sprawled off the edge of his bed, dribbling vomit. An empty bottle of pills lay beside his outflung, inevitably theatrical hand. She had an ambulance come, and he was kept in hospital for a week or so. He refused to explain anything.

My sister said to me recently that she never, as a child, came home from the church's weeknight meetings without feeling sick, as they approached the house, expecting to see, beyond the long rise in the street which hid our place, the sky light up with fire.

My mother contacted the town's nursing home. In an interview she told a committee that the way the family was being forced to live around my father was not good for her daughter, who could have no one call. My father's name went to the head of the waiting list, and soon he was admitted, into a place to which he had said she was never to send him. He went off between the ambulance men, calling back over his shoulder like an affronted child.

When I came to visit him at the home, maybe six months later, everything seemed to have settled down. He had the scrubbed look of normality – a strangely naked-seeming face. I was reminded of the first line of a poem by W. H. Auden, on Herman Melville: 'Towards the end he sailed into an extraordinary mildness.'

Dried out, that was how he was with me; I heard that he was still difficult for the hospital. Not long before my visit, an old drinking companion of his had come to see someone else, had begun talking with my father, and had been persuaded by him to bring spirits, the next day. Of course, they were found out, and the friend was forbidden to visit him. This man said, with the sentimentality of the pub, that he thought 'an old digger' should have his last wish. He was so persuaded by this credo that he sent another 'old mate' on the same mission; but they were all suspect by then: a brisk, furtive visitor of an arthritic age with a bulky newspaper under his arm was watched for, coming down the path, and questioned about his business there. The old men's dedication to their project proved not to be great.

My father showed he was pleased to see me in a brusque way, by calling me 'lad' and 'young fella'. The years of my visiting him in Sydney had apparently created a friendship between us: there was a detectable warmth from him. He even reminded me that we had always seen 'eye to eye'. None of that religious nonsense, eh?

Watchfulness for any pun that could be wrung out of a situation had become, more than ever, my father's response to the world. He bristled with puns and allusions and word play. On my first visit to the home, as I was leaving, he called after me, with as much charm as he could gather, that it had been pleasant, but that he hoped for a more spirited conversation next time. I replied he would have to be disappointed; it was no use me running up against the management, if he wanted a visitor. 'Never mind, then, never mind,' he agreed, in a manner at once more stark.

When I arrived to see him, he would liven up at once, laying down his newspaper. I still had hair to my shoulders, and he once announced, on noticing me enter the common room, 'Ah, here he is – the hair apparent.'

My mother would make my father decorative small cakes for her children to take him as a treat. (She left all the visiting to us.) I presented a biscuit tin of them to him, and opened it, to let him see their brightness and smell the aroma, and he said, 'Yes, yes, I see – some more of your mother's flour arrangements.'

A young doctor was filling in a questionnaire on a clipboard when I came into my father's room. I leaned against the wall and waited. Responding to 'nationality', my father said to him, 'Australian. But it may be relevant to know that my background is Sottish.' He winked at me, having caused a moment's confusion.

Once I went to see him on my way home from the beach, after I had spent too long there: my shirt-sleeves were rolled up on inflamed forearms and my shirt was obviously uncomfortable on my back. He said, at once, 'You have been dealt a summery justice, I see.'

During the last years of my father's life I was the recipient of further grants from the government's arts funding body, and so could visit him fairly often. I had never grown bored with the train journey. On one visit he said to me, 'I hear that you've published a book. I think it would be better if I didn't see it. You weren't intending to show me, I can tell. Very wise. If I liked it, I would be jealous and find fault, and if I didn't like it I would be even harder on you, so it's best that we pass over the matter entirely.' This was said in a tone of generous concession.

On that same day, it may have been, we had gone out to sit on the verandah, as we often did, and my father said, 'You know, I've always wanted to write a book, myself. But I wouldn't have known where to start.' After a while he continued, 'I might have put together some remarks about life, *aperçus*, I suppose. I could have called it "Drafts".' (This is what I thought was the word.)

'Not bad,' I told him. 'Tentative. Speculations.'

'No, no,' he said, 'you've missed it. I mean the cold wind that comes under the door. Draughts. And instead of a contents page, I could have had a "discontents".'

Once, as we sat out, on what was just a cement porch, with ironwork, pot plants and plastic chairs, in the late afternoon, the valley between the hills and us became filled, in a moment, all adrift with the benign pollen of sunset. We could see through its fine golden mist the blue trees on the hilltops, and below us a paving of modest roofs. 'Hills like faintly blue elephants,' I remarked, but could not tell whether he noticed the allusion; he just grunted. Then he scraped his chair irritably backward and threw out his hand, into the vast twilight. 'Here we are, then,' he said; 'here we find ourselves, cooped up in this place. In a desert, in the midst of an oasis.'

In a notebook from 1974, I have found a single entry about my father, written while going into the country on the train. There is, firstly, a quotation from my reading on the journey, from Raymond Chandler, about an alcoholic character of his: 'The whisky won the fight, as it always does. He took a long savage drink out of the bottle and then screwed the cap on tightly, as if that meant something.' Under this I have written: 'Dad's boozing – never any question about it, for him. Only for the first time realise this. It caused so many problems for us, we assumed he had a problem, too. But he never joined AA, or would have dreamed of doing so; never went on the wagon, showed the least regret, apologised, wavered, or wanted to change. No struggle. He was a functional alcoholic, not a binge drinker. His only problem was our objection. His relentless conceit, self-centredness. A determined wastrel. Almost admirable, in his independence.'

I bought him a book by Patrick White. It was probably an excuse to let on that I knew the great man – something to talk about. I had seen he had one of Patrick's books at home. 'I may be a social outcast,' he said, catching sight of what I held, 'but things haven't got so bad that I need to read Mr White's mystical delusions about that condition.' I told him that I knew the author. I had overlooked that Patrick was primarily seen by Australians as someone who was publicly queer. I imagined my father would think of him as a writer. 'Oh, really?' he said. 'You're friends? He's one of those petulant people, isn't he? The ones who get excited about each other's waste-disposal apparatus. I don't approve of you having anything to do with such people.'

'There's no need for you to worry,' I said, irritably, 'I haven't told him, "Get thee behind me, Satan".'

He didn't grin. Other people's jokes were of no interest to him, at the best of times. He looked anxious. I saw that in his inept way he was concerned for me. Perhaps he thought I was sufficiently out of key with normal life, already, and that it was partly because of him.

Despite a subtly disdainful manner – a characteristic gesture was to brush something invisible off his sleeve or off the blade of his trouser-leg while speaking to you – my father was not snobbish. He never showed any sign of racism, and he always thought of himself as on the workers' side. I asked him about his interest in communism, which I remembered from boyhood. He waved the topic off. 'It's too good for us,' he said. 'Capitalism is where we belong. That's human nature. The other thing is an ideal, and is totally exploded. And yet, it remains, you'd have to say. Something remains. There is always going to need to be agitation, in the interests of the slaves. If that impulse fails, the human race is completely degraded. The capitalists will say they're looking after you, but don't believe them. They part with as little as they can. Miserable, at the expense of the working people – that's the

fundamental activity of their minds. Anyone who says there isn't a class war is a blackguard.'

'You've done all right out of the system,' I said. 'I mean, here you are getting medical care, and your wife doesn't live in poverty.'

'That's only because I went to the War. I earned that.' He saw my look. 'If I didn't get shot, there was the chance that I might be.'

I believed him, that welfare would be 'taken away tomorrow, if it weren't for the vote.' It had all become too ideological. He gave me some advice from his old stand-by, Housman, waving all the rest away –

Never fear lad, nought's to dread,
Look not to left or right;
In all the endless road you tread
There's nothing but the night.

My father was one of the few people I observed in our town who showed not the slightest condescension toward the Aboriginals, which was unusual then. At most, there might be some ruefulness in his manner, if he spoke about them. The native people lived at the edge of the town, below the highway, in smoky dark shacks with littered yards. I remember my father reprimanding one of us for a disdainful tone when mentioning those people. 'Do you know Mr Kelly?' he asked. 'Stan Kelly? The bloke who always wears a felt hat. He lives out in that dump – he has to. You've seen him walking into town, on the side of the road, with those two little girls of his. His wife's dead. Those kids are a credit to him. You could put them on the stage. And you've seen how he's turned out himself. He's always sober as a judge. You wouldn't see a better-looking family, anywhere. He won't be remembered, won't be considered as anyone of importance, but he's a gentleman. There are only individuals. Someone who can't see the distinctions among a group isn't using his brain.'

If I came to visit my father in the morning or early afternoon, I found him in the common room, where his Gallic nose gave him the look of an aristocrat of the Revolutionary period, shoved into a cell among the people. He held the best place, at one end of a large couch, leaning on its padded arm, and he read, while most other inmates shuffled about, or blurted inanities, or slumped in their wheelchairs, dribbling. A couple of other old men passed their days in reading, but all stayed strangely aloof from each other. A group of people sang along and clapped hands, as they were urged to do by a woman with a guitar. The air was thinly smeared with a smell of watery bowels.

When he saw me, my father would call out, unnecessarily, 'Over here!' waving the walking stick that had stood beside him. 'This is my son. Make some room, now. My son wants to sit here.' Once, as I crossed the room, he began using his stick like a billiard cue on some of the old women who seemed invariably to crowd about him. He prodded them with the rubber ferrule, announcing

'I sink the navy polka dots. I play the floral print off the cushion. I pocket…the execrable whatever-it-is…'

'For God's sake Dad, what are you doing?'

'I'm getting rid of these old biddies. They always want to sit here, and then they loll around, playing with the hairs on their chin and acting cute. We need some room. Out with you, madam. This one puts up a bit of a struggle. She's called "Vile Jelly"…'

The nurses had nicknames, also. One of them was young and unusually pretty; my father liked her. I will call her 'Rosie Hughes', a name similar to that which he gave her. She and I became friends.

I arrived at the home one day and the cry went from being 'Mr Gray's son is here, where's Mr Gray?' to 'Mr Gray is missing! He's got away again!'

It was Rosie Hughes who came running outside with a wheelchair (I didn't know her then), and she and I set out to find him, along the broad, mown frontage of the street, which was half as deep as people's yards and planted with a row of large trees, as well as being overhung with trees from the gardens. 'Does this happen often?' I asked her. 'Pretty often.' 'Which way does he go?' 'He sometimes ends up down near the creek, and that's a worry, but he usually heads for the turn-off, towards town. He got around the corner, one day, and hitched a lift. The driver brought him straight back to us. You've seen how he drags his leg about – it's amazing he gets away as far as he does. Hey, I think I see him. He's right at the bottom of the hill, in the shadow of that hedge, near the jacaranda.'

He was lying on his back, fully dressed, with knees drawn up, waving his stick feebly above him. He looked like an overturned beetle.

Nurse Hughes and I talked as we went toward him. I took the wheelchair from her. 'You must love your father,' she said. 'I hear you come up from Sydney, and when you're here you seem to visit every day. It gives your family a nice break. He gets more visits than just about anyone, and you don't look in and then run straight off again.'

'I wouldn't say I love him,' I told her. I saw my mother cutting all the crust off a half-loaf of bread, and picking the mould out of what remained. 'I'm bothered by him. His life has been such a waste. He's not a particularly nice man, as you probably know. I suppose I ought to apologise for him.'

'He's a lot nicer to me than the others in there.'

'Well, most of them have lost their marbles, haven't they?'

Nurse Hughes was buxom and fair, and so healthy she looked polished. She was both sweet-natured and down to earth.

'What's your first name?' she said.

'My name's Richard, but I don't mind if you want to abbreviate it.' (I'm afraid so. Nothing too rarefied, I had decided.)

'Ha, ha, ha. I know your name and it's not Richard.'

'I suppose you're going to tell me your name's Virginia.'

We were still laughing as we struggled to get my father into his chair. 'What's so bloody funny about it?' he said.

She was often on night shift, and I would meet her outside the nursing home when she finished work, in what I made her grin by calling 'the birth-wet mornings'. She had brought her swimming costume and we went straight to the surf. Then we went back to her house, her parents having gone to work.

'How's your mother?' my father asked. 'She hardly ever comes here, you know, and she won't let me go back to my own house. She's got all my pension.'

I said, 'She has you home for lunch once a week, and I know she goes to a lot of trouble about it. And half of your pension goes to this place.'

'I'm sick of this place. Why doesn't your mother let me come home?'

'Because she can't look after you. She's old herself.'

'Why is she old? She's ten years younger than I am. What's she done to be old? What's wrong with her?'

'She's tired. You've given her a hard life. She can't worry any more about you. This is the way it has to be.'

'You can't even cut your food with the knives in this place, or I'd finish myself off.'

Nurse Hughes confided to me about my father. 'He went out at night, when it was raining,' she said, 'and fell down on the grass, beyond the lights. He was supposed to be in bed, but was wearing his dressing-gown. Luckily some visitors saw him, at the edge of a streetlight, in the dark. They got a real shock. He wasn't saying a word – he was just crouching on one elbow, trying to get up. He could have caught his death.'

My father had to share a room, with a bed-ridden, somewhat older man. He hated sharing, and set about getting himself transferred into one of the few single rooms.

I had brought him a copy of Edgar Allan Poe's short stories, as mentioned earlier, and he used this to have himself declared socially unacceptable. He began reading aloud from it, whenever he was alone with his room-mate. Amongst what he read, to that large-framed but now timorous and anxious old farmer, were no doubt passages like this: 'The "Red Death" had long devastated the country. No pestilence had ever been so fatal, or so hideous... There were sharp pains, and sudden dizziness, and then profuse bleeding at the pores, with dissolution...'

Of course, he would have selected 'The Tell-Tale Heart': 'True! – nervous – very, very dreadfully nervous I had been and

am, but why *will* you say that I am mad? The disease had sharpened my senses...I heard all things in the heaven and in the earth.
I heard many things in hell...'

Undoubtedly he lingered over some parts of the tale: 'I think
it was his eye! yes, it was this! He had the eye of a vulture – a pale
blue eye with a film over it...I made up my mind to take the life of
the old man, and thus rid myself of the eye for ever.'

His room-mate complained to the nurses that my father kept
going on and on about death, when they were both supposed
to be resting of an afternoon, and again at night. My father said
that he had to read aloud, as he had always done. It was the only
way he could maintain his concentration. Reading was all that he
had...The matron decided he was generally incompatible with
other patients, and we were told, apologetically, he would have to
be put by himself.

'How could you do that?' I said to my father, having overheard
that older man tell his story, quaveringly, to his relatives and to
staff, in the common room.

'Have you ever had to share a room with someone who has a
hearty appetite and who sits on a bed-pan, at any hour of the day
or night?' my father asked me, curtly.

I hoped he had not found it necessary to read aloud from 'The
Premature Burial', but could not think that he would have done so,
for his own sake.

I took my father a book of stories by Jorge Luis Borges, and the
next afternoon he handed it back and asked my opinion of it.
I said I found Borges rather cold-blooded, and (perhaps unfairly)
that he seemed 'a parasite in Poe's greasy black hide'. This was
ignored. 'So they're not good enough for you, but you thought
I would like them.'

'You're the one who likes Poe; I thought you might be

interested in what comes after him. I hate Poe. I hate all horror stories – except *The Turn of the Screw*, if that's one.'

'I find Poe utterly puerile.'

'But I remember you always quoting him. I thought you admired him.'

'That was just for easy effect. Nothing more. You adjust your style to your listeners – you'd know that if you knew anything of Cicero. The bits I quoted would have been garbled, anyway. No, Poe uses too many expressions like "tremendous", "unspeakable", "ghastly", "unearthly", "unbearable" – all the obvious words. Your estimate of my taste is quite wrong, you see.'

Soon after my father achieved a room of his own, he died there. It was unexpected. He had been considered relatively strong, among the patients in the home. I was in Sydney, working at the book-shop. I came back from lunch one day and was told by the owner that my brother had rung to say my father was dead. Did I want to take a longer break? 'I'm perfectly all right,' I said. 'I'll look after the desk. He was an old man, you know.' He was seventy-two.

My father had composed his epitaph. He told it to me, one day: 'You find me in a grave condition.' I had groaned. He quickly stressed that he wanted to be cremated and his ashes scattered. (This was before Patrick White's similar preference.) The only other thing he said about his approaching end was, 'Do you think I am facing a fate worse than birth? I can't believe so.'

I had no premonition that a certain visit of mine was the last, but when I looked back I seemed to remember that as we sat out on the verandah his gaze had mingled with the distance like smoke.

My father had instructed there was to be no religious service for him; he remained convinced, as he hobbled out along his dark promontory, that religious believers are self-deluding. This tenacity seemed to me dignified. I had half expected he would befriend a priest. But my mother wanted to give him a Jehovah's Witnesses funeral, from the undertaker's chapel, and I decided to make no objection. Funerals are for the living. I thought he owed her that much comfort.

My father would have hated what I had connived in. The whole congregation turned up, out of respect for my mother. He was patronised, in death, by those whom he had thought invincibly ignorant. They were all, it seemed to me, faintly self-righteous, and of course unmoved. None of his drinking mates were notified – in fact, my mother would not allow a notice in the paper, so as to keep them away – but I saw some old men lingering together on the pavement for a while, uncomfortable among the plastic hand-bags. I imagined myself having to report to my father that, except for my sister's, there was not a wet eye in the house.

My mother was shaken and stoic, supported by my brothers. I went to join them in the front pew, and she reminded me sharply, 'You can't sit here. You should go to the back. I want only my believing sons with me.' After the service, a few of the Witnesses nodded to me, as I stood on the footpath outside, but none spoke. When everyone had left the chapel, I went in, bowed my head and said pointlessly, 'I'm sorry about this.' The coffin was going to another town, to the crematorium there. Since there was no burial, we all dispersed. I called at home and picked up my bag, to fly back to Sydney. My mother kissed me and held my hand, relaxed now.

A few weeks later I returned, at her request, and she showed me a plastic box, about the size of a house brick, but much lighter, which held her husband's ashes. No one knew what to do with them: they thought I might have some idea.

My brother Billy was still living at home, and he and I got up in the dark next morning and drove to a place well known to me: to the highest peak that was approachable by road in the national park, where it looked out on the ocean. We left the car at the edge of the dirt road, in darkness, and climbed a bank, and then struggled up through the dense rainforest with the help of saplings, on a staircase of roots. We wanted some sense of natural ceremony, and hurrying on, hurrying among the wide dark boles of the fig trees, stepping across fallen branches, we emerged onto an open ridge, just as full sunlight flooded out of its engorged tunnel.

The great eucalyptus trees were driven straight upwards into the white energy of the sky. The sea was white and swollen. Dirt-stained from climbing, we wiped our hands on the long wet grass. Then I tried to open the box of ashes. I used my pocket knife to prise it, and that slipped sideways and sank into the flesh beneath my thumb. I sighed with pain, yet felt instantly this was right. With the dripping hand I scooped up the ashes and strewed them, although I glimpsed my brother's distaste. In a vast relinquishment, I felt the pity of it all. The dark hours of my father's life were done, and I saw how we rise and are consumed, infinite particles, driven before the light. A phrase came unexpectedly into mind, from Heinrich Heine. 'You, proud heart, you have what you desired.'

21. A Tomb in the Winds

My mother lived for almost thirty years after my father's death, to the age of ninety-four, the last ten of these in a nursing home herself. During the time that she was widowed, she developed diabetes, suffered a cerebral haemorrhage, and was diagnosed with Alzheimer's disease, after which she had to be insistently taken into care.

My youngest brother left home early in that period, and Max, who continued to live in the town, called on her every working day, for his lunch, and took her to religious meetings at weekends. It was he who found her after her stroke, lying in the backyard, beneath the breathing bedsheets that she had pegged out, barely breathing. She was flown to Sydney in a small emergency plane, coming back to consciousness, fearfully, during a rough passage through a storm.

With time, as her dementia slowly flourished, she became increasingly eccentric, but it also seemed that she relaxed into the original sweetness of her nature, as I remembered it from childhood. Her last years were probably the happiest of her life.

I used to go home to visit my mother about twice a year, for a week or so, and I have a memory that stands for all of those occasions.

I am woken in the spare bedroom early in the morning by a regular bumping sound. Gradually I realise it is my mother, who is up early, folding away some small things of the wash, at the kitchen table – thumping them into shape with the heels of her hands. I drowse off, but soon there is a jiggling noise, the bottles in the refrigerator door, which gets stuck and has to be tugged; and then she replaces the milk; and has forgotten something and has to go there again. And there is the loud squawk of the back flyscreen door, which also gets jammed, so that something will have to be done about it; and the hard, splayed-out sound of a tap, opened fully into the cement laundry tub. I remember how the brusqueness in the way she did things irritated my father. As background to all this, finely within the pores of the air, the high fine sound of cicadas, their one shrill note of static, very high and constant, on what is already a hot morning at the start of spring. The fretted leaves of the hibiscus lean on the glass, and I hear the clacking shrill noise of honeyeaters, jumping about in the flame tree at the front gate. Red pods of blossom are being shaken onto the toasted grass and the hard white clay, and just beyond there is the white road that leads into town. Lying in bed on the first morning home, my youngest brother long gone to work, I listen to my mother bustling around. The flushing of the indoor lavatory that she has achieved in this life; and in the kitchen she drops a teaspoon, and bends to pick it up with a groan. She will look in soon to see if I am awake and return with a hot drink, and I'll say, 'Come on, please sit down. I'll bet you've been running around for hours. Billy can get his own breakfast by now, you know. Tell me all about what's been going on in this dump of a town.' Although, I don't say it quite like that.

Max told me that he realised how old our mother was becoming while they were at one of the Bible meetings. He rang me that night. 'You know, Mum can't even find the books of the Bible, any more. We're supposed to be looking up First Colossians and she's over there in Psalms. You'd think it would be second nature, by now.'

With age, my mother's comments on things became more than ever dry, and more naïve. She came to visit me in the city, and meeting her at the airport, I saw again her unworldliness. It was almost unprecedented for her to fly, but that was the only way she could travel, by then. She appeared among the incoming crowd, looking vaguely around, like a child who is calm and trustful on her first day at school. Her hands were placidly folded, a handbag on her arm. For the flight, I saw, she had made herself a large name-tag, cut possibly from a cornflakes packet, written on in biro, and attached with a safety pin to her lapel: 'Nina Gray – No Blood Transfusion.'

As we strolled along, to pick up her bag, she kept pausing to look out of the large viewing windows, at the jets parked about, or skidding up abruptly, strangely silent, off the earth. Following her observations, she turned and solemnly informed me, 'You know, man is a clever brute.' Then, as we went on, we saw a large poster in a case on the wall, an advertisement featuring the Sydney Opera House. 'That's our Opera House,' she told me, confidingly. 'It certainly is a marvel.'

While she was staying with us, my mother heard Dee make a telephone call to a reflexologist, leaving a message on an answering machine: 'I'm calling because I saw the word in the telephone book and I was wondering what it's all about, what it can help. Give me a call if you have the time to explain.' (This was before home computers.) She received a return call and had 'an interesting conversation'. My mother thought this was marvellous, this was the spirit in which to approach life. 'I wish I was a young woman these days,' she said.

Before she had settled onto the ground of her good nature, there were some difficult moments with my mother. Her doctor told Max that since she had diabetes it was necessary for her to avoid sugar. My brother, as instructed, went through her cupboards and removed all the forbidden products, and explained to her, again, that her meals would be delivered every day by a social worker. But when Max came to eat his lunch at her house, to keep her company, he continually found the meals provided for her untouched and my mother eating sweet biscuits or bread and jam, which she had gone to the shops to buy. One day my brother drove up to her house just as my mother arrived, too, with a supermarket trolley full of shopping. She had pushed it, heavily laden, a half-mile from town, on the gravel edges of the streets, and was negotiating it down the front path. He was aghast to see that the trolley was filled to teetering point with every sort of sugary food: apple pie, biscuits, chocolates, ice cream, tinned fruit, cakes, packets of sugar, fruit bread, pickles, TV dinners. In his agitation, he threw the trolley over, scattering its load on the lawn. Then he had to repack it and wheel it back to town. My mother shut herself inside, claiming her rights from a window, which she opened and then slammed down. My brother told me about this, in embarrassment, on the phone. I consoled him. He had been the one who had discovered her unconscious, in the past; he should not have to find her in a diabetic coma. Anger was all right in a good cause. Hadn't Jesus overturned the moneylenders' tables in the Temple? I detected this was taking the argument too far.

My other brother came from Melbourne with his wife, to visit my mother. The woman who had enticed her last son away from home was not popular with my mother, although only someone who knew her well would have noticed the reserve. I paid a visit, too, since this was at the time I was staying about twenty miles off, caretaking Joe's house, in the forest. My mother revealed to me her distance from her daughter-in-law by complaining privately about the young woman's voice. 'I can't stand that accent. It's all I can do to put up with her, the way she keeps on saying "darl" this and "darl" that, in such a tone.' I laughed. 'You sound like Dad,' I said. 'I like her. She's sweet. All that bustle and efficiency are just practice for motherhood. And some actresses have made a career out of a voice like that.'

There were enough people in the house; I said I would go back to the bush for the night. My brother offered to drive me there, in his hired car, which meant I could miss the afternoon bus. It was dark when we left, and we both did some shopping at the supermarket, on the way. A heavy storm came on before we arrived at the cabin. Lightning exploded in the bush, rain made a full-scale assault on the forest walls, and overran the cleared hillsides. The car scrambled up the greasy earth track into the clearing where Joe's place stood, and I gathered together my paper bags of shopping, from about my legs, in the darkness, and made a dash for the porch. My brother wanted to hurry straight back. When he arrived at my mother's house, the milk he had been asked to buy was missing. They guessed I had picked it up with my things. 'Silly Robert,' said my sister-in-law, irritably, 'off in a dream, as usual.'

This crossed a line, for my mother. 'Silly Robert, silly Robert! You're calling him silly? Out of my house, now.' My brother could not take this seriously. He and his wife went quietly to bed. But my mother kept wandering through the house, late into the night, slamming doors and keeping them awake. They had to get up and go to a motel. The next morning my brother rang me and asked that I come and intercede. He had unchangeable airline tickets for their departure and could not afford to stay in a motel until then. I persuaded my mother that my sister-in-law was quite right. I was often vague. I was certainly impractical. She and I ended up laughing about it. Then she became concerned. 'You must try not to be silly,' she said to me. 'You shouldn't think you'll get any smarter as you get older.'

My mother took to saving her bathwater and carrying it out of the house in a plastic bucket, to water the garden with, even when it was raining. She commandeered the rinsing water from the washing machine, for the same purpose. Though she lived in a climate of plentiful rainfall, she was remembering the habits of her childhood.

Her preferred diet became bread and tinned meat or tinned fish, or bread and jam, with tea, which was also a remembrance of bush life in her young days. Fortunately for her, bananas and lemons were recognised as acceptable food. The meals brought by the social worker were packed in the refrigerator, until they ended up in the garbage bin. My brother had to clean away these and much else – leftover cakes, things the neighbours had brought – amid her protests. He said it was like hacking a clearing in an icy swamp.

My mother also took to toasting bread by dropping it onto a hotplate of the stove, as if onto the stones or coals of an open fire, and lifting it off with a fork. Often she then forget to turn off the heat and my brother would come and find the kitchen sweltering, the stove ablaze like a branding iron. She made tea by measuring the leaves in the palm of her hand and throwing them into a saucepan of boiling water, but the saucepan was often allowed to boil dry and black. She would take already fallen, usually blighted flowers into the house, so as not to 'waste them'. All through the house were breakfast bowls, saucers, cups, even eggcups, with frangipani, azalea, camellia or hibiscus blossoms floating in them, in various states of withering. I have come home and imagined for a moment that the place had developed leaks, so many bowls were strewn around.

When a social worker called to enquire about her health, my mother would only talk to her through a locked screen door. If the visitor mentioned that she could send a cleaner, or someone for company, or talked about the comforts of a 'retirement home', my mother took hold of a broom that she kept by the door and drove the woman off the porch and along the path. But when a travelling salesman came door-knocking, she bought from him a six-place dinner service in bone china, and accepted a lift into town to draw the payment from the bank. (My brother complained to the company and the deal was cancelled.)

In those years, I talked to my mother once or twice a week on the phone. If I told her of something I had published, she would say, 'That's lovely, dear,' and ask for a copy of the book. But she never read it. I saw her one night sit up in bed and open a book of mine with resolve. After a few lines, she laid it down. 'Very nice. I'll go on with that later.' My poems are not difficult. It was something to do with the elevated reputation of the form, I think, and the concentration of its effects. On hearing any good news of mine, about my writing, she would remark, 'With all this success, you don't want to go parading yourself, you know. You won't be a better person. Fuss just spoils people – it makes them discontent.'

I told her: 'That's a good thing about poetry. You're not likely to think you matter too much. Very few people ever hear of you.'

'It is a good thing. I don't like people to change and have opinions about themselves.'

In our phone conversations, she would say, about my 'news', 'Have you told the Gray girls, dear? Olga will only credit it all to your father, you know, even though she despised him. I wouldn't let on, if I were you.'

After my father and then his sisters had died, my mother remembered them with an emotion that was almost too reflective and accepting to be called bitter. 'Deep-rooted conceit and vanity like that usually come a cropper,' she said quietly, about her sisters-in-law. 'You can't tell me they were happy, for all the airs and manners they put on.'

She remembered her father-in-law. 'The old fellow was just a playboy. He and Mrs Gray thought I'd look after Geoff for them. That was the only reason they were ever nice to me.

'Margaret was civil, always very civil, but stand-offish, you know. Olga loved to belittle people. She was continually slinging off, just like your father. They knew everything. Margaret was the only one with some decency. Geoff told me she used to say, "Oh, give him a chance", when they were laughing about some young man who'd come calling at their house. That's a quality she always had.

'Geoff slapped Olga's face, one day, you know. The whole house was in a turmoil. I'm sure she deserved it.

'Your father never got the good out of a banana plantation. If he had a good season, it never made him think any better of the work.

'He might have gone out swimming where no one else would, or something ridiculous like that, but he was a coward. He couldn't face up to a woman. He knew he didn't have a leg to stand on. His mates! They were the sort who'd sound the horn and leave him out on the roadside. That was his famous mates, for you.'

After he had died, I told my mother I wanted to write about my father, and asked if she would answer some questions for me; I wanted to get it right. She said, 'Any lies you told about your father, you'd be doing him a favour.' Later, she informed me he was 'fastidious to the last grain of sand' about himself and what affected him, but not about anything that concerned other people.

She saw my drawing book, in which there were mainly landscapes but also some nudes.

'I don't like you going to those classes and drawing naked women's bodies.'

'I don't. They're all drawn from memory.'

'Oh. Well, that's all right then.'

When I was at home for a visit, we sat together on the couch of an evening, watching television. My mother would sometimes take my hand, without saying anything, and fall asleep. She had told me she lay awake for most of the night, so I kept still when she slept in the living room. One hot night, as she drowsed beside me, a large cock-roach flew in where the gauze door was ajar, and landed on Rowan Atkinson's face just as he began to make his features squirm, in his role as Mr Bean. He continued working his face about, but the cockroach clung there, with seeming determination. It stayed in place through the changing programmes: the presiding presence in the world news, and the unmoved mover of a hectic panel debate. I sat with the loosening flesh of my mother's hand cool in mine, while she slept unusually well. Outside a dog kept barking, in the distance; an occasional car went by, almost silently; a boy came out of a house nearby, shouted once, and slammed a flimsy aluminium-frame door. The cockroach stayed on. I read a newspaper with one hand, looking over at the television now and then, and once there was a shot of the world from outer space, the old RKO symbol at the start of a film, with that black shape straddling it. My mother sat propped up, a cushion behind her head, in the raw sounds of her sleep. I would have liked to point out that image of the world to her, a view of things which we had in common. Our difference was that she thought the world had gone astray and that it would be redeemed.

I knew how much my mother was changing mentally when I saw what she was reading. Instead of her Bible study aids, of so many years, there were now women's magazines strewn on her bed quilt, with covers that advertised articles like 'Cher's Sexual Torments' and 'My Night of Passion with Di'. Most of the articles seemed to be concerned with the dangerous course of a woman's life, between anorexia and overweight. She requested such magazines by name when I said I was going shopping and read them over and over. She no longer talked to me about religion. Yet she did not seem to have gone through a crisis, nor to have changed her values, nor to be unhappy.

My mother was put into hospital for observation of her diabetes: she had cuts, scratches and insect bites that were not healing. I came home with the intention of having a free hand in cleaning the house. When I had tried to do this while she was around, every object that I wanted to be rid of had caused her to protest. The fastidious standard of housekeeping my father imposed (and which in her younger days my mother perhaps shared) seemed now a contract she had ostentatiously torn up.

I was amazed at what I discovered, once I began really looking into it, into kitchen drawers, cupboards, spare rooms, and beneath the house. I found shoals of plastic spoons and forks, in cardboard boxes; washed and stacked-up plastic food containers; hundreds upon hundreds of plastic bags and sheets of tissue paper from around fruit, crammed into cartons; washed tin cans, with their almost-removed, serrated lids tucked inside them; a collection of keys from sardine tins; many wooden spatulas for eating ice cream; advertising circulars by the garbage-bagful; mummified black mango seeds; empty seed packets; torn-out recipes, mainly for baroque-looking cakes; ancient drafting patterns for children's clothes; rolled-up tubes of dried white shoe cleaner; single shoe-laces for every sort of footwear from tennis shoes to Rugby boots; dusty pencil stubs; many strips of black photographic negative, stuck together; loose dominoes and a broken snakes and ladders board; how-to-vote cards; pine cones; bicycle tube patches; the handle of a milk jug, the head of a porcelain shepherdess, the tail off a plaster dog, each of these in tissue paper; great stacks of uri-nous-yellow newspapers in the laundry and spare rooms; plastic ice cream containers full of rusty nails, staples, leather washers, candle stubs; rusted hacksaw blades; clothes brushes with the bristles almost worn away; tracts from the Mormons; a pamphlet, 'What Do Catholics Believe?'; Weetbix cards; a plastic duck I remembered, with a stupidly jaunty look on its face; and on top of the unused beds, piles of washed clothing, from years gone by…

Under the house were bottles in gritty stacks, for peanut butter, lemon cheese, tomato sauce, pickled gherkins, methylated spirits, lemonade, calomine lotion, vanilla essence, cod-liver oil, pilsener, sorted into different pyramids by size. Beside these lay rolls of wire netting, coils of garden hose, bundles of tomato stakes, spades, mattocks, axe handles, digging forks with tines twisted or missing, and rotting piles of hessian sacks. Over it all hung cobwebs, and beyond them cobwebs, like a dense smoke.

I saw assembled on the back lawn of my mother's house, at nightfall, a black monument to her insecurity.

While she was in hospital for treatment of her diabetes, my mother was diagnosed with Alzheimer's disease and transferred to a nursing home, her wishes overridden. It was a different place to the one where my father had been, and much superior, with the improved regulations of the intervening years. Apart from one incident, in which she disappeared from the home and was found sitting on the front steps of her old house, unable to get in, she settled there, and discovered that she liked it. In the midst of death, she was in life – the bustle and company and interest she had been missing for many years. Despite her dementia, she was unfailingly pleasant, and became a favourite with the staff. Her refrain, on the phone, had always been, 'I'm very lucky; I'm so good for my age. I can't complain about anything.' She continued like that, until she died. When I came to see her, she always answered my enquiry with some variation on that theme. 'A person in my situation would be very ungrateful to complain. I think I'm remarkable for my age. What age am I? No! Well, I'm very good...' I thought she was able to be so calm because she was without pain.

But, when she began to fall and injure herself, regularly for a while, she continued in that manner. After visiting her at night, and seeing her in bed, I would drop by the next morning and find her in a wheelchair, with two black eyes and a swollen nose, or with what seemed a piece of snapped-off black fishing line protruding from her lip, where she had been sewn up. She would be unable to say what had happened. All she could answer was, 'I've got a bit of a headache. But I'm all right, I'm fine. I'm very lucky...'

One would wince, coming into her room and seeing the purplish-yellow spectacle of her face, the blood caked around her nose and mouth and on her split forehead. Before long she was demoted to a wheelchair, continuously; but she didn't think of it in that way. 'This is a most considerate invention,' she informed me. 'I'm a very lucky woman.'

I had a nightmare about my mother, which kept recurring during her last years. I was out skating vigorously on a lake, like Wordsworth in *The Prelude* (the part about him skating is one of my favourite pieces of writing). I have never actually been skating. It was dark, and I was alone on a wide expanse. I came back to the shadows of the bank, where I sat on a rock to remove the skates. All at once, between my feet, I saw a face under the ice, faintly illuminating the darkness with its fluorescence. It was my mother, lying there like an effigy. I knelt closely above her, trying to make out her features, within the soft, floury light, unable to believe what I was seeing. She was speaking, although her eyes were closed. Then she opened her eyes and looked up in horror, pressing the frozen roof with the palms of her hands. I tried to break the ice, under my heel, my fists, but it was as heavy as a steel vault. I ran off wildly for help. When I came back, an obscure troupe of dark-coated figures behind me, I could not see her, at the place she had been. I went staggering about, peering by torchlight, doubled over, trying to find where she might have drifted. The figures with me stood back, silent, embarrassed, their miners' tools on their shoulders. I ran out onto the ice, slipping and falling, crawling on hands and knees, with a torch, away from the impassive crowd on the shore. The water was moving rapidly, close beneath me.

In the decades after I left there, the town continued to grow: 'going ahead', as my mother said. She was delighted to hear that it had traffic lights, and she wanted me to count the supermarkets for her. Prosperity also meant a botanical garden. On my return visits, this was what I liked most. I took my mother there, going

from the nursing home in a taxi (when we arrived, a wheelchair was available). It was an unusual and subtle kind of garden: twenty acres of dense, almost untouched, swampy bushland, simply fenced around and provided with boardwalks and cinder walking tracks (and with unobtrusive signs). Seemingly nondescript, it was extremely rich, when you were closely curtained by it. One boundary of the garden was the creek, whose twenty-yard deep border of mangroves was included in the grounds, by having a boardwalk go zig-zagging through it. There were reed-beds with paperbark trees, and above it all – over the swamp oaks, the burned-out tree stumps – were great, ancient hardwood trees, standing densely together, or in sunstruck isolation. Exotic plants had an area of their own, on high lawns, in the open.

I pushed my mother in her wheelchair through the gardens, the boardwalks barely wide enough (but she was unconcerned by that). We saw blue cranes taking slow flight, off the sinewy limbs of the mangroves, across a pale, soapy-green bend of the creek. We trundled along our carved-out way, walled in by paperbarks. The bigger trees were anciently fire-singed, their furry trunks the grey and black of a cattle dog. The sky was stained-glass blue, broken among the branches and the high leaves. There was usually no one else to be seen. The place concentrated the feeling of the bush – silent, passive, watchful-seeming, and empty. My mother, gazing about, tucked in her plaid blanket, seemed as impressed as I was: we were elevated on more than boardwalks. She looked up backwards at me, shading her eyes, and said, 'I'll remember this outing till the day I die.' Wanting to lighten the moment, for myself, I said, 'Or until this afternoon. So we had better do it again.' She laughed and threw up her old hands (scoured like driftwood), as if catching at the floating scraps of light.

Every day after lunch, my mother was laid on top of the bed in her room for a nap; she spent the afternoon there under a blanket, with a radio playing softly. When I came to visit, the nurses thought it a good idea to sit her up, so that she would talk. Often I had the newspaper and if I offered to read from it she was interested. Although I censored the news, her comment usually was, with a bemused shake of the head: 'Man certainly is a fallen creature.' If a person had done something remarkably clever or humane, however, she would take heart: 'We were meant to be just a little lower than the angels, you know,' she would tell me. 'You can see that.'

The other patients were somewhere downstairs at a musical after-noon, for which volunteers came and played the guitar and the keyboard, or vinyl records. She had not wanted to join them, but lay down for her nap, the blinds half closed. I read to myself, with her bedlamp directed toward me, in the hot afternoon, having become bored with telling my same few bits of personal news over and over, even though they were treated with surprise each time. As I leaned there, self-enclosed, I reached out my hand, a little guilty about neglect, to stroke her thigh, and I felt the muscles of her leg were moving rhythmically to the music we could faintly hear through the almost closed door. I noticed, in the shadowy room, that her foot was busily keeping time.

My mother became mostly confined to bed, and when in her wheel-chair had to be tied in place, to keep her from slipping downwards. Arrived from Sydney, I wheeled her out of the home for a little tour of the neighbourhood. She was ninety now and getting weaker. Her mind was as hard to gather as a ball of thistledown. I parked the chair under a large pine tree at the corner of the street, and sat on the grass, so that we could look across the town. 'That's the old post office, you know that. And there's the road to the jetty. Over here's a new block of flats, which they've nicely stuck right in front of Robinson's Hill. And that's where Dr Yarad used to live, that red-painted roof, to the left of the group of trees, there...' She claimed to recognise it all. As I was wheeling her back up the concrete drive toward the nursing home, she shook one chicken-bone finger out of the sleeve of her dressing-gown and pointed it toward the façade of the building. With this help, she pronounced the words 'S.T. A.U.G.U.S.T.I.N.E.'S. N.U.R.S.I.N.G. H.O.M.E.,' and then abruptly screwed her head part-way toward me and growled, alight with all the prejudice of her childhood, 'I'M NOT IN HERE, AM I?'

'I'm afraid you are.'

'Well...well...Well, those sisters are very tricky. They don't wear their whatyamacallits any more. (She had decided the employees must all be nuns.) But – they're very kind people, I have to say that,' and she sank back into her chair.

'You know, if I thought I'd be here for long, I wouldn't be able to make it,' she confided to me, as we went in through the glass doors.

I came to the home and saw her propped up in a wheelchair in her blue bedjacket, in the noisy common room. Most of the other patients were being led through a word game. At ninety-three, she was now the longest-serving inmate. I was struck by the way she was staring into the distance: you could almost feel the concentric pulsations emanating from her black-encircled eyes. She was staring at a completely nondescript corner of the walls and ceiling, across the jumbled-looking room.

'What are you thinking?' I said, as I came close.

She didn't glance at me; it could have been anyone whom she answered. She said, from a distance beyond that corner, with the utmost frankness, 'I was just thinking, what a terrible thing it is to die.' Her attention stayed fixed, grappled onto whatever symbol of absence she found there.

Not long afterwards, I came upon her staring off in a way that seemed, this time, to be wilted. She felt me standing next to her, and said without looking sideways, and without being asked, 'He never comes.' None of us had mentioned my father in all the time that she had been there.

'Who never comes?' I said, to help her out.

'The Saviour.' Barely audible. 'He promises, and promises. But he never comes.'

I thought she had forgotten about religion.

She was not eating well, so I used to bring her treats. My brother and his wife did the same. There was a list in our heads that we went through with her before the next visit. Peaches, bananas, stuffed olives, pickled cucumbers, crackers with Vegemite, hot potato chips...? Anything she wanted. On many occasions, I remember, she would name her preference (which she knew I thought an unhealthy choice), by assuming a look of great wisdom, and advising me, 'Chips are a very economical purchase.'

But her favourite food, which she considered an extravagance, and which was not available long, was a mango. In the season, we brought her mangos, or sometimes peaches. I would wheel her up to a far corner of the back garden, to a small, latticed summer house, and take from my haversack a bowl, a knife and fork, and tissues, and from its paper bag the mango. I would show her the fruit, which, with any luck, was bronze, like a girl's shoulder, with a few freckles and a little pinkness to it. Newspaper was spread on my mother's lap, and on the floor, and I stripped the peel from the mango and fed her slices of aromatic, orange, dripping fruit, from the bowl with a fork, or if the flesh was too soft, out of my fingers; all the while dabbing at her chin. I fended off a bee with the back of my hand, when it came out of the lavender, and another that wandered from among the wisteria vines that grew along the fence. My mother ate silently, with great seriousness, her sustained intention present in her eyes. When she had finished a mango, once, I asked her, 'Well, how was that?' and she answered, 'That was – a worthwhile experience.'

I had not been to see my mother for a while, for six months, and I felt anxious, in case she would not remember me. The last time I was there, she had wished me goodbye by saying: 'I don't know who you are, dear, but thank you for calling. It's been a nice chat.' Arriving at the town in the late afternoon, by train, I took a taxi to the nursing home without leaving my haversack and my bag of work at a motel. On the way, I had the driver wait, while I ran into the best supermarket. Then I went to her room, and of course she was asleep. I took a mango out of its paper bag and held it, as large as a bullock's heart, just under her nose, where she was propped on her pillows. She opened one eye, and looked out at me, steadfastly, opaque, without speaking. Finally, she growled, with a sticky, dry mouth, 'There are not too many people who don't like a mango. Is that yours, mister?'

However affronting to our dignity as a species the world revealed by science may seem, every unfounded belief must withdraw before it, because nothing is so useful as the truth. Genetics tells us that behind their masks, it is always the same performers who appear in the organic world, the molecules of DNA – chemically encoded information which makes possible the replication that is life, carried in our cells and nourished by us. The particular genes, each controlling a separate character or heritable trait, are immutable for long periods, novelty coming among them through copying errors, or occasionally through them swapping places in their sequence.

We 'strut and fret' in what we think our own voices, our gestures, our personal mannerisms, but if we could stand on a promontory high enough above time, such peculiarities, or most of them, would be recognised as having precedents in our ancestry. As much as our more obvious physical inheritance, the moles, the cleft chin, the tone-deafness, the sickle-cell anaemia, the hairy palms, so also an ambitious or melancholy nature, and our most spiritual responses, have a chemical basis, are given us by chance, and cultivated by circumstance. The genes may be switched off and on by our environment, but that is also something given. A little observation shows that our personal qualities are not things that, from childhood, were chosen by us. The whole panoply of ourselves is visited upon us. The genes have come up through

the conduits of the spreading family vine, over thousands upon thousands of years, to where we have appeared, at the tips of its tendrils.

The genetic code is the overreaching life in humans, stepping from one fugitive existence to another, providing our potential. This is the real metempsychosis: the transmigration of molecules. It has been found that we are not a blend of the attributes that our parents or ancestors had, but an endowment of qualities that remain discrete, each with its specific place on the DNA's complementary, entwined ribbons. So someone in the distant past stood at a window, and long before that at a slit in a wall, and looked out on the grey northern fields and wondered at life, with eyes that are now mine. Further off, these genes that I have, in their rampage to reproduce themselves, sealed off and secreted from outside influence, existed in a lineage that goes back through a shaggy lemur, a dog in a pack, a lizard, a summer fly, a mollusc, a dripping fern, the grass that first brought beauty to the earth, and the algae on smoking oceans.

To adapt a line of Christopher Brennan's, 'How old is my heart, and did it ever go forth with song when the world was new?'

Since she died, I have recognised it is mostly my mother's nature that survives in me, and only with her descendants, among whom it will randomly reappear, will it really end. I can feel her warmth, as a person, possess me; her unworldliness lives on among my senses; I know her calm in isolation; her persistence; her sectarianism, perhaps – the feeling that if we could only get things just right, in our beliefs, we would be transformed; her sense of *vanitas*.

Tolstoy says, 'The fear of death is the fear of not having lived.' Similarly, my fear about my mother's death was the thought of her having had no life. So much of life had been wasted for her.

The day came, which as a boy I had felt would be the worst I could have; the day that I would not know how to bear. But I could bear it – because she was so old, and because she had chosen to die. With a weird strength, my mother one morning locked her jaws and turned her face away from food and drink, forever; even from the sacrament of tea.

When that happened, the nursing home rang and asked me to agree that she not be put on life support. My brother urged me to accept their advice, and I did, after irrational hesitation. Then, to everyone's surprise, she took four days to die, without food or water, unconscious almost all the time. I did not take a plane to her bedside.

There was a memorial service, by her old friends, austere and unemotive. Then, some time later, Max and I loosened her ashes on the air, where our father's had been strewn. Nowhere else seemed possible. The day looked thwarted and metallic. It was chill out on the hillslope, amid the wide sluice of silver grass. The grey sea, stiff as mud, was barely stirred. Her ashes were smoky, and were quickly carried off, standing upright, like someone in a chariot.

I could not overcome my disgust that rattling dice should decide what one's single experience of life would be. Both of us made, with its brutal irony, an open, immemorial gesture there. 'This hopeless garden that we sow/ With the seed that will not grow.'

That night, from the train, I was shown a farmhouse window, in a dark, surging mountain; and, at daybreak, a dangling river, more crystalline than a chandelier.

My mother died quite differently from my father. Her life evaporated in the night, with no one noticing. She was typically gentle, isolated, self-effacing. My father died while making yet another attempt at escape; there was a crashing noise from his room at about one in the morning. He should have been long asleep, but they found him fully dressed in his day clothes, except for the tie that he had been putting on. He died before a full-length mirror fitted on the inside of his wardrobe door. Life exceeds art: in his heart attack, he fell forward, and was left kneeling, his forehead propped against his broken image.

This project has been assisted by the Commonwealth Government through the Australia Council, its arts funding and advisory body.